AUSTRALIAN
PRACTICAL
GARDEN
PLANNING

AUSTRALIAN PRACTICAL GARDEN PLANNING

GEORGE WILKIE

CHILD & ASSOCIATES
AN ALL-AUSTRALIAN PUBLISHER

First published in Australia in 1990 by
Child & Associates Publishing Pty Ltd
5 Skyline Place, Frenchs Forest, NSW, Australia, 2086
Telephone (02) 975 1700, facsimile (02) 975 1711
A wholly owned Australian publishing company

First published 1990
Published for Child & Associates by Weldon New Zealand
a division of Kevin Weldon & Associates Pty Ltd
372 Eastern Valley Way, Willoughby, NSW 2068, Australia
© Kevin Weldon & Associates
© Design Kevin Weldon & Associates

Publishing Manager: Robin Burgess
Edited by Robin Appleton
Illustrators: Greg Gaul
Beth Norling
Designer: Kathie Baxter Smith
Index: Jacquelin Hochmuth
Printed by Griffin Press Limited, Australia
Typeset by Savage Type, Brisbane

National Library of Australia
Cataloguing-in-Publication Data

Wilkie, George.
Practical garden planning

ISBN 0 86777 423 1

1. Landscape gardening–Australia
2. Gardens–Australia–Planning I. Title

712.6

CONTENTS

THE CONSTRUCTION STAGE

THE PLANTING STAGE

WATER FEATURES

BUILT FEATURES

THE PEOPLE FEATURES

GARDEN BUILDINGS

BEHIND THE SCENES

GLOSSARY

INDEX

ACKNOWLEDGEMENTS

INTRODUCTION

This is a book which discusses how to create features in the garden which complement and enhance the established plants in a made garden, and also deals with the design of a garden and its built features from the beginning, on an undeveloped allotment. The author impresses on the reader that the garden, its buildings, and the house should be in harmony, and that the garden is something to be viewed from within the residence as well as without. When people decide to re-design a garden there are many aspects to consider. It is necessary to observe the angle of the sun to the area, the distance from boundary fences, the effect of the new structures on the garden, house, and neighbours. He is mindful of environmental factors and advises the reader of the steps to take to make the garden design on paper a reality, and in accord with the surroundings.

It is a manual for people who want to know what can be done, what to do, how to do it, and it explains why certain precautions and procedures must be taken to ensure soundness of structures and safety.

Some of the questions asked when people are thinking of changing their private outdoors areas, be it

an inner-city terrace courtyard, a suburban bungalow garden, or a weekend retreat are:

- How does a gardener build a gazebo, a fish pond, a barbecue, and what are the pitfalls and methods of construction?
- What materials are needed?
- Is local government approval necessary?
- When does the help of a landscape architect, structural engineer, surveyor make the job easier?
- Does the budget for the garden cover the costs involved in the design for garden buildings, drainage, and plants?

Hundreds of sketches and diagrams help the gardener to become more familiar with the process of construction to be undertaken. The author also provides details of the kind of tools or machinery required for each new project described.

Practical Garden Planning is a reference book which gives answers to many outdoor planning and constructional problems while inviting more questions. Its contents challenge any gardener to extend individuality and impose that personal concept in a well-planned garden. It matters little if the improvements are minor or major. Design is an integral aspect of every garden and must be implemented with consideration given to its impact on the surroundings.

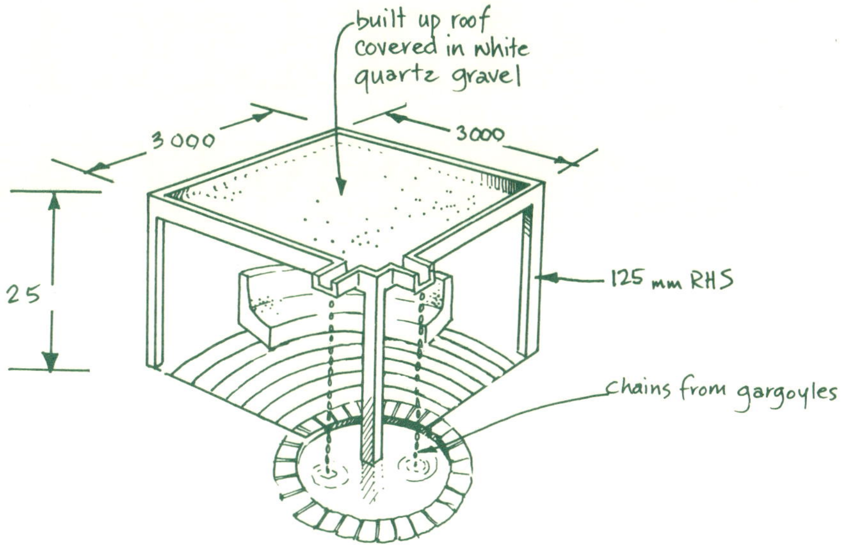

built up roof
covered in white
quartz gravel
3000
3000
25
125 mm RHS
chains from gargoyles
PLANTING
granite or marble bench
stone cobbles laid in
radial patterns
600 mm
2400 mm diam.
reflection pool with
water plants
chain

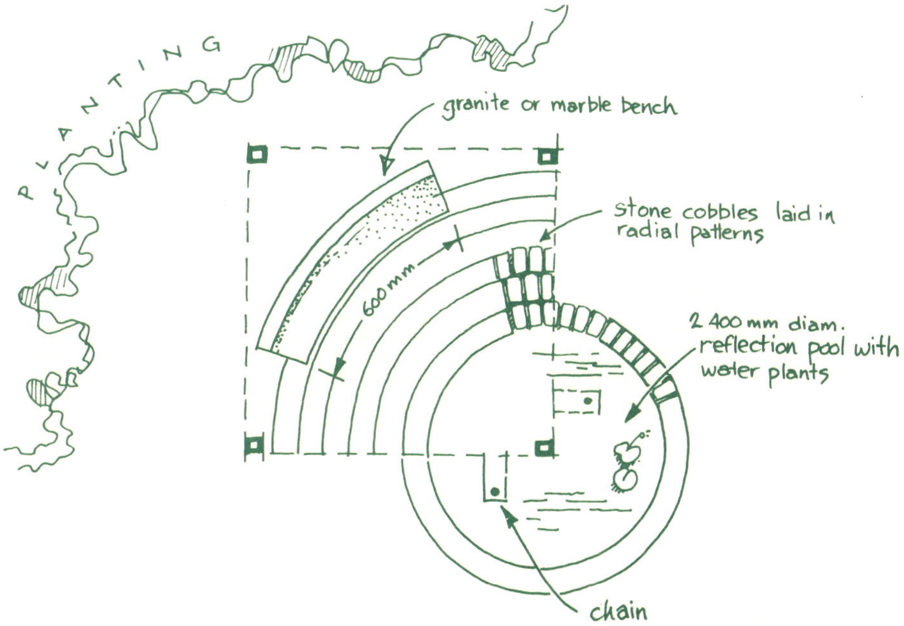

soft light
directed up
into trees

History of Garden-scaping

COTTAGE

Garden Design

In a garden, design is the plan that links the need to create or change a garden environment and precedes the labour-intensive activities which put the design into practice.

Design is about deciding the product's appearance before the event.

Design is about aesthetics. It is the combination of beauty which allows a variety of individual components to be seen as a whole when in combination. Just as many plants are judged individually to be beautiful their beauty can be overlooked in a poorly designed garden if they are not considered as part of an overall composition.

Design is about form. It is the control asserted over the environment being altered, in the built and nurtured as well as the space shaped by the modification of the natural.

Design is about function. It is all those considerations of sunlight, shade, soil, watering, drainage, fertilisation, and many other functional factors.

To begin a garden without a design can be disastrous. There are people who are able to develop a perfect garden without a design on paper but most of them, if pressed, would have clear designs in their heads. Garden design does not require every path, every plant and every bank to be planned on paper and then followed without deviation. This would tend to lead to a visually sterile garden.

Gardeners and their ideas are an important component of the development of a garden design; the garden that surrounds a house does not need to be similar to the landscaping that surrounds a factory or even to public parks. In good garden design whimsy should be the factor that elevates the garden to its highest visual presentation.

Very few people believe that a garden design should define every factor for every season for every year until the smallest seedling has grown into a mature tree. Trees can take decades to mature and few of us live in one house long enough to see a tree mature. Fashions change and native gardens are in vogue at certain times and at other times exotic gardens are popular.

The garden design should be a framework that allows for the personalities of the resident family to be expressed. It is likely that parts of the garden are especially attributable to an individual and that other parts will reflect the combined influence of a number of family members. The garden design should be one that can live and grow through the input of many resident families and provide a pleasing environment for guests and casual observers.

Gardens are normally associated with planting, but it is possible to provide a highly aesthetic, functional and well formed garden with no plants at all, by the use of contoured textured sand, selected rocks, and statuary. At the other extreme, but of similar value, a garden can be designed using only lawn and rocks — where even the patterns left by planned mowing can give intricate visual complexity.

The form of gardens varies from one extreme of attempting to mimic nature in using only indigenous plants, the so called native garden, to grand formal gardens using exotic hybrid plants tortured by the topiary shears and set in patterns and colours reminiscent of a Persian rug. Few gardens are without a plan of some kind but some never seem to succeed. There are also those gardeners who seem able only to grow weeds among the derelict car bodies.

A trip by train through the suburbs of a large city is often a revelation. From the street most houses present some attempt at a planned garden but the views from a train running on elevated embankments often show little sign of planning in the backyards of houses. For all the desire that is expressed by people for spacious residential properties it is amazing how poorly many allotments are used.

Not everyone can design a garden that others will accept as being of a high standard, but this should not deter them from attempting to understand and develop their own skills in garden design. There is an important place in society for the professional landscape architect and the gifted designer but their skills are not accessible to everyone.

Give design a go. What follows is a selection of often technical information that should help in understanding many of the factors that make up sound garden design. Use this text as a source of information to provide the basis of the development of individual local knowledge, combine this with experience, and extend by observation and other reading.

PRE-DESIGN SURVEY

Before designing a garden it is important to know what exists within the area under consideration. To some people this can mean simply walking through the existing garden environment and absorbing the conditions. This method will work only if the designer is extremely gifted, extremely confident or the garden area is very small, flat and barren. Most people will need to check some information and take measurements and photographs.

This plan can be simple or complicated but it makes sense to take more care the more complex or expensive a garden design is likely to be.

Steeply sloping sites will need well-constructed retaining wall or bank design and thoughtful drainage systems. It is logical to measure the slope of the land accurately. Few people can judge the slope of land with the naked eye, not even professionals like real estate agents. They only advertise flat or gently sloping land but there may be a deeper meaning why they can never see slopes greater than 1 in 20.

Try this test: ask a number of people to estimate the slope of the piece of land, then check it and see if anyone came close. A guess that is 5° out on a piece of sloping land 60 metres (200′) long, will mean that there is a 5.25 metres (17′) greater or lesser slope on the land than estimated.

Size and area

The dimensions of the garden to be designed are not always critical to basic garden design, but they become increasingly important the more complicated the proposed design is and are essential when designing gardens of more than 2 000 square metres (21 530 sq ft).

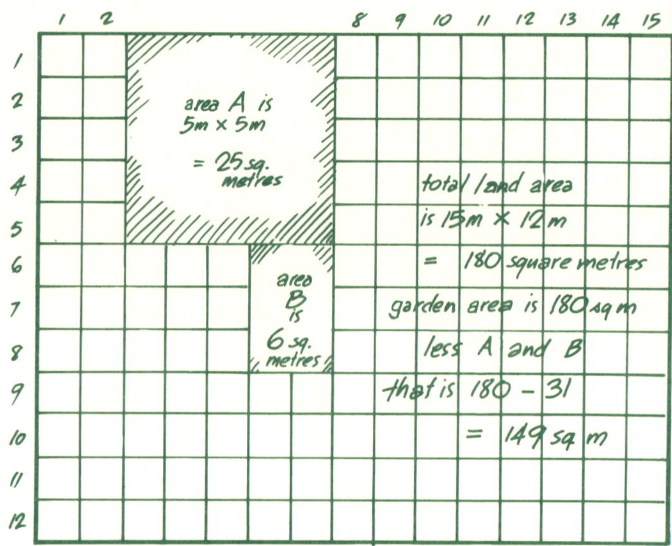

Most residential land has title deeds of some sort and on this document there is normally a plan of the land which shows its boundary dimensions. It is important to know that these dimensions are expressed as horizontal measurements — they do not follow the slope of the land. Some title deeds give the area of the land, in some countries modern ones are expressed in square metres or on larger parcels in hectares instead of square feet and acres. Pre-metric titles may give areas in perches and roods. Take care when doing any conversions.

terraces and driveways and this will result in the nett garden area. Make a scale drawing of the garden using graph paper. Convention recommends one of the following scales: for large gardens 1 to 200 can be used but 1 to 100 is a more suitable scale if the garden plan will fit on the paper size available; for small gardens or for special sections of a garden, a scale of 1 to 50 allows for greater detail.

To calculate the area of the garden take the total area of the land as shown on the title deeds. If it is not provided you will have to calculate it using geometry and trigonometry. Then subtract the area of the residence and garage. Obtain this area by measuring the length of the outside walls, making a sketch and calculating the area. Do not use the area of the house stated by the builder or real estate agent when it was purchased. Because of faulty memory or original overstatement most houses are smaller than their owners believed them to be.

This will give you the gross area of the garden. Now subtract the area of hard sections such as paths, patios,

Slopes

Most land has some slope and if it is to be used as a garden a gentle slope is valued in areas of moderate to high rainfall. Too little slope leads to a risk of swamping, too great a slope and there is a danger of erosion. If there is very low rainfall then land slope is not important for its water-shedding ability but it is valued for its interest. In most parts of the world, land with moderate slopes, situated on ridges with views of water or valleys, is highly sought after.

Take care in measuring sloping land. Although the statutory requirement is to measure land horizontally, a pathway up a slope is as long as the true length of the

path measured along its length. Try telling the paving supplier that you measured the path on a plan — which will provide the horizontal dimension not the true measurement of the length of the path — and he will understand why the extra pavers are needed.

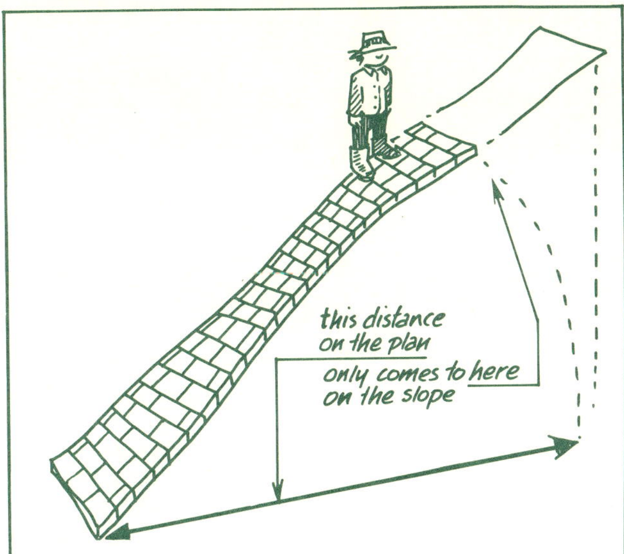

For land with a gentle slope the difference between the horizontal and the sloping measurements is of little significance over short distances. When land slopes are greater than 15° from the horizontal then the difference between the horizontal measurement and the slope measurement becomes significant even over short distances. A horizontal dimension of 10 metres (33′) becomes 10.6 metres (35′) at a slope of 20° and 11.5 metres (38′) at a slope of 30°. A path on the 30° slope which is 1 metre (3′) wide is 1.5 square metres (15 square feet) larger in area than its horizontal dimension calculate or in other words the pavers order for standard brick pavers is 60 pavers short, given that the pavers measure 230 (9″) mm x 110 (4½″) mm.

Orientation

The sun rises in the east, moves through the northern sky and sets in the west, in the Southern Hemisphere. In the Northern Hemisphere it still rises in the east but moves in the southern sky. At sunrise and sunset the angle of the sun to the ground is effectively zero. In a valley the sun's rays make a positive angle; on a mountain top the angle of the rays is negative.

This means that the shadows early in the morning and late in the afternoon are very long and overshadowing of planting beds by buildings and other plants can be an important factor in the choice of plants.

The sun does not rise and set at the same points on the horizon every day. In summer it rises to the south of east and in winter to the north of east; sunsets are south of west in summer and north of west in winter.

Not only does the sun shine for a longer period in summer than in winter but it also climbs higher in the sky in summer than it does in winter.

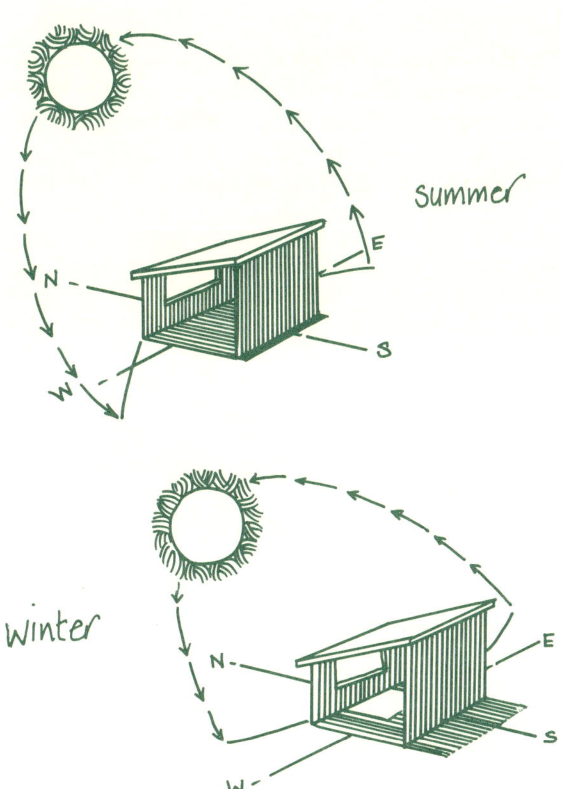

Tracking the sun and applying the information gathered is an essential component of garden design. Every garden has its own solar characteristics related to its latitude, longitude, orientation, elevation, slope, vegetation and the built environment.

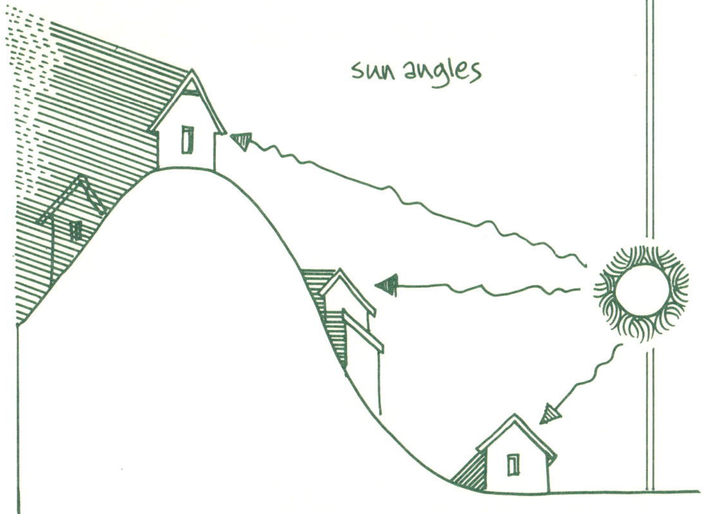

Some plants will thrive in full sun, some like to wake to the morning sun, others like the dappled sunlight of the undercroft. All have to be considered when designing a garden. Sunlight is the most important element in the garden design for without it there is no germination, new growth or flowers. However there can be too much sunlight in some gardens. Use sun-hardy planting or

purpose-built structures to protect those plants which
are damaged in the full sun.

There are plants which seek to grow away from the
direct sunlight and these include mosses, lichens, and
fungi. Though some mosses and fungi, particularly
edible varieties, are deliberately planted, most appear in
the garden without intervention. Many mosses, lichens,
and fungi are welcome intruders into the
garden design and an experienced garden
designer can predict where these will
occur. Some lichens and moulds,
both of which have fungi
connections, can be a
nuisance, turning
shaded pathways
into dangerous
slippery slides.

Prevailing weather

A cardinal rule for all garden designers is to stand on
the land of the proposed garden in all weather conditions, particularly in a storm. Personal experience is
an important factor in garden design.

In most areas wind and rain will come from a narrow
sector of the compass and so gardens can be designed
to mitigate against the worst excesses of inclement
weather. In areas where the weather is less predictable,
there may be two, three or occasionally more directions
from which bad weather can arrive and this increases
the variables to be considered when designing a garden.

Sometimes the land with the best aspect and spectacular views is on the edge of a cliff facing into the
prevailing weather. In this case forget the garden and
enjoy the view. Mostly it is possible to select the land
for a garden so that it has as much natural shelter from
the excesses of nature as possible.

Gardens need good ventilation and most plants
thrive in areas of good natural rainfall but few plants
will survive a windy stormswept environment for very
long. Where they do it is hard for plants to thrive while
resisting a 30-knot wind.

Views

Where a garden is blessed with views beyond its perimeter then the garden designer has the added task of
integrating the view into the garden vista without
reducing the value of either. Views can often be
enhanced by sympathetic foreground planting or the use
of planted or built framing devices.

Views should be carefully studied at morning, noon,
evening and after dark in summer, autumn, winter, and
spring before a final design is decided upon. Panoramic
views should be assessed to determine whether they are
at their best in super-wide cinemascope or would have
more value divided into cameo views. A mountain
framed by an arbour formed by an avenue of trees may
have greater impact than the mountain diminished by
largely uninteresting distant rolling hills.

A study of the views will allow exciting garden
design concepts to emerge. Consider a garden with a
view to the west over ragged hills. On a winter's evening
the sunsets are spectacular but in summer the late

afternoon sun is excessive to the garden planting, and to its human occupants. One solution is to plant a screen of deciduous trees. If you select trees that have an interesting shape when devoid of leaves, they will provide a foreground screen to enhance the winter sunsets and their full foliage in summer will form an effective natural sunscreen.

Access

A garden is not all vegetation. A significant proportion consists of buildings with their associated driveways, paths, terraces, and decks.

Most able people can use access paths that are a combination of level, ramped and stepped sections, although society is becoming more aware of the problems of the physically disabled.

Before designing a new garden or redesigning an existing area work out carefully what options there are for access on to and throughout the property for pedestrians. This is particularly important on steep or undulating sites but subsurface services can restrict the location of driveways, even on perfectly flat sites.

Other than people, motor cars are the most frequent visitors to residential gardens and there are some people who never enter or leave their own property except in a car. Cars are bigger than people and do not climb steps nor steep ramps and cannot negotiate tight corners. They are an intrinsic part of modern life and so a place for a car must be provided for within the garden. Cars need a driveway that leads from the street to a parking place in the garden whether this is exposed to the elements, roofed as a carport, or fully enclosed as a garage.

The area of the average suburban property is about 800-square metres (9 000-sq ft) and commonly has a 150-square metre (1 500-sq ft) residence, 30-square metre (300-sq ft) terrace, a 40-square metre (400-sq ft) garage and 40-square metres (400-sq ft) of driveways and paths. This leaves 540 square metres (6 400 sq ft) for vegetation and other garden design elements.

The residence

The house is an important component in the development of a garden design as it is normally the largest single item on the land. Gardens can be used to complement the appearance of a house, particularly when the house is of significance, or they can be used to conceal houses or parts of houses which are not attractive. The existing house on the land should be studied carefully before commencing the garden design so as to integrate the two harmoniously.

Where a new house is to be built as part of the garden design, an architect who is sympathetic to the garden designer's ideas for the garden should be chosen. A house may dominate the garden if that is what is wanted by the garden designer but it should intrinsically appear to belong in the garden.

Houses that require extensive alteration or additions should be designed in concert with the proposed garden design.

Outlook

Do not forget to look at the garden from inside the house as well as looking at the house from the garden. Windows are where the architecture of the exterior of the house and the decoration of its interior meet. The view from a window is one of the important elements that makes up our judgment of how much a room is liked.

Many illustrations of award-winning gardens show only the garden; few bother to show the garden as it looks from inside a window or doorway. Windows do not have to be large to provide a view of a garden and some of the most interesting views into a garden can be provided with modest-sized windows.

Garden design should be about creating a total concept where the interior of the house is fully integrated with the garden and the exterior of the house complements the garden and is, in turn, complemented by it.

Shadows

Buildings cast shadows and it is important in preparing any garden design that the designer knows where the shadows are. Many plants will not thrive in shade; others will.

When measuring shadows, remember there is an angle from the top of the wall casting the shadow to the ground. This means that, although the shadow may stretch several metres out from the wall, many plants will be in shadow only at their base and will be in sunlight higher up.

At any time in a day, shadows will be longer in winter than in summer. This may be significant for some plants, particularly deciduous shrubs and trees which need sun in summer but are unaffected by being in the shade during winter when they are dormant.

Employing a land surveyor

Land surveyors are trained to measure land, to determine its slope, locate built improvements, locate trees (including their height) and draw site plans and contour diagrams. There is value in employing a surveyor to measure a parcel of land accurately, to plot buildings and trees and to take levels and issue a contour diagram, but this value can be significantly reduced if the garden designer is not trained in the use of surveyor's information and the conventions employed.

Surveyors use terms including 'datum point', 'reduced level', and many others to issue precise information to architects and builders. Much of this detail is not required by a garden designer preparing a design for a normal relatively flat suburban allotment.

Survey information is needed on larger gardens, particularly those with undulating topography, especially if re-contouring, banking and earth retaining is being considered.

If the location of existing utility services is not readily identifiable then the surveyor can be used to prepare a plan showing the location of all services.

THE AUTHORITIES

Generally, the government agencies and other statutory bodies exercise very little control over what individuals can do within their private gardens. The planting of trees, shrubs, lawns, and flowers are mostly unrestricted, but it is worth checking with local authorities when you move into a new area to find out if there are any restricted plants. Such restrictions usually exist to control weeds and pests. Many areas of natural bushland and even some national parks have been blighted by the introduction of non-indigenous plants. Lantana, blackberry, Crofton weed, and water hyacinth are a few. Sometimes they spread from adjacent residential gardens, or are grown from seeds carried by wind, water, or birds; or worst of all, unthinking gardeners have dumped garden cuttings in the natural reserves.

Restrictions on improvements

In most places a building permit is required before a house can be erected. In a few areas a permit is needed to erect a garage, a shed, a fence, an ornamental pool, a swimming pool, a lych-gate, a pergola, a gazebo, a summer house, and even an outhouse. It is the responsibility of a landowner to check with the local authorities to find out what permits are required.

Restrictions on garden buildings are often justified by local government authorities on the basis that the community needs to be protected from poor development. There is conflict between the need of gardeners to have a shed in which to store tools and the potential that a shed will be used for human habitation. But gardeners have some rights and what happens inside a garden boundary should not be of concern to government authorities, except where there is a clear case that other people will be adversely affected.

Pool water is a major worry for our legislators, who are under pressure to require every pool and lake to be surrounded by a 1.2-metre (4') high childproof fence. Child safety is important and every child drowned is one too many, but it is doubtful whether the fencing of all garden water can completely eliminate this danger.

However water is an important component of many garden designs and designers should take great care to ensure that an unnecessary danger is not being

created. If gardeners are careless and child drownings continue then legislators will be forced to bring down restrictive laws.

Locating pipes, cables, and easements

In many places the title deeds to a parcel of land show the location of easements, which normally exist to allow an authority to bury pipes, erect powerlines or drive vehicles through private property as a right. Planting is generally allowed in drainage and powerline easements though there may be some restriction on the type of planting and the species of plants allowed.

Planting is not encouraged in right-of-way easements, even though no vehicle may ever use the right of way. This limits the use of the land and generally only lawn is possible.

Locating pipes and cables is not always easy. Even when an authority keeps records of where it installs services, these are often inaccurate. The local sewer authority will provide you with information and a diagram of where the sewer is on your land for a fee. Other utility authorities normally offer a similar service. Some authorities do not keep records, so take care. It can be expensive and dangerous to break or damage a utility service while creating a garden of great beauty.

SOIL TESTING

Much of the plant life in a garden is out of sight below ground, in the form of roots. It is generally the roots that pump the moisture out of the ground up into the plant, and without healthy roots and sufficient moisture most plants will die. Plants vary in their need for nutrients, water retention and drainage in the soil surrounding them. When planning a garden it is important that the subsurface conditions are suitable for the plants that are to be grown and compatible with the improvements to be made. Poor soil will lead to poor plants while good soil generally means healthy, vigorous plants.

Tests for suitability of soil for a garden should be taken on every property to be designed or redesigned. Include checking for nutrients, pH balance, moisture retention, drainage, and rock.

Detailed information is required on the subsurface condition of a garden before certain improvements are undertaken. It would be foolhardy to consider removing 3 metres (10') of soil from the top of a low mound with a mattock and spade, if information was available to show that it has a basalt core only 1 metre (3') below the surface.

It is relatively simple to check for rock close to the surface by driving steel spikes into the ground and digging exploratory holes. Check that any rock found is not an isolated floater.

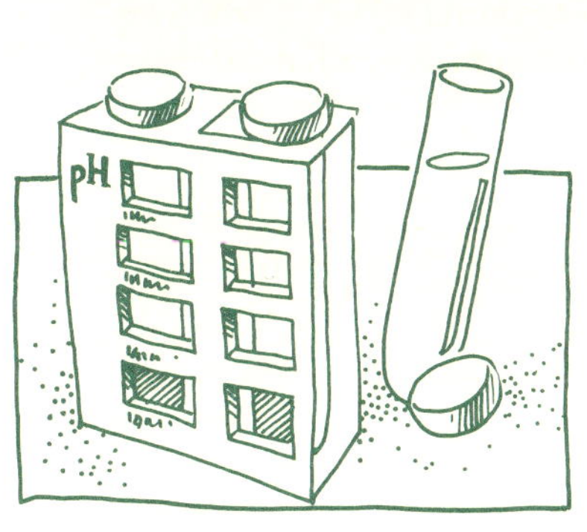

Other reasons for checking the subsurface conditions are:
- With what angle of slope can the subsoil be formed into a battered bank without slip or excessive erosion?
- What footings are needed to support any proposed buildings adequately on the available foundation?
- What are the natural drainage qualities of the substrata?

Taking samples

Gardeners can take their own soil samples from their gardens and then check them through a number of simple tests. To take a soil sample, dig a short trench into the ground to a depth of a spade or the ground is too hard to dig with a normal spade. The person digging the hole may find the trench will be shoulder-high.

A number of checks can be made with this simple trench. When soil is hard to dig with a spade, roots also find it difficult to penetrate. Check the variations in the soil colour as the hole is being dug. If the soil is dark brown in colour and has an open texture, it contains humus and should drain well.

Soil with a sandy coarse texture and with little colour is likely to contain insufficient humus, so water will drain away too quickly. If the soil is close textured and of a yellow/orange or grey colour, then it is likely to be a clay which is not easily penetrated by water or roots.

A garden will generally have topsoil with a high humus content and an open structure. Although this type of topsoil will hold sufficient water for plant growth it will also drain easily to maintain a sweet environment.

The topsoil will vary from only a few centimetres (inches) thick to over a metre (3') deep. Under this should be a layer of well-drained soil over the clay, shale or rock base.

The depth of the soil available will determine the type of trees and other plants that should be planted in the garden.

Checking samples

Samples taken from different levels in the test trench can be checked for cohesiveness, that is, the stickiness of the soil. The soil must be damp to carry out the following test. Take a small handful of soil from the trench and try to roll it into a ball — about the size of a golf ball is suitable.

If the soil will not hold together to make a ball, the soil is non-cohesive, that is, it has very little or no clay content and minimal humus. This soil will need to be enriched with well-rotted organic material if most plants are to thrive.

If the soil makes a ball then it is considered to be cohesive, that is, it contains clay and maybe some humus. Roll the ball into a thin sausage and attempt to bend it into a horseshoe shape. If the sausage crumbles easily then it is likely to be rich in humus and a good gardening loam.

The sausage may bend to form a full circle indicating it has a very high clay content. Such soil will usually require the addition of humus, and in some extreme cases, sand may also have to be added. Note that a significant proportion of sand has to be added before a noticeable difference is apparent in the quality of the soil.

To gauge the proportion of organic matter, sand and clay in a soil sample, place some soil in a glass jar, about a third of the volume will do. Then fill the jar with water and attempt to stir and shake the soil into solution.

Let the contents settle for at least seven days and then check it. The organic matter will have floated to the surface in the form of a dark scum. If there is no scum, wait a few more days and check it again. If there is still no scum, then the soil contains very little humus and other organic material.

The thicker the scum, the richer the soil. Check the bottom of the jar. If there are sand granules visible as well as a scum of humus and organic matter, the soil has good potential. The grey / yellow / orange section in the middle is the clay.

Strain the water from the jar through a coffee filter, then place it in a glass saucepan and simmer it gently until all the water has evaporated. If there is a salt-like white residue, then the soil may have a high saline content and should be checked further. It is *not* a good idea to taste the residue as many toxic compounds could have been added to the soil.

Employing a geo-technical consultant

If the site proposed for landscaping is in steep terrain or is in an area known for landslip, it is prudent to seek the advice of a geo-technical consultant before starting garden-site work.

Landslip is a problem generally associated with steep garden sites. The following factors are indicators of a possible landslip location:

- Steep ground slopes, that is, greater than 25° from horizontal
- The presence of slip scarps or tension cracks in the ground surface
- Hummocky or irregular ground surfaces
- Dead, inclined or curved trees
- Persistent soil saturation or seepage

Combinations of these features may indicate that the area is unstable (or may become unstable) if subject to cutting or filling earthworks or if soil moisture contents and drainage patterns in the area are altered.

In these areas seek advice from a consultant about the requirements for retaining walls, drainage systems, and earthworks controls. Where a bank is excavated or filled by shifting more than half a metre of soil there is potential instability. Unless the excavation or filling is retained properly larger scale instability may result.

In areas where there is already extensive earthworks even a minor change in the natural topography can result in a increased potential for land failure.

Overwatering or the introduction of drainage water in areas of steep land will increase the potential for instability to develop. Designed retaining walls and controlled drainage provisions may be required.

Rock faces and large detached blocks of rock (floaters) can also be destabilised if subjected to excavation, additional loading, to the effects of increased or concentrated water flows. The growth of tree roots into open rock fractures or joint planes can result in the localised destabilisation of rock faces. If these conditions exist or may develop in the proposed garden area, get advice about any remedial or preventive measures that may need to be incorporated into the garden works.

AVAILABLE SERVICES

Whether you are designing a new garden or redesigning an existing one, it is important, and in some cases, critical to know the availability and location of utility services.

All gardens need a water supply and most gardens need a drainage system. The water supply can be as simple as relying on natural rainfall, and drainage can be by natural landfall assisted by absorption and transpiration. In most planned gardens, however, irrigation systems and agricultural drains are important components of the design considerations.

If a garden design is to grow and flourish over the decades, and even over generations, it is important that the existing services are located and all available information is collected and documented before beginning the design. Connections will need to be made to these services, and as roots can cause massive damage to pipes and cables these matters must be considered.

Stormwater drains

Stormwater drains carry excess rainwater from collection points to convenient places of disposal through channels and pipes. On a parcel of land that is bare, except for the residence and garage, it is common simply to collect all the water running from the roofs of the buildings and from any large paved areas and pipe it to the nearest convenient main drain or to an on-site absorption disposal system.

This total loss system works well if there is no need to supplement the garden irrigation system and there is an abundant supply of clean free water. It is wasteful in many locations where the rainfall is irregular or the cost of water is expensive.

Many locations have limited supplies of reticulated water and when there is a particularly dry period, commonly at the height of summer, often garden watering is restricted or banned.

For a well-designed garden, work out a system that makes the best use of rainwater, which is generally the purest water available — and it is free. Every garden will have its own requirements and problems. If rainwater can be made to pass through the garden before being disposed of, this is a definite bonus. If surplus water is still available after routing it through the garden, then some form of holding pond or tank to store the water for use when there is insufficient rainfall should be available.

Today, with the availability of relatively cheap uPVC extruded plastic piping most handy gardeners can install their own stormwater systems. It is important to follow a few basic guidelines:

- Check with the local authority controlling the disposal of stormwater before starting any work that will be connected to a public stormwater drain (including natural watercourses), as many authorities have regulations that need to be obeyed
- Lay drains to even falls. Remember, water in an open-ended system should not be required to flow uphill, and a fall of around 1 in 40 is reasonable
- Lay the pipes in trenches so that there will be sufficient soil over the pipe to avoid damage from

heavy loads such as cars, and to allow for normal planting; a cover of about 300 mm (1′) is sufficient
- Lay pipes on a bed of packing sand, if possible, to provide continuous support for the pipe and reduce the danger of cracking
- Provide cleaning eyes or pits at changes in direction or in very long pipe runs to facilitate cleaning at a later time

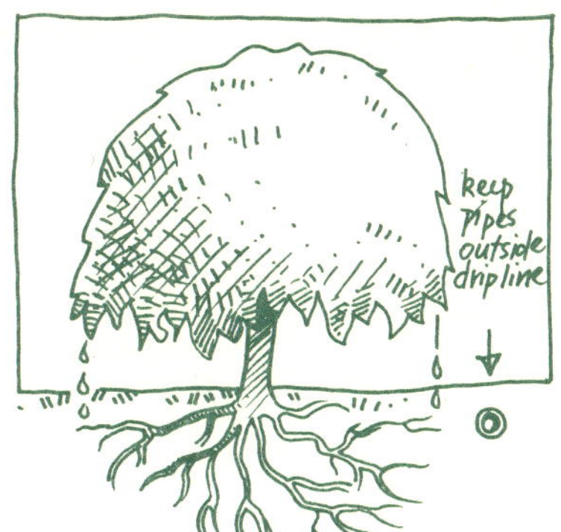

- Keep pipes clear of tree and shrub roots, particularly those plants known to send their roots into pipes (like willows) and remember, trees grow and their roots commonly spread out to the drip line of the tree
- Provide a silt trap pit in the line immediately before any pipes that pick up surface water enter into a main stormwater drain. A silt trap pit is a brick or concrete pit which has the inlet pipe above the bottom of the pit and the outlet pipe slightly above the inlet pipe. Provide the silt trap pit with an easy-to-remove lid, preferably in steel, so that the silt build-up can be removed as part of regular garden maintenance

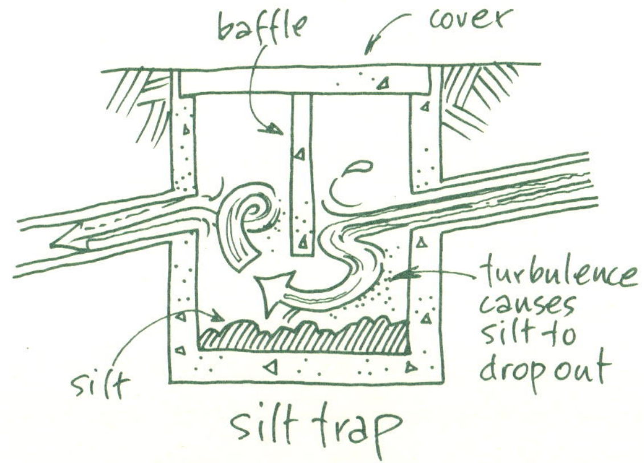

Rainwater from the roofs of buildings can be directed through a bed of pebbles or crushed clean stone on the surface or below the surface. Use this as a slow-release water supply by connecting it to a system of

perforated pipes running through the planting beds.
Allow the stored water to slowly percolate into the soil
adjacent to the plants. The ends of these pipes should
be connected to a drain that allows excess water to run
to waste or ponded storage to avoid waterlogging the
soil or causing swamp-like conditions to develop.

Open drains, whether lined or earthen, can be used
in some gardens but these often require regular maintenance to avoid stagnant water or breeding ponds for
mosquitoes.

Sewer drains

Sewer drains are for removal of septic waste products
(generally described as sewage) containing human waste
products, and the liquid waste from preparing food,
washing clothes, and general ablutions.

Except in the most remote locations sewage disposal
is strictly controlled and all services must be installed by
qualified and registered tradespeople. From the garden
designer's point of view, the sewerage system will not
play any role in the garden other than potential pipe
damage by tree and shrub roots or by excavation.

All sewer lines should be plotted and checked before
starting any work on a garden design. It is cheaper and
more convenient to relocate or protect a sewer line
before the garden is planted rather than after.

Trees are not the only things that affect sewer lines.
If a swimming pool is planned there is sure to be a sewer
line under the chosen location.

Agricultural drains

Agricultural drains are the gardener's friend and a well-
designed system of subsurface porous drains can help to
maintain a stable moisture content level in the soil.

These drains have two main functions:

- To remove surplus ground water from parts of a
  garden where there is too much water — behind
  retaining walls, at the foot of steep banks, at the
  uphill boundaries of the property and other similar
  locations
- To distribute water from surplus watersource to a
  suitable place where it can be absorbed by the
  surrounding soil and then taken up by plants and
  transpired into the atmosphere or lost to the
  atmosphere by evaporation

Most agricultural drains today are constructed by
excavating a trench into the ground with even falls to
its bottom. This trench is part-filled with clean hard
crushed rock and a flexible perforated plastic pipe laid
over. Crushed rock is placed around and over the pipe
to give cover of about twice the diameter of the pipe,
a sheet of plastic is placed over the crushed rock and the
trench is backfilled with sand to the level of the topsoil.
The trench is finished by completing the filling with
topsoil.

The plastic sheeting is to avoid too much silt getting
into the pipe, thereby reducing its flow or even blocking
the pipe, so space should be left at the edge of the trench

to let water flow through. Overfill the trench with topsoil to allow for natural settlement.

Cleaning eyes into the pipe system will allow the
pipes to be flushed out periodically and reduce the risk
of system failure, and all-too-common fault in agricultural drainage systems. Always place a slit trap pit
between an agricultural drain and any stormwater pipe
that it enters.

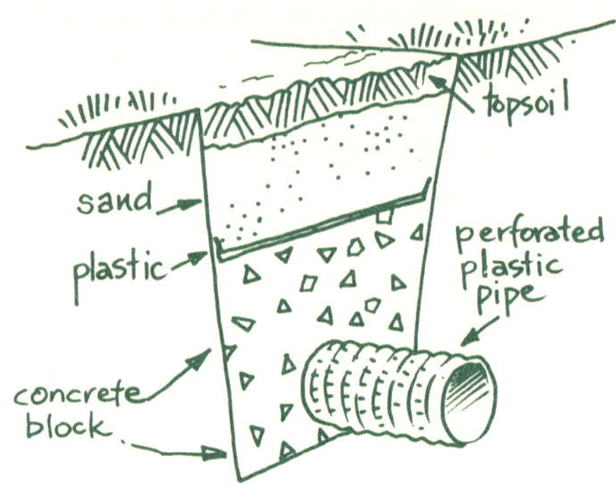

Septic systems

Septic system is a generic term for all the many types of
sewage treatment systems which can be used in areas
not connected to a main sewer system.

Some septic systems are complete treatment plants
that produce clear water liquid waste and solid waste
that is biologically safe and easy to dispose of, but these
are the exceptions rather than the rule.

Commonly, a septic waste system connected to a
residence is a single chamber tank which relies on bac-
terial action to reduce the solid and liquid waste
components to a relatively harmless liquid. This is then
disposed of through a network of absorption trenches
or a simple transpiration bed which uses special grasses
to draw up the excess liquid and expel it as water
vapour into the atmosphere.

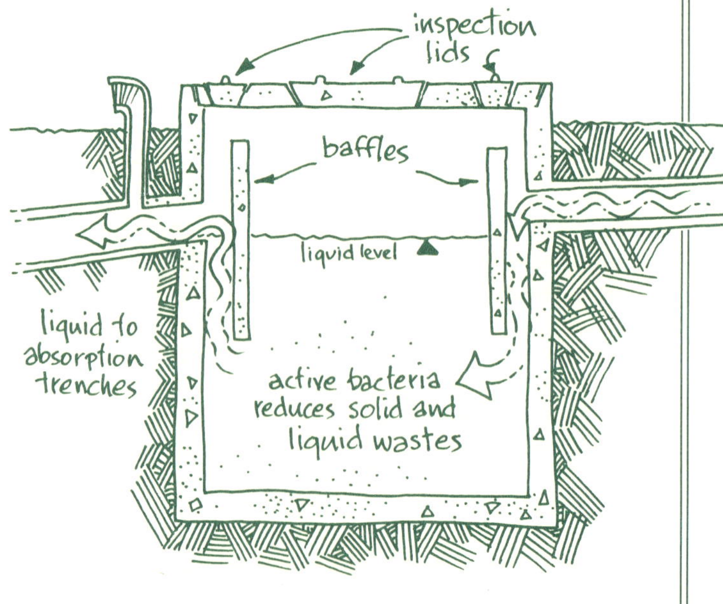

In ideal locations the common septic tank does a passable job of disposing of sewage. Few locations are ideal and there is always a risk of poorly treated septic waste coming to the surface in a garden, which is unpleasant, possibly a risk to human health, and toxic for some plant life.

It is important that the absorption trenches and transpiration beds are located as local conditions require and that you take all necessary care to avoid upsetting the system when designing a garden.

With a septic tank there is frequently a sullage disposal system. This is the system which receives the liquid waste from baths, showers, laundry tubs and the like. Sullage is water contaminated by dirt from bodies and clothes as well as the residues of detergents and other chemicals used in washing.

Sometimes described as grey water sullage water has the potential to be used for watering gardens. Do not use grey water to irrigate plants which may be adversely affected by chemicals in the water. However there are many plants which tolerate these in a diluted form particularly lawns.

Where grey water is stored in an underground tank and further diluted by clean rainwater (particularly in areas with poor water supply), then more water is available for garden use.

If a tank 3 metres (10′) in diameter and 3 metres (10′) deep were built to store grey water its location in the garden design is important. With an approximate capacity of 21 cubic metres (750 cu. ft) or 21 000 litres (4 500 gallons) it would only take about 160 showers to fill the tank. An average bath or shower uses between 100 (20) and 150 litres (30 gallons) of water. For a family of 3 bathing every day in less than 2 months the tank would be full. By comparison a house with a roof area of 150 square metres (1 500 sq ft) would need rainfall of about 140 mm (6″) to provide the same volume of water.

Water supply

Turn on a tap and out comes water by the hundreds of litres. The rate varies from place to place but if it takes 10 minutes to draw a bath containing 150 litres (30 gallons) of water then the tap is providing 15 litres (3 gallons) of water per minute. Leave two hoses spraying water on a garden for 6 hours a day for two days a week adds up to 75 000 minutes a year and over 1 million litres (225 000 gallons) of water is sprayed onto the garden.

Gardens need a lot of water and the watering system to provide it should be designed into every new garden.

Spraying water into the air and hoping it will land on the plants that need it is not a scientific approach and it is a waste of a precious resource.

A well-designed garden should incorporate a system of plant irrigation which maximises the value of every drop of available water. Design the garden watering system so that water is distributed where it will do the most good.

Plastic pipe reticulation systems which provide plant by plant sprays and drips are available from most garden supply shops and can be installed by handy gardeners. If the watering system is cross-connected to the mains water supply, storage ponds and tanks, even the largest garden can be watered economically. All the equipment to do this is available and for a small investment, combined with thoughtful design, a sophisticated system can be assembled.

After designing a watering system that waters the plants and not the concrete drive, the house walls, and the neighbour's lawn, the system can be connected to a valve system programmed to turn on the watering system at predetermined times for controlled periods of time. It waters the garden when the gardener is not at home as well. There are times when plants are more able to take up water, often overnight, and few but the most dedicated gardeners will set the alarm clock at 30-minute intervals throughout the night to go out and change the sprinkler.

Garden water can be drawn from the mains supply, permanent watercourses, local catchment dams, and from bores. Sinking a bore and pumping water up from the aquifers or other underground watersources is one way to avoid water restrictions and have a constant year-round water supply. Local authorities and engineers will know the availability, depth, and water quality of bores in a local area. Although nearly all bore water is suitable for garden use, some is not, and there are very few places where the bore water can be drunk by people.

Sinking a bore is a major expense in setting up a garden, but in many areas it ensures that water is always available to keep the plants alive and flourishing.

Water storage

Many different methods are used in gardens to store water and some of these have been discussed earlier in this chapter. Generally, water can be stored above ground, at ground level, or below the ground.

Above ground storage of water has traditionally been associated with circular corrugated iron tanks but there are many alternatives including reinforced concrete (either poured in place or pre-cast off-site), fibre glass, plastic membrane and masonry. Tanks of any of these materials are likely to be quite large, tall units and need to be located in a garden plan carefully, to minimise their visual impact (some can be contained in a folly), to take into account their overshadowing effect and allow for a spillway. The spillway is required in case the tank fails or there is excess run-off after heavy rain so, the water that is released will do minimum damage to the rest of the garden.

Ground level water storage can be incorporated into a garden in the form of ornamental ponds, pools, brooks and even lakes if the property is large enough. Open storage ponds are often quite large in area compared with their depth and therefore lose a significant volume of water to evaporation. Waterlilies and other water plants can be nurtured in ponds but they can become polluted with algae and provide an ideal environment for breeding mosquitoes.

To control algae the pond can be stocked with fish usually from the carp or trout families. Care must be taken to avoid sucking fish into any pumps and it is a good idea to pump water from a small pool separated from the main pond with an effective strainer for fish and vegetable matter.

Most unprepared ponds will leak and so do not provide useful water storage. Leak-proofing a pond can be as simple as lining it with plastic pond-liner membrane or spraying the underwater surfaces with concrete.

If the pond is to be used to store water for irrigation purposes, it is best to make the sides of the pond nearly vertical. This reduces the visual impact of varying water levels. If the sides are shallow small changes in water level will expose a proportionally large area of bank; in this case, consider the use of sandy banks to give a beach effect.

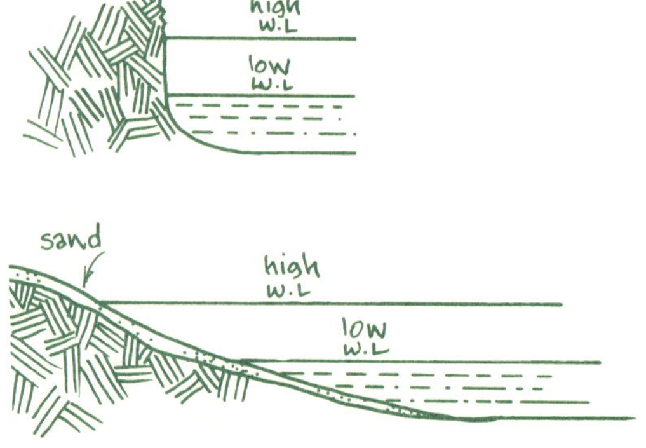

Some local authorities may require approval to construct a pond and safety railings to prevent toddler drownings. You may need a spillway if there is any chance of the pond overfilling from its supply source. A spillway allows the overflow to be discharged into a drain or watercourse, without damaging any plants.

Underground storage of water can take two forms: the first is by tanking and the second is by the construction of a false aquifer — that is, a space underground. The area is filled with hard crushed rock where water can be stored around the stones.

Underground tanks can be constructed to hold large quantities of water but these take up room which could be used for tree roots although the tanks are out of sight, only light shallow-rooted planting can be used over most tanks. There is special danger with underground tanks: if they are empty and the watertable around them rises they are liable to float out of the ground.

The false aquifer allows for normal planting above, although take care not to plant trees which are known to search for water. The storage capacity of the false aquifer is much smaller than an equivalent-sized tank but it has a relatively low impact on the garden and can be any size the garden designer requires. With a special pump and correct installation water can be pumped easily out of the false aquifer.

Electricity supply

Electricity is very dangerous, particularly if it is being distributed at 240 volts. You should be sure of the location of any wiring in the garden area. One shovel cut into a live electric cable is enough to kill most people. Do not take any risks with electrical connections. Always use a registered electrician, approved by the supply authority. If mains voltage power is used, connect it through an earth leak core balanced circuit breaker, this device will cut off the power almost instantly if a circuit is shorted to earth.

Plan carefully the position of all pumps and other equipment requiring electrical power and ensure that the wiring follows a path which will protect it from damage by growing plants, and the likelihood of it being cut by gardening tools, manual or power-driven.

If possible, use only low voltage lighting in the garden. There is a minimal risk of accidental electrocution with such fittings and allows for untrained individuals to alter or add to the electrical lighting system.

Telecom services

Telephone services are often connected to a residence with a small section cable buried in the ground without any added protection. Find the wire and mark its location before forming the garden.

Gas services

Locate any gas lines that pass through the garden and mark the area carefully. Any damage to a gas line can result in an explosion and fire. Many gas lines are very old and are severely corroded and can break with very little force. If there are old gas lines in the garden being designed, have them replaced or sleeved with a plastic lining. As natural gas is connected to properties old gas lines can be removed if they are exposed during garden excavation. It is necessary for this to be done by a licensed gasfitter.

CONSULTANTS

Consultants are those people who, by training, experience, and sometimes government registration can practise in a specialist profession. Not all garden designers will need or want the assistance of professional engineering, landscape, or horticultural consultants. They charge fees for their services and these should be examined carefully. It is important to gauge the cost-benefit relationship before briefing a consultant.

- Where is help required?
- Will a consultant provide the extra input that will ensure the best result?
- If a consultant is not engaged will the designer alone be able to handle the task?

There are many other questions that could be asked but these will serve to illustrate why you might engage a consultant. If your budget for designing the garden is more than adequate and time is of the essence, then consultants will help to spread the load and add to the available knowledge to get the job done.

knowledge of the gardener. They design and develop whole gardens to satisfy the commissioning brief issued by the garden owner, they give advice on what plants will thrive, where or which gravel makes the best path in a specific area, and everything in between.

Many garden designers seem to envisage only the result of their plans in 25 to 30 years. But people do not close their eyes until the garden is fully grown. A landscape designer should be able to prepare sketch drawings of the garden as it grows and develops towards maturity — a view of the garden in two years, five years, eight years, 15 years and 25 years for instance.

Landscape architects will model a garden to give it new style and form, provide you with an efficient watering system, nominate the best plants for a project, carefully shape and refine vistas, and generally offer you a complete design and documentation for a managed garden.

Horticulturalists

Horticulture is 'the science . . . of growing . . . flowers and ornamental plants . . . the cultivation of a garden' (*Macquarie Dictionary*) and a horticulturalist is someone who, through training and experience, has a sound knowledge about the cultivation of plants.

Unlike a landscape architect, a horticulturalist does not have extensive training in the design of garden layouts although most courses would include an introduction to garden design. Horticulturalists know

Landscape architects

A landscape architect, in most places, is required to have a recognised diploma or degree from a college of advanced education or a university. This involves three to five years' study.

Landscape architects combine the spatial manipulation skills of an architect with the botanic

about plants, soil and fertilisers, about planting times, flowering times and pruning. A horticulturalist is a great help to someone who is designing a garden and wants to ask questions about plants.

Horticulturalists come into their own when it is time to plant the new garden. They should know how large the hole should be, how to place the plant in the hole, how to backfill the hole, and how to fertilise the plant for the best results.

When the plants are growing, horticulturalists can be employed periodically to prune, transplant, carry out winter maintenance, and generally keep the garden in good health.

Architects

Architects only touch on landscape and garden design in their courses but special garden features like summerhouses, follies, and bridges are often better designed by an architect. Most of what is required in a garden are small feature buildings so do not skimp on good design.

Consider the garden design in harmony with modifications to the residence — new decks, terraces, verandas, and new windows and doors. There is little point in having the best garden in the district if you can appreciate it only from the outside.

Engineers

Engineers are involved in garden design only in a small proportion of gardens, but if engineers are required they can often lead to the success or failure of the design. Engineers are needed to design very high retaining walls or ones on suspect soil. They are needed when special designs or long-span bridges are required to span creeks or gorges, and they are needed to design tanks and dams.

Under specific circumstances specialist hydraulic engineers are employed to design complicated water storage and reticulation systems.

PRELIMINARY SKETCHES

Most gardens are designed, laid out and planted without the aid of drawings and many of them are very successful. But a garden which is designed and has plans prepared for it has a distinct advantage over a garden without a plan: its goal is clearly defined and all the people who work on the project know what is to be done. Without plans the complete design is held in the brain of the designer.

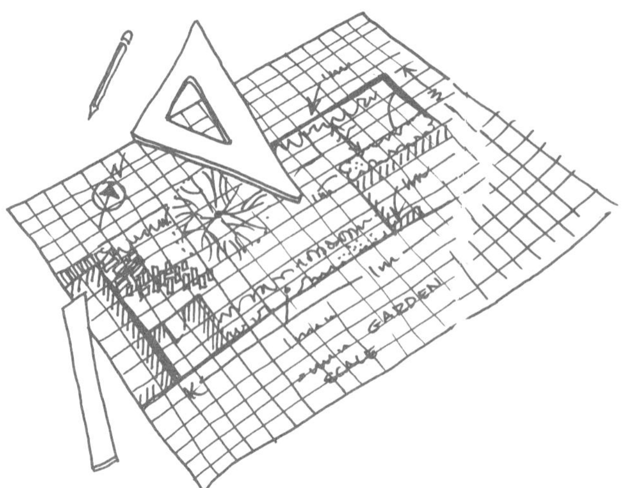

Preliminary sketches should be drawn to scale; they can be created on graph paper, mechanically on a drawing board, or electronically using a computer. Whichever method is chosen it is advisable to prepare the sketches to one of the accepted international drawing scales — 1 to 200, 1 to 100 or 1 to 50. These are the scales that surveyors, architects, and engineers are most likely to use.

If the garden is very large, scales of 1 to 500 or 1 to 1 000 can be used but they will show very little detail and are useful only for the general layout. For small gardens or detailed parts of larger gardens, scales of 1 to 20 and 1 to 10 can be used, particularly if there is detailed construction or complex planting to be designed.

Graph paper and scale rulers can be readily purchased in any of these scales. If the drawing is made on cheap transparent paper (commonly referred to as butter paper) laid over graph paper, the sketch is easier to read. Many sketches can be prepared and reviewed at the end of an intensive design session.

To draw every new thought on a separate sheet of paper, rather than rubbing out previous concepts when trying a new concept, avoids backtracking if the new concept is not as good as the previous one.

Preliminary design sketches should concentrate on the overview of the concept being developed, moving to the particular and the detailed design only when the general concept is well developed. Start with simple concepts and sketch only the information that you need to visualise your ideas, before moving on to another stage in the design development.

Preparing a brief

Designers appreciate it if clients provide them with a clearly written summary of the factors that should be considered when preparing their design. This saves the designer and the client valuable and sometimes expensive time in reaching a preliminary design scheme.

Gardeners who are designing for themselves will find it useful to jot down points for consideration in preparing the garden design. See the list as needs which are important to you in the design.

For example, it is better to say:

The western wall of the residence should be shaded in summer but warmed by the sun's rays in winter

than

Plant deciduous trees on the western side of the residence — or again it is better to say

Rainwater from the house roof should be stored on-site to supplement possible inadequate water supply during summer

than

Provide a 10 000-litre water tank.

Here designers can use their experience to suggest alternative methods to meet the needs listed in the brief, and widen the range of potential design solutions.

Identifying the issues

When the brief is ready there is a tendency for the designer to rush to the drawing board and start sketching, but this may not be the best move. The brief is generally only a shopping list of items that needs to be included in the garden and frequently written briefs do give in detail the reasons why a garden is required at all.

The designer needs to analyse the brief and search for the real issues to be addressed in the design. If the designer is also the garden owner this is relatively easy. Identifying and ranking the reasons, or the issues, of why the garden is to be designed is an important factor.

In the brief you may have written the requirement is the garden should be fast-growing.

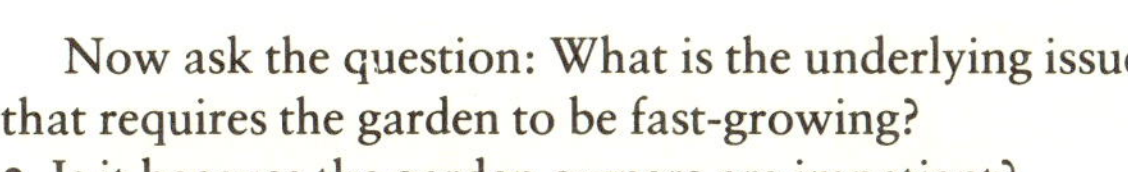

Now ask the question: What is the underlying issue that requires the garden to be fast-growing?
- Is it because the garden owners are impatient?
- Is it because the garden is around a house that is to be sold soon?
- Is it because the garden owners are elderly and hope to see the garden flourish in their lifetimes?

Issues emerging from analysis of the brief and research, allow for a systematic procedure of ranking and re-ranking of the issues to begin. The questions generated by the issues are answered (or generate further questions).

Refining the issues

Issues generating questions can generate more questions so that putting design proper into effect seems to move further away with each new question.

If the garden being designed is a 'botanic garden' with specimen vegetation in highly developed micro-climatic environments and has to last many generations, the issue, research and systematic analysis may take a significant period of time.

Most residential garden designers do not have such aspirations but hope to work out any difficulties before starting the work on the garden. This needs assessing the questions and answers being generated from the issues analysis. The designer must determine when to stop the answer chase before the system becomes self-breeding.

Making further sketches and the concept of scale

After preparation of the brief and the analysis of the significant issues identified, there should be a clear set of facts that will allow you to begin sketch designs.

The sketches can be on paper to an appropriate scale, as discussed earlier, or they can be full-scale diagrams scratched into the soil with a pointed stick on the real site of the garden. This is a good method when the garden is of a manageable size but can be a problem if you are dealing with a very large area, or complex topography is involved.

Designers prepare sketches so that ideas can be seen and re-communicated to their brains for further development. Then they can share their sketches with others. It is possible to do all the designing within the human brain and go straight to the realisation of the design without any sketches or other external assistance but not many people can do this satisfactorily.

Comments from others is often the best way to test ideas and extend the information resources available to the designer.

DEVELOPING THE DESIGN

When the preliminary sketch design reaches the stage where all the major features of the garden are placed and the items in the brief appear to be satisfied, the next stage — design development can begin.

Now all the special details and materials are identified and developed. On the preliminary sketches a retaining wall may show as a simple line separating two levels in the garden; it is now time to determine how the wall is to be constructed, its height, and what materials are to be used.

When you move from preliminary sketches, which are drawn to approximate scale, to the more developed design, you need to know the correct dimensions of all the components you will be using.

A timber·deck may be drawn on a sketch plan in its correct location and size. In developing the design you need to know what will support the decking and how high it will be above the ground surrounding it. The weight of the deck will determine if a balustrade railing is required or the ground level should be raised. There may also be a need for steps to the deck. Decisions need to be made about the materials for the steps and where these will be placed.

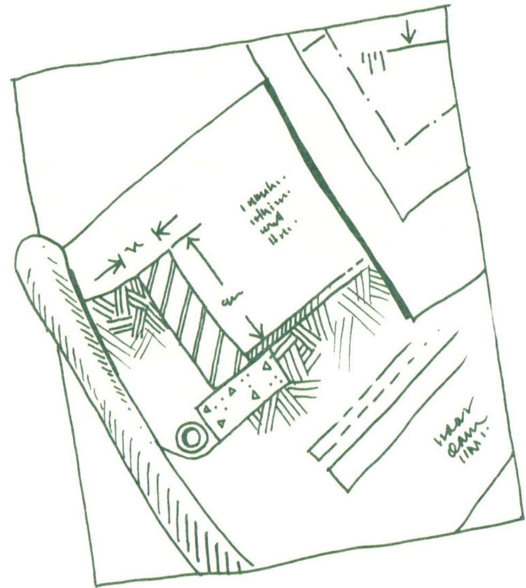

Progressively the sketch design must be developed and refined so that all the individual parts act in harmony and little is left to chance. Garden design has a number of factors that separates it from other types of three-dimensional spatial design. The most important of these differences is that the designer has to combine the manufactured materials with the natural.

When architects design a house they know, within narrow limits, the size of the people who will live in it. It is relatively easy to design a bedroom to accommodate a baby's bassinet, a toddler's cot, a teenager's bed, or even seaman's hammock.

For the garden designer it is necessary to consider such things as a sketch plan showing a pergola in the garden with a tree growing through it. There is a good chance that the tree does not exist when the garden is designed. With the sketch plan reaching the design development stage, the designer has to decide whether to build the pergola and hope that the tree will grow from a seedling to a mature tree and neatly penetrate the pergola where a hole is provided or consider other alternatives to accommodate the tree.

Largely design development is the assessment of alternatives and the selection of the one that will cause the fewest problems. The garden designer can break down the preliminary design into stages, spread over a

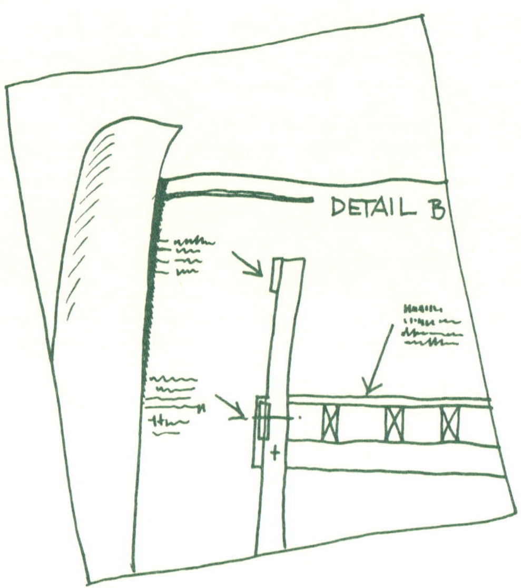

number of years so that reasonable compatibility is reached between plant growth and built features. This is done by drawing sketches anticipating the growth of planned and planted vegetation, over time in relation to the garden structures and built environment.

Dreams and the reality

At the preliminary design stage, some of the concepts that are thought to be important components of the design may appear to be resolved. However on closer analysis during the design development stage, some of these may be found wanting.

When preparation of your brief was discussed earlier it was suggested that it was better to state that shade from the western summer sun was required than simply provide deciduous trees to the western side of the residence.

Now the wisdom of this advice can be explained. If deciduous trees are planted on the western side of the

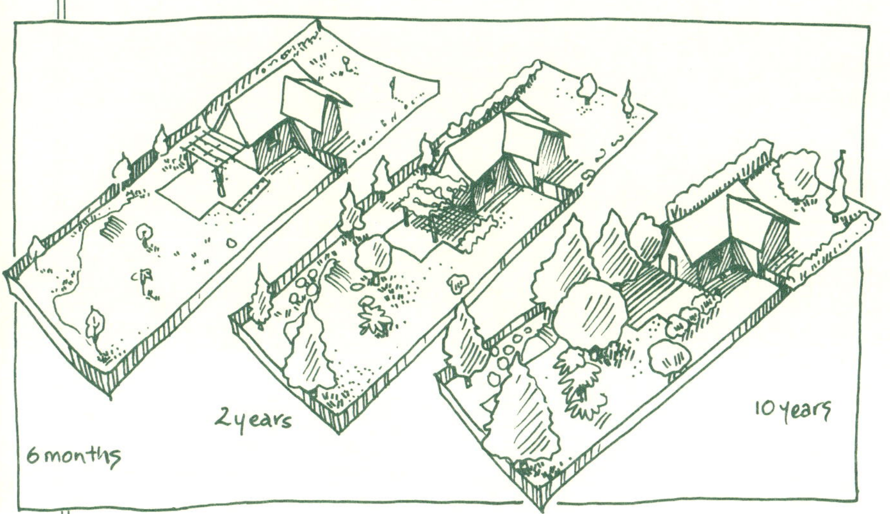

residence and they are 1 metre (3′) high seedlings they will offer little protection from the rigours of the summer sun for many years. If fast growing species are chosen then the delay can be reduced, but deciduous trees are relatively slow growing regardless of species.

Other alternatives can be explored; for example, a temporary pergola could be erected and planted with fast growing deciduous vines which will provide the shade required while the deciduous trees grow to a size where they become effective sunscreens.

Consider the concepts in a design, search for constraints, propose alternatives and at all times, remember a garden is in a state of continuous change — plants germinate, grow and die and the materials used to construct paths, walls, and fences change from new to mellow, to old, to decayed and ruin. These are the factors that make garden design exciting, challenging and never ending.

Testing the design for strength

When the garden design has been thoroughly developed, when all constraints appear to have been considered, suitable compromises found and a staging schedule worked out — go back to the brief.

Does the design satisfy the needs expressed in the brief? If it does and the garden will present well when it is first completed, and through its maturation, then a strong design exists.

If it does not satisfy the original brief look to why not. It may be a good garden design but the brief may not have been sufficiently developed. Make sure before deciding on the final design.

Checking estimates against budget

Gardens seldom cost less to construct than the money available. Most people are aware of this but live in optimistic hope that the garden will not cost more than they can afford.

Where the gardener spends a lot of time in the garden to be developed, having an over-budget design is not necessarily critical although it can be very frustrating to have grand plans which take so long to fulfil that the enthusiasm for the design is blunted.

It makes sense to design the garden within the budget available and to schedule the stages so that these are in line with the likely availability of funds. When the design is nearing completion and before a final commitment is made to its implementation, make a

careful estimate of the likely cost. If necessary then adjust the design to bring the anticipated cost of the development within the realistic budget.

Vast amounts of material can disappear into a garden; for example, if a garden of 500 square metres (6 000 sq ft) is to be raised by an average of 300 mm (1′) it will require 150 cubic metres (220 cu. yds) of filling, or about 15 truck loads.

DOCUMENTATION OF THE DESIGN

After the garden has been designed and the budget estimates checked, the design needs to be documented in such a way that the people who will be constructing and planting the garden know what they are to do and which materials to use.

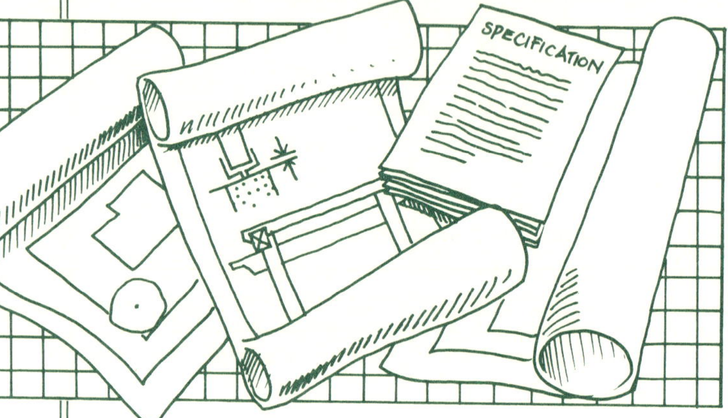

If the designers are also the garden owners intending to do most of the garden construction and planting, then a few notes on the final design drawings and some pamphlets and brochures from material and product suppliers probably will suffice.

However if the garden is to be constructed and planted by contracted workers then more detailed information is required to communicate clearly the scope and quality of the work to be done.

The work can be contracted to one person or a company with agreement to do all the work, either within their organisation or with assistance from specialist subtrade contractors, or the garden owners may choose to superintend the work and let out special sections of the work to other experienced people.

The choice depends on the experience of the garden owners, the time that is available, and the size of the budget. Most people can carry out the tasks involved in constructing and planting a garden with help from others where special skills, experience or heavy work is required.

Drawings to communicate quantity

Drawings are the simplest way communicating the extent of the work to be performed and the size and location of the components used. Often these drawings are called the 'working drawings' as distinct from the 'design drawings'. They follow conventions for symbols, dimensions, scales, descriptions, and layout that are understood universally by contractors.

The working drawings are split into a three-level hierarchy:

1 Location drawings
   These show general plans, sections, and elevations of the work to be undertaken and are normally drawn at scales of 1 to 500 to 1 to 50. They communicate the general location of all the parts of the project.

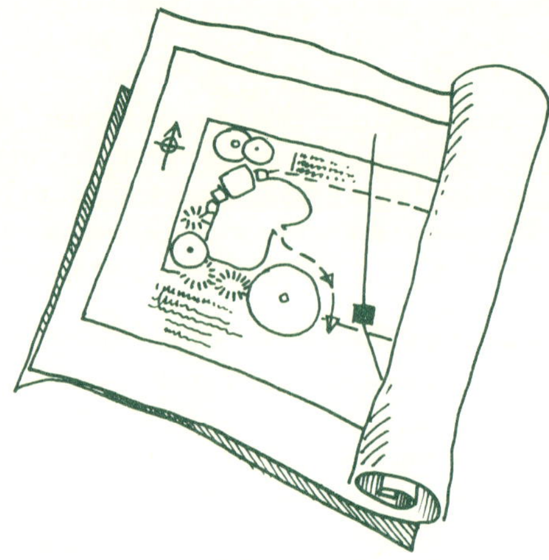

2 Assembly drawings
   These show by the use of plans, sections, elevations, and three-dimensional drawings, how to assemble or construct specific details of complicated or specially designed parts of the project and are normally drawn at scales of 1 to 50 to full size.

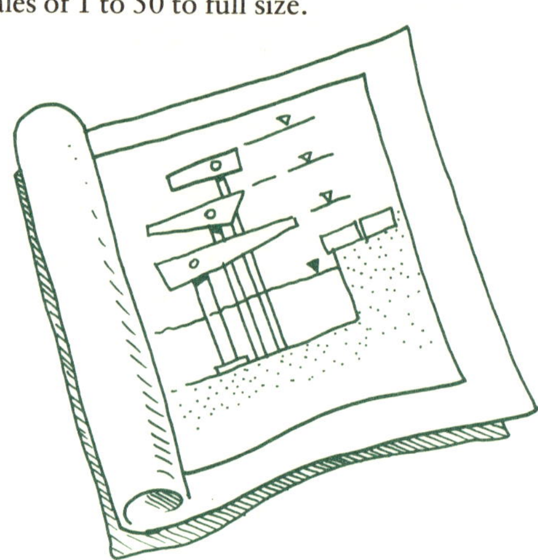

3 Component drawings
   These show information on specific components of the works, particularly items which are prefabricated and brought to the site ready for installation. Component drawings use similar drawing types and scales as assembly drawings but in some instances, may make use of a manufacturer's brochure.

For example, the design may call for a special fountain to be made for the garden. The location of the fountain in the garden would be shown on the location drawings, together with the general location of the main water supply and drainage pipe lines. The assembly drawings would show the footings and the on-site construction method for the base work and water reservoir, plus diagrams of the pipe assemblies, pump fittings, extent of rendering, and other materials to be used. And the component drawings would describe the specially made fountain feature and possibly the type of pump that is required.

The working drawings for a simple garden design may contain the complete information for all the trades on one set of drawings, but if the garden is complicated then separate working drawings may be produced for general construction and specialist subtrades. The most likely special subtrades drawings are for plumbing, drainage, electrical, paving and planting.

Specifications to communicate quality

Drawings are used to communicate quantity but they may have notes on them which will indicate a degree of quality. For example if a particular paver is nominated on the drawing, this is an immediate reference to quality.

The notes on the drawing may be sufficient to communicate the quality of the work required, particularly if the work is being carried out by the garden owner—designer, but if specialist tradespeople are employed more information may be required.

If a brick fence is to be constructed in the garden then the name of the brick can easily be noted on the drawings, but it becomes much harder on the drawing to fit all the information that may be needed to describe the standards, materials, and methodology required. Items better describing fully the quality of a brick fence may include: what standards are applicable, what concrete strength and steel reinforcement is needed in the footings, what quality and type of sand, cement, water, and admixes are needed in the mortar, how the mortar is to be mixed, how plumb and level the wall is

to be, what type of joint is required in the mortar beds and perpents, whether the wall is to be rendered and painted; and what is expected of the tradespeople in the way of cleaning up after their work is over.

The specification is a written document, normally divided into trades sections, which provides all of the above information. Many gardens and buildings are built without using a fully detailed specification, relying on the trades to carry out the work to an acceptable standard. This is in order if the tradespeople are well known to the person employing them, but on large and more complex projects conflict between the proprietor and tradespeople will be less likely if the quality required is clearly specified.

Schedules to aid ordering

The use of tables to schedule finishes, fittings, components and plants is a suitable method of providing information and can reduce the number of drawings and specifications required. If a schedule indicates the extent, type and colour of a product such as a paver and notes that it is to be laid to the manufacturer's recommendation, then many drawings and words can be saved.

Schedules also allow easy ordering of materials, fittings, and plants and are an important component of a well-administered cost—control system.

Tenders and contracts

The completed working drawings, the specification and the schedules should contain all the information that is required to construct the garden.

The basic rule for the employment of all labour and the purchase of all materials is: find out how much it is going to cost before allowing any person to begin work or any supplier to make a delivery. Tenders (or quotations) give opportunities for competitive pricing and contracts and help to avoid misunderstandings.

If practical, obtain at least two quotations for all labour contracts and supply orders. Take care that all tenderers are quoting in the same way — the safest method is to call for a firm price lump-sum quotation and for the work to be completed or the goods supplied by a definite date.

Unless the person responsible for superintending the works has wide experience in administering contracts avoid rise and fall or cost-plus quotations. Both these forms of contract protect the contractor and offer few tangible benefits to the proprietor.

A *rise and fall contract* is one where the tenderer offers to carry out the works for a lump-sum price but is entitled to obtain from the proprietor any increases in the cost of labour and materials which occur during the contract period — if there is a reduction cost the proprietor will be given the savings — there are seldom any savings.

A *cost-plus contract* is when the tenderer offers to carry out all work for a set fee, either a nominated sum or an hourly rate and to charge the proprietor only for the invoice value of all labour and materials used. This can be a useful form of contract on certain projects but the danger is that the full cost of the works is not known in advance. There is a risk that under-the-counter discounts are given to the contractor by the subcontractors and suppliers used, and these discounts are not always passed onto the proprietor.

Where possible the proprietor should nominate the form of agreement to be used in the contract as contracts published by industry groups protect the company providing labour or supplying materials — to the disadvantage of the proprietor. Any contract or legally worded order or other agreement should be checked by a lawyer but where this is inappropriate, try and keep the agreement simple and avoid using words or phrases which do not have a clear meaning.

Contracts seldom make projects run smoothly and are often only read and applied if there is a breakdown in communications between contractor and proprietor. When selecting a contractor, or supplier, always meet the contractor face to face. Even if their offer is the cheapest, when you do not think you can negotiate with the person you meet, employ another contractor.

The best bargain is to have the work done or the material supplied at a fair price, on time, and of the quality required. Never pay for work in advance unless there is no other alternative, conversely always pay on time and in the manner agreed upon.

Approvals where required from authorities

When the design is fully developed visit the local authorities responsible for approving the work to be carried out. The authorities most likely to require application for consent to carry out work are local government, electricity supply and water and sewerage authorities.

Allow time for authorities to consider any applications that are required as some may be very slow on requests for plans, advice, applications for alterations and extensions to services.

Local government involvement in approving garden plans and structures varies from place to place. In some municipalities the local environmental planning codes and regulations require every garden design to be approved in minute detail, particularly if they are protected or environmentally sensitive areas.

Most authorities do not impose controls over what can be planted in a residential garden though many will impose a tree preservation policy. This can be troublesome when a garden designer has a mature native tree in a garden that is planned to be exotic. Some authorities need to approve earthworks planned and most will impose rules and regulations to control any garden construction.

EMPLOYING THE TRADES

Perhaps the greatest problem for people constructing a garden is the method of employing the tradespeople to undertake the work. Local tradespeople who arrive on time, finish on time, and charge what they quoted, are a scarce resource and their names are often jealously guarded by the local builders and the long-term residents. Where tradespeople can be found in the close family or among the trusted acquaintances of the garden owners this gives the owner an immediate advantage. Many people building a new garden have only just bought the property and therefore are far from their relatives and acquaintances.

Do not rush into employing tradespeople; do some local research before spending your hard-earned cash. Ask locals to give you names of the best local trades-people but they may be guarded. Be inventive, drive around the neighbourhood and look for gardens where similar trades are being used. Keep watch on the work for a few days to make a judgment on quality and productivity.

If the tradespeople's work seems to be of both high quality and productivity then they are suitable candidates to approach to give a quote to you. If they are working on private property wait until they leave the land before approaching them. However, the truck they use may have the telephone number on it so note that down and ring at a time when they are able to give you their personal attention.

Look through the local newspaper or the Yellow Pages of the telephone directory for local trades. Discuss with all tradespeople who are submitting a quotation what projects they have done before and whether you can inspect these projects.

Choosing tradespeople

Once potential tradespeople have been found and investigated, the task of choosing the right people for the job begins. Tradespeople can be chosen by competitive tender where the lowest quote is accepted from tenderers of integrity and good working record.

Only employ tradespeople with whom there has been a face-to-face meeting. These people are to work in your private garden. It is unwise to take risks.

Qualifications vs experience

There is the vexed question of whether it is better to choose a worker highly qualified or to employ one with years of experience. There is no answer. All educated people benefit from experience, and experience is generally enhanced by some book learning, but a practised worker with years of experience may be more productive for some jobs in the garden. Do not be biased. Attempt to make all selections of tradespeople on the basis of who will do the best job, on time, and within budget.

Checking previous work

The quality of the work done by any tradespeople can be judged by asking for a list of similar projects they have undertaken. Driving past and casting a quick eye over the gardens listed is insufficient. Talk to one or two of the owners to confirm that the tradespeople are what they state they are or, even, in extreme cases, who they are.

Lump-sum vs hourly rate

Whenever possible accept only lump-sum quotations, those from tradespeople's and suppliers' quotations where there is agreement to do all the required work for an agreed sum of money. The quotation should not be

subject to any claims for extra money unless extra work is done over and above the quotation and agreed to by the proprietor before the extra work is carried out.

If the work is not suited to a lump-sum quotation then tradespeople can be employed on an hourly rate. If you have not employed them before, make sure they work and their employment can be terminated, without penalty, on an hour's notice. Some workers will require that they are paid for a minimum period of time, often a half or full day, or they are paid while travelling to the job. On most occasions these requests are fair but the arrangements must be made clear at the time of engagement.

Payments in advance

It is now common practice for many tradespeople to request payment in advance and almost universal for suppliers. Tradespeople are required to pay in advance for materials they use so they ask the proprietor to meet the cost of such purchases.

In many cases this is fair but occasionally the money you pay for materials, is not used for that purpose. Materials purchased by, and delivered to tradespeople, even at the site of the works, under some conditions are not the property of the proprietor until they are finally built into the project.

If tradespeople cannot afford to purchase the materials required to start in advance you see them as the best people for the job, then purchase and take delivery of the materials personally. You may find that you can negotiate significant discounts and that your credit-worthiness may allow delivery before payment or cash on delivery.

Payment in advance does not always disadvantage you. Tradespeople need to be paid regularly, weekly or fortnightly, and if they are to give good service for work complete payment must be prompt and calculated correctly.

Taxation responsibility

In some areas a person employing tradespeople is responsible for preparing and lodging returns to taxation departments. Generally, for projects say under $10 000 there are no special requirements, but keep accurate records of payments made, and be sure that the person you are paying is a bona fide contractor and cannot be considered your servant employee. If the taxation department considers the person as a servant employee then the employer may be responsible for deducting taxation contributions as if the person were

a casual, part-time or full-time employee. When you act as an owner-builder, detailed returns on all employees and contractors may have to be lodged. On larger projects (in excess of $10 000) this should be checked with the authorities having jurisdiction at the time the work is being carried out.

When you apply to an authority to carry out construction of any type, they may inform other authorities, including the taxation department, of the work undertaken. Take care and check with the local authorities and with a taxation accountant or solicitor before proceeding as there may be stiff penalties for non-compliance.

Long service leave and superannuation

In many areas there are special laws which require anyone who employs another person to lodge contributions to portable long service leave and superannuation funds with an authority. Check what the local requirements are before employing anyone on more than a one-off casual basis. As for taxation responsibility there could be penalties for non-compliance.

Insurance

Many gardening projects may appear to be of low risk to people or property, but closer examination will quickly show that a person up a tree with a chainsaw creates the potential for serious injury. There is also the risk to anyone in the vicinity of the tree and the chance of damaging property should a bough fall on a neighbour's land or house.

When employing people and carrying out garden construction discuss the insurances that are needed with a reputable insurance company or specialist insurance broker.

Workers' compensation

Workers' compensation is the insurance that covers the loss of earnings suffered by workers who are injured or killed while carrying out their work. In most areas it is compulsory to take out workers' compensation insurance to cover any employees on your property. It is foolhardy trying to save the insurance premium, for accidents on jobs do happen and the financial responsibility for the injured worker is likely to rest with the property owner.

In some areas insurance can be purchased to cover casual employees doing some garden maintenance at a private residence, but this cover may not extend to people employed to carry out specific projects. Most contractors will have workers' compensation policies to cover their workers but the gardening industry has many employers who are not practised administrators and may not have insurance for their staff, or have, for some reason, let it lapse.

Even if all the people employed appear to be covered by adequate workers' compensation, and current paid-up policies have been sighted, check with a reputable insurance advisor before allowing anyone to begin work on a project.

Public liability

Many people constructing a garden will be prepared to take the risk of damage to their property during the construction project but check the general property insurance policy to see if it covers damage to the residence caused by construction work.

Insurance to cover injury and damage to third parties is essential for anyone undertaking any construction work. As the property owner you are liable to find yourself responsible for compensating any person who suffers injury or property damage at the time of construction.

By way of example consider the possibility of the neighbour's property being undermined by a collapsing retaining wall excavation. If there is heavy rain the night following excavation the excavation could collapse. The neighbour is unlikely to be convinced that this is an act of God.

Injury to people is of even greater concern, as the effects of many injuries are lifelong. There are too many incidents of wandering children falling into excavations or being injured by machinery, and in many cases the garden owner is liable to compensate the injured party, even if they were intruders on private property.

Insurance is to protect people from risk. Check the insurance required carefully. Do not take any risks.

PURCHASING MATERIALS

During the construction of a garden many different materials might be purchased. Some will be quite expensive. It is sensible to list all the materials in advance and check their probable cost.

When working out quantities of material special care should be taken. In most cases it is cheaper to order the correct amount on the first occasion rather than to have to purchase top-up quantities during the project, particularly if there is a delay in delivery or the product is a special one that cannot easily be matched.

Over-ordering can be a much a problem as under-ordering, to remove 1 000 extra pavers from the property can be costly even if a buyer can be found. Many barbecues have been built from surplus bricks.

Check with all your labour contractors whether there are materials they need to be delivered before they start work. Many contractors will offer a price to supply and construct but there may be an expectation

where the purchase of some materials will be your
responsibility.

Choosing a supplier

In most areas there will be more than one supplier of
the materials and before one is selected check on their
record of delivery:
- Do the suppliers deliver when they say they will?
- Do they supply the product ordered?
- Do they supply materials of consistent high quality?
- Do they organise the delivery or is that the
  purchaser's responsibility?
- Do they offer good back-up for under-orders?
- Do they take back unused material if it is in good
  condition?

Avoid suppliers with a patchy record, even if their
prices appear to be the cheapest.

Delivery and receiving

When ordering any material which cannot be taken
immediately, check what arrangements can be made for
delivery and receiving. Most suppliers have a small
delivery charge based on a set charge per delivery to a
project no matter how much or how little material is to
be delivered in a single truck load.

Try to order all the materials needed for one project
to minimise the number of deliveries and costs of
delivery. Ask about the size of the trucks which are
used. For large volume items like topsoil this may be
important. Where the truck is small there may be a
higher delivery bill but if the truck is oversize for the job
it may not be able to make the delivery close to the
work site. This will lead to a lot more on-site handling.

Confirm the delivery date. Ensure someone is on-site
to receive the goods. Check the delivery. This reduces
the risk of having to contact the supplier after delivery
to complain about the material being the incorrect type
or of a poor quality.

With no supervision the delivery may be dumped on
the newly planted roses, or roughly handled during
unloading. There is always a danger of short delivery
which may or may not be the suppliers' fault as building
material theft abounds. It is amazing how brazen thefts
occur in daylight raids, even when the adjacent
neighbours are mowing their front lawns.

Liability during deliveries

It is likely that the property owner is liable for any
damage to property or injury to people caused during
the delivery of materials to the property once the truck
has left the public road. Make sure you have insurance
to cover this.

Discounts and payment terms

Always ask for a discount at the suppliers. It is often
given if the order is large. Payment in cash can attract
a discount. Payment by credit card often leads the
supplier to pay a premium to the credit card company.

If there is a significant amount of material to be
bought from one supplier it may suit the supplier and
the purchaser to arrange for a monthly account to be
opened. Check the terms of any extended payment
scheme to make sure your discounts are not lost or
reduced to your financial disadvantage. Ensure that the
account can be paid when it is received or within the
terms extended by the supplier. Some suppliers give a
percentage discount for full payment made within a
stated period, over and above the original discount.

Invoices and statements

If materials are supplied on terms keep all delivery
dockets and check these against the invoices and the
periodic statement. All materials returned should have
a credit note.

Any discrepancy in the documents issued by the
supplier should be discussed with the supplier
immediately along with unresolved matters on a
statement. All account items in the order should be paid
by the due date. Withholding money owing to a
supplier is only acceptable where there is a genuine
grievance.

The delivery truck is bogged

Many things can go wrong while materials are being
delivered, and often there is dispute between the
deliverer and the receiver. A common problem is when
a heavily laden delivery truck arrives at a garden project
and the driver is asked to drive onto the property to
make the delivery. The truck may be driven over a
newly filled drainage trench and sink to the axles,
bogged. Just who is responsible for dragging the truck
out of the bog and paying for the cost of a tow truck

or similar vehicle, or how to account for the loss of time suffered by the truck driver is unclear. In many cases the property owner will be responsible. The truck driver gave a special service in making an on-site delivery and should have expected that the grounds be able to support the truck's loaded weight.

The situation is further complicated if the truck enters the property without the owner's invitation, but is the driver liable if there is no sign warning of soft ground, and who is responsible for any damage that may have been caused to the excavation or any drainpipes?

Again there are many possible answers and the problem is unlikely to be resolved by a violent argument with the truck driver. The logical answer is to take care in advance and make sure if a delivery onto the property is required that there is sufficient room to manoeuvre and the ground can support a loaded truck.

We put it on the nature-strip at 4.30 am

Deliveries out of normal working hours are made sometimes. However, all efforts should be made to restrict deliveries to times when there is a person to accept and check the materials delivered. Ask for deliveries to be made at predetermined times — allow some flexibility — and make sure, by letter, that the supplier knows that deliveries made at times when the goods cannot be checked for quality and quantity, will not be accepted. As well as the possibility of theft, there is the danger of materials being damaged by exposure to the elements. Topsoil left on a street verge can be washed away by a sudden downpour of rain. Timber can warp and twist in the sun.

GARDEN-SCAPES EXAMPLES

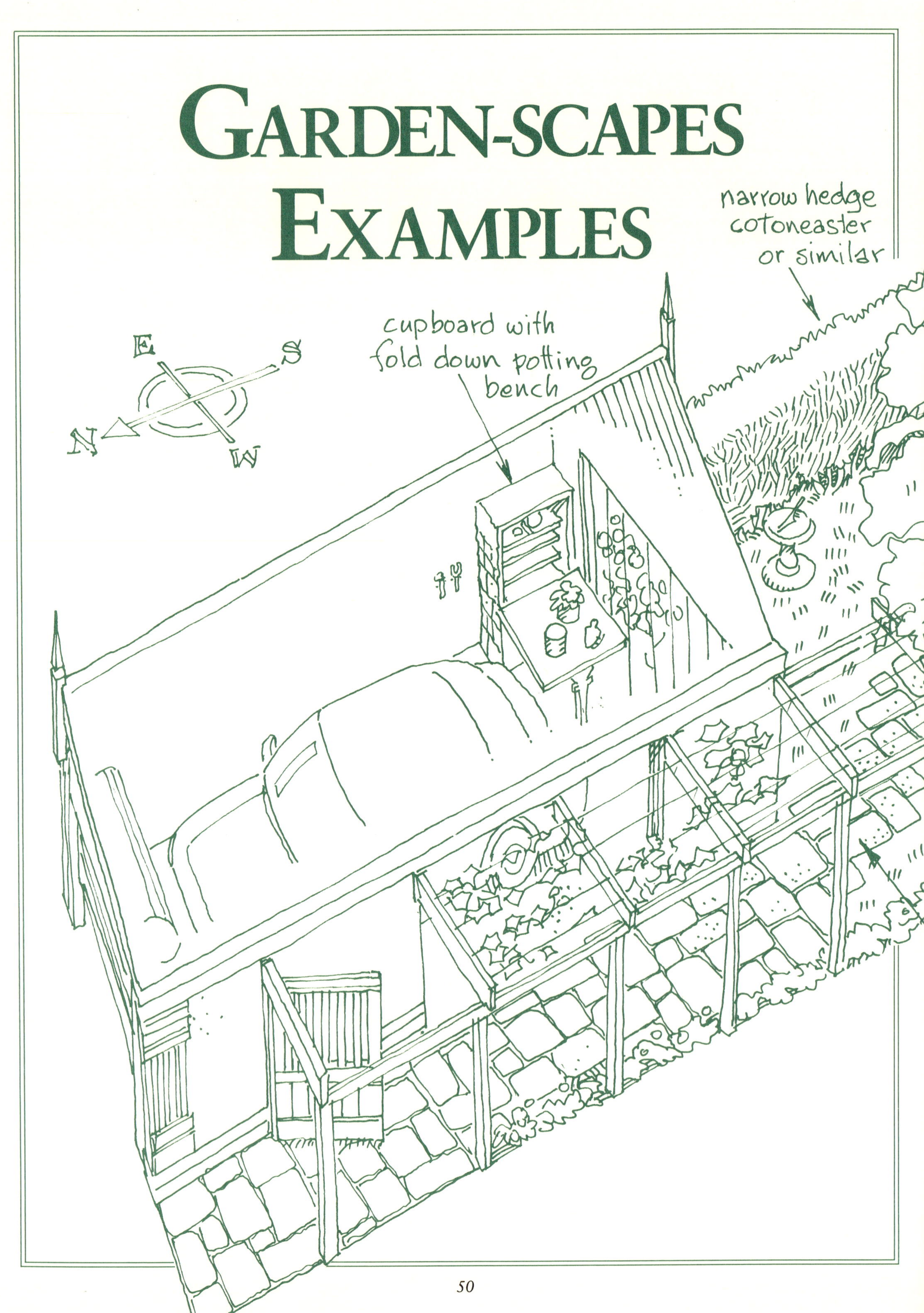

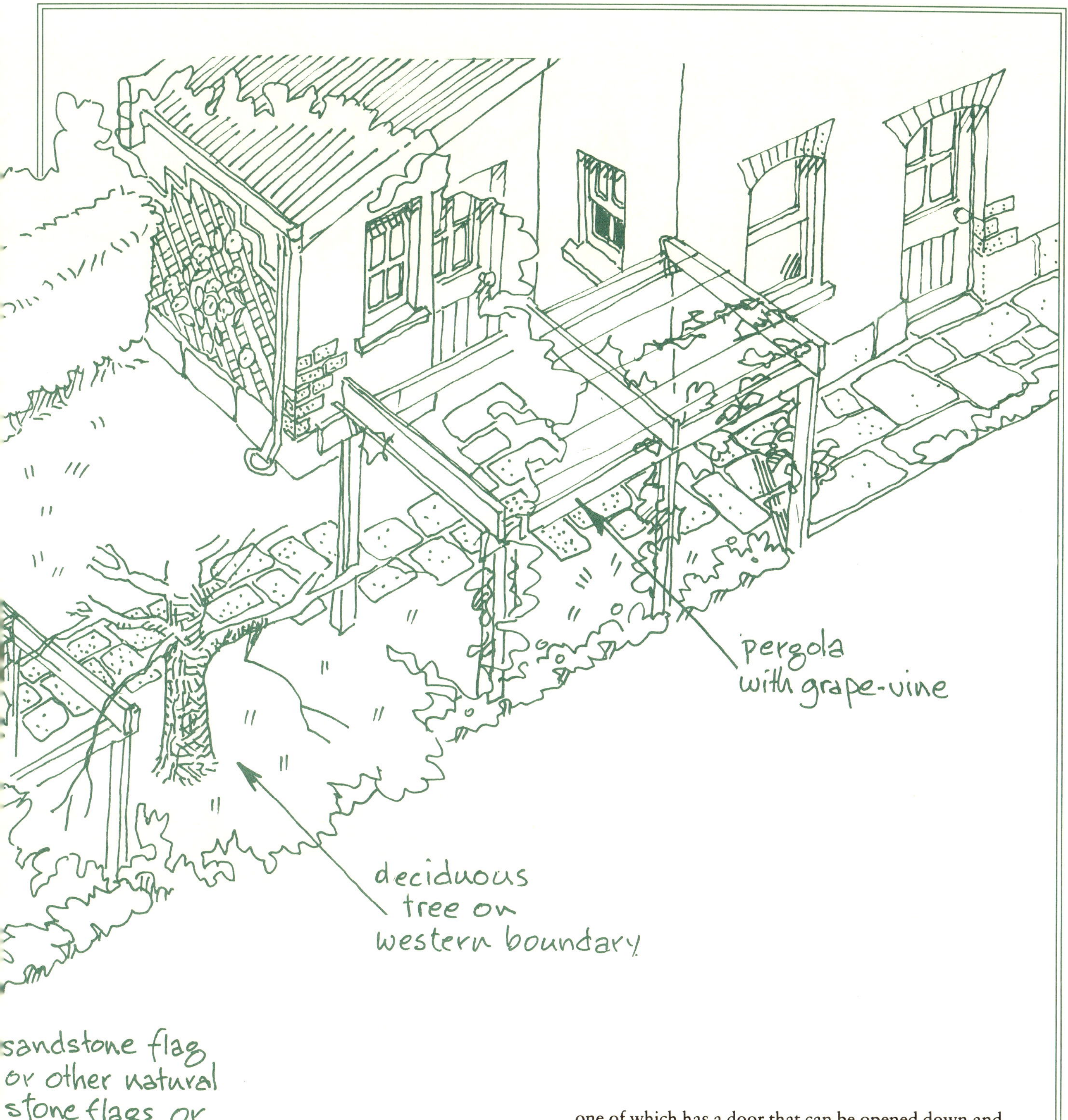

AN INNER-CITY COURTYARD

The small backyard of a Victorian terrace needs careful planning as often available space will have to be shared with a garage.

In this example the garage has been kept to the minimum size and incorporates two storage cupboards, one of which has a door that can be opened down and used as a work table.

A pergola links the gate entry from a rear lane through to the back door of the terrace house. This can be used to support vines which will, in turn, provide a visual barrier from overlooking windows.

Much of the garden is paved for convenience and many climbing plants have been planted.

It is difficult to provide any views from the inside of a terrace house into a rear courtyard garden, without major planning and structural alterations to the building.

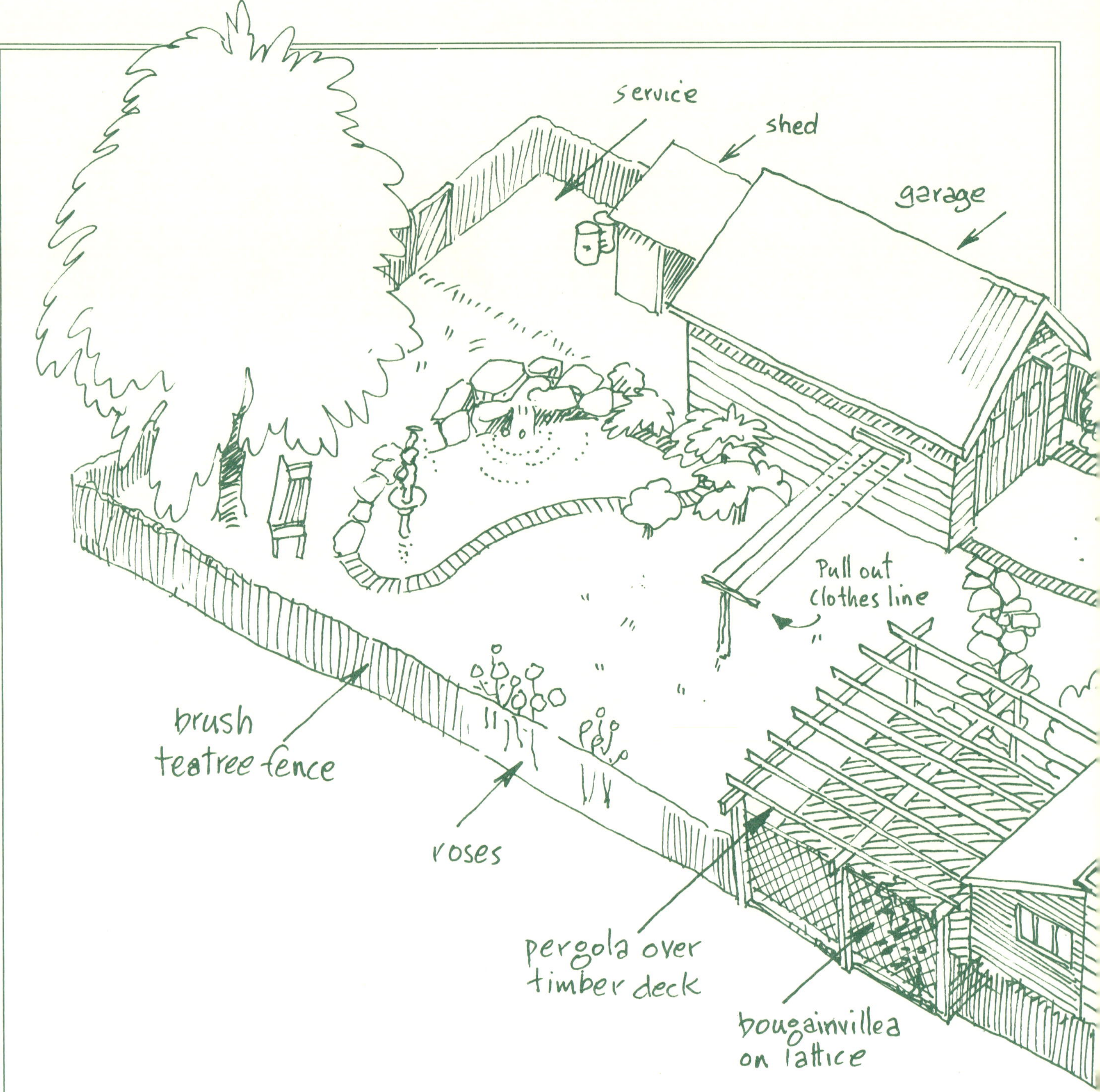

SMALLER ESTABLISHED ALLOTMENT

Many of the subdivisions in the well-established suburbs are quite small with houses that are not well oriented to the sun, climate or garden. The advantage of these subdivisions is that they are often in convenient locations with extremely good amenities.

Careful replanning of the garden can improve many of the disadvantages of these allotments. Some reordering of the house plan with the addition of a family room or conservatory, designed to take advantage of the rear garden can change the whole environment and enrich home life.

If the garden has healthy plants, in good shape, and especially if there are plants which have taken many years to mature, these should be kept and incorporated into any new garden design.

The new garden plan should be in sympathy with the streetscape if there is a consistent garden form in the street. With a house of a definitive architectural style, an appropriate garden design will enhance both the house and the garden.

In most cases the two most important aspects of garden planning for this type of allotment is to allow the sun to enter the garden and the house, and to provide reasonable privacy within the garden to improve its usefulness.

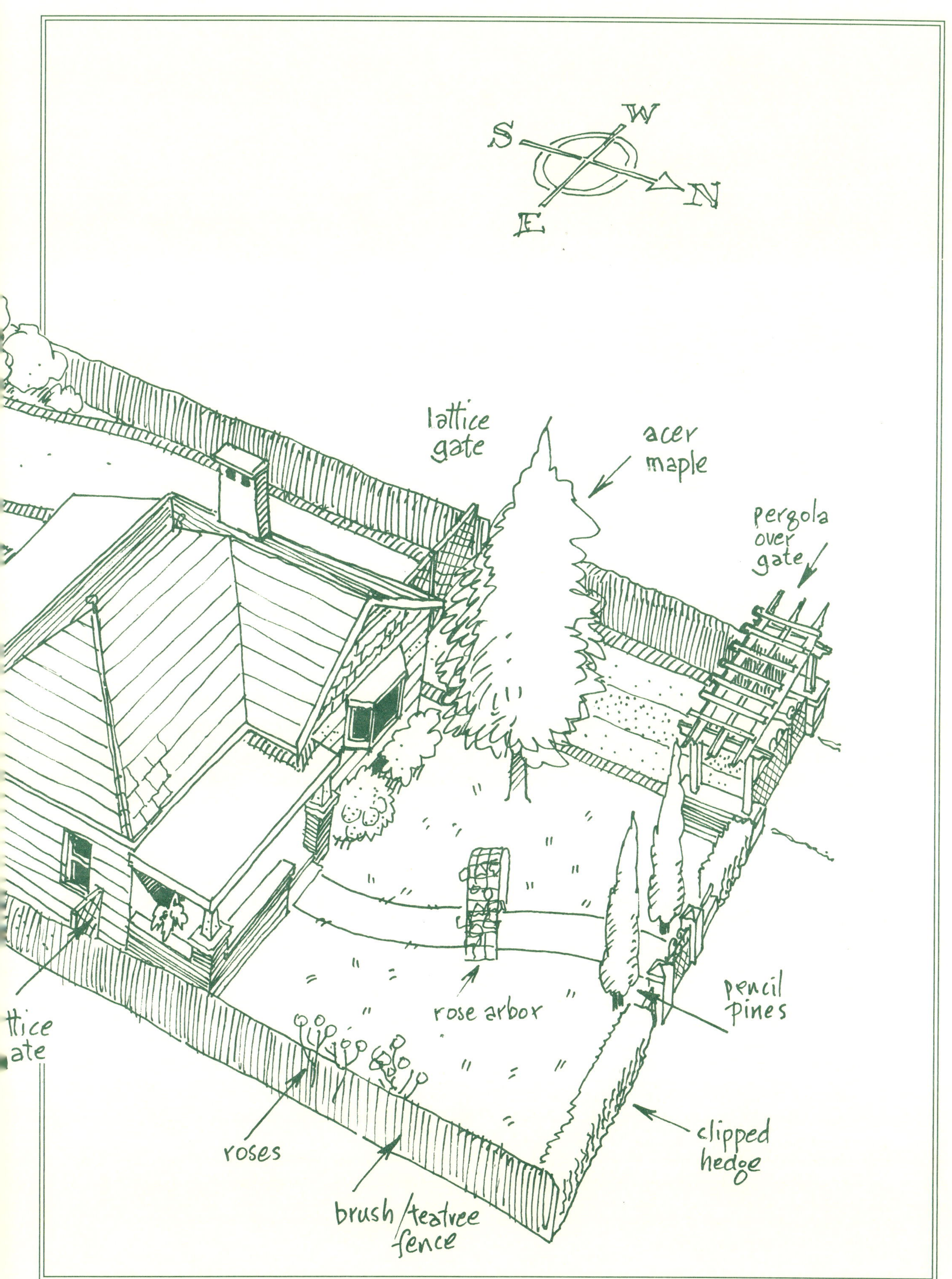

S
W
N
E
lattice gate
acer maple
pergola over gate
pencil pines
clipped hedge
rose arbor
ttice ate
roses
brush/teatree fence

E
S
N
W
lattice fence
concrete
cobble
banksia
or bottlebrush

54

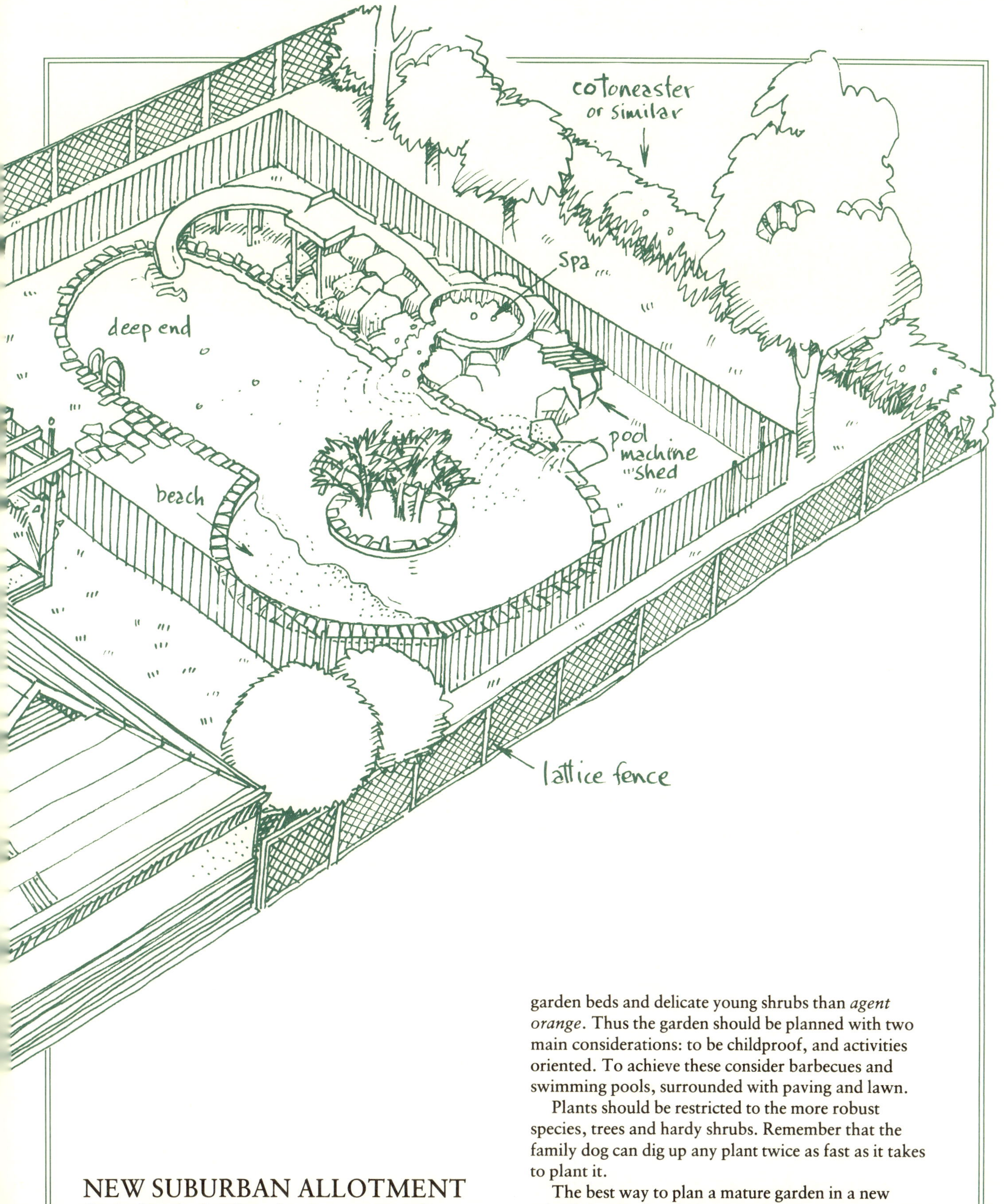

NEW SUBURBAN ALLOTMENT

Out in the suburbs where the cows once grazed, planning a garden can seem like an overwhelming task with the piles of builder's rubbish, clay-filled trenches, and weed-infested pasture spread as far as the eye can see.

These are the houses where families grow up, where six or seven children at play can do more damage to garden beds and delicate young shrubs than *agent orange*. Thus the garden should be planned with two main considerations: to be childproof, and activities oriented. To achieve these consider barbecues and swimming pools, surrounded with paving and lawn.

Plants should be restricted to the more robust species, trees and hardy shrubs. Remember that the family dog can dig up any plant twice as fast as it takes to plant it.

The best way to plan a mature garden in a new suburb is to make a long-term commitment to wait until the children leave home, then there is a short respite in which to establish the garden before the grandchildren invasion happens. Take solace in the fact that if you can design the best playground garden in the street where the children will congregate, you will know then where your children are.

ash
elm
cottage
conser
picket
fence
box
hedge
garage
cypress
hedge
6 to 7 m
high

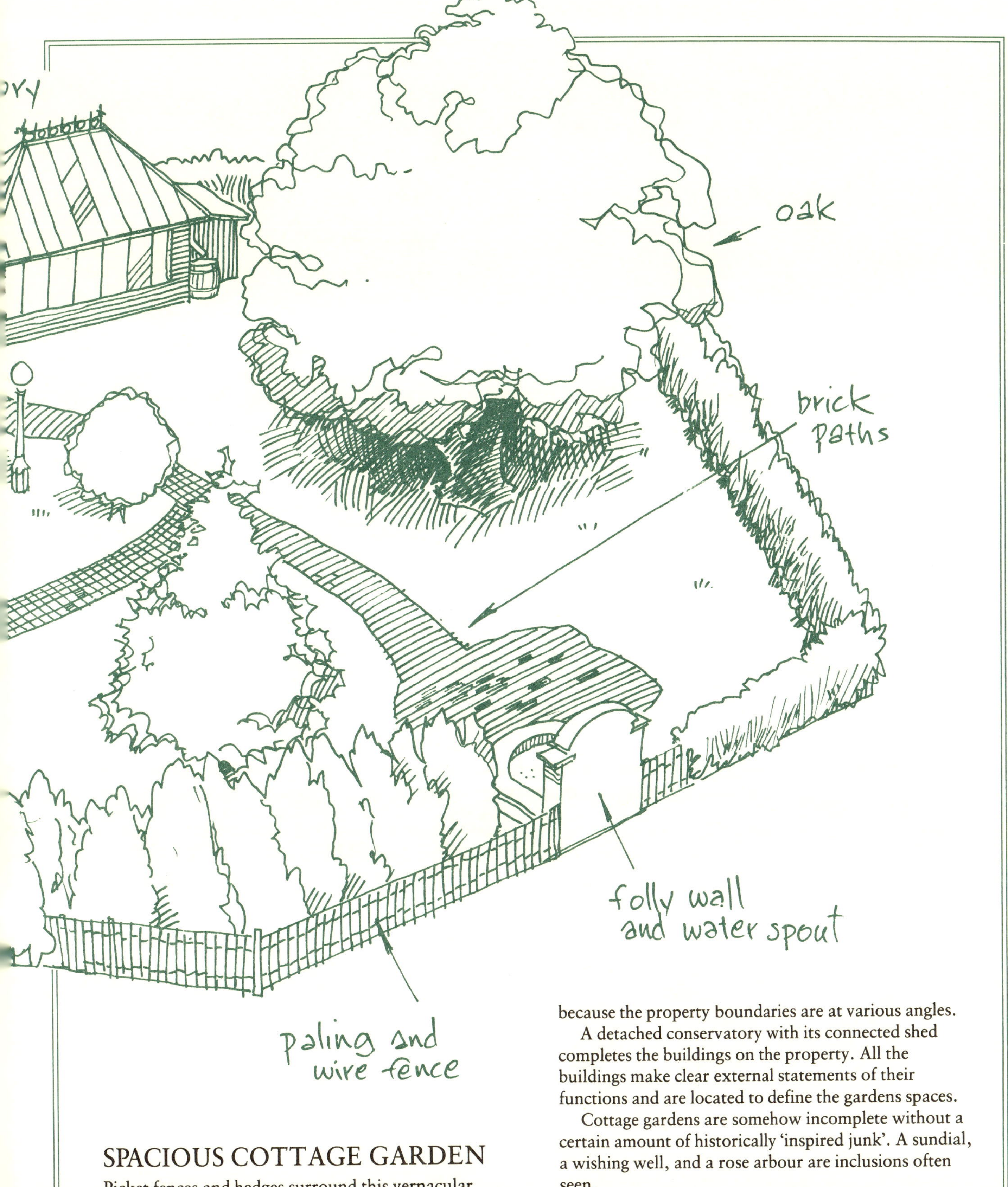

SPACIOUS COTTAGE GARDEN

Picket fences and hedges surround this vernacular stone-built cottage. There are gables and dormer windows into an attic room, and the plants are in the cottage genre.

The garage is set at a different angle to the cottage residence and has the style of a stable and loft. This tension of using different orientations for the buildings within the property is made easier in this example because the property boundaries are at various angles.

A detached conservatory with its connected shed completes the buildings on the property. All the buildings make clear external statements of their functions and are located to define the gardens spaces.

Cottage gardens are somehow incomplete without a certain amount of historically 'inspired junk'. A sundial, a wishing well, and a rose arbour are inclusions often seen.

There is no concrete to be seen. Any material not available in the Tudor period has to be considered very carefully. Stone flagging, gravel and brick-paved paths, are important inclusions as are the appropriate trees. Here the trees are deciduous hardwoods and conifers, traditionally associated with cottages, but some species of eucalypts can fit in to a cottage garden.

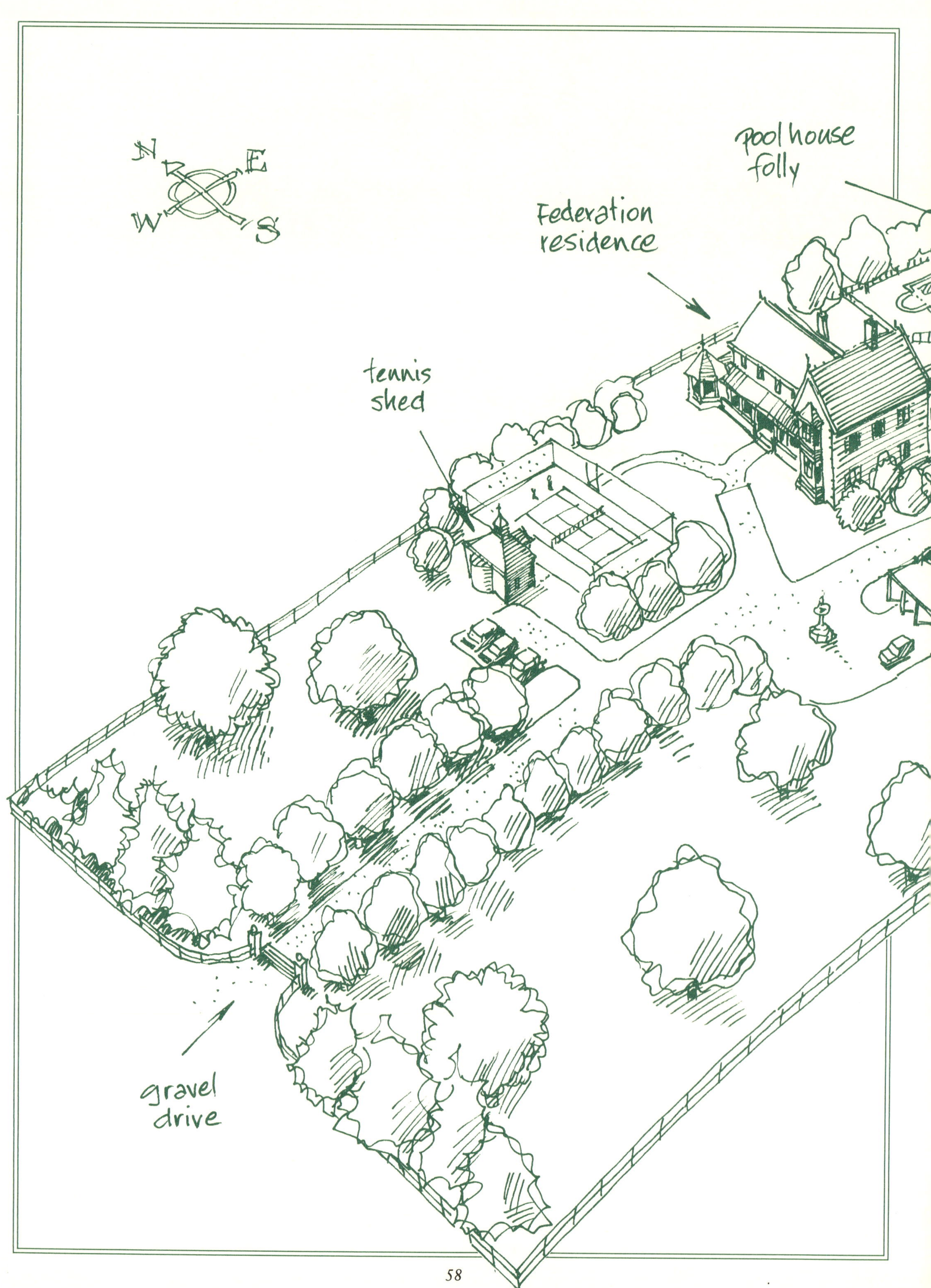

N
E
W
S
pool house
folly
Federation
residence
tennis
shed
gravel
drive

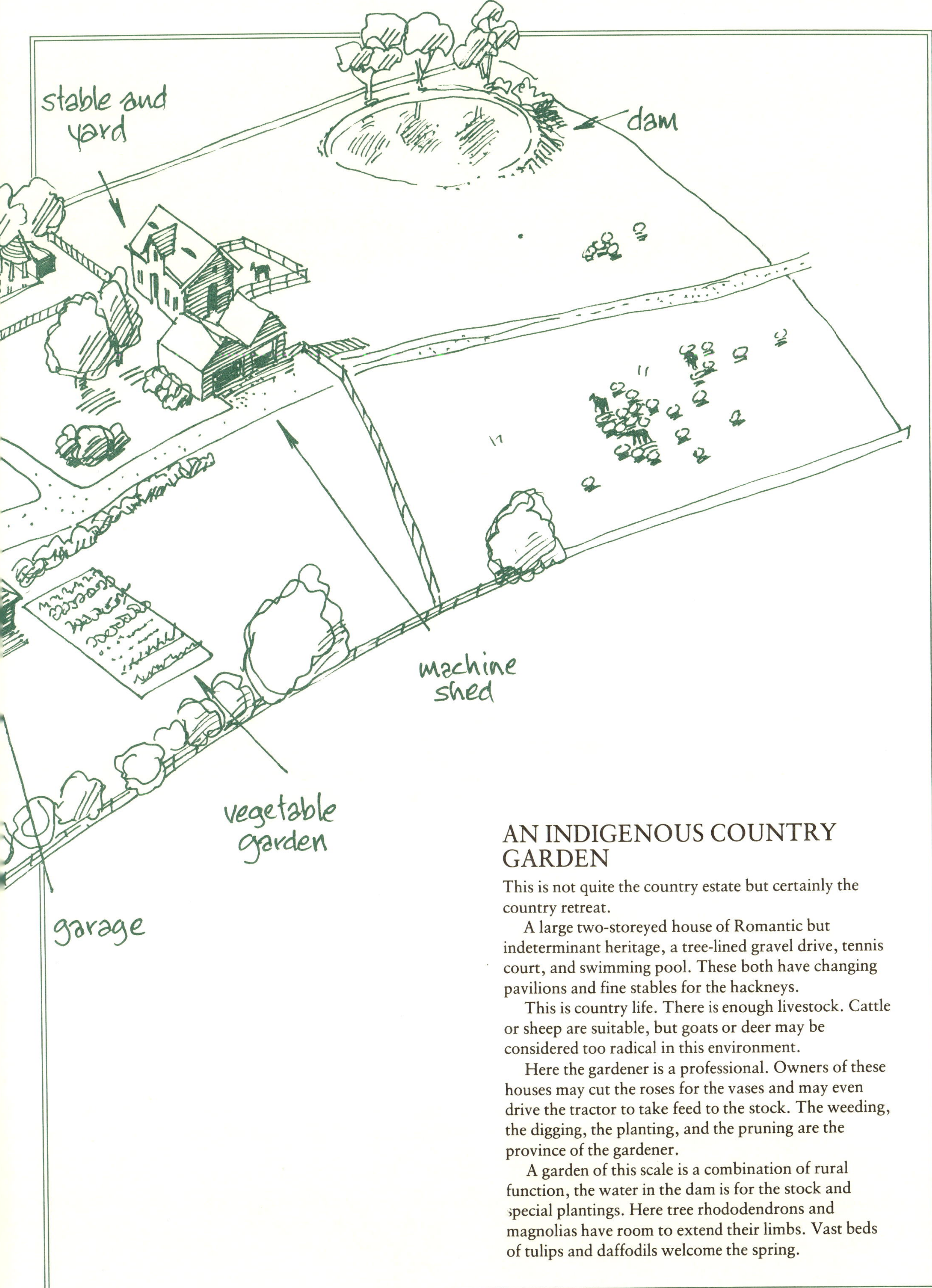

AN INDIGENOUS COUNTRY GARDEN

This is not quite the country estate but certainly the country retreat.

A large two-storeyed house of Romantic but indeterminant heritage, a tree-lined gravel drive, tennis court, and swimming pool. These both have changing pavilions and fine stables for the hackneys.

This is country life. There is enough livestock. Cattle or sheep are suitable, but goats or deer may be considered too radical in this environment.

Here the gardener is a professional. Owners of these houses may cut the roses for the vases and may even drive the tractor to take feed to the stock. The weeding, the digging, the planting, and the pruning are the province of the gardener.

A garden of this scale is a combination of rural function, the water in the dam is for the stock and special plantings. Here tree rhododendrons and magnolias have room to extend their limbs. Vast beds of tulips and daffodils welcome the spring.

A LARGER FORMAL GARDEN

This is a bit 'over the top' but some people do aspire to this obvious display of wealth, if not elegance. The circular drive, inherited from the days of horses and carriages.

The porte-cochere rivals a fair-sized hotel and the neo-Regency facade is suitably palace-like.

A formal avenue of fragrant roses leads from the centrally located and featured wrought iron gates to the imposing entry. The less formally located, but strictly balanced, specimen trees provide shade to the front lawns.

The rear of the house has a large elevated terrace overlooking the lawn that sweeps to a swimming pool. This pool reflects the glory of the line of trees that define the rear boundary of the property, but keep guests guessing if the garden continues on the other side.

To add to the exotic affectation of the property a large conservatory butts out into the garden from the rear of the house.

There are no garages or sheds on this property. These are kept on an adjacent property, chauffeurs bring the cars, and gardeners bring their equipment.

A STEEPLY SLOPING SITE

This is a property that is awkward to 'garden' in the traditional sense of the word. There would be little value in having a lawn that is so steep that no one can mow it, let alone sit on it, or play ball on it.

The answer is to maintain the property in the manner that nature intended, either by leaving the natural vegetation when building the residence or, if that is not possible, planning and planting a garden to support nature.

Often these steep properties are released on the edge of existing residential areas and the natural vegetation has been infested with introduced and invasive plants and weeds.

Build a residence with a small footprint, use poles, posts and piers for support, and avoid cut-and-fill excavations. This reduces the danger of inducing landslip or surface erosion.

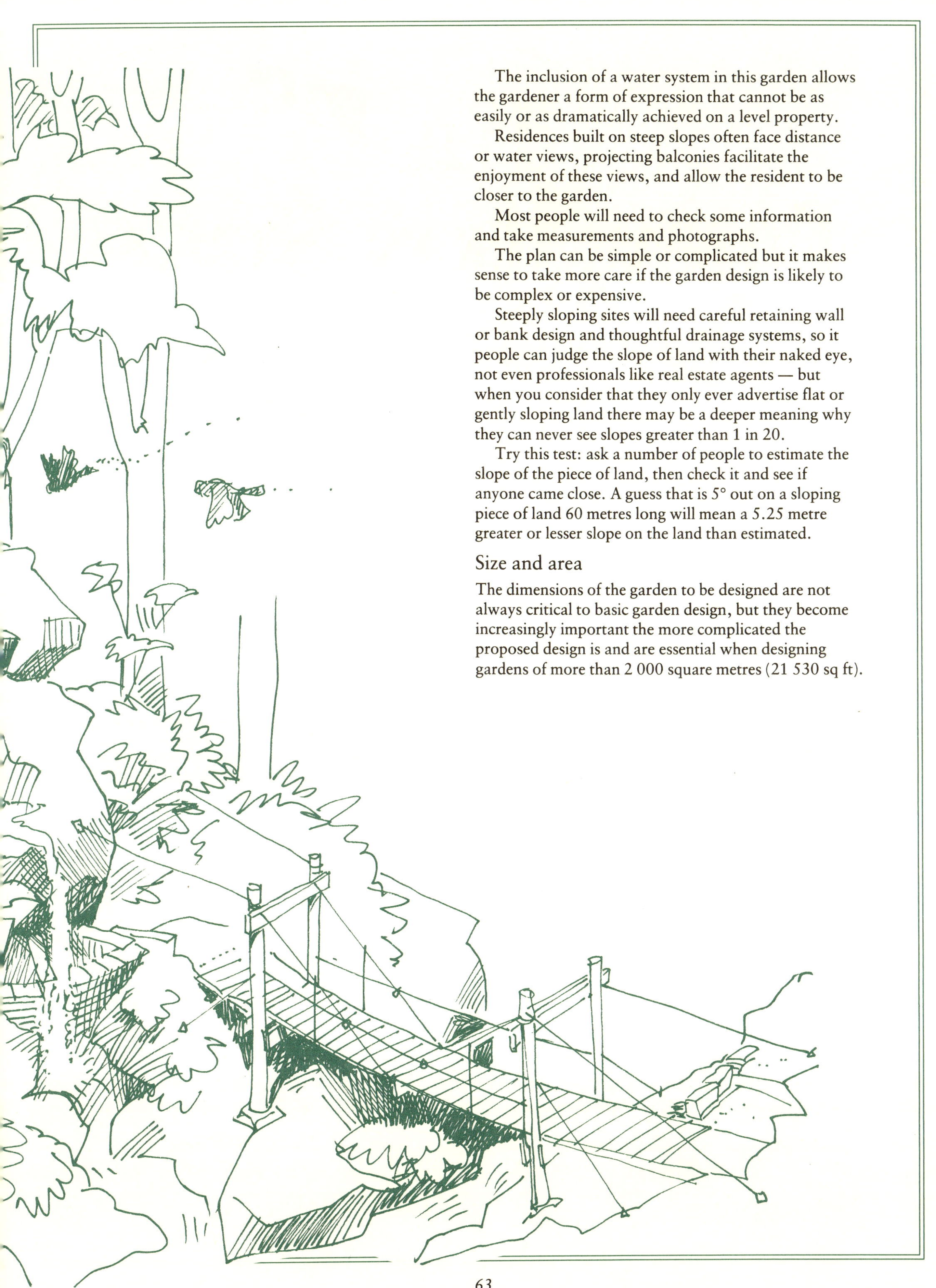

The inclusion of a water system in this garden allows the gardener a form of expression that cannot be as easily or as dramatically achieved on a level property.

Residences built on steep slopes often face distance or water views, projecting balconies facilitate the enjoyment of these views, and allow the resident to be closer to the garden.

Most people will need to check some information and take measurements and photographs.

The plan can be simple or complicated but it makes sense to take more care if the garden design is likely to be complex or expensive.

Steeply sloping sites will need careful retaining wall or bank design and thoughtful drainage systems, so it people can judge the slope of land with their naked eye, not even professionals like real estate agents — but when you consider that they only ever advertise flat or gently sloping land there may be a deeper meaning why they can never see slopes greater than 1 in 20.

Try this test: ask a number of people to estimate the slope of the piece of land, then check it and see if anyone came close. A guess that is 5° out on a sloping piece of land 60 metres long will mean a 5.25 metre greater or lesser slope on the land than estimated.

Size and area

The dimensions of the garden to be designed are not always critical to basic garden design, but they become increasingly important the more complicated the proposed design is and are essential when designing gardens of more than 2 000 square metres (21 530 sq ft).

THE
PREPARATION STAGE

A garden is only as good as its preparation. Poor preparation will lead to deterioration of the improvements that are made and prevent the best growth and presentation of the planting.

Nature may provide a good basis from which to develop the intended garden design and planting program but the requirements of a designed garden are mostly different from the conditions which existed in the unimproved state.

All structures, whether a simple path or a complicated building require stable foundations. In its natural state most land is covered by topsoil with high humus content so detailed preparation is required before any building can take place.

The natural soil is unlikely to have all the qualities needed for any new planting which is to be carried out. With the removal of existing vegetation the soil character will change and is unlikely to be correct for the proposed planting.

It is sensible to work with the natural environment wherever possible. It would be foolish to build a structure on areas of poor foundation or to plant a tree with deep roots on a rocky outcrop.

SETTING OUT THE GARDEN

To ensure the proposed new garden or alterations to an existing garden conform to the design that has been prepared, it is essential to set out the plan of the garden at full size. Setting out the garden on the ground will help the garden builders to realise the work that is required and to visualise where re-contouring and other earthworks and buildings are to be constructed.

This helps to set out the key points and axes first as these can be used as reference points for the more detailed setouts required for the actual construction program.

Hurdles and offsets

When setting out a straight line or series of straight lines the recommended method is to place timber hurdles beyond the setout line with the top of the hurdle approximately at right angles to the setout line.

The hurdles should consist of two stout pegs 75 mm (3") x 50 mm (2") x at least 600 mm (2') hammered well into the ground, with a piece of timber fixed between them. The top piece of timber should be of sufficient strength so that it will not bounce when nails used to fasten the strings are driven in. These hurdles are left in position throughout the construction period but the stringlines can be removed and replaced at will.

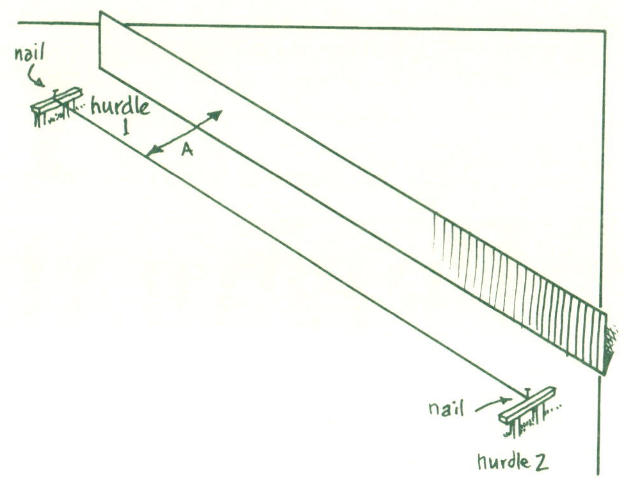

This allows for measurements to be made from known points — property boundaries or existing buildings — to a stringline held taut between a pair of hurdles, and for the string to be moved on top of the hurdle until the correct location is achieved. When the correct location is established, then a nail can be hammered into the top of the hurdle and the string tied off. Repeating of this procedure at the other end of the stringline will result in a straight stringline between the two hurdles.

To set out a pathway, the stringline should be positioned along one edge of the path. The width can be measured as an offset from this line. Too many hurdles and stringlines lead to confusion or they may be knocked over as manoeuvring room on the site is restricted.

If the pathway has changes of direction, further hurdle and string setouts can be made and if the path is to be curved offset measurements can be calculated from the stringline and used to locate the curved edge.

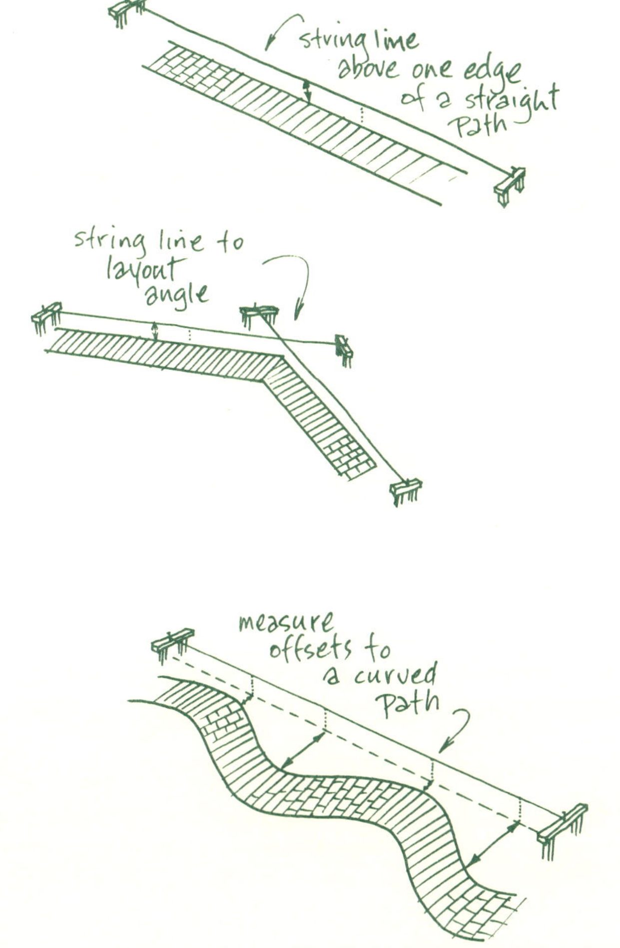

For a simple building like a rectangular shed four pairs of hurdles and stringlines are used. When setting out for a building or any straight-walled structure it is usual to locate the stringlines along the outside face of the external walls.

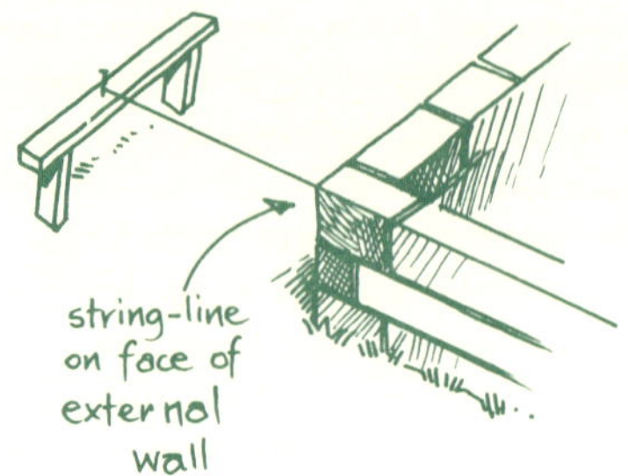

The first pair of hurdles should be positioned so that these can be located by offsets from a known line or the extension of a known line. The second pair should be set at the correct distance in the other direction from a known point or line. When the first two pairs of hurdles and their stringlines are in place with the string of the first pair nailed in their final location, only the string at the ends of the first pair should be finally nailed.

The loose end of the second string may be tied to the hurdle. Once this is done the intersecting corner of the two stringlines can be checked for square before the string is attached to a nail.

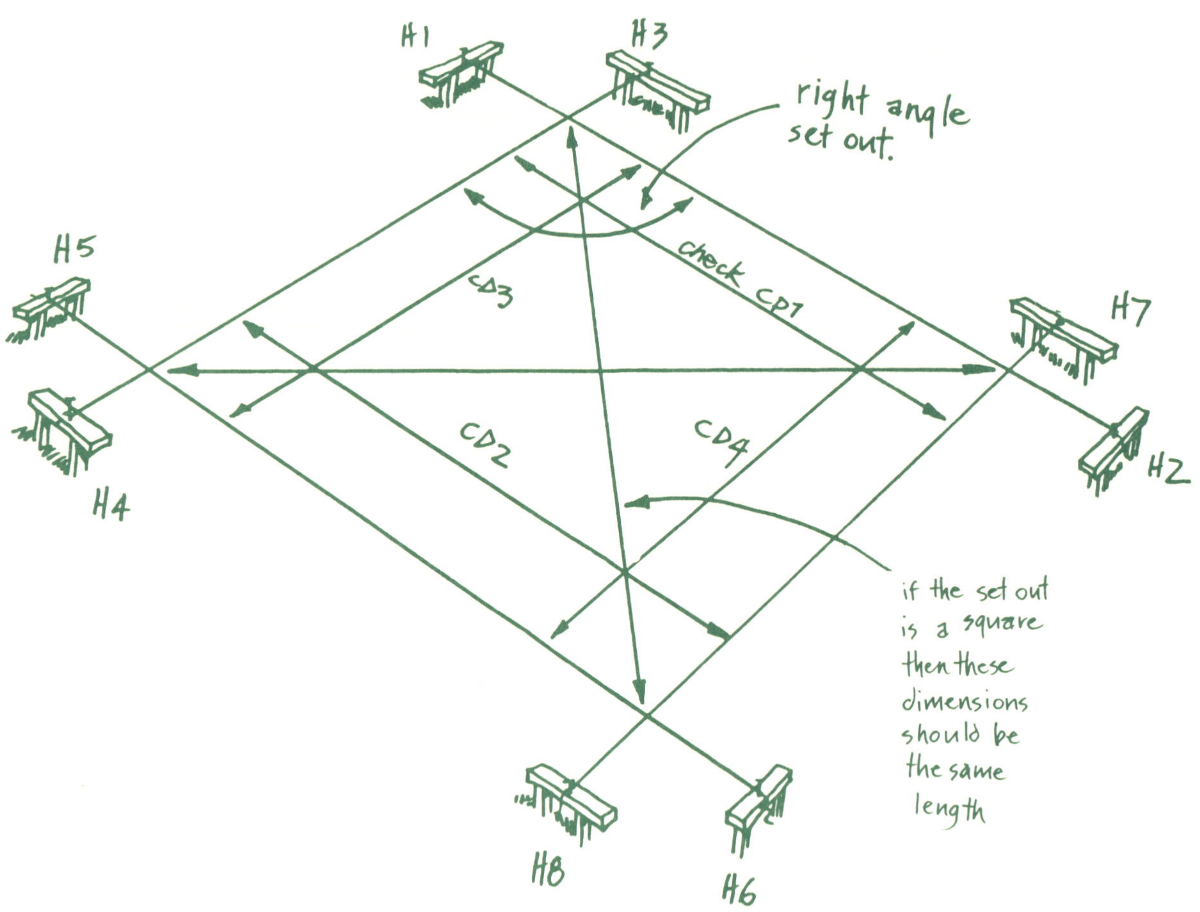

When the first and second stringlines are at right angles, check that their location to the known lines and points is correct, then construct the remaining two pairs of hurdles. By measuring from a point near the ends of the third and fourth stringlines across to the first and second stringlines respectively, the third and fourth lines will be the correct distances apart and be parallel to the first and second lines.

Stringlines can be used to locate the centres of posts, fountains, trees and the like by crossing two stringlines. The lines should not cross at the real centre of the construction or tree because they would be in the way,

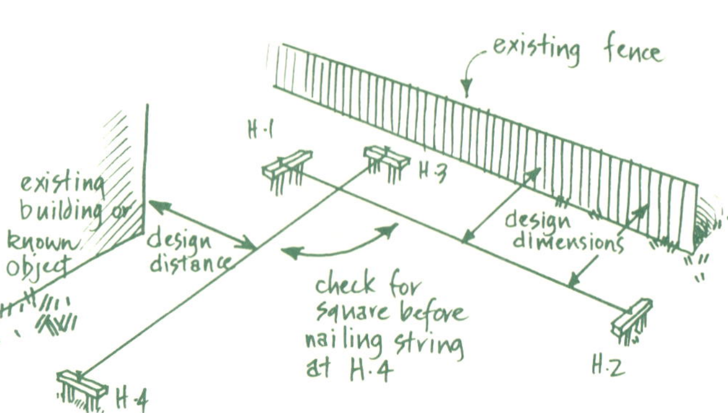

they should cross at a known distance, preferably the same distance in both directions, from the centre. By keeping the crossing of the stringlines away from the real centre and using offset dimensions accurate locations for objects can be achieved.

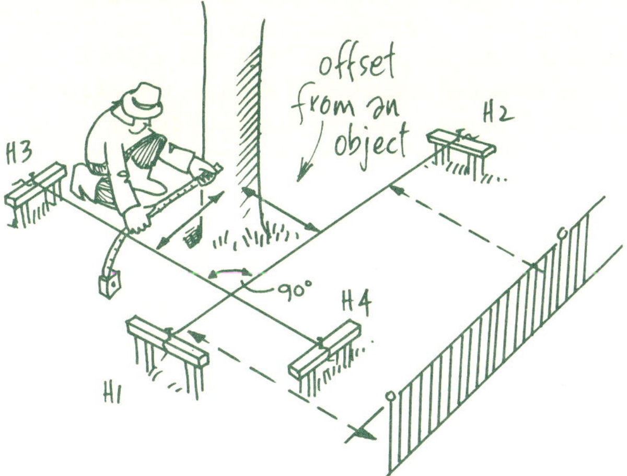

Measuring horizontally and vertically

Although gardens predominantly follow the natural or modified slopes of the land, accurate measurement of horizontal and vertical dimensions is a common requirement.

Dimensions that are shown on plans are horizontal measurements and when used to set out a garden they must be measured vertically as well or errors because of the slope of the land will occur.

There are a number of ways in which horizontal measurements can be made. Some need only simple tools, others are more sophisticated and need special equipment. The first step in taking a horizontal measurement is to ensure that both ends of the tape measure are on the same level. For relatively short distances this is easy but if the tape measure is too short or the slope is very steep, more care is required.

The first method makes use of a piece of garden hose. To use a hose to locate points of the same level, first insert short lengths of clear plastic or glass tube into both ends of the hose. Take the hose to the place where the horizontal measurement is required and hold both ends upright. Fill the hose with water until the water is visible in the clear tubes at each end.

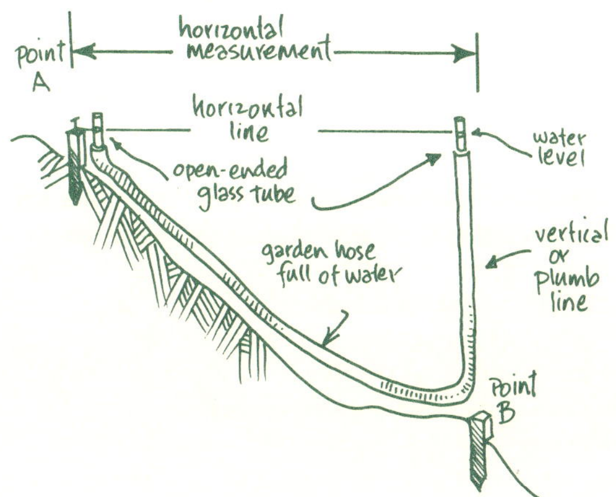

Water in the two arms of a vessel with open ends is always at the same level, so the water visible in the tubes is at the same level and the line between them is horizontal. Attach the hose to a vertical staff at each end and the staff at the end of the known location is vertically above the known point, then when a tape measure is used from the known point on the horizontal line between the two ends of the hose then a horizontal measurement can be taken.

To transfer the horizontal measurement to the ground surface, a plumb-bob can be hung down past the required length on the tape and where the centre of the plumb-bob touches the ground it will give a reasonably accurate horizontal measurement from the known point. This method can be inaccurate and is not recommended for critical dimensions such as statutory setbacks.

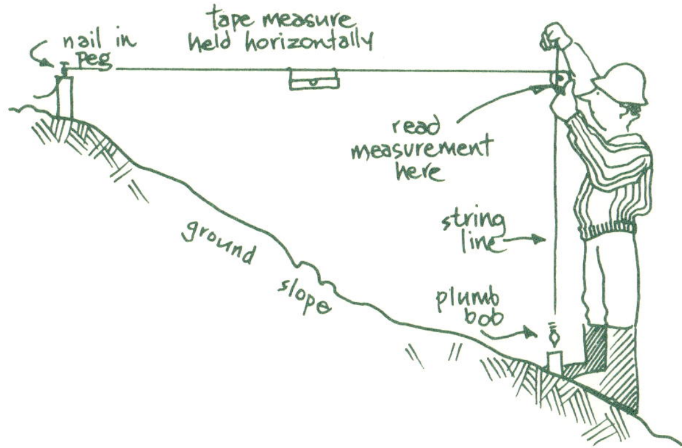

An alternative method of obtaining a horizontal dimension is to use a string level. This is a lightweight spirit level with small hooks on it so it can be attached to a normal stringline. Using a similar technique to the one using the water hose, a measurement can be taken along the stringline which has been set level using the string level and transferred to the ground again using a simple plumb-bob as before.

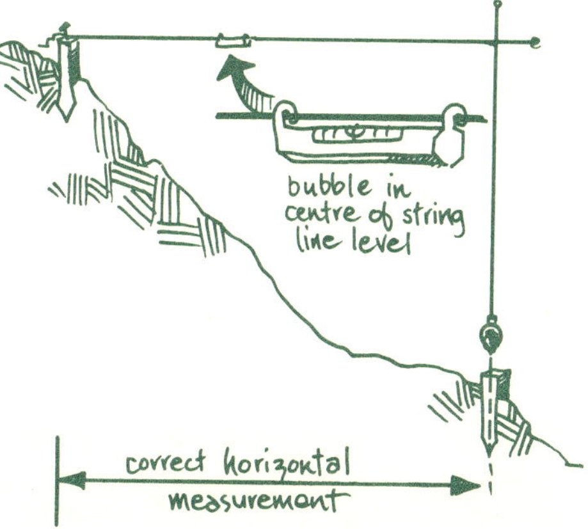

A more sophisticated method is to use an optical level and to find the same level at the known point and the point to be be measured using a levelling staff. The measurement is then carried out as before with tape and a plumb-bob.

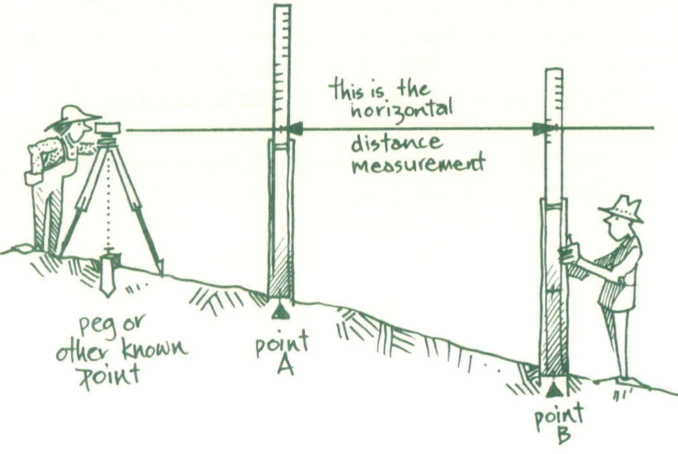

If there is a lot of work for a level in the project, it is worth learning how to use an optical level and hiring one from one of the builders' equipment rental companies. If the budget can be stretched a little further, a laser level can be hired. This magic equipment will send a horizontal light source out in all directions from a rotating head and wherever the light hits is at the same horizotnal level.

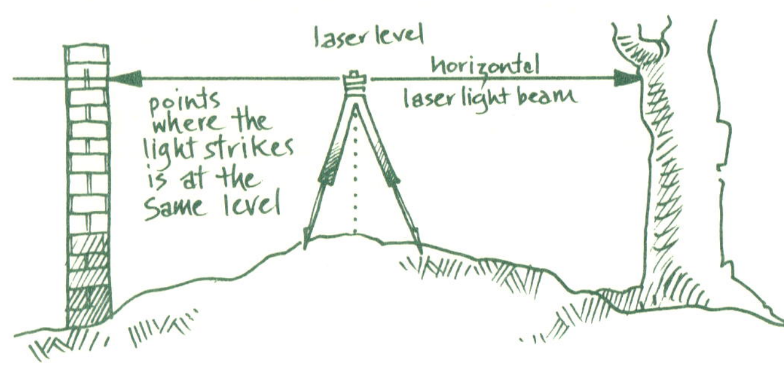

Finally, if all else fails and the planned garden is large and complicated a surveying team can be commissioned to take all levels and mark all important setout dimensions and points.

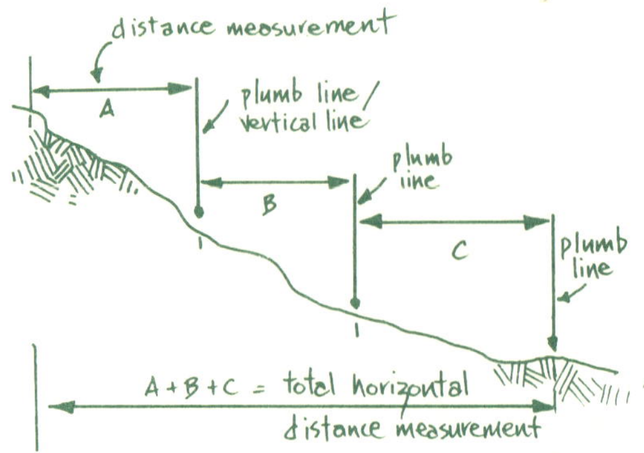

Some dimensions cannot easily be taken in one measurement because they are very long or very steep. Twenty metres (60′) is close to the maximum distance that can be measured accurately by most people. Holding a tape measure taut while standing on a step ladder has distinct disadvantages. In these cases it is easier to divide the measurement into workable sections and follow the contour down in a series of steps.

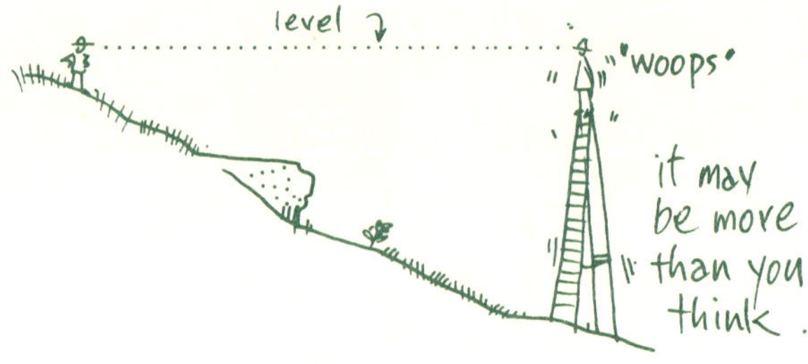

Vertical dimensions can be taken by measuring from the ground to the level line in the case of the hose and string level methods. Take measurements at both the known point and the point where the vertical height is required. Subtract one height from the other to find the vertical difference.

If an optical or laser level is used then readings are taken on the staff, which is marked off in 10 mm (⅓″) increments, and subtracted in the same way.

Plumbing

The term 'plumbing' means finding a vertical line. This has traditionally been done by hanging a lead weight on the end of a string (the term 'plumb' comes from the Latin word for 'lead'). Modern plumb-bobs are generally made from brass or stainless steel and equipped with a sharp end to help locate exact points. Even modern surveyors equipped with laser theodolites and satellite equipment have not perfected a more accurate localised method of finding a vertical line.

Plumb-bobs are accurate in all but very windy conditions. To counteract the wind, place the bob in a can of oil which will act as an anchor to stop the string line being blown off the vertical. A plumb bob can be inconvenient to use under certain circumstances, particularly when laying masonry.

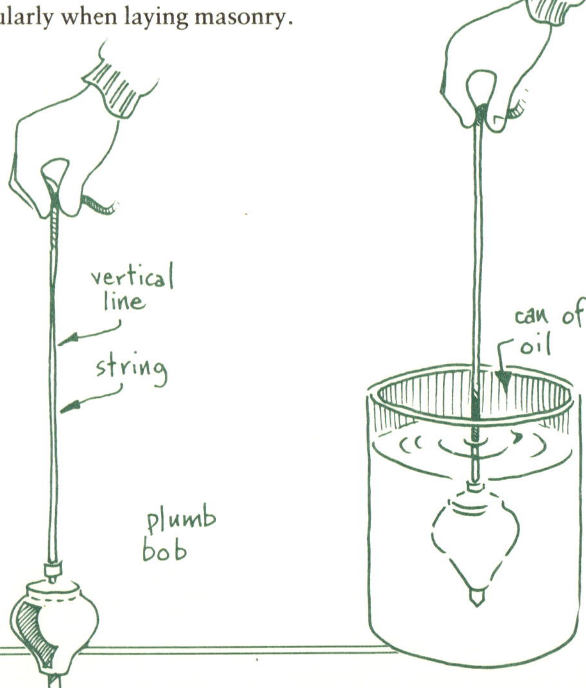

A modern builder's spirit level is equipped with at least two spirit levels — one to read the horizontal and the other to read the vertical. Bricklayers have been known to call their spirit levels, 'plumb sticks'. A good spirit level is a worthwhile piece of equipment for every garden builder.

Levelling

Levelling is the procedure by which all the critical levels on a site are referenced to a known level called a 'datum'. This datum can be a standard datum set by government edict, used by all utility services, road construction and other authorities to maintain a coordinated system, or it can be an arbitrary datum for use on an individual site.

In garden construction it is common to refer all vertical dimensions back to one known point called the 'site datum'. The site datum can either be given an arbitrary value or it can be a standard datum. Generally, a round number such as 10.000 metres is a good arbitrary value because it allows any levels which are less than the site datum still to be given a positive number value. If the standard datum is used then a known standard level is needed from which to set the standard datum within the site.

For convenience in garden construction an arbitrary site datum is normally sufficient. It is usually located towards the lowest point on the site as this generally means easier reference if an optical level is used. If the optical level is used with a level located towards the high point of the site there is a risk that levels taken from some parts of the site will be lower than the height of the eyepiece of the optical level which can mean taking extra readings.

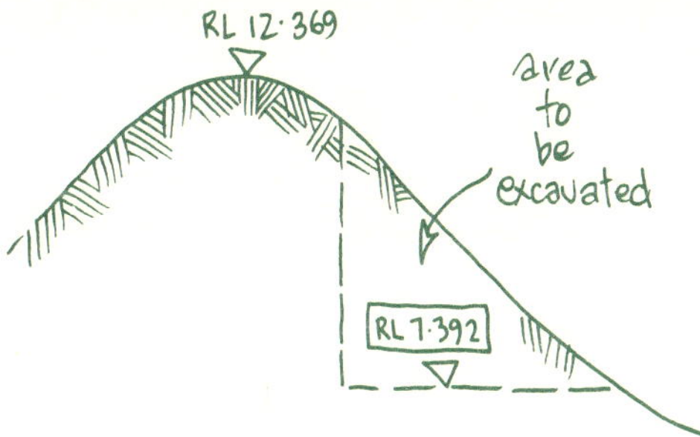

Points taken on the site are called reduced levels (RL) and expressed as a numeral referenced to the site datum. If a point is 3.789 metres above a site datum given the value of 10.000 metres, then the reduced level will have a value of 13.789 metres. If a point is 2.450 metres below the site datum then it will have a value of 7.550 metres, that is, 10.000 less 2.450 equals 7.550.

If a level is 12.225 metres below the site datum then its value will be -2.225, which is confusing and inconvenient. If this happens increase the value of the site datum to 20.000 metres, to avoid negative numbers.

When levels are shown on a plan drawing of the garden they should have the letters RL (reduced level) in front of them; from our examples RL 13.789 and RL 7.550. If the level already exists it is written RL 13.789; if the level is to be excavated or built up it is written in a box [RL 13.789].

Sometimes points of the same level are joined together on a plan by continuous lines called contours. These are very useful in garden design but they would usually be the work of a surveyor as their calculation is complex.

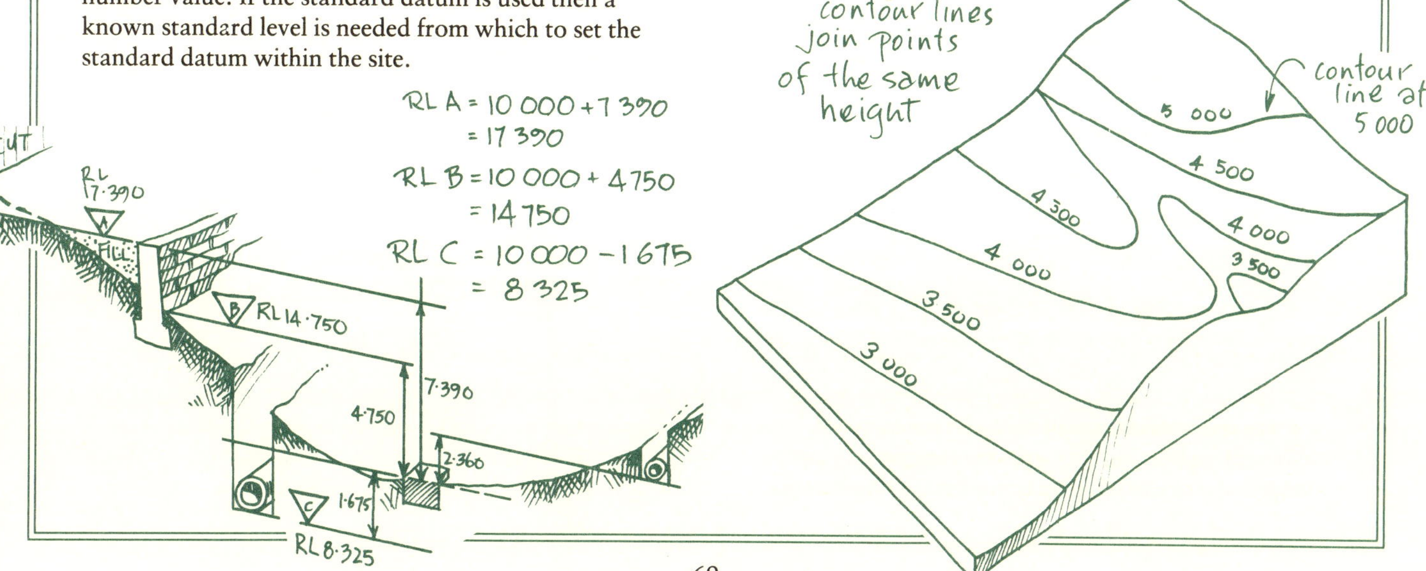

Squaring

Garden plans often call for square corners but it is not easy to judge a right angle on the ground. The simplest way to check that the intersecting corner is square is to make up a large triangle from timber battens using dimensions based on the 3–4–5 triangle. A triangle with its three sides in the ratio 3 to 4 to 5 will always provide a right angle at the intersection of the 3 and 4 sides. A triangle 3 metres by 4 metres by 5 metres is unwieldy so make one that is 1.5 metres by 2.0 metres by 2.5 metres. If it is much smaller than this it becomes difficult to achieve an accurate right angle (an imperial triangle could be 6′ x 8′ x 10′ or 3′ x 4′ x 5′).

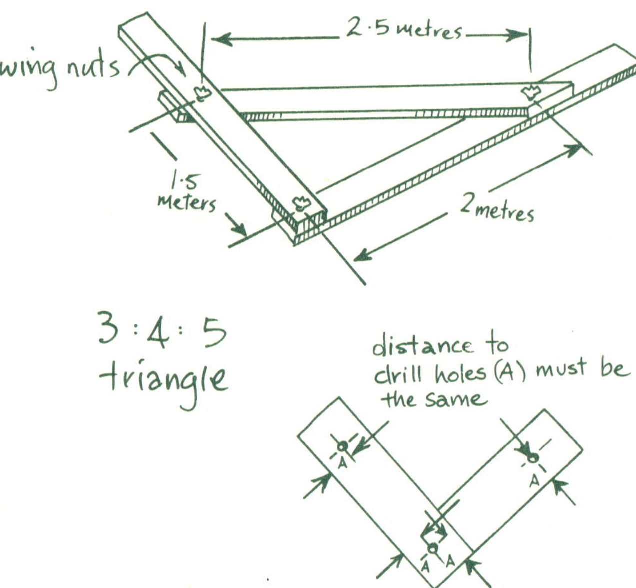

It is also possible to construct the right angle by using stringlines and pegs, but this method needs some practice and it is less convenient than making a large wooden triangle.

THE EXISTING VEGETATION AND IMPROVEMENTS

In most garden designs certain plants, paths, constructions, and buildings are likely to remain. Few people demolish the house on a property to construct a new garden, though some do. The existing improvements must be considered when working on the garden construction as there is always a chance that damage may occur during or because of the construction. There is little point in designing a new garden around a special mature tree if the tree dies as a result of the new work.

Protecting wanted plants

Most plants are vulnerable to damage during garden construction, particularly if heavy machines are used or there is limited space in which to work. Protect all plants within 3 metres of any work area by erecting stout stakes hammered well into the ground.

If the existing level of the garden is to be changed as part of the garden design, great care must be taken to ensure any large shrubs and trees do not have their roots damaged during excavation. This may mean that mounds have to be left around some existing planting. Be sure that a tree will accept disruption of the topsoil before proceeding with the work. It is worth checking with a horticulturalist.

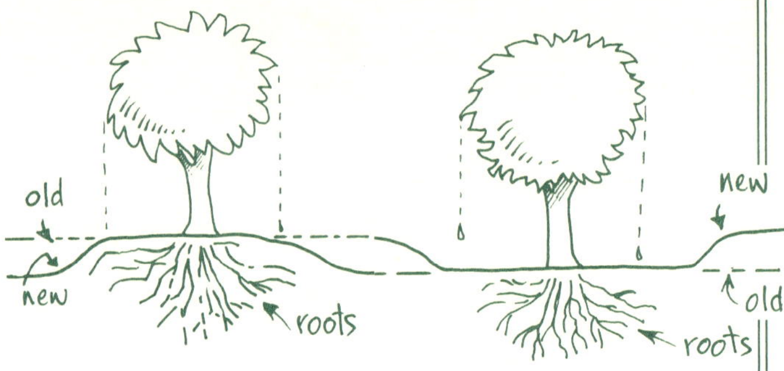

Whereas many trees and shrubs will accept being left in a mound, most will not accept having the level of the soil raised around their trunks and if the surrounding ground is raised but the tree left in a hollow there is danger of the hollow becoming waterlogged when it rains. If a tree has to be left in an area of filled ground, particularly if it is a tree that will not accept an increase in the height of the soil around its trunk, make sure that the hollow area around it is well drained.

Some trees will tolerate an increase in the height of the ground around them if the difference in height is filled with a crushed rock fill which is well drained and ventilated. This only works for some trees and requires careful construction.

Protecting existing improvements

Buildings on the site of a garden being modified can be adversely affected by the garden construction work. The worst danger is that of introducing damp into a building. This can occur throught the ill considered raising of the natural ground level. If the new ground level is above floor level of the building or above the damp-proof protection built into the base of the walls, the chance of dampness occurring in the building is increased.

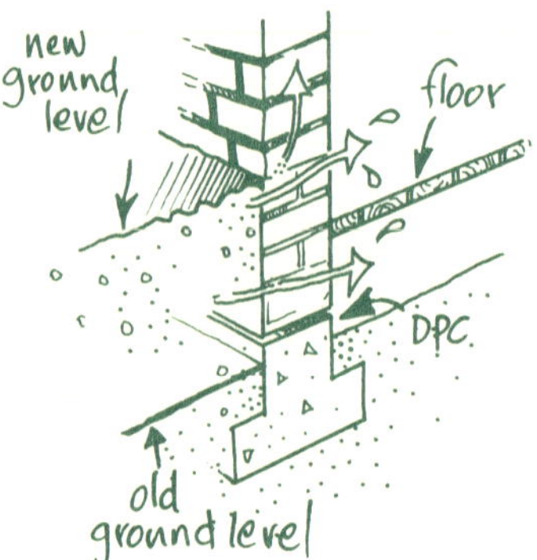

Conversely, the foundations of the buildings can be disturbed by excessive lowering of the existing ground level. Many modern residences are built on concrete raft floor systems and it happens that the concrete edge beam surrounding these floors to be only 200 (7″) or 300 mm (12″) below the natural ground level. Any excavation close to such buildings can cause irreparable damage to the residence as the building is likely to settle further into the ground causing differential movement of the structure and resulting in large cracks or worse damage.

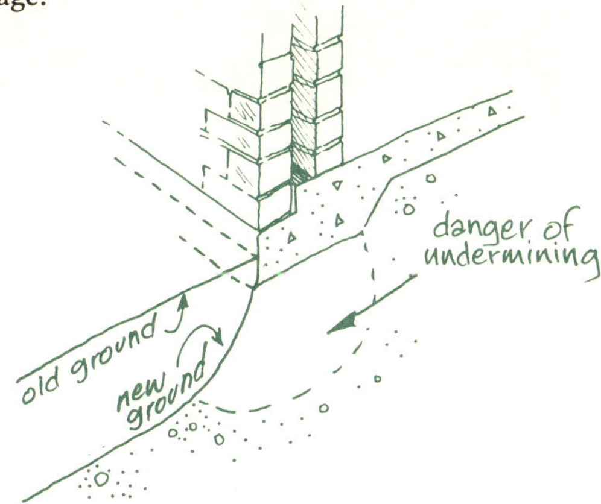

Even buildings with deeper footings can be damaged by quite small excavations around them. Excavations can upset the subsurface drainage around the building again leading to cracks appearing in the building fabric.

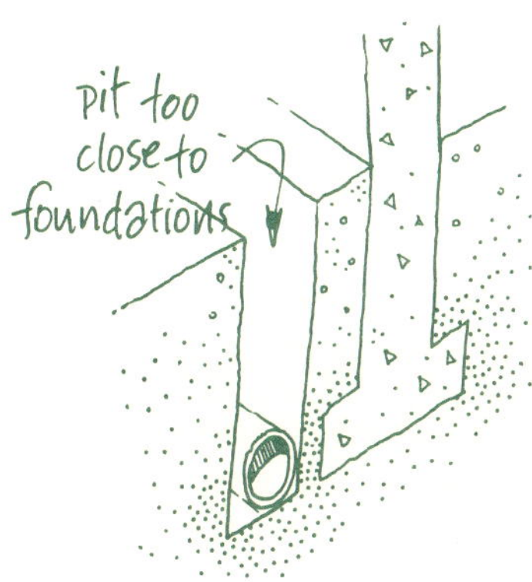

These activities are less likely to cause structural damage in buildings that are built on well-drained land or on rock. If the natural substrata of the garden is clay, there is a fair chance that the soil is reactive; that is, it expands when it is wet and shrinks when it is dry. These are the soils most likely to give problems if they are disturbed.

Investing in a well-designed subsurface agricultural drainage system around buildings on clay soil is sound. If the subsoil is well drained it has less changes in water content and therefore is less likely to cause building movement.

Uprooting plants for future relocation

When uprooting plants for relocation in another part of the garden, take great care to move them carefully and seek detailed local knowledge.

In most cases all the roots are removed as part of the process of taking the tree or shrub out of the ground and this leaves a big hole. It is not always advisable just to fill this hole with the best available soil. If the hole occurs in a clay subsoil, there is a risk that the place where the tree was removed will become an underground water catchment. If this happens the water that is trapped may turn sour and contaminate other planting.

Fill the hole with soil similar to that which occurs naturally at the stratum so that at the end of the backfilling the hole has a similar soil cross-section to the surrounding area.

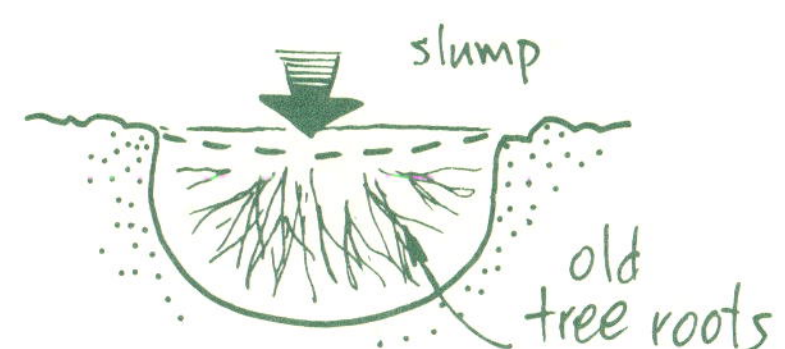

Uprooting plants for disposal

When trees and shrubs are being uprooted for disposal, follow the same advice above for the backfilling of the excavation. It is also important to remove the bulk of the roots from the soil surrounding the place where the tree was removed, particularly if any construction is to be carried out in the same place. With time the roots will decay and rot away, leaving underground voids which may collapse, causing paths to dip, fountains to tip, and pergolas to sag.

De-weeding stockpiled topsoil

When removing existing topsoil to allow for the new garden plan, stockpile if for re-use on the garden when the construction work is complete. This must be stored away from all weeds intact ready to re-germinate in the new garden, and those still in the topsoil.

There are a number of mechanical and chemical ways to treat the soil before stockpiling it so that it is free of weed when re-applied to the garden. Check with local garden supply companies to find out what methods are best in your location.

DRAINAGE SYSTEMS

The construction of drainage systems is very important in the preparation of a garden. Most modern drainage is carried underground in uPVC plastic piping, which is very easy to use. Underground piping of stormwater has always been a potential problem in a garden, particularly one with large trees. Tree roots and pipes are in competition for the space underground and some trees have identified drainpipes as a convenient source of water.

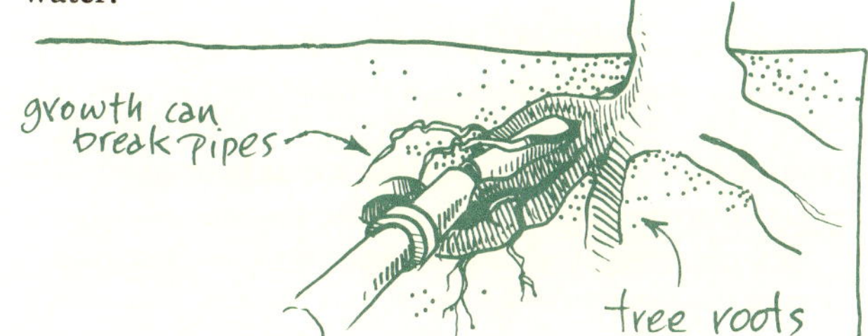

Pipes underground are out of sight so it is hard to tell if they have been ruptured by growing roots or if they are being invaded by water-searching roots. Eventually the system fails completely.

It is advisable to run surface drains where applicable and to keep piped drains to a minimum. Make sure piped drains are of adequate size and in straight runs with cleaning eyes to allow any choked lines to be cleared easily.

Stormwater inter-allotment drains

In some places stormwater is removed from individual properties by a system of inter-allotment main drains. A well-designed system will consist of correctly sized stormwater underground pipe drains, located at a level below the lowest ground level on the properties serviced.

Many areas still make-do with street kerbs as collector drains with minimum main pipe drains serviced by side-entry pits in the kerbs. This system means that the street is, in effect, used as a drain. This is sensible but if the system blocks from leaf debris and other rubbish local flooding can result. The kerb drainage system can only work adequately if the properties along the street are all higher than the kerbing, and this is not always the case.

If the street kerbing is at a higher level than the property being served, the stormwater has to be absorbed on-site or collected into holding pits and pumped up to the kerbside gutter.

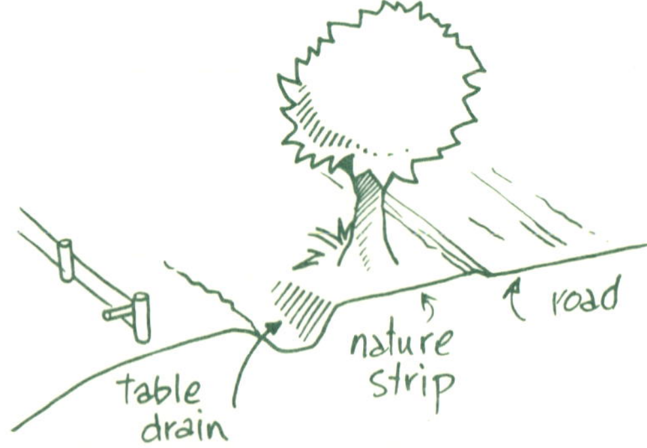

In other areas where roads are only partly formed storm drainage is directed into shallow open drains between the roadway and the adjoining properties. Some properties may make use of natural watercourses passing through the garden. Safety precautions need to be taken when these pass through private property. These can sometimes be enhanced and incorporated into the garden design but take care, they are often public waterways and covered by regulations.

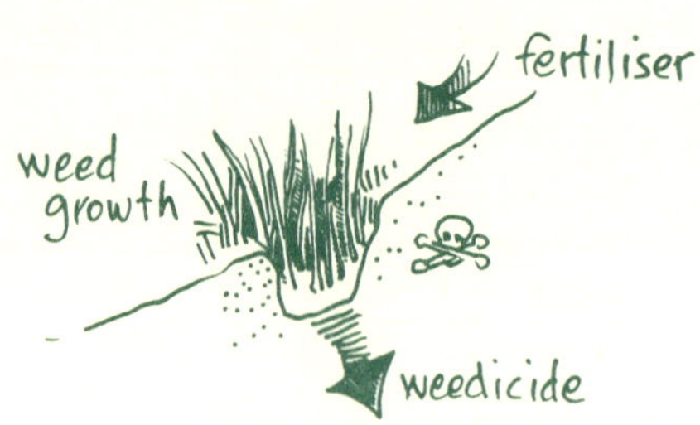

Wherever water is drained from a garden into an earth drain there is the possibility of dense weed growth in the watercourse and on its banks. This is encouraged by fertilisers often from the garden being leached out during rainy periods and deposited in the watercourse. Tackling these weeds with any chemical weedicide needs to be done with caution as the water from the watercourse may enter a sensitive area of native vegetation or be used by other gardeners downstream to irrigate their gardens.

Stormwater house service

The first step when installing a stormwater service is to locate where the water can be discharged from the property. Where there is an inter-allotment main piped drain approach the local drainage authority to provide information on how and where the main pipe can be entered. Drainage authorities disapprove of people who cut holes in their expensive drainpipes without authority as this can damage the system.

Some drainage systems will have connection points or pits built into them and this is where any connections must be made. Others will require you to construct a connection to the authority's specifications.

If footpaths or roads have to be opened to connect a stormwater drain to the main drain, a permit is normally required from the local authorities. In some areas conduits are built under new streets during construction and the conduits are made available to property owners when they are ready to connect to the stormwater outlets.

If it is impossible to connect the stormwater drains to any main drainage system then an absorption system needs to be constructed on-site. There are many different types of absorption systems and the local authorities will be able to give information on the one most suitable for your area.

Absorption systems consist of a series of trenches excavated into the ground roughly parallel to the natural contours. The extent of these trenches is determined by the amount of water to be absorbed by the ground and its ability to take up water. In areas with sandy, gravelly soils the ground can take up large volumes of water without much difficulty but if the soil is dense clay then the ground's ability to absorb water is much less.

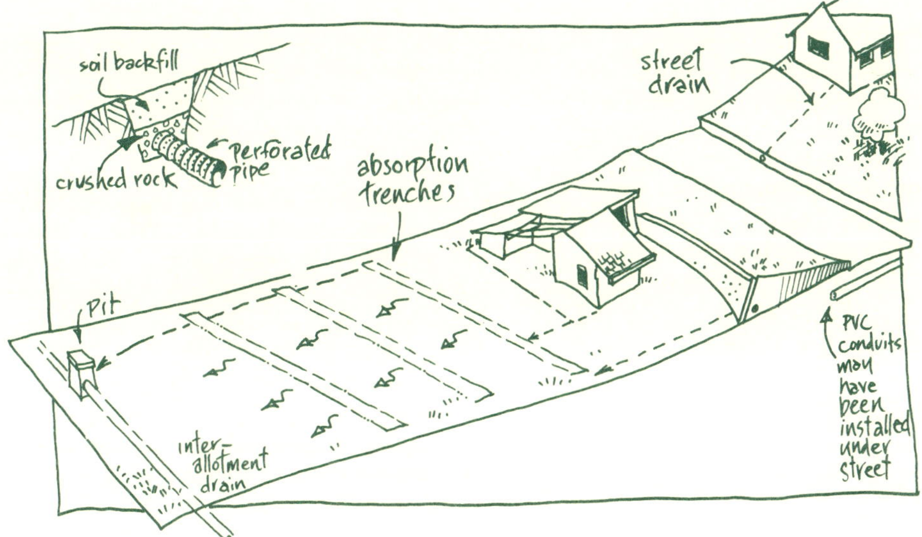

The trenches normally contain agricultural drain-pipes surrounded by crushed rock and are backfilled with garden soil. The stormwater is fed into the absorption system at the high end of the trenches which branch out to provide the required distribution.

Where a pump-out system is required, you will need to construct a pit that will hold enough water to allow for a larger inflow than the capacity of the pump. The difference between the pump's capacity and the probable highest volume of water requiring disposal should be calculated individually for each site. A pump normally requires a sump of water, from which to draw. The critical volume of water the pump can handle is a compromise between a pump that would be too large to efficiently pump away water on a drizzly day and a pump that would be too small to handle rain from a thunderstorm. Pump manufacturers can assist in providing data on the capacity of pumps and recommended operation procedures.

fall of at least 1 in 50 is required for a piped service and 1 in 100 for a hard bottom open drain. A good drainage design will use the minimum number of entry points possible. Don't forget to allow to pick-up of all down-pipes from any buildings on the site. Avoid placing pipes near trees. Ensure an even fall and avoid locations that could cause problems in the future because of ground settlement or root invasion.

Pipes should not be located under driveways where they can be crushed by vehicular weight, nor under any building or place where a building is proposed. Do not put pipes under patios where maintainance or repairs are needed. Significant expense and damage could result.

The top of a drain in a garden should be at least 300 mm (1') below the finished ground level; that is, it should be deeper than the depth of a spade blade or the normal blow of a mattock, to avoid accidental damage from implements.

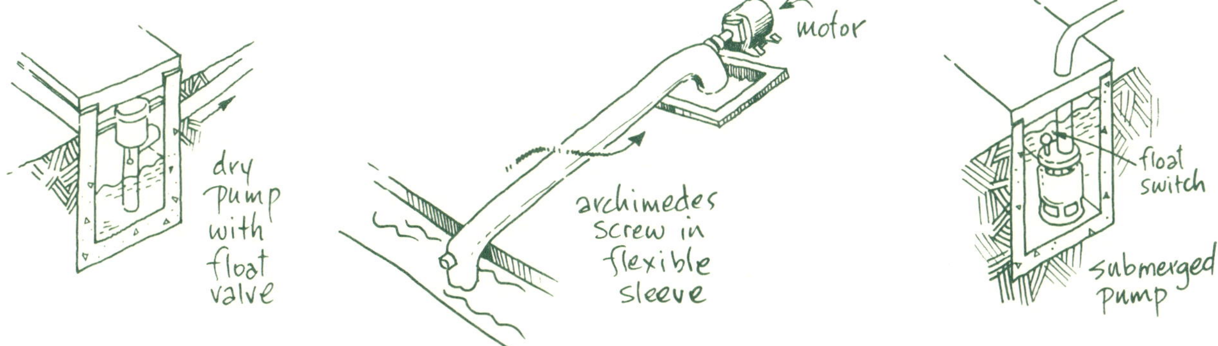

When the point to which the stormwater from the property is to be directed is located, then all the pick-up points for stormwater within the property have to be identified. Water will only run downhill, whether in a pipe or an open drain, unless it is being pumped or siphoned.

The levels at all stormwater pick-up points should be referenced to the point of disposal. In general terms, a

Silt traps

A silt trap is a specially designed pit which breaks the flow of water in a pipe in order to separate out soil particles from the water. These are sometimes used at the entry end of an absorption trench system to reduce silting up trenches and prevent inefficiency.

Silt traps can be used anywhere in a stormwater system where it is desirable to remove silt from the water.

Pits

Pits can be built into any stormwater system and are commonly located at changes of direction. They are particularly useful if the stormwater drainpipes are very deep in the ground, making normal inspection of opening-type cleaning eyes impractical.

Building a pit out of concrete or bricks down to the pipes at a change in direction makes it possible for a person to gain easy access to the pipes and carry out de-choking operations. The pit should be fitted with ladder bars and large enough for a person to crouch down to work on the pipes.

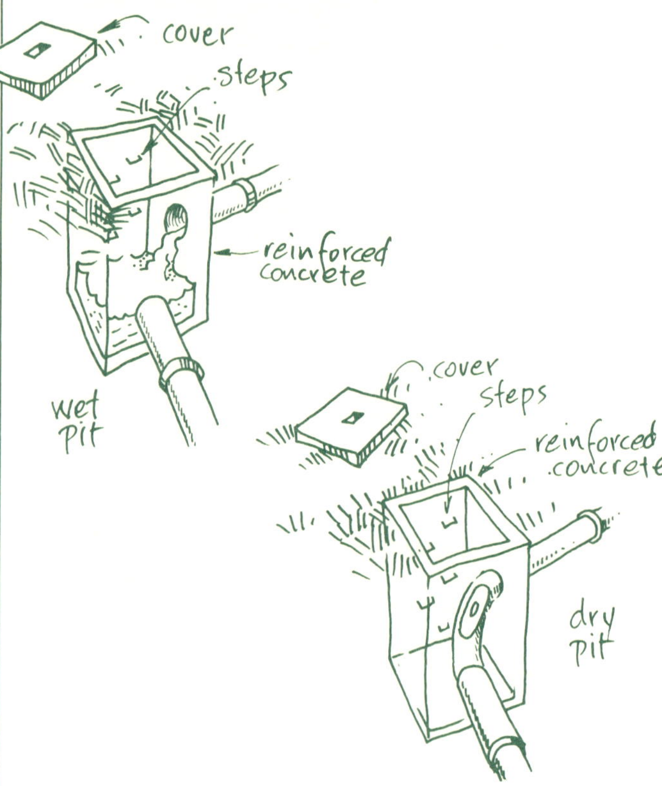

Pits can be dry or wet. Pipes passing through a dry pit are fitted with sealed inspection openings; in a wet pit the water passes through the pit in an open trench. Wet pits are normally used if the top of the pit is fitted with a grating to allow the entry of water.

The pit lid should be made from reinforced concrete, cast iron or fabricated galvanised steel. Do not use timber lids over any pits as they will rot away with time. Such lids become dangerous for an unsuspecting person who may stand on one.

Agricultural drains

Agricultural or rubble drains are used to collect excessive underground water directing it to a place where it can be disposed of. Such drains can be used in many locations in a garden to maintain a balanced moisture content in the substrata.

It is wise to install agricultural drains on the uphill side of any residence within a garden, so rainwater and garden water is not trapped against the footings of the residence. This could lead to foundation movement or contribute to the risk of rising damp.

Agricultural drains should be placed at the base of all retaining walls, at the back of the wall, so that any water dammed behind the wall is carried away before it builds up sufficient pressure to damage the wall. Most retaining walls that fail, do so because water is trapped behind them under pressure, not because the earth they are retaining pushes them over.

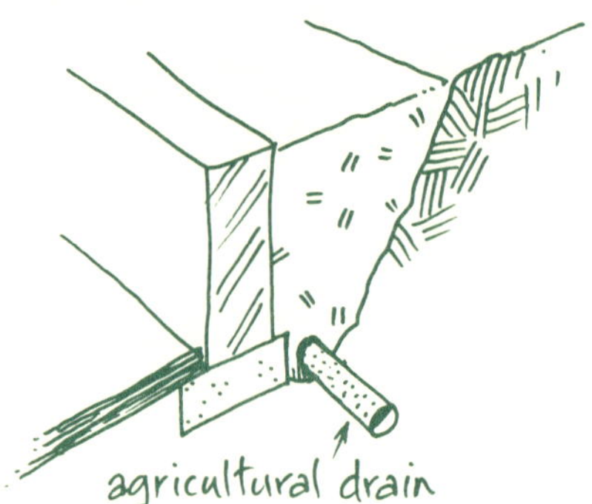

At the boundaries of the garden with other properties that are at a higher level you can use an agricultural drain filled with rubble to the natural ground level to limit the amount of uncontrolled surface water that flows into the garden.

Agricultural drains should have a fall of about 1 in 100 and should be separated from the main stormwater pipe system with an effective silt trap. If the line can be designed so that it falls in both directions from a high point in the system near the middle of the drain, it can empty from both ends, allowing for easy flushing.

Silting of agricultural drains is a common problem. The speed of silting has to do with how well the drain was designed initially, how much water flows through and the composition of the surrounding soil. If cleaning eyes or open ends are designed into the system, it is a relatively simple matter to push a garden hose with the water full on through the drain and flush out much of the silt which has built up.

Responsibility to neighbours

Most people accept that there will be a certain amount of water flowing on the surface of the ground when it is raining and that this water will flow downhill from higher properties to the lower properties in an area.

Problems occur when landowners cause excessive amounts of water to cross from their properties into a neighbour's allotment where the land is at a lower level. Sometimes this can be accidental. As a garden is developed and re-contoured and extra patios, paths, and buildings are constructed, run-off may become much faster than it was previously.

Neighbours who have to suffer a higher flow of water across their property boundary than would be expected naturally have a legitimate complaint. If the flow of water has been concentrated by earthworks in the garden where the water originates, the matter becomes more serious.

Roots and drains

Some trees have roots that cause expensive damage to underground drainage pipes either by entering the pipe in search of water or by damaging the pipe through their growth.

Modern uPVC piping is relatively resistant to root penetration and damage because it is in long lengths with minimum joints and has some flexibility. If roots do penetrate, uPVC stormwater grade pipe can be damaged by the pipe-clearing apparatus, as it has quite thin walls. It is recommended that the thicker-walled sewer grade pipe is used where pipes are in close proximity to trees.

If you believe that the tree roots will damage even the thick-walled sewer grade pipe, then the whole of the pipe can be cast into concrete, but this is expensive.

Grated drains and pits

Grated drains are used to collect water flowing down a driveway or path. They consist of a gutter, generally cast in concrete across the driveway or path, covered with a cast iron welded fabricated galvanised steel or perforated galvanised steel plate.

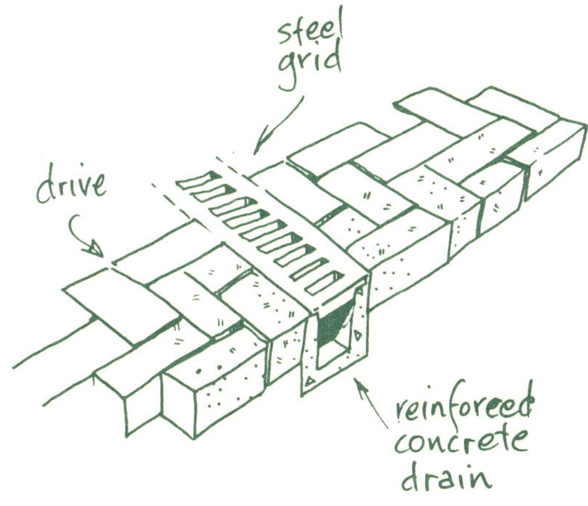

Grated drains are generally located across the entries of buildings, particularly garages, that stand at the end of paths and driveways where water can easily flow into the building through doorways. They are also used to stop excessive rainwater flowing down external stepped paths or ramps and to collect water from areas where it could otherwise be trapped.

Grated pits are similar to grated drains. They consist of a pit constructed from rendered brickwork, poured concrete, precast concrete, moulded fibrous cement and even treated pinus. The pit has a grated cover to allow

the entry of water and is connected to a drainpipe for disposal.

Grated pits can be distributed around a garden anywhere there is a need to collect rainwater and can be built into open drains to complete a system of excess rainwater collection and disposal.

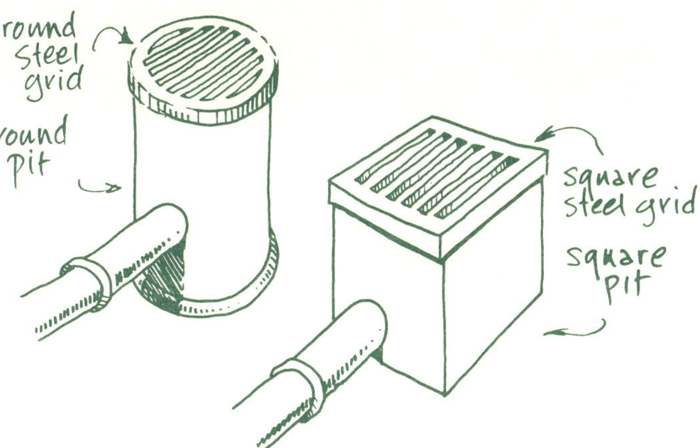

Gutters and ditches

Open drains are a very good way of collecting and channelling rain and seepage water in a garden. A hard-faced gutter is in most cases preferred to an earth drain, but when used with due care, both can perform an important role in the water control system in any garden.

Very good gutters can be formed with poured-in-place concrete or precast concrete units, but these are often visually less suitable in a garden than a gutter constructed from more natural materials. Hard-burnt clinker bricks make attractive drainage gutters and are flexible, so they can be built in whatever location, shape, and form individual gardens require.

The best way to construct an open brick drain is to dig a trench at the site of the drain and prepare a base of packing sand into which you have dry-mixed a binding agent. Cement or hydrated lime is suitable. Do not make the mixture too strong, a mix of 1 part binder to 10 parts sand is sufficient. Shovel the sand mix into the trench that has been prepared and tramp it well down so that there is a flat surface on the top. The top surface should be below the finished level, finish the surrounding area by the thickness of the brick that will be used, plus another 100 mm (4") to 200 mm (8") to allow for the drain sides.

The bricks can be laid flat or on edge. The extruded-type wire-cut bricks are not as suitable as pressed bricks as they must be used on edge and you will require many more bricks. Some people like to fill the joints between the bricks with mortar. This is not required but if you wish to do this, use a very weak mix of sand and hydrated lime so that the drain can absorb ground movement without cracking occurring.

To avoid ponding in the drain, set the fall to not less than 1 in 100. When the base bricks have been laid, form the sides of the drain with bricks to an angle to suit the location. Where the drain is to pick up water from a paved or gravelled area, the sides should be on a slope of about 30° to the horizontal. This will give a reasonable depth to the drain and still allow water from the paved or gravelled area to flow easily into the drain. If the drain is through a garden bed, the sides can be deeper, but it is a good idea not to have any side steeper than 60° to the horizontal. This avoids the sides being pushed over by the adjacent earth.

Natural stone will provide a more natural drainage ditch and can be used effectively either as a dressing to a concrete or brick channel or as a complete stone brook. If the flow of water is reasonably consistent then a babbling brook can be created and this adds the further dimension to the garden by the introduction of the sound of water gurgling over rocks and even a small cascade or two.

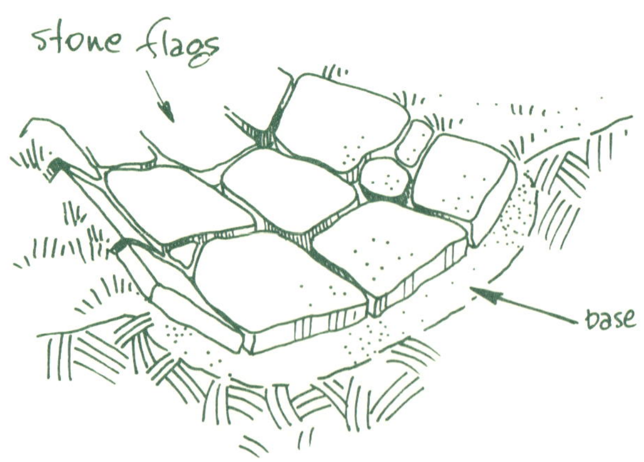

To give a constant flow of water there will have to be a natural spring or regular rainfall. If this is not available, a constant flow of water can be achieved by reticulating water with pumps from a dammed pond at the lower end of the brook. This dam should be designed to overflow in periods of excessive run-off.

Take care if there is irregular rainfall, as a brook-like drain can hold small ponds of water which become breeding places for mosquitoes in the drier periods of the year.

CONTOURING THE SITE

It may be necessary to re-contour the garden to achieve a desirable garden design but any major landworks should be treated with some care; in most cases the natural landform will be the most stable.

At the two extremes of contouring there is the danger of preparing too flat a garden, which may have drainage problems and become waterlogged, or too steep a garden, which has the potential hazard of erosion or possible landslip.

Always check carefully the composition of the substratum of the garden before beginning any deep excavation. If the site has a stable gravelly substratum then significant re-contouring can be considered, without much danger, if the slopes and drainage is well designed.

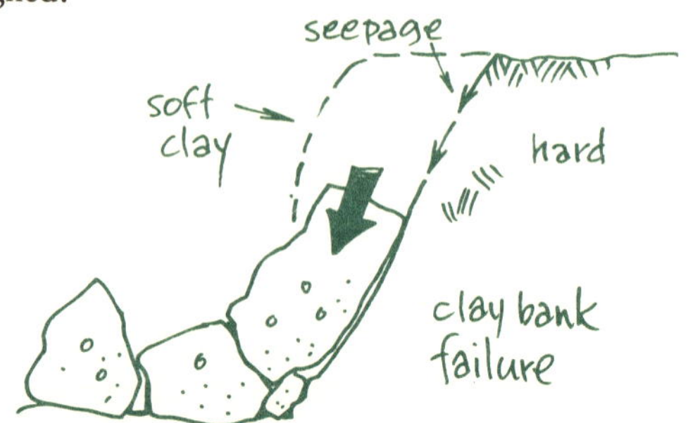

Where clay substrata are encountered, great care should be taken not to mix too much of the clay into the top growing soil of the garden. Clay is a cohesive soil type; that is, when it contains water it binds together. Because of this it is relatively easy to work when it is dry but can turn into a sticky mess if major excavations are carried out when it is wet.

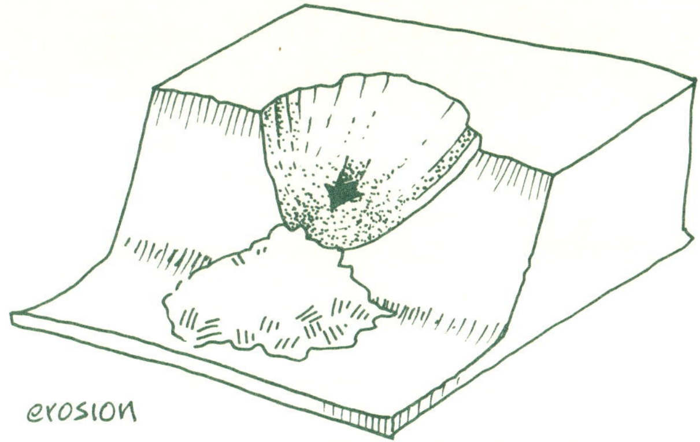

Excavations into clay will hold steep banks, even vertical slopes, when the clay is dry, but when wet it may slip without warning and care should be taken when working steep excavations in clay soil. Most clay soils are reactive; this means that when they are wet they expand and when they are dry they shrink, often to the extent of opening up cracks in their structure. This reactiveness may not be a problem where there is planting but it can be a major nuisance if paved areas or buildings are erected on highly reactive clay foundations, as major structural cracking can occur as a result of the soil movement.

If clay is used as a filling to raise levels of the garden, place the fill in thin layers, 200 mm (8″) deep. The layer should then be mechanically consolidated with a power stamper before the next layer is placed and consolidated. Failure to to this may mean that much of the filling is void; rough filling can be over 30 per cent void. Over time the soil will consolidate naturally through the effects of ground water and pressure and the filled ground will sink leaving hollows at the garden surface.

If you encounter rock in the substratum then at least there is a stable base in most cases but rock is hard and expensive to excavate, requiring extensive use of heavy machinery or even explosives. Most rock substrata will have a layer of broken rock material over the bedrock in the form of boulders and gravel. Some of this material may be useful for rockeries and garden walling or even granular fill in areas needing good water permeability.

Shales, sandstones, and limestones can be excavated by mechanical digging machines although some of the denser sandstones, granites, and basalts require drilling and explosive extraction mining procedures. In most areas the use of explosives is not allowed, particularly in closely settled urban areas. Even in more open rural locations a permit must be obtained to carry out any blasting, and an approved operator must be used.

When backfilling with extracted rock be careful that it is well interlocked and stable as it can shift and settle over time. In some cases the addition of gravel or sand to fill the voids is advisable.

Machinery for site works

Few gardeners will want to carry out any but smallest excavation by hand, particularly when it is realised that an area 3 metres (10′) by 4 metres (13′) by 0.5 metres deep (1′ 8″) contains 6 cubic metres (8.5 cu. yards) of soil with a mass of around 12 tonnes (12 tons).

Small rubber-tyred earth-moving machines (often called Bobcats) can work in confined areas and excavate a hole the size of a swimming pool, in easy-to-work soil, in one day. Other machines, like a tractor with a backhoe attachment, need more room to manoeuvre but are useful for trench excavation and ripping out holes for ponds.

If the excavations are large and there is plenty of room to move then a crawler track bulldozer may be required. For rock excavation a bulldozer with a ripper blade on the back can make short work of the softer rock layers. When earth and rock is excavated the pile of spoil that comes out of, the hole is always larger in volume than the hole it came out of and because it is a pile with sloping sides it takes up at least twice the area on the ground as the hole from which it came. Make sure there is enough space in the garden to store this spoil or arrange for a truck to carry the surplus away.

Pneumatic hand-operated jackhammers may be required for heavier rock excavation or sometimes a pneumatic pick can be used as an attachment on a tractor or bulldozer.

All this means noise, dust, and expense, so plan any excavations required carefully, and only after all other alternatives have been explored thoroughly.

Environmental impact

An important consideration in any excavation plan is the environmental impact it is likely to have. Neighbours are generally unimpressed by the noise, dust, and damage that can be caused by even relatively small-scale excavation. Let your neighbours know when you are about to undertake noisy and dusty work in the garden

More serious environmental impact can result if the earthworks allow dirty clay slurry to flow through neighbouring gardens or adjacent natural countryside polluting watercourses and staining the soil. Poorly designed or supervised earthworks can cause short and longer term soil instability where earth banks erode away over time or fail and slip into the neighbour's garden.

Even small re-contouring projects can have an impact on other people and their property, particularly if there has been a change in the ground water flow. In a storm, water may flow from a garden that has been re-contoured into a neighbouring allotment that has not had any major surface water flows in the past.

Erosion mitigation

Wherever earthworks are carried out there is always a risk of erosion of the soil through wind and water. This risk is highest if there are exposed areas of soil on sloping land where the effects of the weather are at their least favourable.

Rainwater running down a slope is the most obvious type of erosion that is likely to be encountered in a garden and this can be reduced in many ways. An open drain constructed at the top of the slope will divert excess water away, although this does not stop the rain that falls directly on the slope. In this case contour drains may be required on very large or extremely exposed slopes to carry away excess water.

The quicker vegetation can be grown on a slope the quicker the surface of the soil is bound together and the more resistant it becomes to water erosion. There are a number of methods which can be used. To stop grass seeds being washed off a slope there is a procedure where grass seeds are combined with fertiliser, chopped

straw, and a binding agent. Then spray the slope where the mixture sticks to the surface of the ground for as long as it takes for the seeds to germinate and take root. Another method is to cover the slope with chopped straw which contains fertile grass seeds and fertiliser and hold it in place with fine steel netting.

Unless the garden is exposed to violent and regular wind bursts, both of these methods will reduce the chance of wind erosion. Keeping the slope moist will provide reasonable soil protection.

In the second case where a cutting is made into the side of a sloping land, water penetration can have similar results. The most common problem with this type of excavation is that the new bank of the cutting is made too steep; that is the slope is steeper than the earth can retain naturally without supplementary retaining systems. The face of the bank could fail as the earth takes on its natural maximum angle of slope.

The steeper the bank the harder it is for vegetation to take root. In many cases the bank will need to be battered with stone rubble, or faced with and inter-locking concrete, or treated timber crib walling, so that the bank is stabilised and there is better opportunity for vegetation to take hold.

If a really steep bank is required then a retaining wall may be needed to control slippage of the bank.

Stockpiling

When any bulk excavation takes place there is a pile of spoil which has been excavated out of the natural ground. This spoil is likely to contain topsoil, inter-mediate soils, and base material. If this is all allowed to be mixed together the resulting mix is unlikely to be good garden material.

It is sensible to clear the area to be excavated of all vegetation, and for all material containing weeds or weed roots to be removed from the site or if applicable, composted. When the site is clear of vegetation then the topsoil can be stripped and stored in a convenient location for later reuse.

It is sensible to enclose the area where the topsoil is to be stockpiled with a timber barrier made from used railway sleepers or similar large sections of timber solidly staked to the ground by long steel spikes. This enclosure allows for more soil to be stored in a given area and reduced spread of the pile owing to wet or windy weather, and activity adjacent to the pile. If the soil is stored in a windy area, use a covering of hessian sacking to reduce the loss of soil to wind erosion.

When all the general excavation is completed then the topsoil can be redistributed over the garden, ferti-lisers, and other soil enhancement materials can be added conveniently during the spreading of the topsoil.

Filling

Filling usually means levelling a section of sloped land or hollow with earth filling. If the soil is suitable, the easiest way to excavate soil from one part of the site is to fill another.

Cleansing

Where soil excavated from the garden is intended for reuse for filling or levelling another part of the garden, all green matter which may sprout again in the new garden design should be removed carefully. All large roots and fallen tree limbs should be taken away as these will decay, leaving voids under the ground if the soil is used for filling.

Decaying dead timber can also be a host to termites and other timber-eating bugs seldom useful to a garden. After all decaying timber is consumed by the bugs they may turn their attention to eating the residence or live trees.

Cutting

Bulk soil excavation by cutting is generally a choice of two methods. Either by the removal of the top of a mound or by the cutting into a slope to form a flat area of ground. In the first case there are few problems involved, other than making sure that by taking the top of a mound of ground that water does not penetrate the exposed substrata. Water can flow between the denser often sloping substrata and the more unstable topsoil and in extreme cases localised landslip can result.

WATERING SYSTEMS

A garden is limited in size and type by the volume of consistent suitable water available to irrigate the plants. Before any ambitious garden plan is undertaken the water supply should be assessed.

In many areas water supply is irregular, unpredict-able, restricted, limited, and often expensive. It is foolish to plan a garden if all the hard work and expense is reduced to a desert because of a failure of the water supply in a period of dry weather.

Mains water supply

Mains water supply is generally available to irrigated gardens when the system has good reserves in the dams or other supply source. If there is a depletion of reserves then restrictions of garden watering is normally the first step the authorities take to conserve diminished reserves.

Water for drinking, washing, industry, fire-fighting, and food production are all ranked higher on the scale of water usage over watering a residential garden. If there is a chance of water use restrictions in the area where the garden is planned then either the garden should be planted with plants which can resist long dry spells or the garden should be restricted to a size which will allow for alternative watering methods.

Bore water supply

In many parts of the world underground water can be tapped to supplement or even totally provide the water supply for residential gardens. Even where the aquifer is relatively close to the surface, bores are expensive and require regular maintenance of the bore head equipment.

If bore water is to be used to supplement mains water supply the authorities will generally insist that the two systems are reticulated through different pipes. This is to reduce the danger of the mains systems siphoning bore water into drinking water in the event of a system failure. Seldom is bore water suitable for drinking.

This requirement for a separate bore water reticulation system adds a further expense to the use of bore water for irrigation. The authorities generally do not require their consent to sink a bore or to install the necessary pumps and piping, but it is wise to check what local requirements exist.

Make sure any pumps are installed to manufacturer's recommendations. If possible, use an installer approved by the manufacturer to ensure that the system is safe and all warranties will apply. High pressure water pumps can be very dangerous if they are not correctly installed.

Rainwater supply

Rainwater is a gift of nature when it is allowed to take its natural course. If rainwater is stored in tanks, some local authorities may levy a rate as they consider that the householder is avoiding contributing their proportion of the cost of supplying mains water.

The problem of storing rainwater in a garden is that above ground tanks are generally ugly and underground tanks require pumping systems. Both take up valuable space in a garden. If the tanks can be located in a suitable spot then rainwater is worth storing in the rainy period of the year for use in the drier months.

In collecting rainwater be careful that only water, surplus to the garden's need, is gathered and tanked. There is no point in catching too much water and artificially creating a drought in a period of insufficient rainfall.

Remember too that the tanked water is not allowed to be mixed with the mains water supply in most locations even though it can be argued that the rainwater is likely to be much purer than the mains supply. If mains supply, bore water, and stored rainwater are all used on the one garden, then three separate piping systems may be required.

Creek or riverwater supply

The water in creeks, rivers or other permanent watercourses, which flow from, into, past or through properties, generally does not belong to the land through which it flows. The water in most locations is considered a public resource and is administered by a government authority.

If the water is to be used to water gardens, then normally approval is required and the authority will place conditions on the use of this water. These conditions will often restrict the volume of water that can be drawn from the watercourse and specific periods of restriction will be nominated. In some cases dams may be approved but these are often subject to the landholder submitting detailed engineering documentation and the maintenance of a certain minimum water flow to downstream users — even if this means opening the dam to let stored water flow at certain times of the year. Also there may be requirements to maintain the watercourse, its banks and its catchment. The maintenance of the natural watercourse with restrictions on lining, culverts and conduits, often is considered important in environmentally sensitive areas.

Leaving the natural vegetation on the banks of a watercourse is more acceptable than new planting as the alternative planting may affect the natural watercourse adversely, or if the introduced plants drop seeds into the water. These may take root further downstream and be undesirable for the natural environment.

Consider if any change to contours or increased runoff in the garden adjacent to the watercourse will affect it. Damage can result with extra silt filling natural hollows in the watercourse. This would alter the environment for fish and other river life.

Too great an increase in the run-off of surface water from the garden can scour the watercourse, ripping away natural bank vegetation, causing erosion, and undermining banks.

Whether or not detailed restrictions apply to the use of natural watercourses, passing through a garden, the gardener should think of the plants and animals which depend on the watercourse for food as well as the needs of any downstream users. Remember, any chemicals in the form of fertilisers, insecticides and herbicides will probably be leached into the watercourse and be deposited downstream where animals and people may be using the water for drinking.

As watercourses are commonly at a low point in a garden a pump may be needed to draw water. Site the pump and the suction point where it will have the least environmental impact. If a petrol or diesel pump is used, make sure that the fuel tank is constructed in an acceptable manner. The whole unit requires regular checking to avoid any risk of hydrocarbon pollutants entering the watercourse.

Storage of water on-site

Where possible, place any water storage tanks at a high point in the garden so that the contained water can be reticulated by gravity rather than energy-consuming pumps.

Grey water system

Grey water systems which are using non-septic waste water should be located so that their contents can be drained to an environmentally safe place. The water could become unsuitable for irrigation purposes because the quality is affected adversely by a domestic chemical or algae.

Grey water is an extremely useful system to use in a garden where a good clean regular water supply is not available. Remember, this water should not be released into natural watercourses or stormwater systems, and should be reticulated using a pipe or channel system, that will not become mixed with any pure water system.

Piped water reticulation

Where water is to be reticulated from mains supply normally it is required that all of the plumbing is done by a licensed plumber. All pipes and fittings have to be approved by the water supply authority. This restriction is in the interests of public health as there is always a danger of polluted water being drawn into the public water supply.

Garden taps installed by plumbers usually will be of a type that contains a reflux valve which will shut automatically if there is a back pressure of water. This avoids the danger of dirty water entering the drinking water system. These reflux valves are not foolproof and care should be taken so that hoses connected to garden taps are not left in buckets, ponds or pools where a slow back siphon effect can occur.

Plastic pipe garden watering systems are often connected directly to garden taps. Where possible make these connections with all parts of the plastic pipe system lower that the tap supplying them so they will drain naturally when the tap is closed. This reduces the danger of water re-entering the clean water in the main system.

If the garden watering system is not connected to a main water supply or to any other piped water system that is used for human consumption or bathing, then a less complicated system of piping and valves can be used. Piped garden watering systems can often be purchased in do-it-yourself kits and can be installed without the use of a licensed plumber. Most of these use black piping to stop the breakdown of the plastic as a result of ultra-violet light. Such hoses can be run over the surface of the garden where they are not in danger of being cut by lawn-mowers. This use of black pipe in surface installations means that the water that is

trapped in the pipe at the end of a watering period can be easily heated by the sun. It has been suggested by some authorities that the temperature of the water in the pipe can provide a perfect environment for the growth of bacteria. Legionella bacteria which is potentially lethal to humans is one such bacteria. If the system is left for a period of time between use, then consider fitting a relief valve to the end of the line so that all the water trapped in the pipe can be flushed out, rather than be sprayed as a fine mist into the atmosphere where people can breathe it in.

Gravity irrigation systems

Gravity irrigation systems are where a system of pipes and/or channels are used to allow water to flow slowly around the garden to the plants that require the water. A gravity system can be controlled by a series of diverter valves or damming boards in the pipes and trenches.

A traditional low technology watering system, this only requires the water to flow constantly to a lower level in minimum slope pipes and channels to work efficiently. If the channels have too little slope, the water will not reach the end of the system. In the case of too much slope the water does not have time to soak in rendering the system inefficient.

With a little trial and error the correct slope to suit any particular garden can be found and a long-lasting minimum maintenance irrigation system achieved. In hot and windy environments an open channel system can lose much available water to the atmosphere because of evaporation.

A closed system of pipes with small branches which deliver the water exactly where it is required in the correct volume takes a little time to tune but once perfected has very little loss of water to evaporation or absorption into the soil where there are few roots.

Spray irrigation systems

Spraying water into the air to land on a garden in droplets as if it was rain is still among the most common and convenient ways to distribute water over a garden.

Spray watering is ideal for lawns where simple sprinkler heads can be fitted to the end of a normal garden hose. If a lawn is being created or re-developed it may be more convenient to install an underground spray watering system with pop-up spray heads. These systems are generally available as do-it-yourself kits and are not costly.

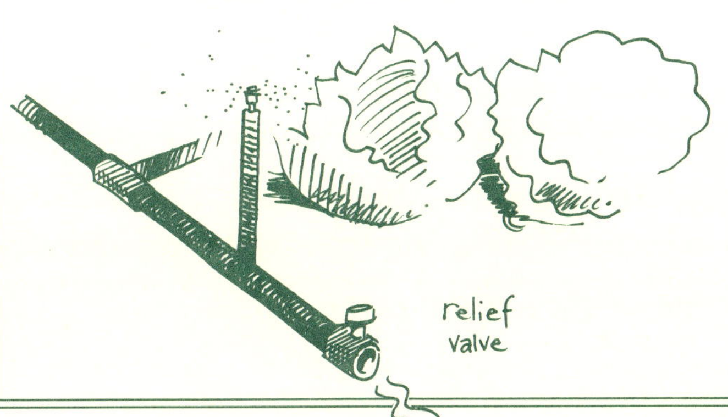

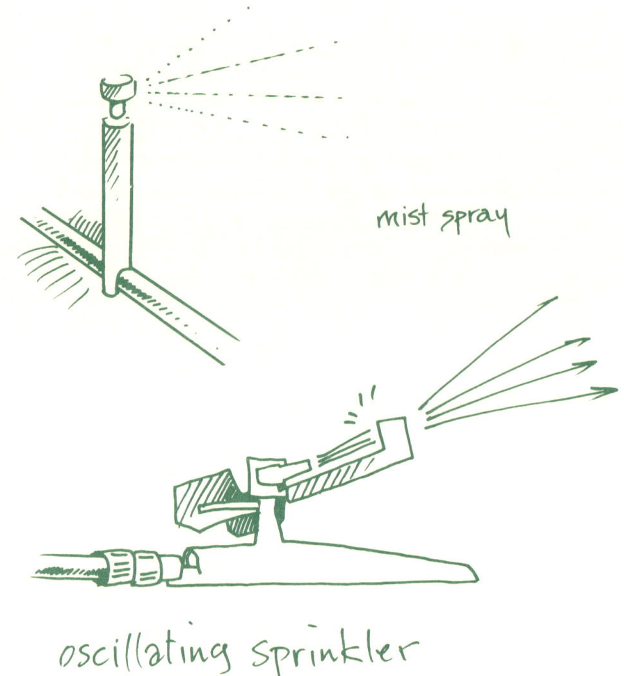

Spray systems can use wide coverage spray heads or very fine local sprays. Carefully plan the type that suits the garden and install them before planting or at least in conjunction with the planting.

Drip irrigation systems

Drip watering systems can be used as a component of any piped watering system and the concept is to develop a system where the major plants in the garden are provided with a steady metered supply of water to the ground around them. This system is considered to be one of the most efficient systems of water conservation devised to date for use in gardens where there is limited water available, particularly in hot and arid climates.

Timers and valves

With the popularity of the do-it-yourself type plastic piped spray, flow and drip garden watering system there has been a parallel development of valve and timer systems.

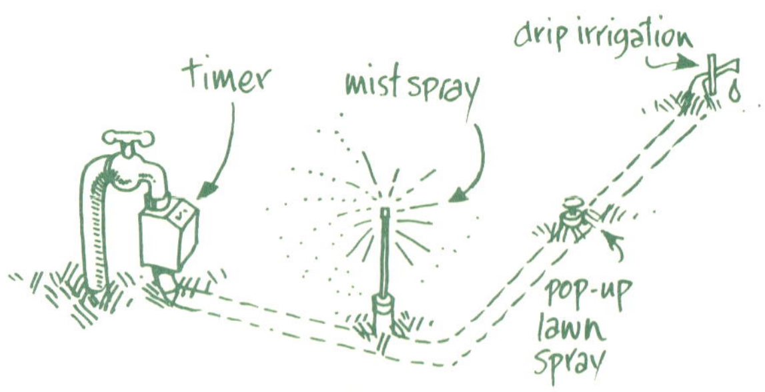

These systems vary from multi-branch valve sets, which are fixed to a standard garden tap and allow for the manual control of two, three, four or even more pipeline systems to complicated electronic computer-controlled valve systems incorporating timers.

By using a valve and timer system a gardener can set and forget, knowing that the garden will be regularly watered to a preset formula. This system has reduced the need for gardeners to change the sprinklers manually and they can go away on holidays leaving the timer to water their gardens automatically.

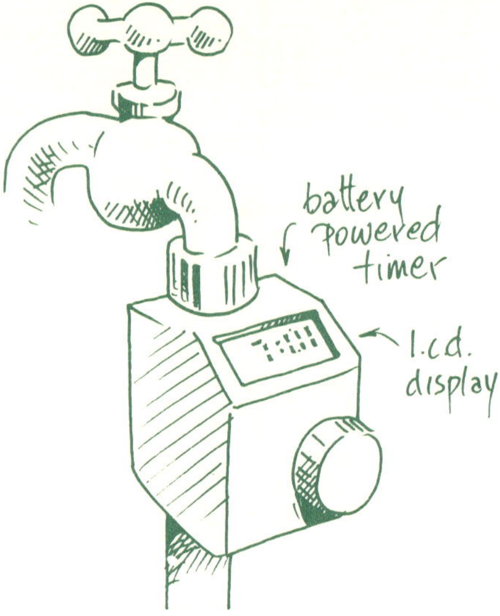

What happens if the system overwaters or keeps watering during a period of high rainfall? The most sophisticated systems have sensors built into critical areas of the garden which alert the *black box* controller when the soil has reached optimum moisture content.

Pumps

There are many pumps available to reticulate water in a garden. Be careful to choose the correct capacity for the volume of water to be handled. Always check with the pump manufacturer for information.

The best type of pump is driven by electricity which are quiet when operating. As the combination of electricity and water is potentially lethal have such a pump installed by a qualified electrician.

Other pumps using petrol, diesel and LPG (liquid petroleum gas) may be used if electricity is not convenient. These should be installed by approved installers because the fuels are inflammable and a poor installation can result in explosion and fire. As liquid fuels are pollutants any leak from fuel tanks on pumps will kill any vegetation they are in contact with.

If the garden is of a convenient size with reliable winds then a windmill-driven pump can be considered. These are quite expensive to install initially but operate on the free energy of the wind. A mechanically simple pump, it is relatively easy to repair, and requires only easy-to-undertake maintenance.

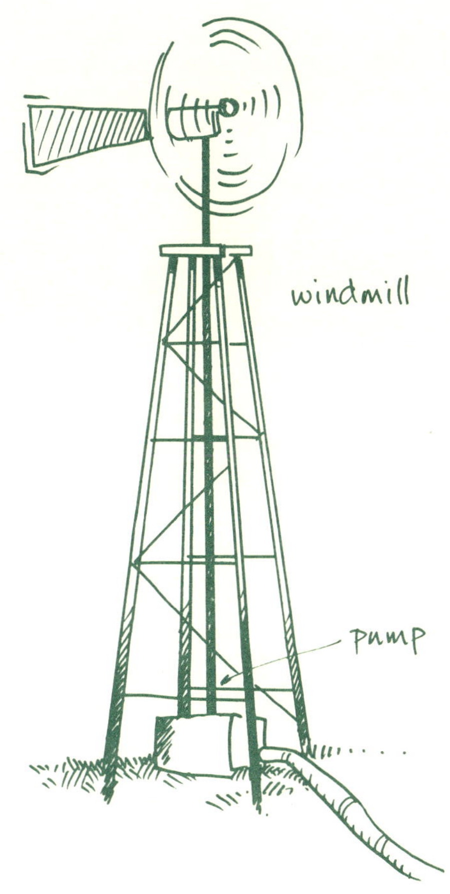

TOOLS AND MACHINES

When preparing a garden much of the back-breaking work can be carried out using specialist tools and machines. All this equipment is expensive. Purchase it with care and keep it well-maintained throughout its use to achieve the maximum use and value from the equipment.

Every garden should have a range of well-made hand tools, a selection of power tools and machinery selected to suit the size and kind of garden to be developed and maintained. If gardening tools and machinery are purchased from reputable manufacturers and suppliers, price is often a good guide to quality.

There are spades on the market which are of very low price but are made from steel that blunts, splits and bends easily and some last only a few hours. If the blade does not fail, the timber handle will. At the other end of the price range there are spades with carbon fibre handles and stainless steel blades. While these will last a lifetime they are very expensive. These do not last any longer or perform any better than a spade with a well-made wrought steel blade and selected hardwood handle, which costs much less.

Power tools and machines are harder to judge for quality, and many power lawn-mowers look good but must be assessed as a practical piece of machinery. Fancy cladding may not mean that the machine is efficient or not but to pay for a lot of show, may not translate to a lot of go.

If a power tool or piece of machinery has been on the market for years unchanged, except for evolutionary improvements, this could indicate it is seen as a useful and successful implement. Unless the budget for tools and machinery is unlimited, it is not a good idea to spend too much on untried revolutionary gadgets. Remember, the gardeners of the Palace of Versailles had only simple hand tools. Fancy equipment does not make a rose bloom any better or faster.

Hand tools

The design of basic hand tools including spades, shovels, picks, mattocks, rakes, trowels, axes, forks, saws, and hoes have changed little, if at all, in thousands of years. In fact a Victorian hand wrought-iron shovel blade was probably better than all but a few of the modern equivalents.

Some hand tools have improved with the use of modern manufacturing techniques, particularly secateurs and similar double-blade cutting tools, but even these advances have been evolutionary, in the main, rather than radical.

Wheelbarrows are essential for any garden. Buy a good quality product, with pneumatic tyres. Do not purchase the largest barrow available unless absolutely necessary as often their bulk can be a nuisance in a small garden. Many people are unable to push a large labourer's barrow.

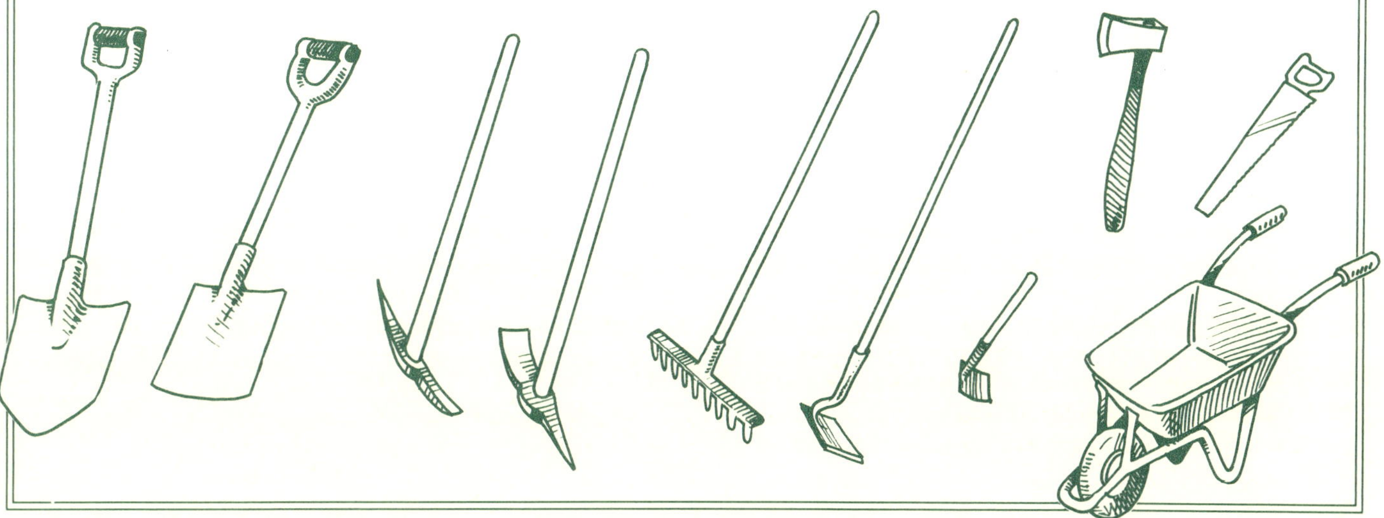

In the past garden wheelbarrows were made from durable timber. This was sensible because they could be repaired if a board or two rotted through or was accidentally broken. Today most barrows are made of steel. If the budget can be stretched, buy one with a heavily galvanised box. Many of the painted barrows will rust through after only a few days of being left in the rain, full of lawn clippings.

Hand-held power tools

Modern gardeners have many hand-held power tools available. These reduce the amount of manual effort needed to undertake many of the once back-breaking tasks needed in the garden.

These tools are either driven by small electric or petrol motors and generally need little more maintenance than being kept clean, having cutting edges replaced periodically, and being stored in a suitable dry shed.

There are a number of lightweight cutting tools which make use of rechargeable batteries to drive cordless cutting implements which can prune, clip, and trim many soft-stemmed plants and leaves. These implements are restricted by the charge in their batteries to about an hour's continuous use but are good for small jobs. As the batteries use low voltage, there is no danger of electric shock or fire that is associated with mains power or petrol-driven tools.

Where a tool is going to be used continuously over many hours, or the work is beyond the stored energy of a small battery, mains power is used. Most modern electric garden implements are double insulated and are safe if used within the design limits of the machine, however if an electric cable is undersized, of excessive length, or is accidentally cut, there is the potential danger of electrocution. Do not use cables that are kinked, coiled, frayed or which get hot during use.

If possible it is a wise precaution to use power supplied from an outlet equipped with an earth-leak circuit breaker which cuts the power supply the instant that a short circuit is detected. Most local electricity supply authorities can provide information on suitable systems.

Electric hedge trimmers have been available for many years and when used with care, can be a useful tool for cleaning up overgrown areas of a garden.

A multifunction hand-held garden tool now accepted by many gardeners, is a device with a long handle which can be fitted with nylon cord slashers, circular cutting blades, lawn edger attachments, and mechanical hoe blades. Sometimes these machines are sold to handle only one function but the more professional models can, by simple changes to the tool head, carry out all of the above functions, and sometimes, some others as well.

The light- to medium-duty long handle tools are commonly powered by mains electric motors but the heavier duty models are often powered by petrol engines. All of these long-handled tools can be used in

small spaces and are extremely useful in a small garden where many tasks cannot be performed by larger machines because of lack of space.

Any high-speed rotating head can be dangerous. Because of their high mobility great care must be taken when using long-handled power tools, particularly if they are fitted with open metal blades. Wear eye protection and stout boots as minimum protection when using these tools. Never attempt to use them wearing only thongs and shorts. Always ensure that no one else is close. These machines are very noisy and the operator may not hear a person approaching.

Even the garden rake and broom can be substituted with power blowers and vacuum cleaners. Before buying one of these machines check that it will do the job you expect of it. Some blowers will not move wet leaves and are only effective in a dry autumn. Hand-held vacuum cleaners are useful when cleaning up leaf litter from garden beds but if they only have a small bag there may be more trips to the compost heap than desirable. If the bag is too large then it can become too heavy for all but a very strong person to carry.

Low wattage power implements

The most common powered implements used in residential gardens are petrol or electric lawn-mowers. The reel and the rotary are the most common.

The reel-type has been available from early in the 20th century, when enterprising people mounted a motor onto a standard manual reel mower. The design has not changed radically over time and this type of mower, which is only suitable for trimming established lawns remains a relatively expensive machine.

The rotary-type was considered only for very large slashing machines until the Australian Victa company perfected a lightweight model for residential use after World War II. The lightweight rotary mowers did not trim lawns as well as the reel-type but they were light enough to be pushed without motorised drive, which was an essential component of the much heavier reel-types. Over the years the rotary mower has become more sophisticated, reliable, quieter and elegant. They even cut lawns to a tolerable quality. Rotary mowers can cut rough grassed areas as well as established lawns and most have an efficient lawn-clipping catcher.

Most rotary mowers use a two-stroke petrol motor and today need little maintenance other than to top up the fuel tank and to change the blades when these are damaged or worn. There are some electric rotary mowers. One of these uses some of the power of the motor to lift the mower above the ground so that it can operate without wheels, which can be an advantage in some terrain.

The tradition of raking autumn leaves into small piles around the garden and burning them has become less acceptable in a world where the pollution generated from these fires is considered anti-environmental. Collecting the leaves for dumping into a big bin for collection has become the task of garden vacuum cleaners. Often quite large contraptions the cleaner is on wheels with a large nozzle at the front, a motorised fan in the middle, and a huge sack hanging at the back. It does not add dignity to an autumn garden as the fragrant smoke from the leaf piles of old but that is pro-

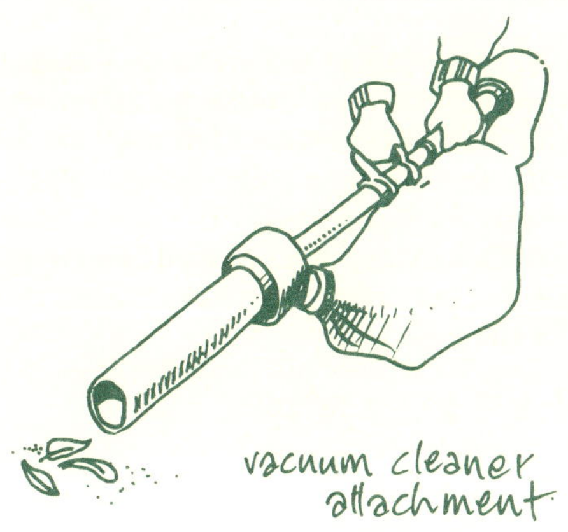

gress. Probably one day this machine will go the way of rotary mowers and take on the visual attire of Grand Prix racing cars.

Even the humble spade and hoe have a mechanical alternative and motorised tillers are produced which will turn over last year's annuals beds quickly. Generally these small machines will not turn over ground that has not been broken and aerated previously but they reduce the backbreaking chore of preparing existing plots for a new season's planting.

When gardeners had lots of time to tend their or their employers' gardens, composting and mulching of vegetable refuse and garden clippings was a leisurely task of periodically turning over the compost heaps in the back corner of the garden. Now science has come to the aid of the gardener with mechanical mulchers. These turn the vegetable matter over in big drums automatically, shortening the time it took a bygone gardener, with some help from nature, to produce mulches and compost.

Medium wattage power implements

There is an upper limit to the size that a rotary mower can be before it is unwieldy to operate by handles, on foot, even if the wheels are motor-driven. Enter the ride-on mower, a machine that looks like a mini-tractor straddling a large rotary mower blade.

The marketing departments have given these machines all the elegance of a cappuccino machine. Some are equipped with headlights so that lawns can be cut at night. Most ride-on mowers have one function, and there is no provision for attaching other implements to this pseudo-tractor. The more functional models are less visually attractive but often provide a range of useful additional functions including slashing, tilling, harrowing, and towing.

When preparing a new garden in an overgrown property, a large professional slasher is a useful implement. It is often of little use in an established garden and hiring one is wiser than buying an expensive piece of equipment that may only be used once. A slasher is not an implement developed for the average gardener's use. Consider employing an experienced operator if you think your garden requires such a machine.

In the same category as slashers are mechanical rotary hoes. These machines are capable, dependent on their size, of breaking-up consolidated ground, but are awkward to operate and are very dangerous in the hands of the inexperienced. They are unstable on rough or uneven ground and hard ground. A correctly sized machine in the hands of an experienced operator can transform a wilderness into arable land in a short period of time; operational in small areas and around obstacles in a manner not possible by any other machine.

Inexperienced operators can use a rotary hoe to turn wilderness into desert if by their inexperience. They dig through the productive topsoils and degrade them with the heavy clays from lower stratas.

If the garden to be developed is a large one and there is a significant amount of material to be moved, particularly on sloping sites, then think of buying or hiring a motorised barrow or other similar machine. These come in many forms and are developed most often for use on market gardens so they are generally utilitarian in appearance, and robust in construction.

Also gardeners who need a ride-on mower should consider purchasing one which has the capacity to tow a small trailer. This way, one motor can perform another task. Take care with any wheel-driven motorised machine when operating it on sloping land. There have been too many accidents caused by runaway or overturning machines.

To reduce the heavier plant waste, such as prunings from trees, mechanical shredders fill a useful role, turning branches into shredded or chipped material which can be used as ground cover mulch. Mechanical shredders come in many sizes, from those capable of reducing fruit-tree pruning, to those which can digest hardwood boughs. Shredders are noisy, use vast amounts of energy, and must be used with great care.

High wattage power implements

Few gardens need to own high powered machines. These are used only to establish a new garden normally. However, if a garden is large enough, a small tractor may fulfil many of the functions discussed above, with the addition of power-take-off implements.

A tractor that has become too old and unreliable for full-time use on a farm may be quite suitable for use in a garden. Good second-hand implements providing a wide range of functions from mowers, trailers, slashers, and diggers to scraper blades, and even tank trailers for fertiliser and water spraying can be purchased.

Storage and maintenance

Most garden machines require dry storage and a garden of any size should include a machinery shed. This shed should be capable of storing all the machines used in the garden in such a manner that they can be taken out without every other piece of machinery having to be moved.

If petrol has to be stored, make sure that all local regulations are met. Store only the amount of inflammable liquids that is essential for operating the machines.

When garden chemicals of any type are bought, read the labels carefully for the recommended storage methods. Dispose of any date-expired chemicals carefully, at a toxic waste receiving centre if possible. Do not put toxic chemicals in the rubbish bin.

Some chemicals are potentially explosive. The most common of these is swimming pool chlorine. It should not be purchased in excessive amounts, regardless of the potential savings in cost.

Most machinery will need maintenance of some form and a clear floor space with a workbench in the machinery shed will assist in ensuring this work is carried out. Machines not thoroughly maintained, are often potentially dangerous, but poor maintenance will shorten a machine's usefulness.

Machinery access ways

A machine is only as good as the ability to manoeuvre it to the place where it is to be used. Make sure adequate access ways are planned into the garden. A small rotary mower is very heavy. Make sure you do not have to carry it to and from the shed.

CONDITIONING THE SOIL

Soil is the medium that holds most of the nutrients needed for plant growth as most plants draw nourishment through their roots. This is used in combination with sunlight and air to provide sustenance and growth. It is possible to grow some plants without soil where plants are capable of growing with their roots suspended in enriched water. This can be useful in farming some crop vegetables but does not provide a pleasant environment for human enjoyment.

Plants send roots out through the soil for two main reasons: the first is to anchor the plant to the ground, and the second, and most important, is to absorb moisture. Under normal circumstances plants will grow sufficient roots to anchor them and to absorb the necessary amount of moisture.

Generally a good garden will have a soil cover deep enough for the selected plants to develop good root growth and be of a type which allows water to be retained long enough for the plants to extract their needs, but then to drain at a sufficient rate to avoid waterlogging.

Through their roots plants will absorb the water in the soil, complete with many other chemicals in solution. Plants need certain of these chemicals for their growth but some chemicals will be harmful to some plants. The quality of the soil has a direct bearing on the plants that can be grown in any garden.

De-weeding

The first task in any garden development project is to clear the site of the garden of all weeds, weed roots, and weed seeds. This is not an easy task and there is no foolproof method of removing all the weeds, but it is easier to de-weed a garden before planting, than to attempt to do it after.

In a garden that is to have completely new planting beds and lawns established, the whole of the top layer of roots and soil can be scraped off and the whole disposed of in a environmentally safe location. No material containing weeds should be tipped in natural bushland as this is propagating the problem in another location where the effect can be more devastating than where it originated.

It was once acceptable to burn weed-ridden soil and to return the residue soil and burnt vegetable matter to the garden. Now considered environmentally damaging to the atmosphere to burn any garden refuse, there are many areas where laws forbid burning garden refuse.

An alternative to disposal or burning, is to treat the soil with weed-killing chemical. Agri-chemical companies maintain that most of the modern chemicals are environmentally and animal friendly.

When stripping weeds from a garden some topsoil as well as some humus material is lost. When buying replacement soil it should contain decayed composted material to a proportion suitable for the new garden planting. The new soil must be of a pH level suitable to the plants going into it, and the soil must be guaranteed to be weed-free. It pays to buy soil from a reputable supplier as not all topsoil sold by garden suppliers is weed-free.

pH testing

pH testing is not an examination to achieve a Doctor of Philosophy in Gardening. It is a scale which indicates the acidity, neutrality or alkalinity of a material; in this case, garden soil.

Some plants like acidic soils, some a neutral soil, and others perform best in alkaline soils. A gardener who selects plants to suit the natural soil type generally has an easy-to-manage garden but if the gardener has a preference for non-local plants then probably a system of pH management will be required.

Kits to test pH can be purchased at many garden supply outlets and in most cases they are relatively easy to use.

If the test kit gives a result which does not seem to favour the planting proposed then certain agri-chemicals can be added to the soil to modify its chemical make-up. Use these chemicals carefully and always follow the manufacturer's recommendations.

Use less additive rather than more as it is impossible to remove excess chemicals.

Organic conditioning

Using organic material is the traditional method for improving the quality of soil, growth rate, and quality of the vegetation.

When farm and working animals were common in cities and towns, as well as in the countryside, there was a ready supply of animal droppings which could be used on gardens. Horse manure was favoured. However, with care and knowledge, the droppings of most herbaceous animals can be used satisfactorily.

Animals' digestive systems speed up decomposition of herbaceous material and it is ready for nearly instant recycling. Composting plant material, often in combination with kitchen waste, is a slow process by comparison, but the decomposed material is a suitable garden conditioner.

Animal droppings can be used today but most of this material is sold in plastic bags, and is often combined with composted material and other additives. Careful preparation of these proprietary mixtures allows them to be specially developed for specific plant types.

Using cuttings and sweepings from the plants in the garden has the benefit of returning to the soil nutrients from where they were drawn. This closed cycle process generally reduces the need to add large doses of chemicals and externally sourced conditioning material.

Inorganic and processed material conditioning

In most modern gardens processed additives and minerals, including certain trace elements, are added to garden soils.

Developments have allowed the agri-chemical companies to offer plant-specific mixtures of chemicals and other material in more and more convenient forms. It is now commonplace to be able to purchase a plastic bag or tub of pre-mixed conditioning material for just about every common garden plant.

Many of these preparations are spread in granular form around the appropriate plants. Application of liquid preparations can be by spray or using automatic water spray mixer attachments on garden hoses.

These preparations are usually easy and relatively safe to use. The manufacturer's instructions must be read carefully before applying the products as many are concentrates and overuse is a common problem. Too much growth enhancer can have a more devastating effect on the plants that they are supposed to help, than by using no additive at all.

Aerating

The correct ratio of void to solid material in garden soil is important if the soil is to remain sweet and water can move freely around the roots. A proportion of non-cohesive material is important in soils containing cohesive clays to avoid the clays becoming non-receptive through the effects of watering and the subsequent binding together of the soil particles to the exclusion of air-filled voids.

Heavy clay soils can be aerated mechanically by digging and hoeing but this procedure has to be carried out regularly. Digging around the roots of trees and shrubs can damage delicate roots and adversely affect the plant.

Sand can be added to clay soils in combination with decayed vegetable matter to improve the aeration of these soils but a large proportion of sand is needed before any appreciable gain in sustainable voids is achieved.

Specially prepared aeration materials can be added to the soil to open up its structure. These products vary in availability from place to place so discuss them carefully with a local horticulturalist before using any of them. These materials which include mica, perlite, vermiculite and expanded shales are quite expensive and specialist knowledge is required if they are to provide a real benefit in a garden.

Mulching

Mulching is nature's way of regulating the evaporation and transpiration of moisture in the soil, and of returning nutrients to it.

Most garden beds will be improved if the leaf debris from the garden is spread over them. Gardeners should keep the mulch sufficiently open to allow the passage of water through to the soil below, and the even circulation of air to assist in the controlled decomposition of the leaf material.

If the mulch is too dense or lacking in aeration, the result is a slimy smelly mess that does little to improve

the quality of the garden. Some lawn cuttings can be
spread into a leaf mulch if extra material is required,
but cut lawn grasses are more likely to become slimy
than leaves so these should be used with care. Also there
is a danger of transferring weeds from the lawn to the
garden beds.

If suitable mulching material is not available from
the garden being prepared, it can be bought from some
garden suppliers. Selected hay can be a useful mulch,
particularly for newly prepared flower beds.

Although woodchip mulches have enjoyed popularity often these are used carelessly and can be of more
nuisance than value, particularly when the weeds grow
up through the chips. Some gardeners have tried to
solve the weed problem by covering the garden soil with
plastic sheeting before covering it with woodchips but
this is a lazy gardner's practice and can seldom be
recommended.

BANKS AND RETAINING WALLS

Most new gardens, unless built on a near flat site, will
require some re-contouring. New banks and possibly
retaining walls will need be constructed if that is the
case.

Banks and retaining walls are functional and add
interest to the garden form but they should be constructed to achieve stability and not to interfere with the
planned planting.

Angle of slip

Before any bank or retaining wall is designed, it is
important to know at what angle the ground to be
banked or retained is, so that it will maintain its own
stability without slipping.

This can be done by making a test bank which is
then treated roughly and watered regularly. This
method is suitable for banks which are up to about 1
metre (3' to 3'6") or so in height and not in a critical
location. Banks that have buildings close to the top or
bottom, or are located on a property boundary, should
be treated with special care.

If the bank is in a critical location; higher than 1
metre; on really poor soil refer to a geo-technical
consultant for appraisal.

No bank should be left if it has a chance of slipping,
whether as an earth bank, an enhanced bank, or as the
earth behind a retaining wall.

Natural slope banks

Natural slope banks can seldom be left with the
substrata exposed to the elements. The exception is
where the bank is cut into rock, shale, or some well
bound gravels.

When the bank has been cut to an angle of its natural
slip, if in doubt about the correct angle it is prudent to
be conservative. The bank should be covered as soon as
possible with soil and planted with well-rooted vegetation.

Where banking cannot be planted out at an early
stage in the garden preparation then it should be
protected against erosion and surface slippage. By
covering it with a proprietary spray-on compound or
alternatively, chicken wire or similar mesh stretched
over the exposed face and pegged down the bank will
be secure until planting.

Enhanced banks

An alternative to using a bank at the natural slope of
the substrata material is to use a system of banking
enhancement. These methods are useful, particularly in
gardens where the natural slope would be very shallow
or where vertical retaining walls are visually unsuitable.

The traditional method of bank enhancement is to
batter the bank with dry-laid stonework, this can be
either in natural rock boulders, rough-cut stone rubble
or in cut stone blocks. In all cases the individual rock
pieces should be well interlocked and bedded into a well
draining base.

Hollow concrete blocks with the open core holes
exposed are a useful alternative to natural stone. These
have the advantage of being able to support interesting
planting in the core holes to completely conceal the
concrete blocks.

A stone batter allows quite steep slopes to be
achieved even in poor soil conditions but care should be
taken with batters over 2 metres (7') high and angles to
the vertical less than 30°.

The joints in stone batters can be filled with mortar
but any water that can build up behind the stones
should be able to escape, before it builds up sufficient
pressure to push the base of the batter away from the
banking.

Another method of bank enhancement is to construct the bank as a series of terraces with low height
retaining walls along their edges. This can be used to
visual advantage in some gardens, particularly where
the terraces are curvilinear. Curving the retaining walls
also tends to increase their stability.

If the terraces are curved with non-parallel curves
and combined with thoughtful planting a very steep
garden can be designed with useable flat terraces
combined with dramatic hanging gardens.

Crib walls

An alternative to a stone or concrete block batter is to use interlocking concrete or treated timber pieces to form a structurally sound bank enhancement system. These systems are manufactured components usually and come with detailed information on how to use them.

A crib wall system commonly consists of horizontal members which stretch along the face of the bank. These are separated by shorter members which link the horizontal members together and extend back into the banking.

The crib walls can be constructed to provide very steep bank faces, within a few degrees of vertical in some cases.

To use crib walling the bank which is to be stabilised is cut to the correct slope for the particular product chosen and the soil type to be stabilised. Then working from a prepared base, the crib wall system is progressively constructed and continuously backfilled with granular fill. The combination of the interlocking elements and the granular fill produces a structurally sound banking enhancement solution which also allows ground water to escape. In the voids of the crib wall plants can give an attractive appearance.

Gravity mass retaining walls

Gravity retaining walls are normally constructed from brick, concrete block, stone or concrete. They use their mass to retain the earth behind them.

There are some simple rules to follow when building a mass retaining wall:

- Always build the wall of a continuous reinforced concrete footing that is on a stable foundation or of the bedrock
- Always place an agricultural drain alongside the footing and drain this to a suitable place
- Always build the wall so that at any point in its cross-section the height to the top of the wall is not greater than three times its thickness
- Always build weepholes into the wall just above its base to allow any water not carried away by the agricultural drain, to escape from behind the wall. Retaining walls fail in most cases because of water pressure acting on the internal face of the wall
- Always fill behind the wall with well-draining granular fill, normally crushed rock is used
- Always build-in masonry reinforcing mesh into the horizontal mortar courses every 450 mm (1½″) vertically.

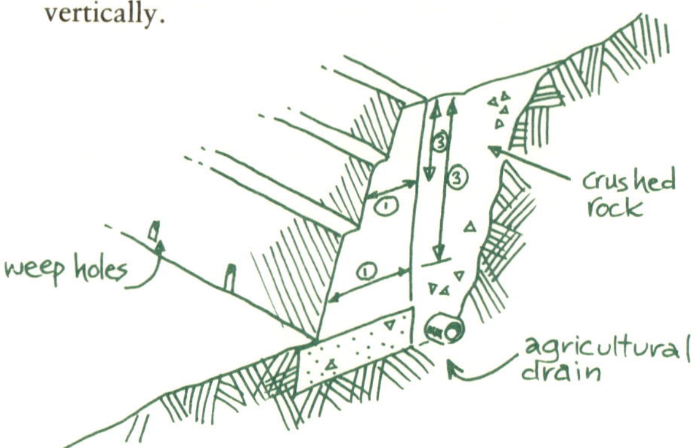

Brickwork

Mass is the primary requirement of a simple retaining wall. Therefore it is advisable to use hard-burnt pressed clay bricks or solid concrete blocks. Unless the voids are filled with concrete during the building of the wall, extruded bricks which have holes in them and hollow concrete blocks have less mass and are less suitable for gravity mass retaining walls.

Probably the retaining wall will be subject to varying pressure along its length and this may lead to some cracks appearing in the wall. This is a nuisance but it does not mean that the wall will fail and fall over.

To attempt to have any cracking restricted to the mortar joints rather that through the bricks, the mortar should be weaker than that of the bricks. By using a lime-rich mortar any cracking should be restricted to the mortar joints, and as lime-rich mortar is more flexible that cement mortars, many minor movements in the wall will be self-healing.

With the use of bed reinforcing mesh it is possible to build the retaining wall with a stretcher bond face but very strong walls can be built using English or Flemish traditional brick bonding methods. These bonding methods provide the face of the retaining wall with an equal mixture of face and head bricks, which are often considered more appealing than the common all stretcher bond face.

Build in changes of directions in the retaining wall where possible. This will add to the wall's stability and look more interesting than plain straight structures.

Build in vertical expansion joints every 5 metres (16′) as some clay bricks will grow after they have been built into the wall and this growth can cause the wall to fail.

Stone

Rules that apply to brickwork apply equally for a retaining wall built from squared ashlar stone.

If mortar-bedded clean sound rubble is used to construct the retaining wall then the height to thickness ratio should be reduced to 2.5 to 1.

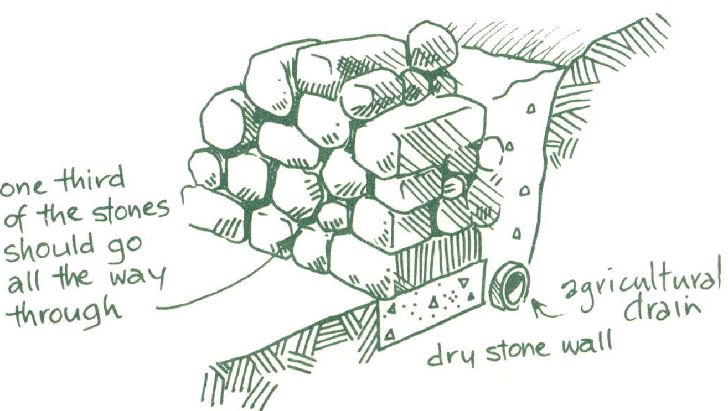

If dry-stone walling is used, attempt to have over 30 per cent of the stones go through the full thickness of the wall. Take great care to achieve well-interlocked stones. For dry-wall stonework in retaining walls use a height to thickness ratio of not greater than 2 to 1.

It is a false economy to build too slender a mass retaining wall.

Propped walls

It is possible to build a satisfactory retaining wall by using posts set well into the ground with boarding fixed against their edge facing the earth to be retained. The posts should be propped with buttress-like props at about 45°, solidly pegged to the ground and cut into the posts.

The posts and props should be of highly durable hardwood and the boards out of either hardwood or treated pine. Posts and props should have a minimum section dimension of 100 mm (¼″) and boards should be a minimum of 50 mm (⅛″) thick.

Timber-propped retaining walls are satisfactory only up to about 1.5 metres (5′) high. They have a limited life unless continuously maintained.

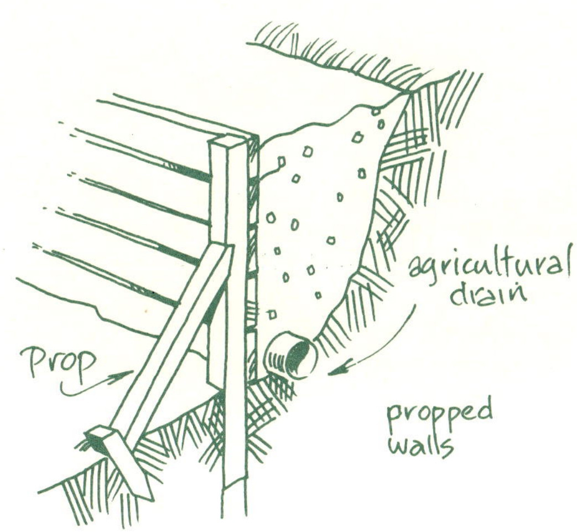

Tied walls

Tied retaining walls can be constructed in the same way as the propped wall but instead of using props, the posts are anchored with cables and pegs. The galvanised steel cables are attached to the post at the top of the wall and connected to pegs, driven deeply into the ground, behind the natural slope angle of the ground being retained.

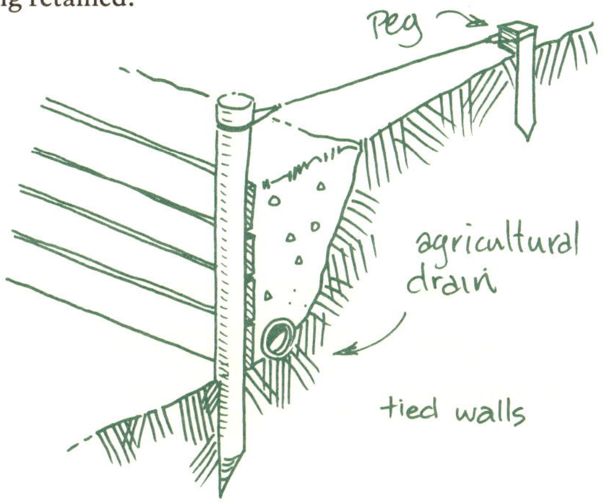

An alternative method is to use steel 'H' sections as posts and to slide reinforced concrete plans into them to form the wall. The posts are anchored then with cables to pegs or alternatively concrete anchors set deep into the ground.

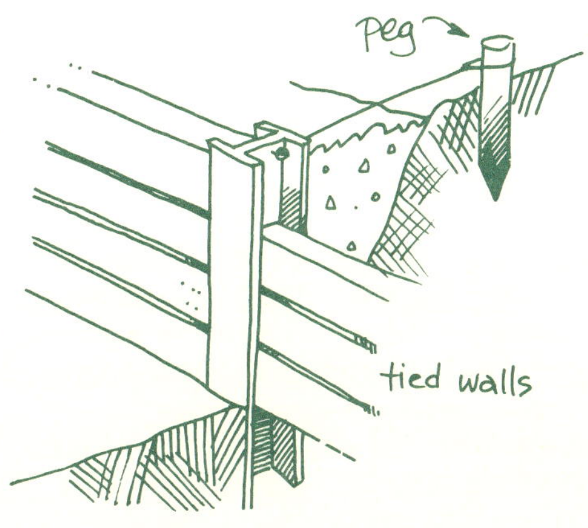

Cantilever walls

Cantilever retaining walls have a wide base and a slim wall cantilevering vertically from it. Traditionally these walls have been constructed from reinforced concrete.

The concrete cantilever retaining wall is very efficient but has to be constructed to critical engineering tolerances. This makes such a wall quite expensive and often out of reach of gardeners financially. When a high retaining wall is required, or a building is to be erected on the retaining wall, or where the retaining wall is on or close to the property boundary, then the cantilever wall should be considered.

Alternatives to the poured-in-place concrete retaining walls are: the precast retaining wall or the reinforced concrete block retaining wall.

The precast retaining wall comes in T-shaped sections which are craned into position. These are available from reputable precast concrete manufacturers and remove the requirements to build formwork, supply tie reinforcing steel and to pour concrete on-site.

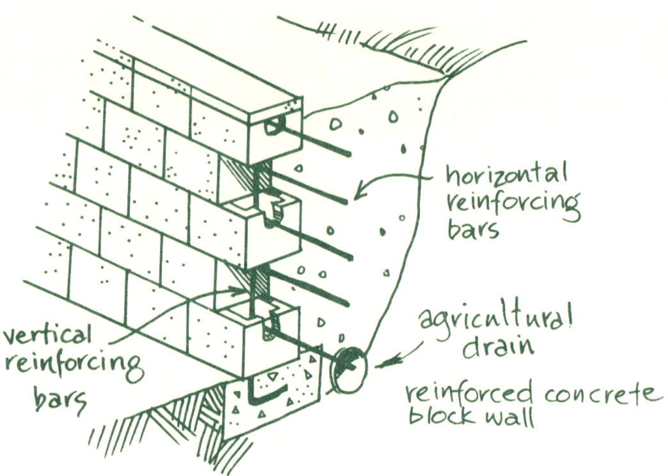

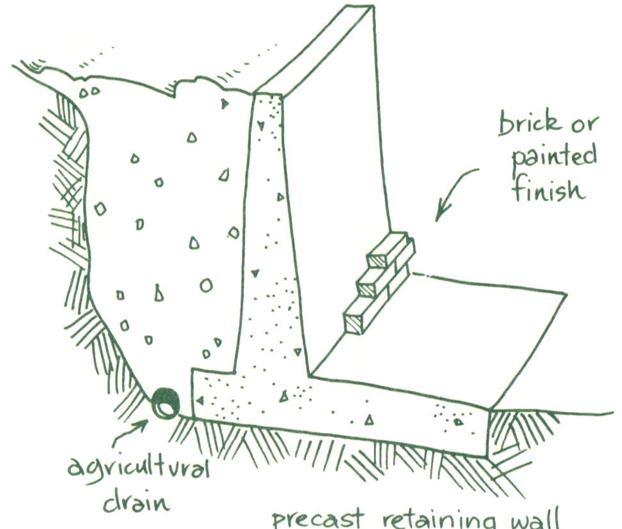

Reinforced concrete-block retaining walls are constructed from specially made concrete blocks which are laid in the same way as normal concrete blocks off a reinforced concrete strip footing. What makes them special is that vertical and horizontal reinforcing bars are built into the block work and when the voids are filled with concrete a very strong retaining wall results.

Concrete is not a material accepted universally as often it is considered to have too harsh an appearance for a garden environment. It is possible to build a brick, block or stone veneer on the face of a concrete retaining wall or to finish the surface with rough cast stucco or pebble dash stucco. In some cases coloured limewash is all you need to enhance the appearance.

The Construction Stage

All gardens need some construction from simple mower strips, paths and driveways to more complicated fences, steps, and lighting.

Many of these constructions are easily carried out by the home gardener without the need to employ specialist labour. The information contained in this chapter is to assist gardeners avoid the major problems that can catch the inexperienced unaware and to offer advice on how to handle some of the tasks.

Materials and construction methods will vary from place to place, the basic rules will remain much the same but it is worth gardeners' time to observe how things are done in their locality.

DRIVES AND PATHS

The visual quality of a garden must have been much easier to control before the motor car replaced the horse and cart. In those days the horse was kept in a laneway at the rear of the property except at grand houses where there were stables.

Today many houses have a motor vehicle driveway leading from the street frontage through the garden to the blank doored garage. These driveways are often hard against a side boundary effectively reducing the opportunity to plant trees on one side of the front garden.

Even when there is sufficient room to plant trees on the boundary there is the risk that their roots will grow up under the drive smashing the concrete and creating an unsightly mess which is costly to repair.

Drives and pathways are a major visual component of any garden and should be planned to give the best possible effect in the design of the garden.

Preparation

When preparing a garden it is important to locate drives and paths so that these do not interfere with the other garden elements, particularly the planting. Land slope and drainage are of critical importance in their location.

Any path or driveway should have a slope not exceeding a slope of 1 in 20 and if at all possible, with an absolute maximum slope of 1 in 8.

Drives need a transitional slope at either end so that the vehicles do not get caught on the underside or scrape their overhangs. This is particularly important if the slope of the drive is greater than 1 in 12, but this should be checked with a motor vehicle before the final surface is applied. Remember some makes of vehicles have less undercarriage clearance than others.

By curving a driveway you can reduce the slope and increase the distance from boundaries, but care must be taken to avoid excessive tightness in any curve or too narrow a drive width.

Also remember that unless a turning circle or bay is available adjacent to a curved or steep driveway vehicles will have to be reversed along the driveway when entering or leaving the property.

Unless the driveway is constructed on consolidated and drained granular natural base material it will require a base foundation of consolidated roadbase material. On a relatively level site this base material can simply be clean packing sand but if the natural substrata

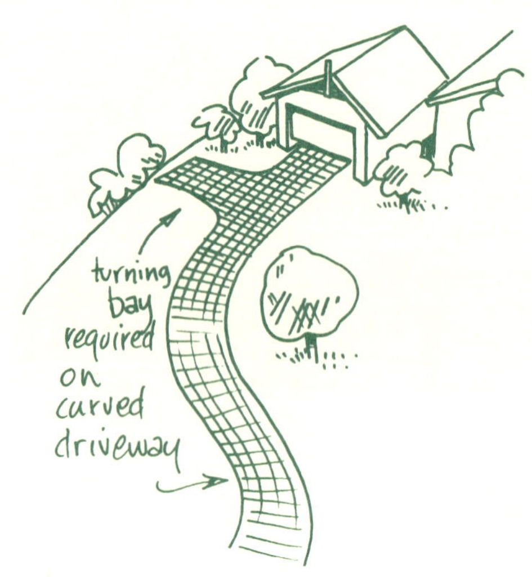

Roadbase is a mixture of large and small aggregate with a cohesive binding agent. This material is commonly purchased as a pre-mixed batch to which a controlled quantity of water has been added, it is delivered to the site in a truck, spread and then consolidated with a vibrating roller.

Reinforced concrete is where ready-mixed concrete is poured onto a prepared bed of packing sand covered with a moisture proof membrane. Steel reinforcing bars or welded mesh supported above the membrane before the concrete being poured in situ. When the concrete cures the steel is locked within it giving a strong and durable slab.

A reinforced concrete driveway can be trowelled smooth, finished with a steel or timber float or textured by sweeping it with a yardbroom. There is no technical requirement for an additional driveway surfacing material, but sometimes a more aesthetic surface is desirable. If a surfacing material is to be added to the reinforced concrete base, then the surface of the concrete is left rough to facilitate a sound keying between the concrete and the surfacing material. Suitable surfacing material which can be used for driveways include; brick pavers, concrete pavers, cobblestones, asphalt, gravel or timber blocks.

is unstable or reactive a more durable base will be required. To check quality of substrata dig a hole about 600 mm (2′) deep, if the soil is very porous and full of roots or other vegetable matter or if it is damp clay, durable base is required.

More durable base materials include:
Stabilised sand which is packing sand with a stabilising material added, such as hydrated lime or cement. The stabiliser is normally dry-mixed into the sand before it is spread under the proposed driveway after which it is wetted down and rolled to obtain reasonable consolidation.

Prepare pathways in a similar manner as driveways but where the sand filling or roadbase may be 100 mm (4″) to 200 mm (8″) thick under a driveway 50 mm (2″) to 100 mm (4″) is normally sufficient under a pathway. While driveways must have a continuous slope, it is possible to build steps into pathways but always consider access for prams and wheelchairs.

Reinforced concrete

If reinforced concrete is used as the finished material for paths and driveways, care should be taken to construct the paths and drives to obtain the best possible appearance. Use sound construction practices.

Smooth, bare concrete is not the most aesthetically pleasing of materials but if correctly constructed it is durable.

Most concrete paths and driveways constructed in a garden will be supported directly onto the ground but in some special cases there may be a requirement to suspend the concrete to span between supports. If suspended concrete slabs are required then these should be designed by a qualified structural civil engineer, particularly where motor vehicles are to be driven on them.

To prepare for a concrete path or driveway to be poured onto the ground the first step is to lay out the extent of the paths and driveways. This can be done by simply pegging the general location. Where the paths or drives are to be curved outline the edge of the area to be concreted on the surface of the ground by pouring lime from a hole in a bag.

When the preliminary location of the paths and driveways are determined then excavate the ground under where the concrete is to be poured to a depth which is free of roots and is of consistent foundation material. When a satisfactory foundation has been achieved throughout the length of the paths and driveways then using steel pegs at about 1 (3′) to 2 (6′) metres apart set out the levels of the centre-line of the area to be concreted.

The foundation for pathways is not as critical as it is for driveways but if root material is left under a path particularly if the roots are from growing trees then local movement can break up the path surface.

For driveways the foundation should be at least as deep as the proposed thickness of the concrete plus the minimum thickness of the supporting base material. On very stable sand or gravel soils a satisfactory driveway can be constructed with a 100 mm (4″) thick unreinforced concrete slab over 50 mm (2″) of packing sand.

Where soils are less stable and the driveway is only to be used by passenger cars a 100 mm (4″) reinforced concrete slab is sufficient in most locations. If any trucks, including furniture removalist trucks, are likely to use the driveway then consideration should be given to using a thicker slab of about 150 mm (6″) thick.

Pathways for pedestrians only can be as thin as 70 mm (3″) and seldom need to be more than 100 mm (4″). Pathways do not need to be reinforced although light weldmesh reinforcing fabric is sometimes used to reduce the incidence of cracking in reactive soils.

The base under paths and driveways may not be required in many sand or gravel soils but some filling sand is generally required to provide an even base for the concrete. Remember sand is generally much cheaper than concrete and therefore, it is sensible to use sand to adjust levels rather than to use excessive quantities of concrete.

In heavier soils a base of at least 100 mm (4″) of packing sand is recommended under concrete driveways and in very reactive clay foundation conditions a 100 mm (4″) bed of crushed rock with 100 mm (4″) of sand over can assist in maintaining a well-drained substrata and improve the stability of the driveway.

Pathways can be any width that suits the garden but are seldom useful under 400 mm (to 1′6″) wide and seldom need to exceed 750 mm (2′6″) wide. If a pathway is to double as a machinery access way then it may need to be wider than this.

Driveways can either be full width in concrete or consist of separate wheel tracks. Full-width drives should not be less than 2 100 mm (7′) wide if they are short and straight, should increase to 2 400 mm (8′) wide if over 7 metres (23′) long and it is recommended that they are 2 700 mm (9′) wide if they are curved.

Separate wheel tracks should be used only on straight sections of driveways. Few people can reverse along separate curved wheel tracks successfully. Most cars have a track of between just under 1.5 metres (5′), so if the centre-line of the concrete tracks are set at 1.5 metres (5′) and the tracks are constructed 750 mm (2′6″) wide then the space between the tracks is also 750 mm (2′6″) and the overall width of the driveway is 2 250 mm (7′6″).

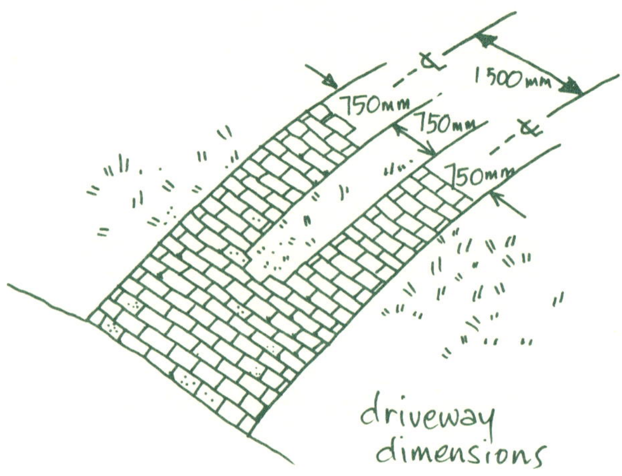

driveway dimensions

When the base has been prepared then the edges of the paths and driveways need to be formed. Usually stout planks of timber are used, about 35 mm (1″) thick standing on their edge, with their top edge set at the finished level of the concrete. It is important that these planks are securely fixed to timber pegs thoroughly driven into the ground. If the ground does not give solid support to the pegs and there is any risk of the planks being pushed out by the weight of the concrete when it is poured, then add braces to the pegs to increase their stability.

It is possible to pour large sections of concrete in one go and this has been made more economic by the wide availability of truck delivered ready-mixed concrete. Gardeners should take care, particularly if they intend to place the concrete themselves not to become too optimistic about how much concrete they can place at the one time. A driveway 2 400 mm (8′) and 9 metres (30′) long will contain around 3 cubic metres (4 cu yards) of concrete. Concrete weighs over 2 tonnes (2 tons) per cubic metre (cu. yard). Imagine moving 6 tonnes (6 tons) of concrete from the truck to the place it is to be poured while the truck driver looks on, and explains that there is an extra charge if the truck is at the site over 20 minutes.

Gardeners who want to place their own concrete should at least divide the paths and driveways into manageable-sized sections. Paths can be divided up into lengths of about 1-metre (3′) long with timber separation strips across the path, driveways are broken into longer sections of about 2 to 2.5 metres (6′ to 8′). The concrete can then be poured into alternative panel lengths in convenient workloads, then after the alternative panels are poured the timber dividers are removed and the remaining panels filled with concrete.

The use of panels of concrete separated with construction joints is the correct method of pouring concrete paths and even when paths and driveways are poured in one go they should also incorporate construction joints. If the path or driveway moves then there is a reasonable chance that the movement will be taken up at the expansion joint minimising the risk of cracks appearing in the concrete slab.

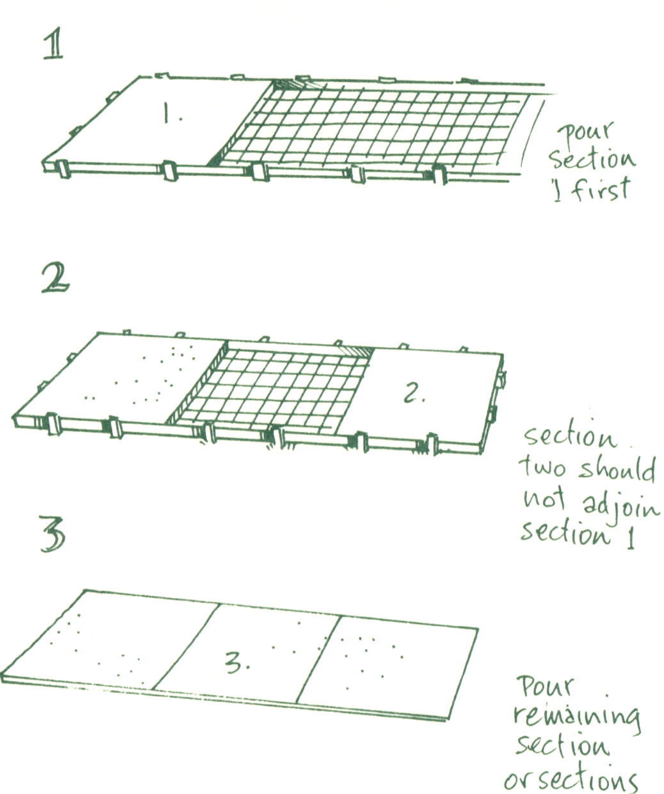

Few people on their own can barrow, place and finish concrete at a high enough rate to justify the purchase of ready-mixed concrete so attempt to have at least two people for every cubic metre (cubic yard) of concrete delivered in a single truck load. As concrete sets quickly and permanently do not do too much in one go. It does make sense to employ labour to assist in barrowing the concrete and to seek the assistance of an expert finisher. Many an amateur concrete finisher has worked until midnight by the light of a torch desperately attempting to screed a concrete pavement.

Many toppings can be applied to concrete from a simple monolithic topping, that is the one that looks like cement, which can be finished smooth or in as many textures as required. Colour can also be added to the concrete or just the topping and aggregates can be scattered on and rolled or tamped into the topping.

Cobblestones, flagstones, and other pavers

Cobblestones, flagstones, and pavers when used as paths and driveways require a sound base on which to be laid. The base conditions outlined for concrete paths and driveways hold good for cobblestones and pavers. The sand base is often stabilised by the dry-mixing of hydrated lime into the sand before it is placed.

Cobbles and pavers come in many forms from natural stone to concrete and kiln-fired clay products and in many sizes from large sections needing mechanical lifting equipment to small hand-sized sections.

Natural stone cobbles make suitable driveways but do not always work as well in pathways. Cobblestones with rounded smooth surfaces can be rather dangerous when wet and lead to falls and twisted ankles.

Almost any hard stone can be used to make cobbles; basalt, granite and the harder forms of sandstone are often selected. A cobblestone is generally tool-finished to have a top surface rather like a loaf of bread that has been baked in an open-topped tin. Varying in size, shape, and colour, cobbles may be as small as 150 mm

(6″) x 100 mm (4″) and large cobbles may be 375 mm (1′3″) x 250 mm (10″). In shape these may be simple rectangles, squares, Voussior wedges or circular.

Cobblestones are generally quite thick in relation to their plan dimensions whereas flagstones are relatively thin when compared to their plan dimensions which are generally larger than cobblestones.

Cobblestones used in one place are normally of the same dimensions or of cobbles dimensioned to present a specific pattern. Flagstones by contrast are less rigid and vary from dressed stones all of the same shape and dimension to random-shaped stones.

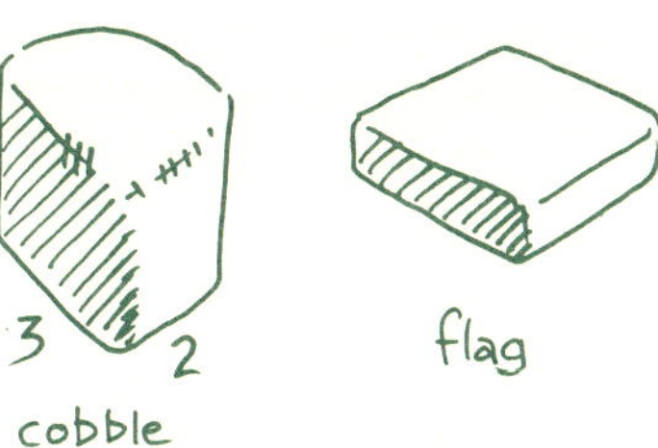

Granite and sandstone are often used for flagstones, slate is quite common, and basalt which does not split easily into slabs is seldom suitable. The large thin stones used in flagging are well suited to pathways, but are less suited to driveways. The heavy point loads associated with motor vehicles are more likely to crack a flagstone that a cobblestone.

When laying cobblestones the two kerb lines should be set out and constructed first as these control the level of the cobbled infill. Cobbled drives can either be contoured to drain towards the centre-line of the drive where a series of grated pits are constructed to collect rainwater run-off or they can drain to the edges. If they are required to drain to the outside, then the edges of the drive have to be raised higher than the edge of the drive proper.

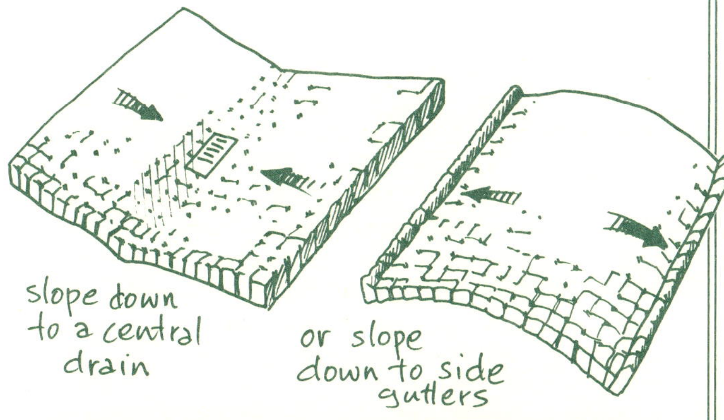

The forming of raised kerbs, with either grated pits for the rainwater or alternatively side entry pits, means that the driveway must be wide enough to allow sufficient manoeuvring room so drivers do not scrub the car tyres on the kerb.

Well-made and laid cobbles are very close to one another and seldom require mortar joints between individual cobbles. Whereas flagstones are not always this precisely dimensioned and often require mortar-filled joints to bind them together.

Dressed squared flagstones or split rubble flags can be used to construct paths either as formal paths or as romantic stepping stones. There is generally no requirement to use kerb construction when using flags and for many low-duty paths the stones can be set onto the ground with minimum preparation except reasonably even bearing. It generally does not matter much if there is some movement in the flags as these can be easily re-laid or left loose to give a more natural appearance.

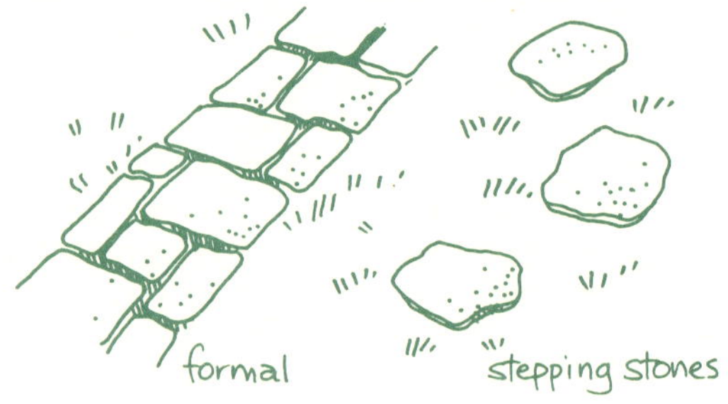

Alternatives to natural cobblestones and flagstones are artificial stone cobbles and flags, concrete flags, vibrated concrete pavers, clay pavers, and bricks.

Artificial stone cobbles and flags are generally a specially prepared product based on moulded concrete with stone-like topping. These products are used as if they were natural stone and the better quality products are used as if they were natural stone and the better quality products have a long life. In some areas artificial stone is more economic than natural stone particularly if there is a shortage of suitable local stones. Concrete flags are available in many colours, shapes, and textures. They are useful as stepping stones but do not give as good an appearance as the other products discussed in this section.

Vibrated concrete masonry pavers and clay pavers come in many shapes, colours, and patterns as well. They are cheap and easy to use with a reasonable life expectancy. They are laid on a sand base as for most pavers with falls to shed surplus rainwater.

The edges of paths and driveways constructed from concrete masonry and clay pavers should be contained at their edges in most conditions to gain the highest durability. Edges can be constructed from durable timber edge strips pegged into the ground. This method

is suitable for pathways only. A concrete edge strip can incorporate a kerb and gutter if required or be made from concrete masonry blocks or clay bricks which match the pavers, set these on a stable base, and lay in cement mortar.

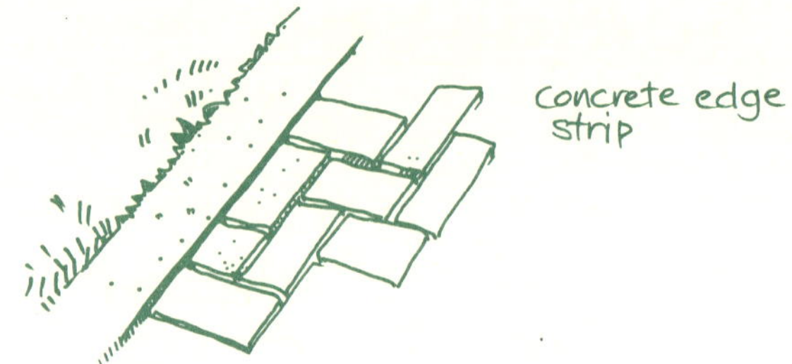

Paving can be carried out using standard clay bricks which come in two forms: the traditional pressed brick and the extruded wire-cut brick. Pressed bricks are more suitable generally for paving as they have a higher mass than extruded bricks, which have holes through them.

Pressed bricks can be used on edge, on flat or with the pressing frog upwards whereas extruded bricks are only suitable to be used on edge. Brick paving is laid on a sandbed at least 50 mm (2″) thick and the edges are constructed as for concrete and clay pavers.

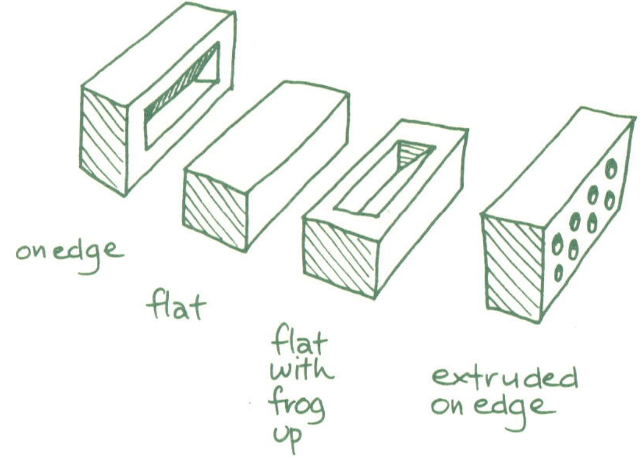

Many interesting patterns can be used to lay cobblestones, flagstones, pavers and bricks. Some examples are illustrated but gardeners should use their own design thoughts to develop unique patterns.

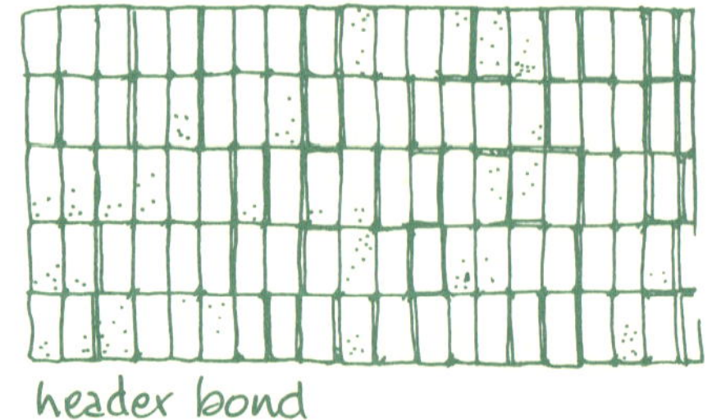

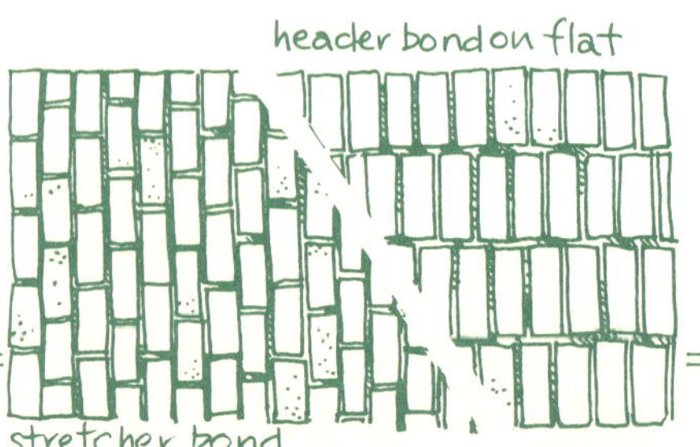

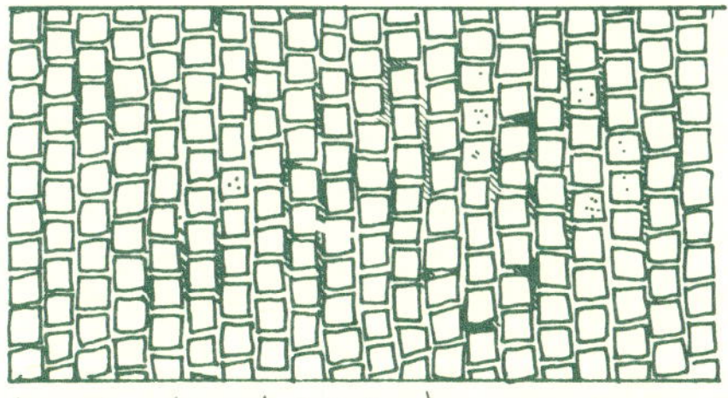

header bond on end

two by two on flat

basket weave on flat

three by three on edge

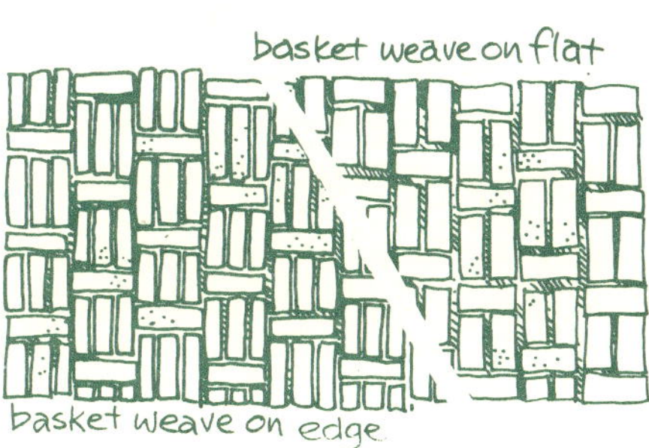

basket weave on flat

basket weave on edge

herringbone on flat

herringbone on edge

Bitumen

Bitumen is often overlooked as a suitable path and driveway, but it is a flexible, durable, and economic paving material. Bitumen paving is a mixture of tar-like materials, cement, and selected aggregates.

It is flexible in two main aspects as it is capable of being laid to a free-form plan without a great deal of effort while following the ground contours; it is also able to adjust to small movements in the ground owing to reactive substratas without damage to its surface.

The most important component for laying bitumen is a sound and stable roadbase of well-compacted gravel and a generally well-drained subsoil environment. The thickness of the roadbase required will vary to suit the local conditions but as a general rule allow 50 mm (2″) to 100 mm (4″) of base under paths and 100 mm (4″) to 150 mm (6″) of base under driveways.

It is also possible to use bitumen over a concrete base and in some places a no-fines concrete roadbase provides a durable base for a bitumen topping. No-fines concrete is concrete mix with no sand in its composition, this means that it is of lower mass and higher permeability than normal concrete, because of the high content of void in its structure.

To build a bitumen topping using cold materials, where solvents are used to keep the tar-like bonding agents liquid during the construction is very messy. It has been replaced largely by hot mix asphaltic bitumen.

Hot mix is where the ingredients of the topping are batch-mixed at a remote plant location and trucked to the site as a hot liquid. The laying of hot mix is the work of skilled labour and gardeners are unwise to attempt to lay this themselves.

A single coat of asphaltic bitumen is sufficient for most garden paths and driveways but its appearance is plain so a crushed stone topping is often applied. Using coloured crushed rock as a topping rolled into the surface of the still warm bitumen gives a very attractive finish.

The crushed rock availabe to gardeners will vary extensively from place to place but hard limestone, quartz, granite, marble river gravels, and some basalts can be used.

The edges of the bitumen pavement should be contained. This can be done using durable timber boards on edge or a brick, stone or concrete kerb. Always form the bitumen surface to drain to grated pits within the pavement to kerbs and gutters at its edges, so no water is absorbed into the bitumen. Puddling can be a nuisance.

Gravel

Gravel paths and driveways give a garden a traditional natural appearance and are favoured by many gardeners. When making a gravel path or drive ensure that there is a sound base of compacted gravel and that the top layer of gravel will remain in place. Gravel does wash away or become scattered in lawns and garden.

Like most paths a containing edge is important and again timber, bricks, stone or concrete are suitable materials. Weeds are the common scourge of the gravel path or driveway and the edge strip should be of a type that will allow easy access to any weeds which attempt to grow into the gravel. Avoid irregular or fancy edges to gravel paths and driveways as these increase the labour needed to control the weed invasion.

Gravel is more porous than most other materials used for paths and driveways and it is recommended that rubble or agricultural drains be constructed under the gravel to carry away excess water. For narrow paths and drives a single drain under the middle of the path will do the job but for wider drives two drains placed under the outer edges of the gravel drive is recommended at 300 mm (1').

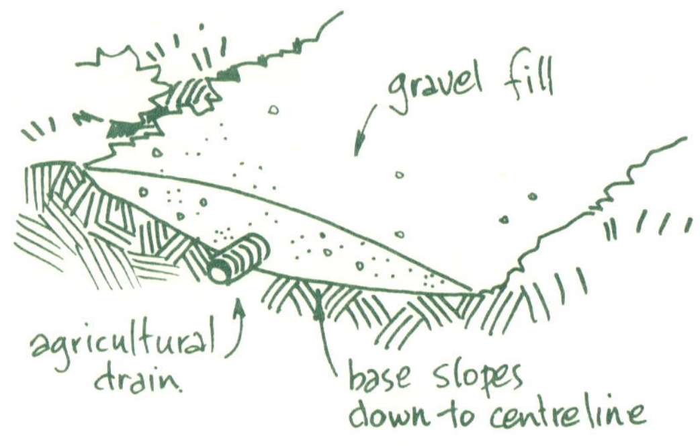

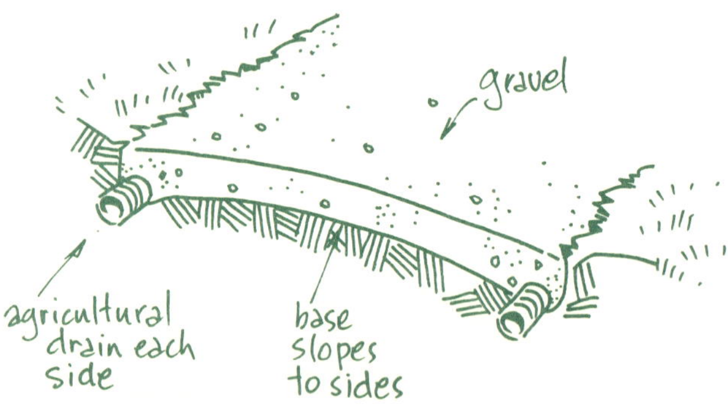

The gravel material available for drives will vary from place to place. Natural gravel sourced from riverbeds and stone formed by volcanic action generally have good binding qualities so the gravel remains where it is placed but the individual stones still show.

Red volcanic stone often referred to as scoria, white-grey river gravel, crushed quartz, river pebbles, crushed marble, crushed granite, and crushed terracotta (which is manufactured from broken roofing tiles), all make suitable gravel paths and driveways.

Allow at least 50 mm (2") thickness of gravel for paths and 75 mm (3") or more thickness of gravel for driveways. It is wise to make sure that the source of the gravel will be available for a reasonable time into the future, for it is likely that top-up gravel will be needed if the paths and drives are to be maintained in their best condition.

Some gardeners have placed plastic sheeting under the gravel in an attempt to reduce the growth of weeds. This is not recommended as it affects the efficient drainage of the gravel and does little or nothing to reduce the weed infestation. In some cases it may assist the weed growth. If the gravel is laid on a well-consolidated base then any weeds will be contained in the gravel topping and should, in most cases, be easy to remove.

The soil under plastic sheet often turns sour and reduces the vigour of garden plants which allows the weeds to gain the upper hand.

Crib blocks

Crib blocks are hollow concrete or terracotta blocks that are designed to be laid as if they were open-topped cobblestones. They are able to support the weight of pedestrians or vehicles. Lawn can be planted in the hollows.

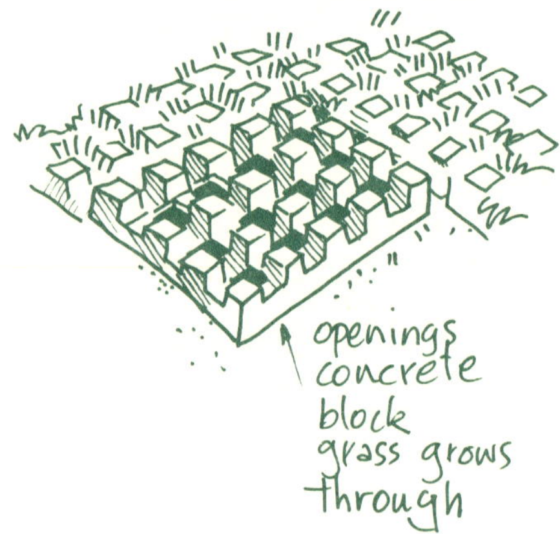

These crib blocks can be used for paths and driveways but their best use is for parking or turning bays in the vehicular area within a garden if there is a disproportionate amount of path material. Terraces can also be constructed with crib blocks.

There are a number of designs and bearing capacities available in crib blocks and these vary from place to place. The manufacturer normally provides detailed information on their recommended methods of construction.

EDGES AND GUTTERS

The layout of most gardens allows for pathways, lawns and garden beds with these functional areas divided, one from the other, with some form of visual separation at, or just above, the groundline. These edges can be simple such as a lawn edge trimmed to a neat border where it meets with a garden bed; a path may be made of paving flags set into the lawn or garden bed.

The edges often fulfil a definite function in the garden plan. Where a lawn meets a garden bed or a pathway create an edge by a simple mower strip made from concrete, brick, stone, or even timber which is about 150 mm (6″) wide and level with the lawn.

Sometimes the edges between the different parts of a garden are of an insufficient variation to have a mower strip as there may be a need to collect surplus water, or to facilitate a change in level of the land.

Gutters are often required at the downhill edges of sloping lawns and at the edges of driveways. These gutters are normally a combination of a kerb and gutter and are used as the defined construction edge of these areas. In a garden it is sensible to have kerbs of a reasonable height so that wheelbarrows and lawn-mowers can be pushed over the kerbs with little effort.

A gutter at the edge of a lawn or driveway should be between 300 mm (1′) and 450 mm (1′6″) wide and slope towards the kerb to form a gutter depth of at least 50 mm (2″). The height of the kerb can be as low as 25 mm (1″) above the low point of the gutter, which means that the kerb height can be as low as 75 mm (3″).

To improve moving wheeled implements over the kerb the gutter side of the kerb can be angled. Where lawn is adjacent to a kerb and guttered driveway it should be at least level with the top of the kerb to avoid water building up at the intersection.

If a kerb and gutter is used at the edge of a lawn or drive, against a garden bed then weepholes can be left through the kerb to allow water to clear from the garden into the gutter, reducing the chance of undermining of the edge of the lawn or drive.

Kerbs can be increased in height or sloped back to retain a garden bed which is higher than the gutter. When this is done greater care needs to be exercised to make sure the kerb and gutter is on a sound stable foundation. The garden bed behind the low retaining wall or sloped stone batter should be filled with hard granular fill with an agricultural drain at the footing level of the structure and weepholes made through to the open gutter.

Setting out

When setting out for edge strips and kerbs and gutters make sure that the levels used will give correct water flows and that those on either side of a strip are integrated.

The garden's division strips should be set out and checked before any finished work starts. The setout should include a series of location pegs which are placed at the correct levels.

Preparation

After the division strips and kerbs and gutters have been laid out then the foundations can be excavated and any form boards located. Only excavate to the width and depth required to achieve a sound foundation and adequate bearing. With too deep and too wide an excavation extra material is required for fill. This will increase the cost of the project.

When the excavations are filled for footings to division strips or kerbs and gutters ensure the full width of the excavation is filled with concrete. If the footing is in bricks or stone, mortar is used to fill out any voids. This is important because earth backfilling even if well-tamped, may not give adequate lateral support to the division strip or the kerb and gutter and it may be pushed sideways causing failure and sinkage to occur at the edges of lawns, garden beds, and driveways.

Where there is any doubt about the soundness of the construction of the foundation for a division strip or a kerb and gutter the two most important things to consider are:

- Is the foundation material stable?
- Is the foundation area well drained?

Reinforced concrete

The most flexible and long-lasting material to use to construct edge strips and gutters is reinforced concrete. Most gardeners, with a little practice can form, place and finish reinforced concrete to provide all the edge strips and gutters necessary in a garden.

To construct a standard mower or garden bed edge strip a narrow excavation, about 100 mm (4″) to 150 mm (6″) wide is dug along the line of the proposed strip. The excavation should be carried down through the topsoil to a reasonably dense sound base.

To form the strip two planks of timber, or if the strip is to be curved, two boards cut from flexible plywood or tempered hardboard, are fixed to pegs located on the outside of the proposed concrete strip. The pegs should be about 1 metre (about 3′) apart on straight sections and closer around curves.

The boards are set 75 mm (3″) to 150 mm (6″) apart, to suit your requirements, with the top of the boards being at the finished level of the proposed concrete strip. Steel reinforcing is not essential in a simple mower strip but if one or two 10 mm (⅜″) diameter steel rods are suspended in the centre of the excavation the strip is strengthened. Steel rods should be suspended with light steel wire hung from battens laid over the form boards.

When the boards have been tested to assess resistance to side pressure (exerted by the wet concrete that is to be poured between them), their location is checked and any reinforcement placed. It is then that the concrete can be poured.

There are a number of ways to buy concrete. The easiest is to order a load from a ready-mixed concrete supplier. In many areas suppliers operate mini-crete trucks for the supply of small orders of concrete to gardeners. Order the correct amount of concrete as the supplier expects to be paid for the concrete delivered, even if it is not used. An extra charge may be made by the supplier if excess concrete has to be taken to another location to be dumped.

If too little concrete is ordered another load may be necessary and often because suppliers specify minimum charges for loads below an economic minimum the concrete can become quite expensive if you need to order more to finish the work.

The minimum volume of concrete from a ready-mixed supplier than can be purchased economically is often a cubic metre (cu. yard) or more. This will provide sufficient concrete to construct 50 metres (165') of mower strip 100 mm (4") wide and 200 mm deep. This is quite a project for a quiet Sunday afternoon.

Where ready-mixed concrete is too complicated to handle a small edge strip project the concrete can be mixed on-site in small batches. Taking into account the physical limitations of the person who will do the labour.

The simplest way to hand-mix concrete is to purchase pre-mixed bags of dry concrete. These can be mixed with water in a large heavy wheelbarrow and then the concrete can be emptied directly into the formed strips.

When the project is a little large for pre-mixed concrete, the ingredients can be bought separately and mixed in a small concrete-mixer in the garden. This machine can be hired from most plant hire outlets.

The materials required to make concrete are cement, which is normally supplied in bags, sand (say it is for concrete, not brickwork or packing), crushed rock aggregate, and clean water. Store the materials carefully and keep these dry until they are used.

Measure the cement, sand, and gravel into the mixer bowl and then dry-mix these before adding any water. For a mower strip a mixture of one part cement, two parts sand, and four parts crushed rock aggregate will provide a strong mix. These proportions are by dry volume.

To mix a batch of concrete of about $1/30$ of a cubic metre, that is approx 35 000 cubic cm ($1/27$ of a cubic yard is 1 cu. ft) in depth or sufficient concrete to construct just over 1.5 metres (4') of mower strip 100 mm (4") wide by 200 mm (8") deep, use the following guidelines:

$1/4$ of a bag of cement
0.017 of a cubic metre of sand ($1/2$ cu ft)
that is a one batching box
    300 mm x 300 mm x 185 mm
0.034 of a cubic metre of sand (1 cu ft)
that is two batching boxes
    300 mm x 300 mm x 185 mm
5 litres (1 gallon) of water

The batching box can be easily made for this purpose from timber.

When the materials are thoroughly mixed the concrete is placed in the prepared formwork. This should have a timber stop board across it at the point where the volume of concrete being mixed will fill.

When the formwork is filled to the top with concrete, work a metal rod up and down in the placed concrete to drive out any trapped air voids. Top up the concrete to the top of the formwork again.

Let the concrete set until it is firm but not hard, the time of setting varies with the weather. To obtain a smooth finish to the top of the strip, dust it with a mixture of sand and cement and using a concretor's steel float slid back and forth on the top of the strip until a smooth finish is achieved. Special tools can be purchased to finish the top of a strip and a small distance down each side if a more professional finish is required.

The formwork can be removed any time after about 12 hours and the new concrete should be wetted down and covered with plastic sheeting to aid curing. Keep the concrete surface wet for at least seven days after placement. The sides of the strip can be backfilled with soil at any time after the formwork is removed.

If the strip is to be of a colour other than plain concrete, oxides can be placed in the initial concrete mix as well as being added to the finishing topping.

It is possible to render over the mower strip instead of simply dusting and floating. Rendering is carried out by removing the formwork when the concrete has set sufficiently to keep its shape unaided. Then a stiff, but not too dry mixture of cement and sand is prepared and applied to the top and sides of the strips as desired. If fine-crushed sandstone or granite is used with a suitable colouring agent a high quality stone-like finish can be achieved.

To construct a gutter or combination kerb and gutter in concrete the procedure is the same as for the simple strip but spacers cut to the proposed profile, are placed between the form boards.

The profile boards are placed about 900 mm (3') apart and the concrete placed and finished in alternative sections. When all these sections are in position the profile boards are removed and the remaining sections placed and finished. The reinforcing, if used, is continuous, that is, it does not stop and start at the divisions made by the profile boards.

Often for a gutter or kerb and gutter the form (profile) boards will be at different heights from each other, to allow for a higher kerb.

A kerb and gutter which is 400 mm (1'4") wide overall and 300 mm (1') deep overall with a 150 mm (6") high and 150 mm (6") wide kerb needs 1 cubic metre (1 cu. yard) of concrete for every 12 metres (40') of kerb and gutter. This is approximately a mix containing half a bag of cement for every 900 mm (3') section.

Brickwork

To construct a mower or garden edge strip out of bricks there are many options from which to choose. The two most common options are to use bricks on end, or bricks on edge. It is not advisable to use bricks on flat as few bricks give a suitable appearance in this way and the strip is seldom deep enough to give sufficient durability. It is too easy to dislodge the bricks if they are knocked by the mower.

The first thing to do when constructing a brick edge strip is to set out the location and height of one edge of the bricks using a stringline fastened to the face of pegs, so that the pegs will not get in the way of the bricks when they are being placed.

Next excavate a trench adjacent to the pegs at least 20 mm (near 1″) deeper than the depth of the brickwork being constructed. If standard bricks on end are being used, then the excavation should be about 250 mm (10″) deep and about 150 mm (6″) wide. If standard bricks on edge are being used, then the excavation should be about 130 mm (5″) deep and about 250 mm (10″) wide. A standard brick is approximately 230 mm (9″) by 110 mm (4½″) by 76 mm (3″).

To lay the bricks, prepare a mortar mix of one part cement to four parts sand. The mix can be quite wet but not too runny. To avoid too much moisture being draw out of the mortar the base of the excavation should be covered with a continuous strip of plastic. Damp-proof course material is satisfactory and the bricks should be well wetted. If the water is drawn out of the mortar, then there is insufficient water to complete the chemical reaction which allows concrete to cure and low-strength mortar will result.

Using a bricklayer's trowel, place a layer of mortar into the excavation about 25 mm (1″) thicker than is needed to bring the brick to be bedded up to the stringline. If a layer of brick reinforcing wire mesh is pushed down into the mortar bed then a more continuous edge strip will result. This will be less likely to be moved around by subsoil forces later.

Push the bricks down into the mortar bed and tamp them until they are vertical and in line with the string guideline. Mortar can be placed between the bricks but this is not necessary and makes the job of laying the bricks more complicated for the amateur gardener.

The mortar placed in the excavation should be sufficient to lay about 10 to 20 bricks at a time. After laying every five bricks backfill the space between the bricks and the sides of the excavation with mortar at least halfway up the brick.

If the work of laying the bricks is carried out carefully there should be very little mortar smeared on the bricks. However, any mortar can be cleaned off exposed parts of the bricks later, using a proprietary brick cleaner available from any hardware retailer. Be careful when using brick-cleaning solutions as they contain acid which can burn holes in people and damage plants. It must be kept away from children and animals, and the empty container disposed of with great care.

To build a brick kerb and gutter the first step is to excavate a trench to a sound base. Then place a stabilised sandbed into the excavation to provide a stable base about 130 mm (5″) below the outside edge level of the driveway.

The gutter is constructed with bricks and edge. The gutter brick is laid with a 25 mm (1″) or greater fall towards the kerb. The kerb is built from a full brick, laid to project half a brick higher than the gutter, and at right angles to the gutter brick.

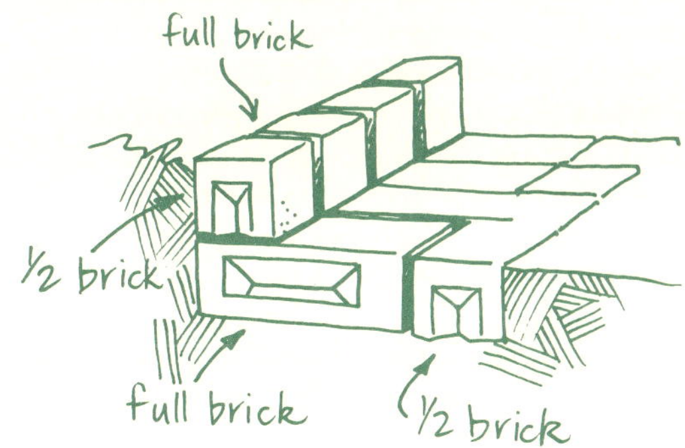

The cross-section of the kerb and gutter is an L-shape formed from two full bricks. Alternative brick rows will have a half brick at the edge of the driveway then a full brick beyond that and a half brick to form the kerb. The kerb can be constructed from bullnosed bricks to give a smoother look to the kerb line.

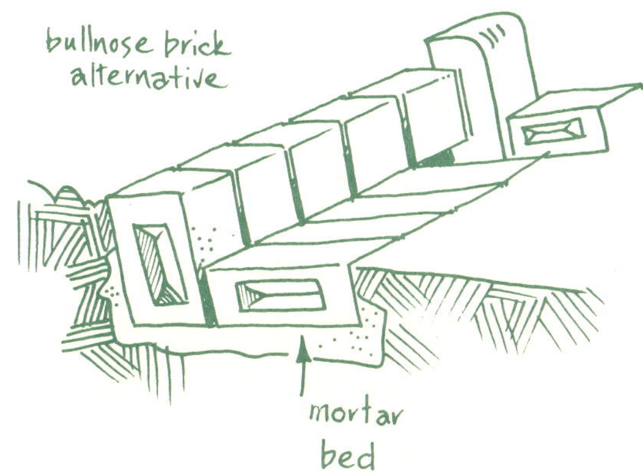

The gutter and kerb bricks are bedded into a waterproof mortar bed with a wide strip of steel mesh brick reinforcing. Any space between the brickwork and the faces of the excavation is to be filled with mortar to about 50 mm (2″) below the kerb and the top of the kerb.

The gutter must fall downhill to all drainage pick-up points, whether grated drains or side-entry pits. The gutter should not be too steep or pick-up points too far apart. If these have to collect too high a volume of water they may choke leading to localised flooding.

The joints between the bricks can have a full 10 mm-wide (⅜″) mortar joint or they can be tight dry jointed. Extruded wire-cut bricks which have holes are not recommended for kerbs and gutters.

Stonework

Edge strips and gutters constructed from stone are well suited to most gardens as the stone is durable and efficient if well built and allows you to present images from rustic to formal.

Almost any stone can be used to build edge strips and gutters. Availability will vary considerably from place to place. Slate, sandstone, limestone, granite, basalt, and marble can be used but care must be taken in selecting the stone. Some stone is too soft for long-life externally. Some marbles, limestones, and slates will erode very quickly with the action of water or break-down by expansion and contraction caused by the sun.

Most sandstone and granite are durable and can be worked with the correct tools to present attractive colours and textures to complement most gardens. Basalts are durable but generally very hard to work. Basalts are often dark blue-grey in colour with little tonal variation.

Basalt pitchers, squared blocks approximately 400 (1'4") x 200 (8") x 200 mm (8"), make durable kerbs and gutters. Many have been in use for hundreds of years.

Stone edge strips and gutters require a suitable stabilised base of gravel and sand if they are to maintain their location and give long service.

Check with the supplier of stone on the best mortar mix for the stone supplied. Where there is any doubt, err to a weaker rather than stronger mortar. A mortar of one part hydrated lime to four parts clean sand will generally carry out the task required and can be removed from the stones at a later time if they require rebedding or are relocated.

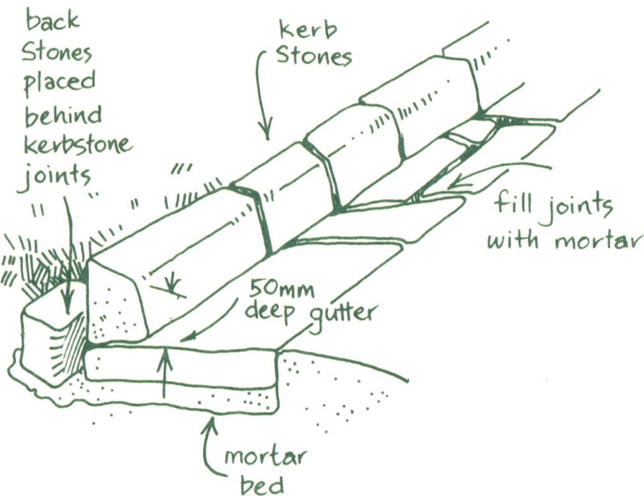

Timber

Only sturdy durable timber should be used to construct edge strips and gutters. Any timber that is susceptible to attack by insects or fungi should be avoided.

Durable timbers include jarrah, ironbark and river red gum in the eucalypts, tanolith and similar treated pinus processed timbers and any timber that is used for railway sleepers. Only the heartwood of untreated timbers is durable, sapwood of most species may still be attacked by termites, beetles, and fungus rots.

In many areas new or used railway sleepers can be purchased. Take care that any new sleeper is of acceptable quality and not just a piece of non-durable timber cut to the same section as a sleeper. Used sleepers should be checked for soundness but dense old sleepers will give many years service as edge strips and kerbs in gardens.

The old sleeper cutters believed that a split, broad-axed and adzed sleeper was more durable than a sawn sleeper, for this method was more sympathetic to the grain direction and other natural structures of the timber. Adzed timber, timber that has had its surfaces dressed, using a special axe shaped like a mattock, has a special character suitable for garden environments.

It is possible to use timber as a guttering material but it is better to combine a timber kerb with a brick or natural stone gutter.

Timber edge strips and kerbs need to be well fixed into the ground and this can be done by using steel spikes which are formed to loop over the timber or by driving a spike through a ready-made hole in the timber. Both methods are suitable and in both cases the steel spikes should be driven at least 300 mm (1') into sound substrata.

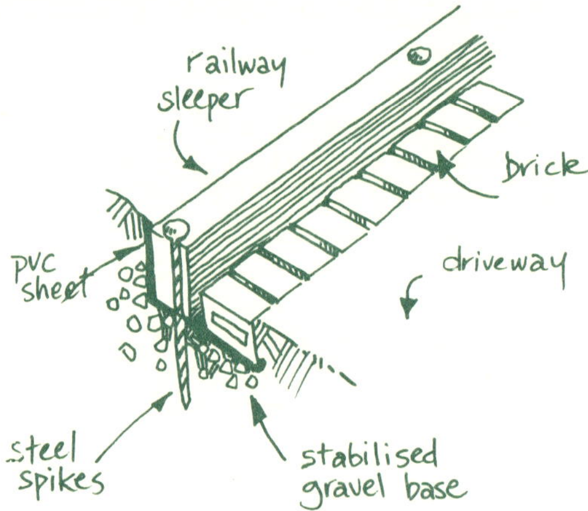

To make a durable hole in timber through which to drive a spike many old hands believe in burning the hole through the timber, using a red-hot poker, rather than boring a hole with an electric drill is better.

Timber used externally and in contact with the ground should never be less than 50 mm (2") in any sectional dimension and 100 mm (4") is the preferred minimum.

STEPS AND RAMPS

Many gardens will have at least one set of steps or a ramp unless the ground is level. There is no minimum angle for when a slope becomes a ramp and no maximum angle at which a ramp becomes precipitous. Common-sense indicates that a ramp is a slope up or down which a person is negotiating a change in height.

Most ramps are in the range from a maximum slope of 1 in 4 to a minimum of 1 in 25. A slope greater than 1 in 4 is too steep for normal people to negotiate and 1 in 25 is so natural that it feels almost flat. Most ramps which are specifically constructed to negotiate changes in level are in the range 1 in 6 to 1 in 12.

Steps are even more prescribed than ramps and fall into tight limits, with vertical rises seldom being less than 100 mm (4″) or more than 200 mm (8″). The horizontal tread of a set of steps is seldom as narrow as 200 mm (8″) and seldom exceeds 350 mm (1′2″). The criterion in judging a set of steps is that they must be able to be negotiated, up and down, with ease.

Steps with a rise of 150 (6″) to 175 mm (7″) and a tread going (G) of 300 (1′) to 250 mm (10″) seem to suit a wide range of people. Note that as the rise height increases the tread width reduces. R is the rise, and T is the tread: 150R/300T and 175R/250T. One formula that is favoured by some authorities is:

Twice the rise plus the going should equal 585 to 625

$$2R + G = 585 \text{ to } 625 \ (23″ \text{ to } 25″)$$

example:

150 x 2 + 300 = 600 (acceptable)
175 x 2 + 250 = 600 (acceptable)

but

150 x 2 + 250 = 550 (not acceptable)
175 x 2 + 300 = 650 (not acceptable)

The compromise between steps and ramps is a system that is called stepped ramps, where the change in level is negotiated by a series of rises between wide steps or short ramps. Stepped ramps allow quite steep slopes to be negotiated relatively easily and naturally. These can be built in simple materials in a relatively rustic manner without having to undertake the precision construction necessary for steps and most ramps.

A combination of steps, ramps, and stepped ramps can provide an interesting system of routes through a garden, adding diversity to the garden-scape.

Setting out

Particular care is needed when setting out for steps as the rhythm is critical to safety. Any flight of steps should have equal rises and goings where they are in straight flights. If the flights are curvilinear then the rises should be equal and the goings should be of a controlled width of a near-equal dimension on the main climb path.

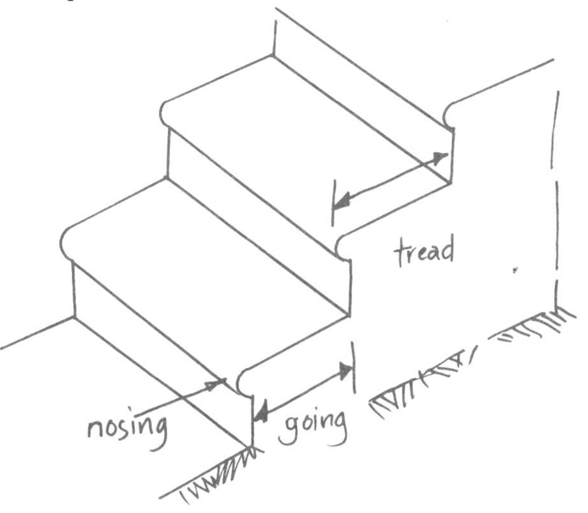

When viewed in plan the line of the nosings on adjacent steps should not vary more than 30° in curved flights. If possible a minimum tread width of 150 mm (6″) should be maintained on the inside of any curvilinear steps. These controls are to avoid constructing steps which have built-in dangers.

It is sensible to construct step flights with four to 10 rises, starting and ending on safe flat areas. Where two or more flights are joined by landings, then allow a landing of at least 750 mm (2′6″) going in a step system that is in line or close to in line. Where a change of direction of 45° or more is taken at a landing the landing should be at least 750 mm (2′6″) square or as wide in all directions as the flights it services.

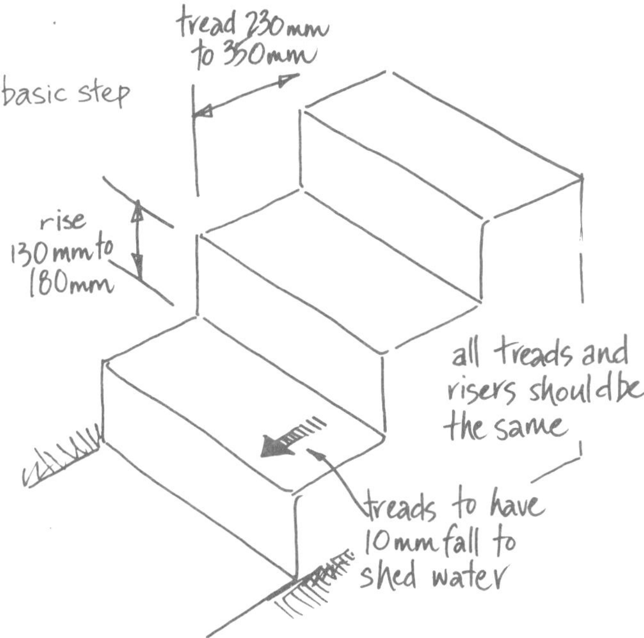

With fewer than three steps in a flight, it needs to be simple as there is a high risk of stumbling if the change in level is not obvious. It is particularly unwise to place a single step in a landing.

The maximum number of steps in one flight that normal adults can comfortably climb is about 15. Do not consider more than 18 rises in a single flight. There is regulatory control of the rises, goings, width and flights of steps in some areas. Check with local authorities before commencing this expensive construction.

Steps should be a minimum of 600 mm (2′) wide; 750 mm (2′6″) to 900 mm (3′) is a good median width. Short narrow flights of steps may not need handrails (unless required by law) but flights of more than six rises and of modest width benefit from a handrail and wider longer flights are improved with a handrail on both sides.

A handrail to a flight of steps should be between 800 (2′8″) and 900 mm (3′) above the nosing and should have a continuous, easy-to-grip capping. Picket fence-type balustrades to steps may look romantic but are not functional unless they have a good continuous handrail attached to the step side.

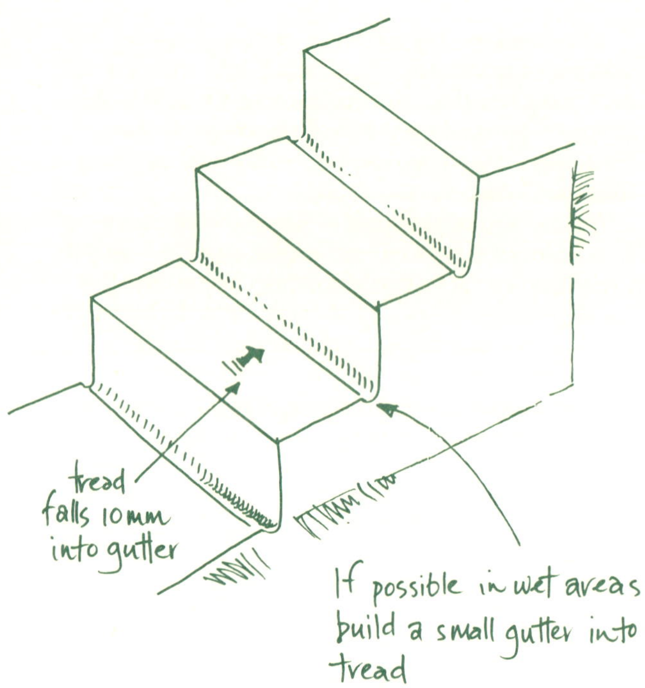

Using this formula, a rise of 100 mm (4″) at every step with a ramp length of 750 (2′6″) and a slope of 1 in 10 would provide a vertical level gain of 225 mm (9″) in every metre (3′4″). This is an equivalent ramp slope of 1 in 4.5 which is much safer than a ramp of similar vertical gain.

When setting out steps and ramps make sure that there is good drainage at the top of the flight or ramp, it is important that the minimum volume of water is allowed to run where people will walk.

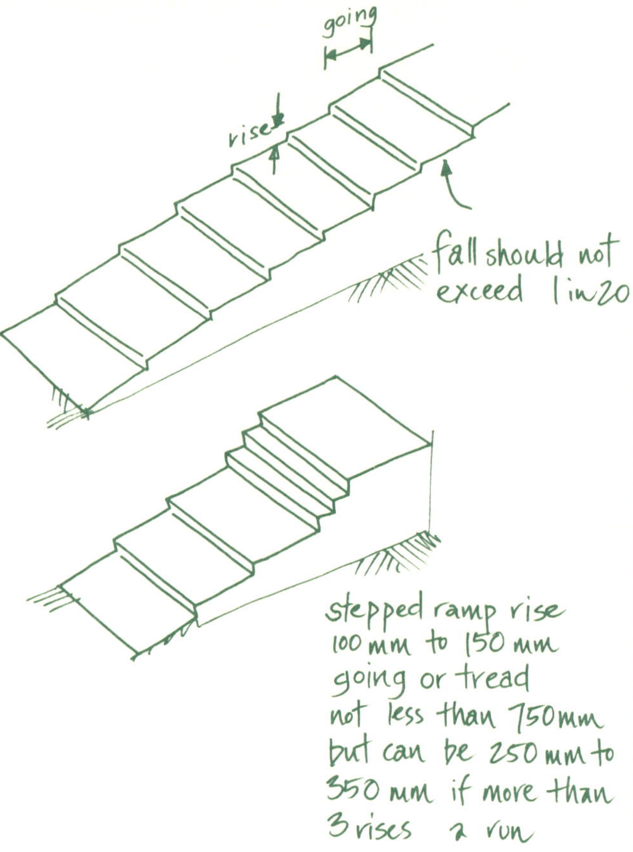

Ramps should be set out to have a transitionary zone at the top and bottom to avoid too abrupt a commencement of the ramp. It is not a problem if ramps change slightly in slope negotiating a climb between two different levels so long as the slope changes are gentle.

If possible build in some cross fall to any ramp of a length over 3 metres (10′). This minimises the amount of water that flows down the ramp during rain. The cross fall can be in one or both directions but the slope should not exceed 1 in 50.

Where ramps are negotiating the side of a slope it is wise to build a kerb on the side of the ramp against the slope to avoid garden soil and other debris being washed onto the ramp surface.

If ramps are to be negotiated by wheeled machinery allow sufficient manoeuvring room to safely enter and leave the ramp at the top and the bottom.

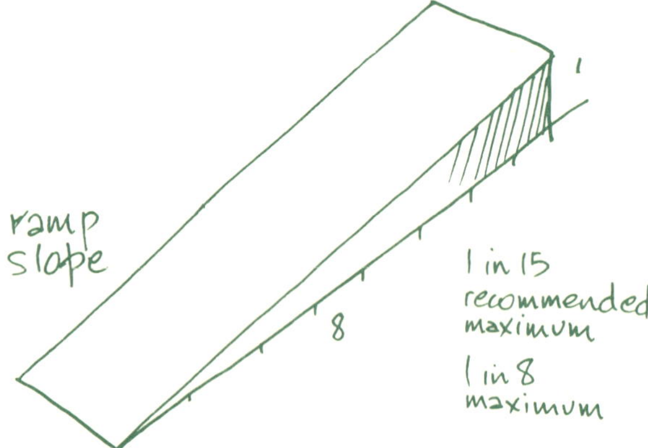

To lay out stepped ramps less precision is required but careful thought should be given to the rise, slope, and spacing of the sections. A rise of 100 mm (4″) is suitable with the ramp steps to be 750 (2′6″) to 1 500 mm (5′) long with slopes not exceeding 1 in 10.

Preparation

Steps and ramps are only as sound as their basis. There is no point in building a beautiful flight of stairs or a sweeping ramp if they are at risk of damage through ground movement. The mass of all steps and ramps must be taken down to stable substrata, whether by the use of concrete pads, strips and piers, or by excavating the unstable topsoil and replacing it with compacted and stabilised sand, gravel or mixed roadbase.

Preparing the base for any construction is the same for all construction. It is not the size of the footings that matter but the quality that counts. The better the foundation strata the less critical the size of the footings. Any support for any construction must be free of reactivity and be fully compacted. Good subsoil drainage systems reduce soil reactivity.

Reinforced concrete

Reinforced concrete can be used to build stable long lasting steps and ramps. It has the capacity to provide quite wide spans and has the flexibility to be cast into any shape or form needed to negotiate the most complicated step and ramp designs.

Mass concrete has been used on and off in the building of garden structures since Roman times. It is only in the last 100 years that gardeners have had the ability by using reinforced concrete to span and since the 1950s–1960s that ready-mixed concrete has been freely available.

When concrete is poured as a base for a ramp, which is to be finished in an integral cement topping, apply the topping when the concrete has not quite hardened. In some cases grooves may be trowelled into the surface to improve surface drainage and, colour or textures applied to reduce slip.

Where concrete is the base for an applied finish of the type where selected gravel, pebbles or other aggregates are bonded to the surface using chemical liquids the concrete surface should be finished as specified by the manufacturer of the finishing product.

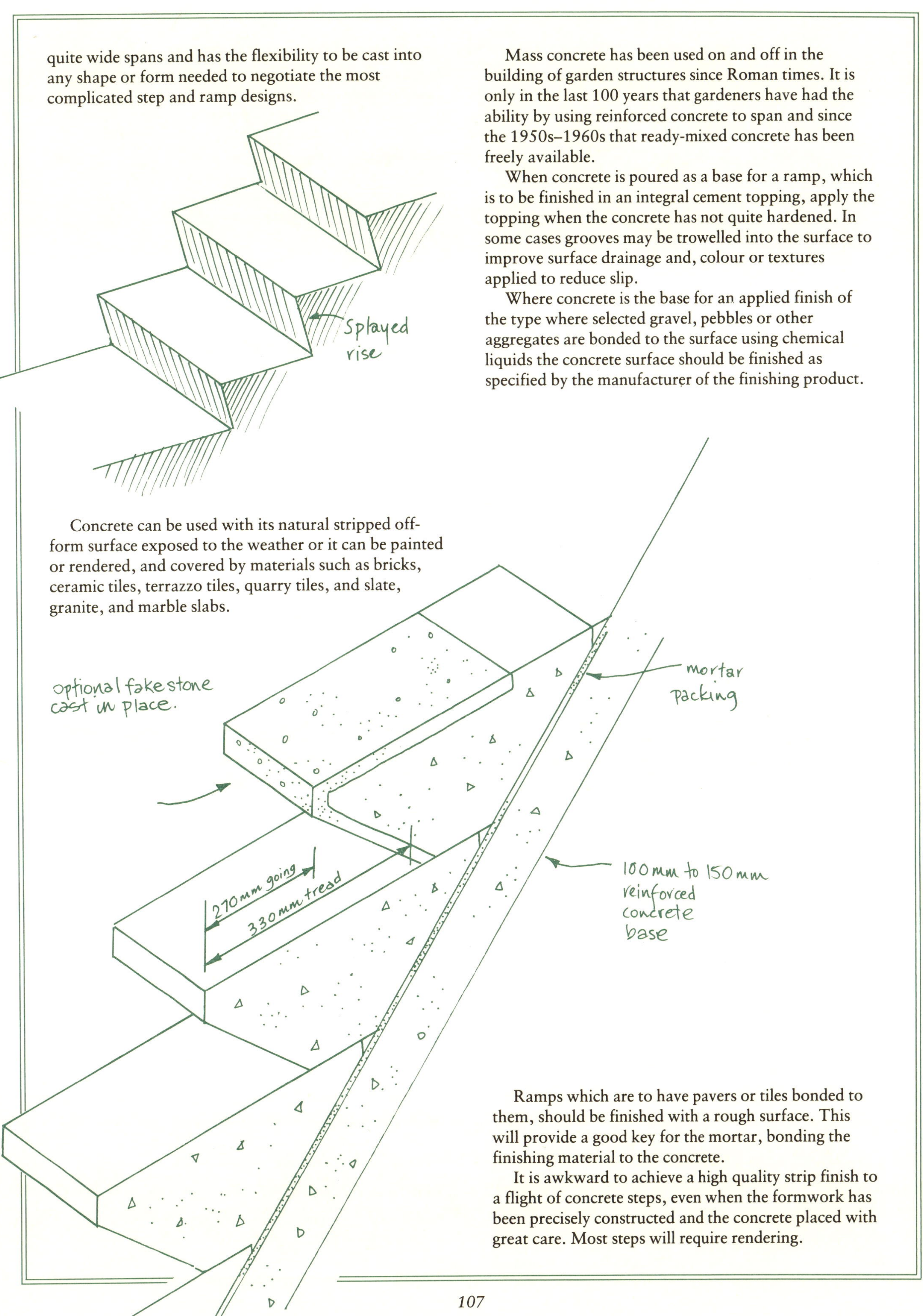

Concrete can be used with its natural stripped off-form surface exposed to the weather or it can be painted or rendered, and covered by materials such as bricks, ceramic tiles, terrazzo tiles, quarry tiles, and slate, granite, and marble slabs.

Ramps which are to have pavers or tiles bonded to them, should be finished with a rough surface. This will provide a good key for the mortar, bonding the finishing material to the concrete.

It is awkward to achieve a high quality strip finish to a flight of concrete steps, even when the formwork has been precisely constructed and the concrete placed with great care. Most steps will require rendering.

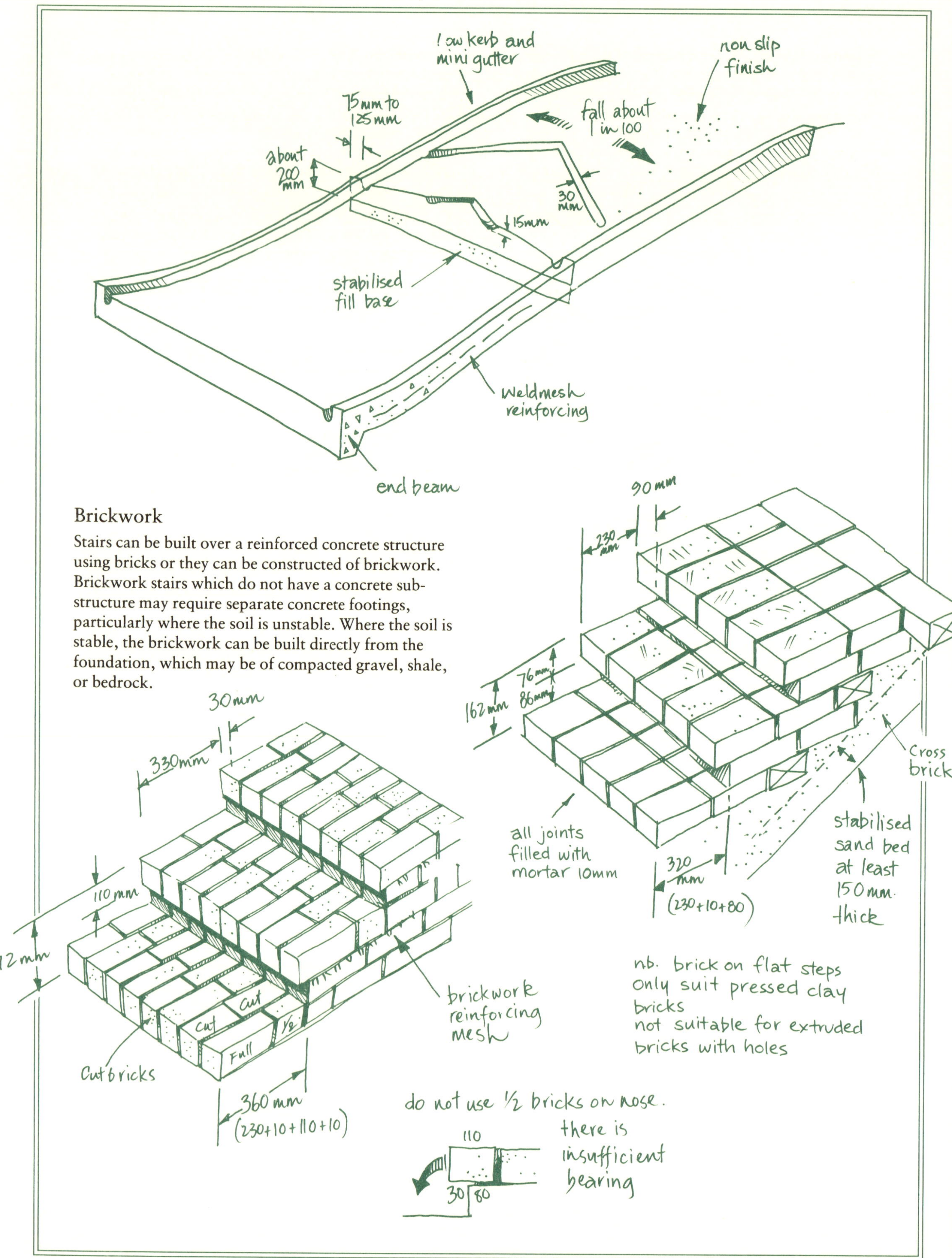

Brickwork

Stairs can be built over a reinforced concrete structure using bricks or they can be constructed of brickwork. Brickwork stairs which do not have a concrete sub-structure may require separate concrete footings, particularly where the soil is unstable. Where the soil is stable, the brickwork can be built directly from the foundation, which may be of compacted gravel, shale, or bedrock.

Brick treads normally are constructed from bricks on edge, which means the brick step features the face of the brick. It is possible to build steps with the bricks on flat, but again not with bricks containing holes. The joints between the bricks are normally kept to brick course size, these joints allow the water that falls on external steps to drain away quickly.

Brick reinforcing mesh should be used liberally in the horizontal bed courses, especially the structure under the treads.

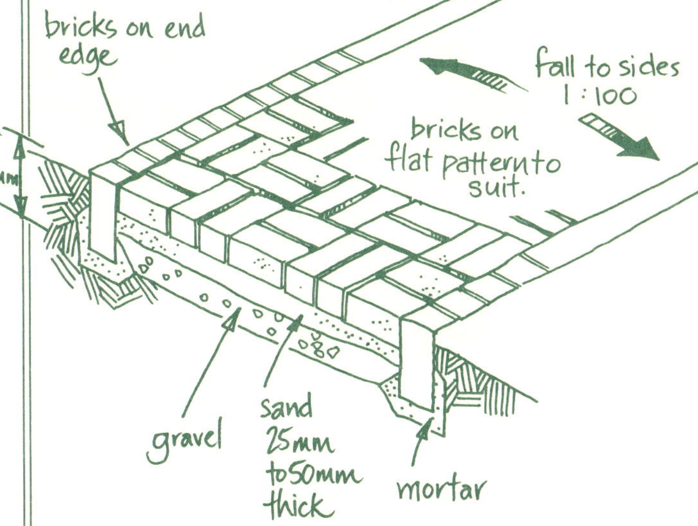

Stonework

Carefully dressed stone treads are normally used to construct stone steps to minimise the danger of tripping. Stones that have been split on natural planes such as slate and sandstone are considered to weather better than sawn stone slabs. Granite and marble with more homogenous construction must be sawn and polished or textured for effect.

If supplies of fair-to-good quality shaped stones are available at a reasonable price the steps can be constructed of stone. Where stone is not available economically then stone facing can be constructed over a brick and/or concrete base structure.

Well-designed stone steps are a special feature of a garden and should be built with great care and be well drained. Stones will become quite slippery when they are wet and need to be placed so that they are bathed in sunlight for some time every day. This is important as heat reduces the growth of mosses, lichens, and fungi on the treads. These plants can increase the slipperiness of the steps.

Timber

Simple timber steps can be constructed using railway sleepers fastened to levelled steps in the natural ground. These steps can look rustic and provide access to parts of the garden which require infrequent attention. They are not recommended to be used as main access steps as they are seldom sufficiently durable or stable.

Railway sleepers and treated round logs can be used as dividers and edge strips for ramps and stepped ramps with a great deal of appeal. Usually this type of construction would be used with gravel or rough brick or stone infilling.

Traditional steps are constructed with timber or steel stringers solidly fixed at the top and bottom to brick, stone or concrete footings. The treads are constructed of durable planks of 40 mm (1½″) or greater thickness.

The stringers must be tied together with steel rods and the treads must maintain sound bearing at their ends. Wherever possible, the timber of the stairs should be kept clear of the ground to reduce the chance of invasion of the timbers by destructive insects and fungi rot.

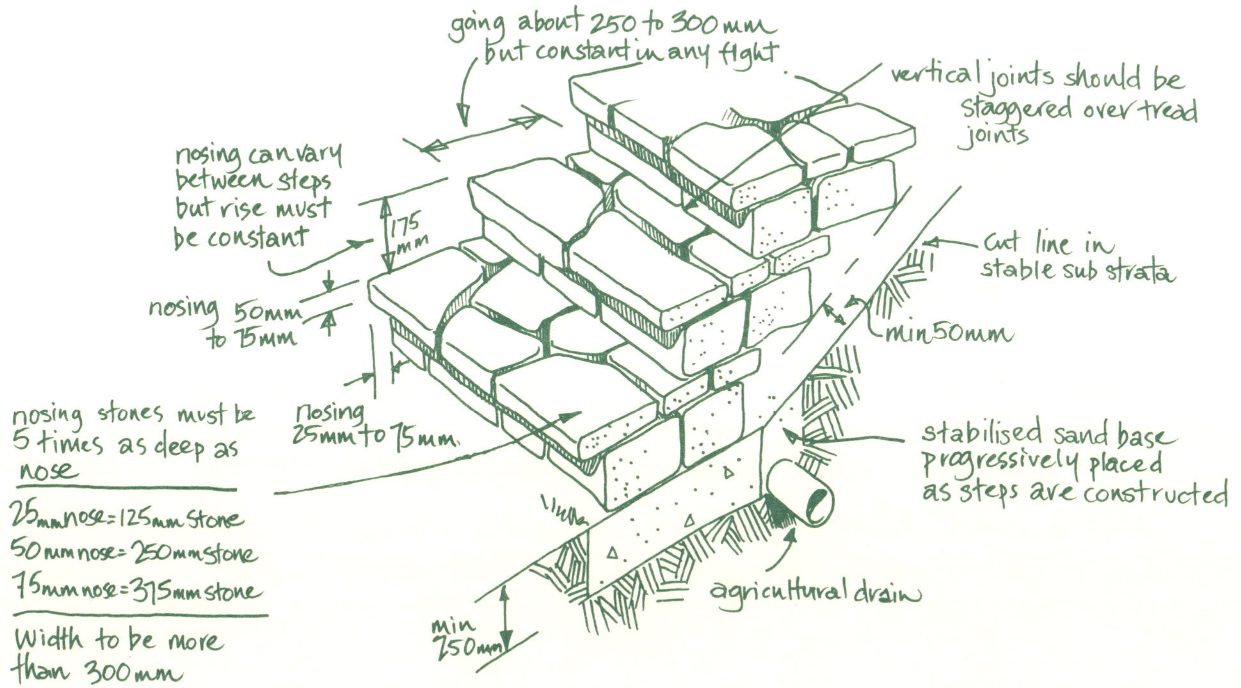

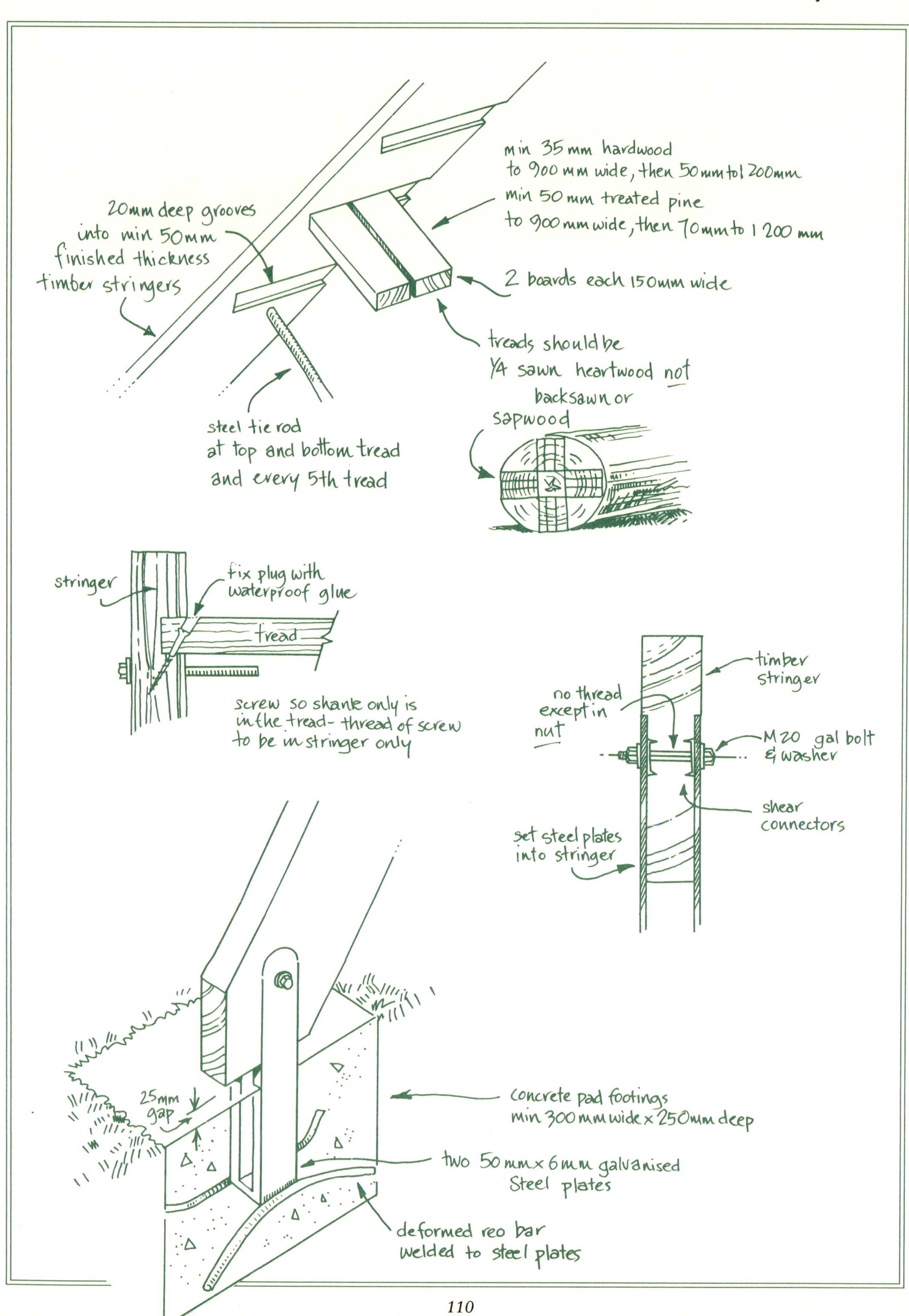

20mm deep grooves into min 50mm finished thickness timber stringers
min 35mm hardwood to 900mm wide, then 50mm to 1200mm
min 50mm treated pine to 900mm wide, then 70mm to 1200mm
2 boards each 150mm wide
treads should be 1/4 sawn heartwood not backsawn or sapwood
steel tie rod at top and bottom tread and every 5th tread
stringer
fix plug with waterproof glue
tread
screw so shank only is in the tread - thread of screw to be in stringer only
timber stringer
no thread except in nut
M20 gal bolt & washer
shear connectors
set steel plates into stringer
25mm gap
concrete pad footings min 300mm wide x 250mm deep
two 50mm x 6mm galvanised steel plates
deformed reo bar welded to steel plates

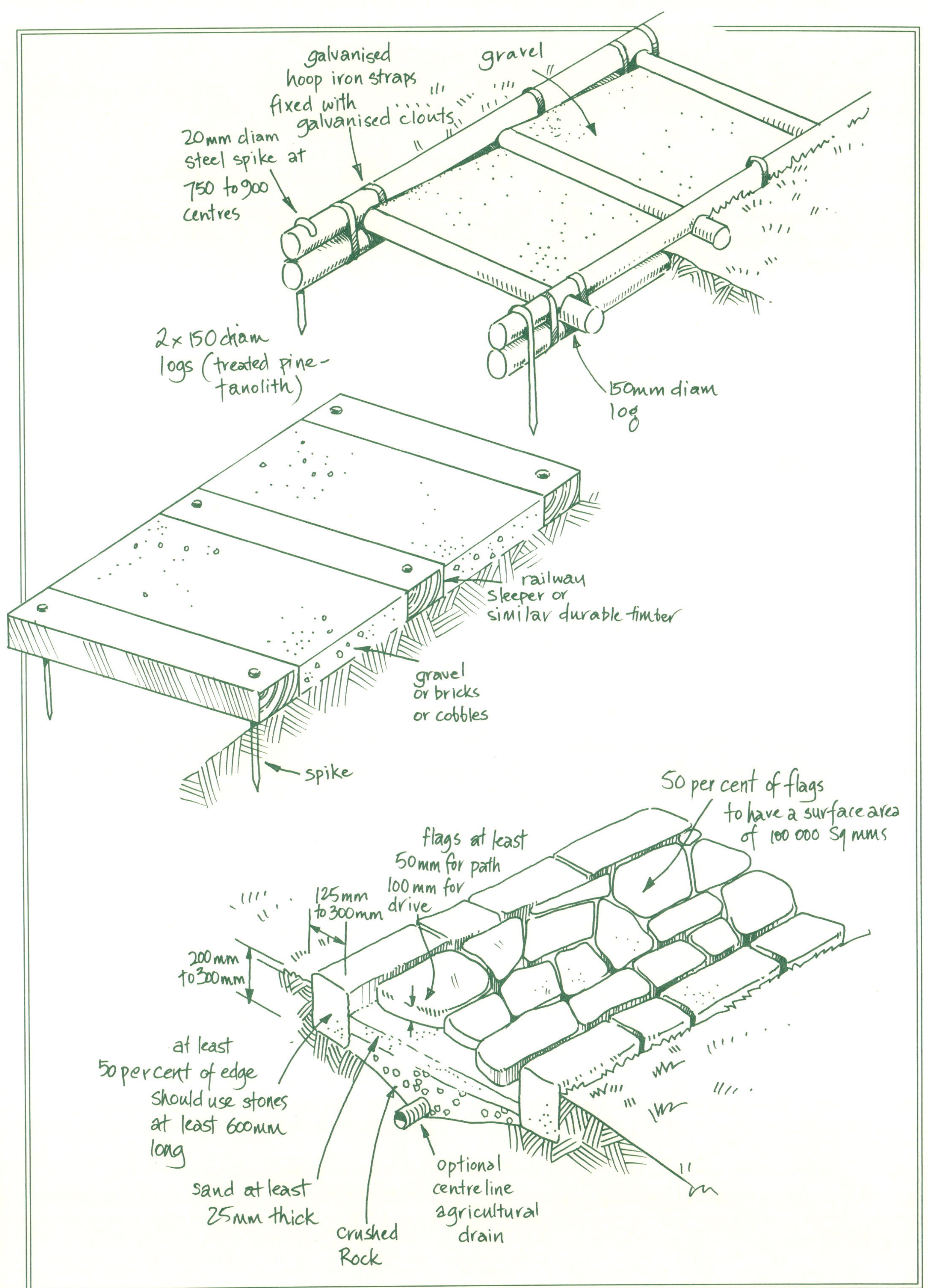

galvanised hoop iron straps fixed with galvanised clouts
gravel
20mm diam steel spike at 750 to 900 centres
2 x 150 diam logs (treated pine - tanolith)
150mm diam log
railway sleeper or similar durable timber
gravel or bricks or cobbles
spike
50 per cent of flags to have a surface area of 100 000 sq mms
flags at least 50mm for path 100mm for drive
125mm to 300mm
200mm to 300mm
at least 50 per cent of edge should use stones at least 600mm long
sand at least 25mm thick
Crushed Rock
optional centre line agricultural drain

masonry fences

FENCES AND WALLS

Fences and walls are very important structures in gardens. They define boundaries and protect the gardens and the residences they surround.

The style of the fences and walls chosen should harmonise with the garden of which they are an integral part.

Different periods of history, availability of materials, various localities, and diverse socioeconomic conditions have led to many types of fences and walls. Consider the towering defensive walls of medieval Europe and the fence-free environments of the open democratic North American suburbs.

There are picket fences where timber is plentiful; stone fences in quarrying regions; brick fences in closely settled urban areas; post-and-rail fences in the country; and wire fences surrounding the mass-produced houses of the labourers and consumers of the industrial revolution of the 1830s.

Choosing a fence in the late 20th century is often a matter of whim and has very little to do with local conditions or availability of materials. Before the industrial revolution began to crowd humanity into urban areas, most fences were seen in rural and semi-rural village environments where their main task was to keep animals in their place. These fences were rustic timber post-and-rail structures, dry-stone fences, or in more closely settled villages and towns, timber pickets.

dry stone wall

Sometimes places of importance such as palaces, mansions, barracks, prisons, and asylums were surrounded by quality masonry fences. With the advent of the industrial revolution in England and progressively around the world urbanisation has become a significant force, and settlement is much closer.

In the Georgian and Regency periods most fences were of the simple picket types. Early Victorian houses were fenced by timber pickets also but styles in fencing were changing and becoming more elaborate.

post and rail

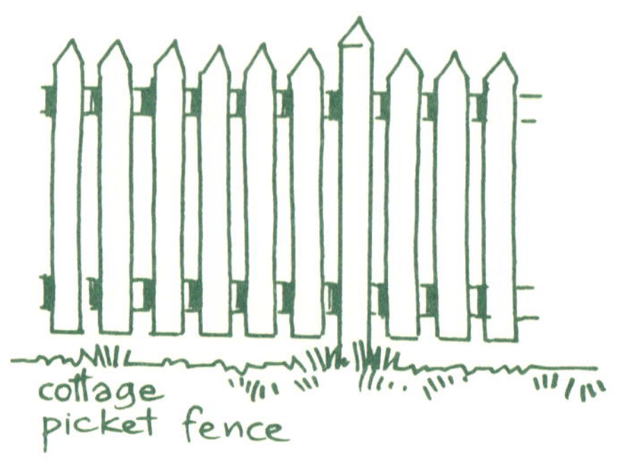

cottage picket fence

Middle Victorian villas displayed stone and iron fences which highlighted the opulence of stone drawn from the walls surrounding those of privilege and the reason for the wealth of the occupants of the villas — the furnaces of the industrial revolution. For those who could not afford the grand stone and iron fence a stuccoed alternative was available.

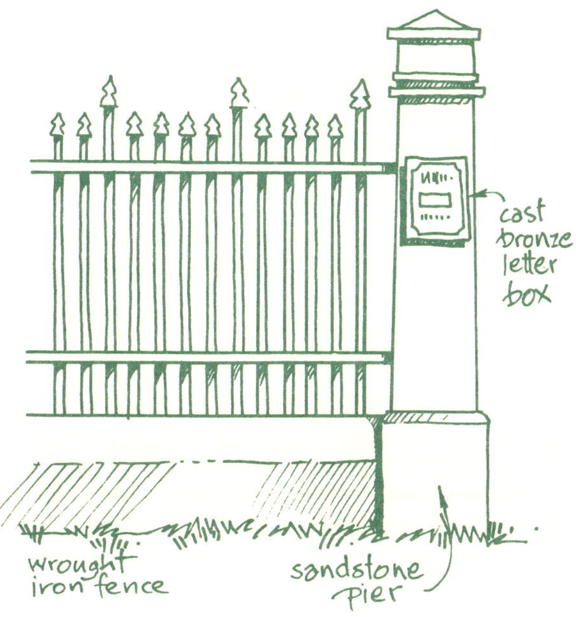

By the late Victorian period the use of stucco had reached its height and instead of being a cheaper substitute for real stone it had become high art in its own right and dominated the built environment, including many very elaborate fences.

With the boom of the late Victorian period on the wane a new humility was emerging in residential style, the Edwardian—Arts and Crafts—Queen Anne Revival movement, which is called Federation style in Australia. The stucco and iron gave way to bricks and pickets.

World War I swept away the Edwardians and the new world was often a confused mixture of old values mixed with cinema images of lifestyles invented by film directors and presented as normal. Everyone wanted a bungalow and a car, this provided a streetscape of narrow blocks of land where the length of the front fence was reduced and a gate added wide enough to allow a motor car to pass into the property.

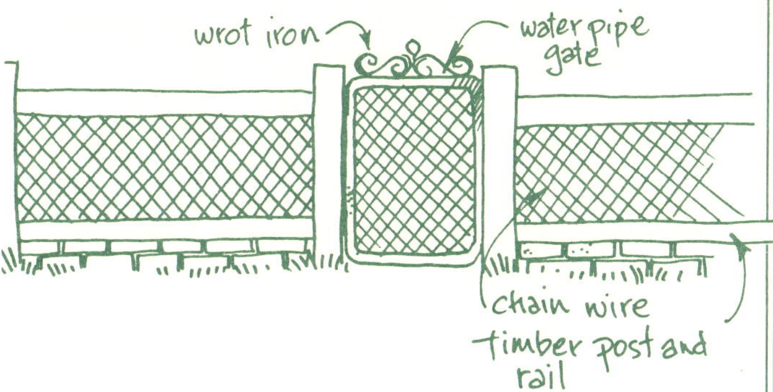

The wide gates needed for motor cars were better provided with steel tube and wire mesh designs than the traditional timber pedestrian gate. Gates in the 1920s and 1930s were generally low, about 1.2 metres (4′) high and built of brick plinths and piers with mass-produced steel tube, scrolled mild steel, and interlocked steel wire.

galvanised "fabric" wire fence early 20th century

For a while after World War II the authorities had a flirtation with the fenceless streetscape, which looked so nice on the North American situation comedy films at the local cinema. Dog excrement on pampered lawns, move towards security and privacy meant that fences slowly appeared again. In the latter part of the 20th century fences vary from 2-metre (7′) high brick security walls to ugly white powder-coated steel tubes with spearheads welded to more steel tubes, fastened to other steel tubes set in concrete appeared.

Consider your choice of fence carefully so that they are in harmony with their garden environment. A fence which is not in sympathy with the garden it surrounds and the house in the garden is very ugly.

Setting out

Fences may be on property boundaries or within the property. There are many different laws, codes and rules covering the erection of fences.

Many local authorities require application be made to them for permission to erect a front frence. Some locations use power under town planning legislation to control front fencing. In some localities the rules controlling front fences extend down the side boundaries to the statuary building line.

Side fences are often controlled by special laws, called Dividing Fences Acts or similar. These laws require adjoining owners to reach agreement on how a dividing fence will be constructed or if necessary resolve the matter in civil court.

Even the fences within a property can be subject to control by the authorities, which often treat these as constructions so that their erection can be controlled.

Government laws and rules can be challenged and if people want to change the way they are applied seriously enough, they will persevere and changes will be made. Most laws, however inconvenient, have some purpose.

The greatest frustration is when there is a rule to which there is no recourse, the title covenant can be such a law. If a land developer at the time of subdivision of a larger property into smaller parcels decides to attach special conditions, that is covenants, over the land these conditions can be registered in the title.

People purchasing land should be alerted by their conveyancing consultant (the name of the agents who carry out conveyancing varies widely) to any covenants that affect it. Covenants are normally in favour of all the owners of the allotments that make up the subdivision. They can be in other people's favour, but usually they favour the collective landowners. Covenants have been used to attempt to make sure that the development of the subdivision is of a predetermined quality, to protect the interests of the individual landowners.

Traditionally covenants require houses to have brick walls and tiled roofs, and it can be seen that once all the houses are built, the covenant ceases to affect the daily lives of the residents. Now consider that a garden is located on an allotment which is subject to a covenant that states that 'there will be no fences built between the front boundary of the property and the statutory building line . . .'

This means that there will be no front fences. The only way that this covenant can be changed is if all title owners affected by the title agree to the exact wording of any change or expungement. This is possible in a small subdivision of a few lots, but many subdivisions which have this form of restrictive covenant contain hundreds of allotments.

Covenants often represent the fashion of the time in which they were drawn up. In the 1960s front fences were unfashionable. There are some covenants which require only specific types of plants can be planted. This could mean that it could be against the rules attached to the titles of a piece of land to plant any shrub or tree that is not indigenous to the area.

Check the rules governing the use of covenants in the area where any garden is being developed and check if there are any restricting covenants applying over the subject land.

When all the matters of which body has jurisdiction over the fences to be constructed, is resolved, then the landowners should ascertain that they know where the title boundaries of the properties are. In some places to build a fence outside the title boundary, or not on the centre-line of the boundary can lead to the fence being removed by the owner of the property onto which the fence has been built, without compensation.

If there are no clear markers identifying the boundaries or if no private treaty can be agreed between adjoining landowner then the boundaries should be surveyed by a land surveyor before any fencing work starts.

For all fences, whether on boundaries or within the property, take care to consider any changes of ground levels which may take place during the construction of the garden. Note that in some places changes of level by the use of retaining walls are not allowed on property boundaries.

Foundations

Foundations for fences are often overlooked but when a fence can be over 20 metres (70′) in length (and 50 metres (165′) and more are not uncommon) they can be critical. If the foundation material varies in reactivity or is subject to other ground settlement or movement conditions, then the fence that is constructed onto it has a risk of distorting.

Take the foundations of a fence down to the same bearing capacity for the full length of the fence and to only use flexible fencing materials such as timber and steel in areas of highly reactive foundations that cannot be economically controlled.

Footings

The footings of the fence are the concrete, brick, stone or timber posts, piers, pads or strips which transfer the reactions of the fence to the ground. The footing will transfer the mass of the fence to the ground, that is easy to see, but it may be harder to see that the footings will transfer the wind loads acting on the fence and also be required to resist the local overturning load imposed on the fence, when anyone tries to climb over it.

For a post-and-rail fence, most picket fences, as well as paling fences and rail and wire types, the footing is made by pouring concrete around a post which is suspended for about 1/3 of its length into a foundation hole. If the foundation hole is excavated by using a mechanical post hole auger-type digger, mounted on a tractor or similar machine, then deep holes can be prepared that are well socketed into the stable subsoil. Hand-excavated holes are unlikely to be as deep and the risk of a high paling fence being blown over in a gale is increased.

For masonry fences, whether they are all or part masonry in construction, the footing should be a continuous reinforced concrete footing. The continuity of the footing and its resistance to vertical and horizontal forces is more important than the footing's simple ability to transfer the mass of the fence to the foundation soil.

If the stable foundation level is too deep (over 1 metre (3'6")) to simply excavate a trench, then piers can be bored at regular intervals down to the stable sub-strata. The piers are filled with concrete and a reinforced concrete beam is poured over and between them to act as a continuous beam. If a stable footing is provided then the fence should be without the movements which cause cracking.

It is a good idea to extend the strip footing across all gate openings, this means that the gate posts are less likely to move independently of each other.

Always discuss any changes to dividing boundary fences with adjoining neighbours before commencing any excavations which extend over the title boundaries.

Some local authorities will not allow any part of a front fence to intrude into the public land of the street reserve, this is sometimes interpreted to mean footings. Also care must be taken to avoid digging up utility services when excavating for the fence's footings. It is essential to check where the following services are located.

telephone wires
electricity cables
gas supply pipes
water supply pipes
sewer service pipes
stormwater pipes

There is a reasonable chance that these are located close to the front boundary fence and most of them will pass through this boundary to service the residence.

If a main telephone line is cut, the person who cuts the line is subject to be invoiced for the cost of the repairs to the cut line, plus any loss of income suffered by the telephone authority as a result of the severance of the service.

This fades into insignificance when it is considered that a crowbar into a high voltage electricity cable may mean instant death or a pick axe through a pressurised gas pipe could lead to a devastating explosion.

Brickwork

High quality durable fences of pleasing appearance can be built in brickwork. If built taking into account some simple rules a well-constructed brick fence or wall will have a potential life of many decades. In contrast if poor construction practices are used natural forces can reduce a brickwall to a pile of rubble in a few years.

After ensuring that the brickwork will be constructed on a sound footing the next important task is to choose a suitable brick. Fence bricks should be tough; those well-burnt in solid clay or well-cured in solid concrete are generally the best types. Hollow bricks of any type are generally less durable when used in fences and more susceptible to cracking. Bricks of the calcium/silica type, which is a clean white brick, have to be treated with great care as they discolour very easily in a garden environment.

Most modern bricks are dimensionally stable after delivery to a site but it should be realised that some clay bricks, even if very well fired, grow after they are built into walls owing to a slow chemical reaction within the bricks. Damage because of brick growth can be minimised by building expansion joints into brick fences within 2 metres (7') of corners and at 4-metre (13') intervals in the run of the fence. Check with the brick manufacturer if further information is required about growing.

There is a dilemma that faces a bricklayer when deciding what mortar mix to use in a fence. If the mix is strong and cement rich it will not erode out of the joints during unfavourable climatic conditions. If the mix is made lime-rich to remain flexible, so it can accommodate some movement in the fence without cracking, it may be eroded over time. There is no definite answer for all locations and situations but as a general rule, a composite mortar containing cement, hydrated lime and sand is a reasonable compromise in most situations.

When choosing bricks for a fence consider how much of the bricks will be visible. Most bricks have only one face and one head that are select quality while the back, reverse head, top and bottom of the brick varies in visual qualities.

It is almost impossible to build a brick fence where some of the non-select faces are visible. It is a good idea to dry-lay any brick fence before laying the final brickwork so that the design can be modified and the best compromise selected. Bricks are made with a select face and head, the obverse face and the reverse head are often marked with colour bars and other scars. The top and bottom of bricks are not made to be exposed except if specially ordered for the purpose.

The two most common visual problems associated with brick fences are:

A brick fence the thickness of a single brick exposes the back of the bricks and while some bricks look satisfactory when laid this way, others are ugly and of colours and textures totally unrelated to the select face. Some bricks have inconsistent thickness which only allows one face to be flush.

Wire-cut bricks used to construct copings to piers and fences often lead to the multi-holed tops and bottoms of these bricks showing. If the brickworks does not manufacture solid core bricks, then the choices are to use a masonry saw to cut mitred bricks or to use a different brick or even a different material for the copings.

Every brick selection should be checked carefully.

Most brick fences are constructed of single skin walls with brick piers at regular intervals. Sometimes the piers are expressed as pilasters, in other cases they are treated as functional stiffeners only. There is a lack of imagination in many brick fence constructions although they are often expensive to construct and dismal in appearance.

A brick fence where there has been expressive use of piers, panels, plinths, and copings, particularly if subtle colour variations and special shaped bricks are used, can provide an excellent backdrop to many plants.

Brick fences can be formal or informal, even rustic, in appearance but they should never be poorly built as they have to resist most of the elements as well as ground movement and plant-root growth.

Brick fences should be as thick as possible, be as stiffly piered as possible, contain wire mesh reinforcement and have changes of direction if possible. A straight slender brick fence, will almost certainly begin to lean in time and eventually fall over. A 1.5-metre (5′) high brick fence with piers engaged on one side of a single skin wall only has to lean about 170 mm (7″) off the vertical and the centre of gravity of the fence will be outside the base of the brickwork.

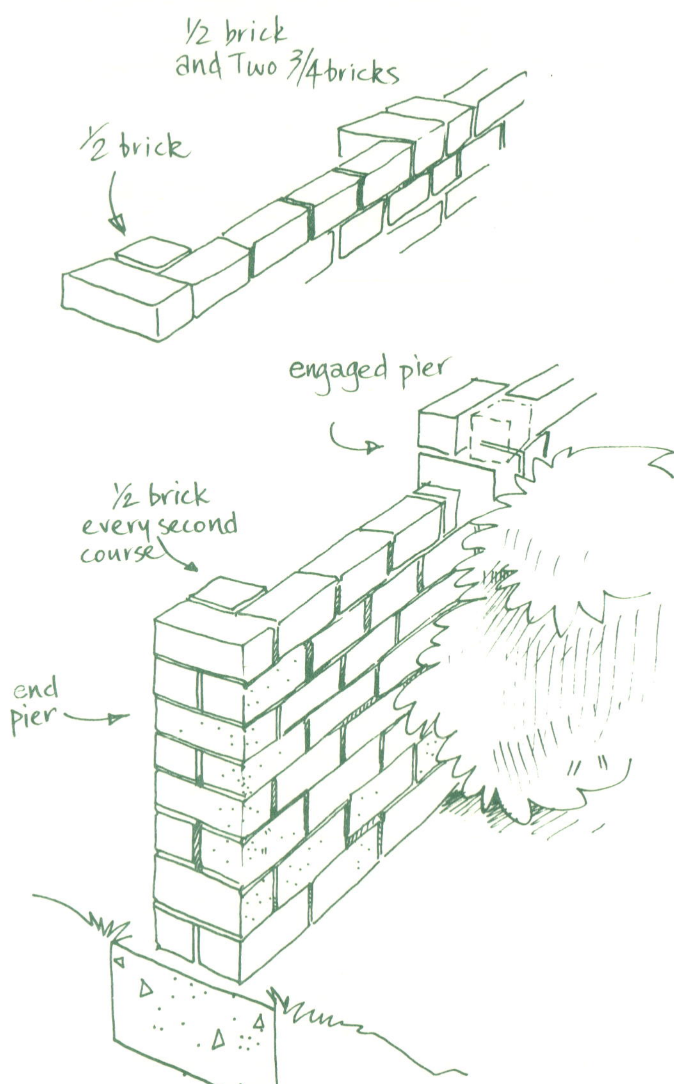

Stonework

Stone fences can range from the most rustic dry-stone walling to the most formal dressed stone edifices. Few materials give a gardener as many opportunities of expression as stone when used to construct fences.

The traditional stone walls of English farms were often constructed by the farmer simply picking up the larger stones that were in the immediate area. That way the act of building the wall satisfied two requirements of the farmer, the stones were cleared from the fields making them easier to work and barriers were erected which defined boundaries and contained the livestock.

This type of simple dry-wall fencing is valued highly by many gardeners. It combines simplicity with structural integrity not expressed in more formal fence designs.

Dry-walling is, as its name suggests, when a stone wall is constructed without the aid of wet materials, that is the stones have no mortar bedding. This simple concept requires patience and care to construct a fence that is sound, durable and with an even mix of stone sizes along its length.

Almost any stone can be used in dry-walling but some are easier to build with than others. Flat plate-like sections of sandstone and slate are probably the easiest stones with which to build a dry-wall. Spherical smooth quartz stones from a riverbed are among the hardest rock types to use.

In between these extremes are all of the other possibilities of naturally occurring stones or shards, including basalt, pumice, limestone, granite, and marble. It is possible to use some of the softer rocks which would not normally be considered suitable for any type of construction, including shales and claystones. These softer rocks will weather quicker than the harder rocks but in many gardens they will give quite long service in a sheltered area.

It is possible to use machine-split stone to build dry-walls and after a period of weathering there is little difference from an authentic dry-wall built of natural stones. Some working of the stones is needed in most dry-walls, there are some very fine examples of dry-wall where the stones are smooth-cut to the face of the wall.

To provide a suitable footing for a dry-wall a trench should be excavated to a stable foundation, under the site of the fence. This trench then should be filled with sand or gravel to within 100 mm (4″) or so of the groundline. The base course of stones should be of the largest size available and should be worked well into the footing material to provide a fully supported wall.

Skilled masons can build dry-walls to heights of over 2 metres (7′) with thicknesses as slim as 400 mm (1′4″), a ratio of 5 to 1. Most amateur gardener masons should keep wall heights to below 1.2 metres (4′) and start with a base course 400 mm (1¼″) thick, a ratio of 3 to 1.

Though not strictly authentic, many dry-walls have their top course, that is the coping course, set in mortar. This reduces the danger and nuisance of the coping being dislodged accidentally. Dogs are a common

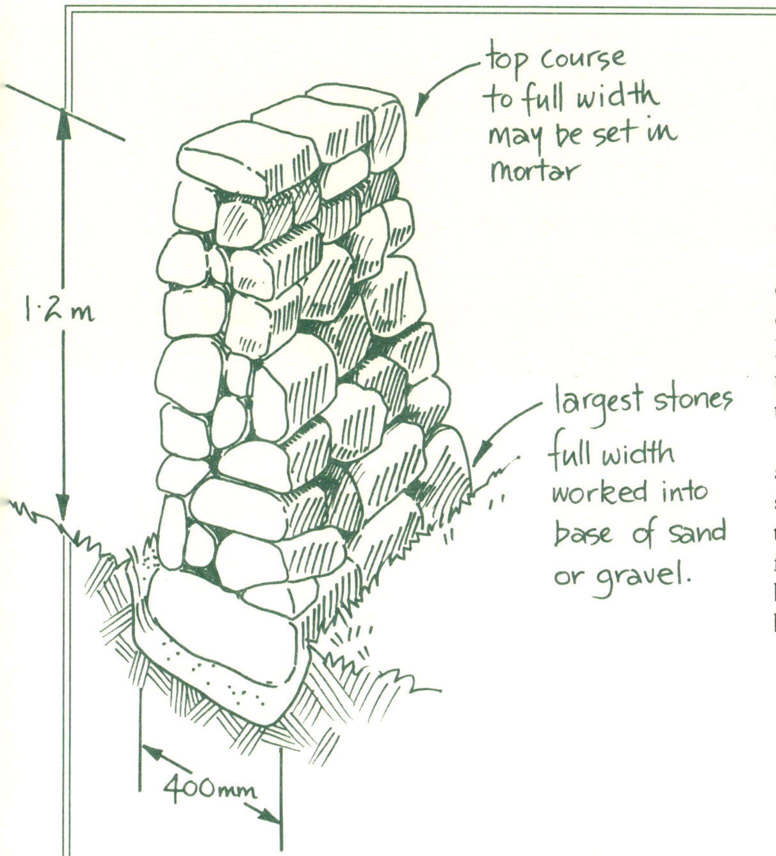

The footing for a rubble wall can be stones as for the dry-wall or reinforced concrete. A reinforced concrete footing is often more suitable if there are gateways and openings in the fence. Here it can be poured continuously under openings, linking both sides and reducing cracking.

The entry of water into the top of a rubble fence can cause early deterioration of the structure and if the top of the fence is left with hollows these can fill with dirt. It is then that weeds appear, as if by magic, from the top of the wall. It is advisable to build a sound coping to the top of rubble fence.

If the top of the fence is above normal eye level then a coping or waterproof cement mortar render with a slope to shed the water will suffice. Where the top of the fence is in view then it is better to build the coping from flag-type stones which are close jointed and well bedded. Alternatively neatly dressed coping stones can be bedded to the top of the rubble fence.

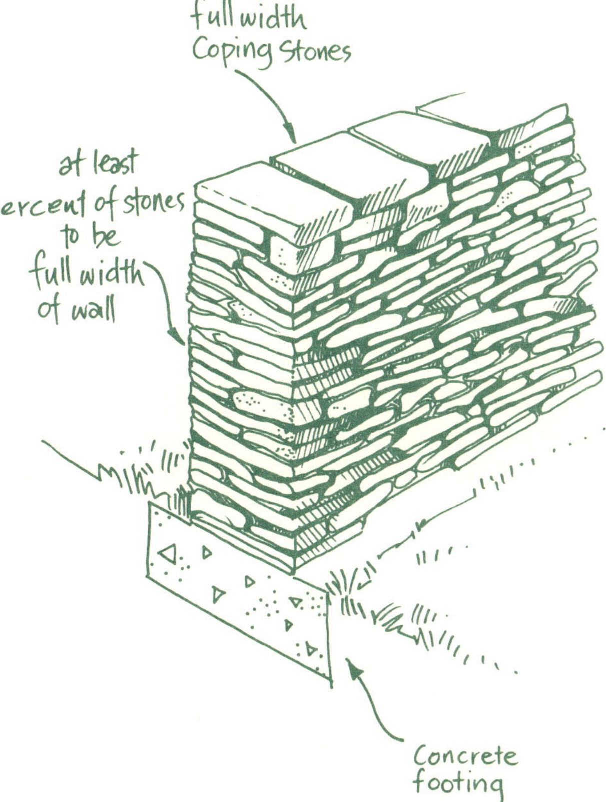

problem by dislodging stones if they scale a fence. Examples of these dry-walls can be seen in many older council parks.

Rubble walls are built from irregular stones set in mortar, and can be of rubble that has been graded for size and shape or even from partially worked stones. Skilled masons can construct durable walls from rubble, the life of the wall only being limited by the quality of the stone and mortar used.

There are rubble-built walls thousands of years old, particularly where the climate is dry and hot.

It is difficult to build a rubble wall with relatively parallel faces, without cutting many stones, if all the stones in the wall pass through the full thickness of the wall. It is easier to maintain parallel faces if some of the stones are only visible on one face of the wall and any internal voids filled with stone chippings and mortar.

It is important that some stones pass right through the wall to bond the two faces, about one-third of the area of the faces of the wall should consist of bonding stones. The number of bonding stones can be reduced if brick reinforcing mesh strips are used in the wall to enhance the bonding.

Care must taken to avoid near vertical joints, over two or more courses, these will be weak spots in the fence and if there is any ground movement, this is where the crack will appear. Where possible use rubble at the face of the fence which will provide a majority of stones which are twice as long as they are high. This should ensure reasonable face bonding.

There are two ways of building a rubble fence, random rubble and coursed rubble. Random rubble is when there is no attempt to line up any of the horizontal courses however in a well-built fence it would be expected that the lower stones were larger than the stones higher in the wall. Coursed rubble is where at intervals up the fence there are horizontal courses, these can be equally or irregularly spaced but would normally be 400 (1′4″) to 900 mm (3′) apart.

Dry-walling and rubble wall fences are capable of being built by many gardeners after some practice. Try laying a rubble wall in wet sand while practising. Do not use permanent cement or composition mortar until high skill levels have been achieved.

Dressed stone masonry is a fine tolerance craft and should be left to experienced masons. There are so many ways, so many different stones, and so many designs available that is impractical to give a detailed appraisal of them all. The accompanying drawing attempts to give a small visual presentation of some ideas for stone fences.

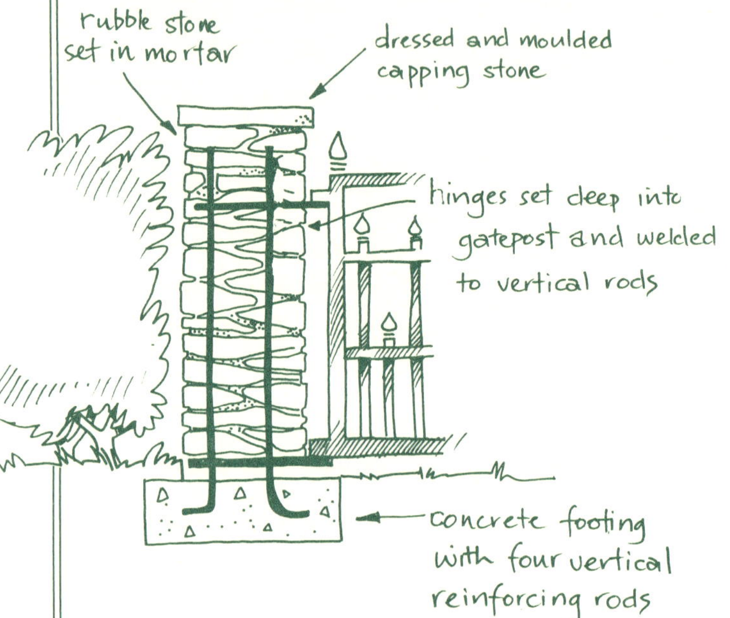

Timber

The first timber fences were simply thornbush entanglements. These were used by early people as a defence against attack by wild animals and intrusion by other human beings. Later logs were set side by side, with one end in the ground and the other with a sharpened end, standing vertically or at a defensive slope. Log palisades and even thorn entanglements are still used.

Pickets, palings, posts and rails are more closely associated with fences today but even their roots probably extend back beyond recorded history. Certainly rude timber fencing has been used by most isolated people exposed by European explorers and conquerors.

Modern brushwood, sapling, and lattice fences are also modifications of traditional fencing methods which were constructed using grass or vine bindings and green wood interweavings. Galvanised wire, mass-produced nails and sawn timber have changed the appearance of these fence types over time but each kind remains well suited to a garden environment.

Durable brushwood is harvested commercially and is therefore available in most locations. It can be purchased ready-cut, suitable for use in fences from 900 mm (3′) to 1 800 mm (6′) high, rising in 300 mm (1′) intervals.

To construct a brushwood fence, timber or galvanised steel pipes are set in concrete-filled footings at about 1.5 (5′) to 2 metres (7′) apart. The posts should be vertical in all directions and end posts should be restrained or braced to allow steel wires to be stretched between the posts. Space the wires at about 300 (1′) to 450 mm (1′6″) apart.

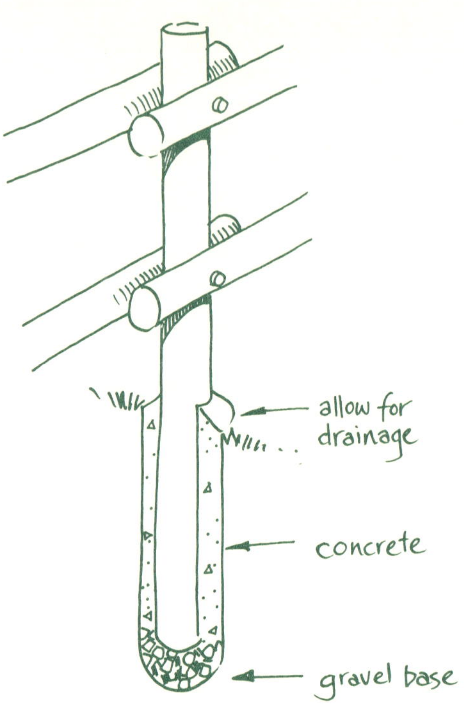

The brush is now fastened in vertical bundles of about 100 (1′) to 150 mm (1′6″) in diameter to both sides of the pre-stretched wires. The brush is woven onto the wires, using other pieces of wire. Sometimes the brush is placed between two strands of wire, the wires then being clipped together every 300 mm (1′) to 450 mm (1′6″).

Traditionally the top of a brush fence has a thatched capping. Modern examples can have weathered timber copings or even galvanised and painted steel channel copings.

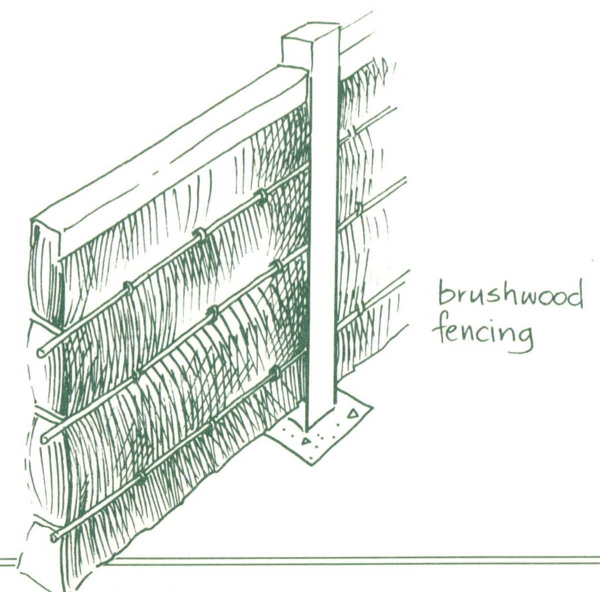

Brush fences make a good boundary fences or provide excellent internal garden screens to effectively hide the composting yard.

Sapling fences are constructed using a simple timber post-and-rail system, posts of a section 125 (5″) x 50 mm (2″) or 100 (4″) x 75 mm (3″) with 75 (3″) x 50 mm (2″) rails are commonly used. The rails are set about 600 (2′) to 800 mm (2′8″) apart, between vertical posts which are concreted into the ground.

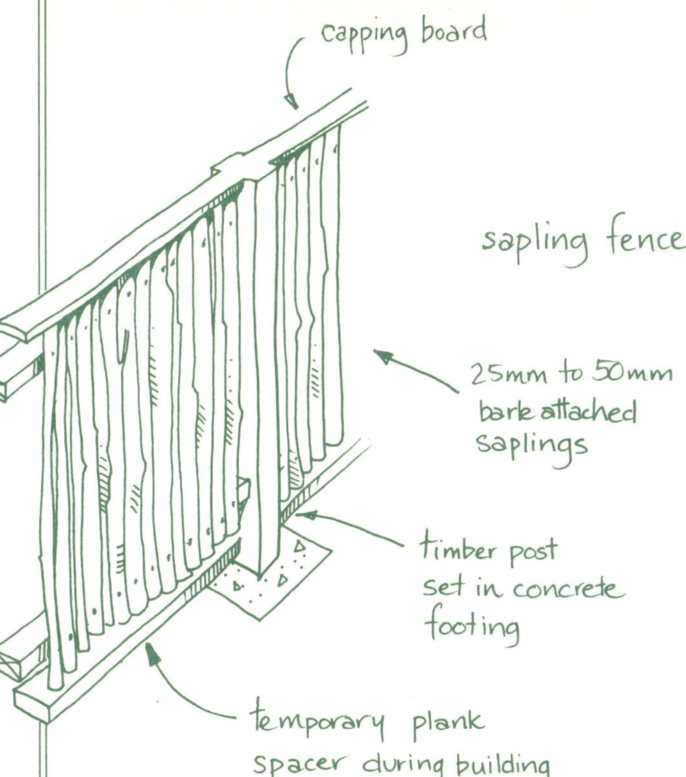

The rails may be horizontal or they can follow the natural slope, the sapling infill should always be vertical. The saplings which can be any species of bark attached round section timber of between 25 (1″) and 50 mm (2″) diameter. Fencing suppliers in most areas will be able to supply durable timber species with attractive and interesting barks.

It can be good fun for you to cut your own saplings but always check with the property owner before beginning the harvest. Removing saplings from the natural bushland is forbidden in many areas. Telephone the local authorities to find out the necessary information.

Saplings are nailed to the rails using flat-headed galvanised nails. The saplings can be graded in size if they are purchased from a fencing supplier or they can be used ungraded to provide more rustic appearance.

It is a good idea to place a plank on the ground under the bottom of the saplings to keep the bottom line even and provide a gap between the ground and the bottom ends of the saplings. Most saplings will give a longer life if there is an air space below them. There is no need to cut the saplings to length as they can extend vertically

and then be cut to the desired line later.

A safe timber preservative can be applied to any timber in contact with the ground but care should be taken to make sure that plants and animals will not be adversely affected by any of these chemicals.

The top of the saplings can be left but many people prefer to use a timber or metal channel capping, fixed to the top of the posts.

Lattice fencing originally was made by weaving young green branches or split strips of timber. The patterns ranged from simple vertical and horizontal under weaves and over weaves, or diagonal weaves to complicated weaves similar to those used to weave cane baskets.

This traditional type of latticing is also called wicket fencing. When the green timber seasons then it locks the weave and provides a secure fence. As wicket fencing uses young green sapwood it usually has rather poor durability.

Wicket-type lattice fence is a rustic but suitable alternative to modern lattice. It can be used as a base support frame for a creeper hedge and allows the propagation of very interesting hedges. To construct a creeper hedge a series of posts are driven into the ground along the line which is to be hedged. If a wider fence is required drive in a parallel row of posts. The posts should be 200 mm (8″) or so shorter than the required height of the finished hedge. One row of posts will provide the base for a hedge approximately 300 to 600 mm (1′ to 2′) wide dependent on the vine used. When two rows of posts are used then allow at least 200 mm (8″) extra to each side of the post lines for vine growth. If a vine or creeper hedge is required to be 750 mm (2′6″) thick then the internal wicket frames should be about 350 mm (1′2″) apart, 200 + 350 + 200 mm = 750 mm (8″ + 1′2″ + 8″ = 2′6″).

While the vine hedge is growing the wicket frames provide support and by the time the wickets rot away the vine has provided an alternative supporting framework. The result is a more natural-looking hedge than is usually possible when modern machine-made lattices are used.

With machine-made nails available at a cheap price and battens were able to be bought from sawmills, the appearance of lattice changed significantly. Timber battens of approximately 20 to 35 mm (¾″ to 1½″) × 8 to 12 mm (³⁄₁₀″ to ½″) cross-sections are used. These battens are laid out in a jig for the horizontal (or vertical or diagonal) members, then in the same jig the vertical (or horizontal or diagonal) members are nailed where these cross. It is important that the nails project through the battens and are bent over to clench the battens together.

Nailed timber lattice panels can be folded like a concertina to aid in their transport and to increase their width/height flexibility. Most lattices are of an even square or diagonal pattern where the space between the battens ranges from about the same as the batten width to twice this width. There are no rules and some very interesting effects can be developed — by using battens of varying widths and thicknesses; by varying the spaces between battens; by fixing battens at various angles. There are many more options than can be dealt with here.

Timber latticing was manufactured from painted hardwood with galvanised nails in the attempt to give it reasonable longevity in the past, but lattice is difficult to repaint and even galvanised nails eventually rust. Now much of the latticing being used in gardens is manufactured from treated pinus battens which are fixed together with stainless steel staples. This pinus does not require painting as it is a greeny/yellow when new which weathers to a greeny/grey over time, blending into most garden environments.

More durable lattice can be obtained by using fibrous cement lattice, this is a sheet product with square or diamond holes to give the appearance of lattice.

When building a fence from lattice it is important to realise that some maintenance will be required to the battens over time. The posts for the lattice fence should not be set too far apart 1.5 to 2 metres (5′ to 6′8″) is about right. Whereas it is possible to use lattice to build a fence by simply nailing it to the face rails, this seldom gives a fence of quality.

To build a visually good quality lattice fence use at least 90 mm (3½″) square posts set well into concrete footings. The posts can finish under the fence capping or project above it with either a simple weathered top or a special turned design. The posts at gates can be larger in section; 140 mm (5¾″) square is suitable for most lattice constructions.

Bottom plates should be morticed into the sides of the posts clear of the ground and horizontal. The plates may step at the posts. Capping plates should be morticed between posts when projecting posts are used or diagonally screw-fixed from the underside where the capping extends over the top of the posts. They can be screwed through the top of the capping but this provides a weak spot for the entry of water into the timber and this should be avoided if possible. The top of the capping should be double-splayed to shed water.

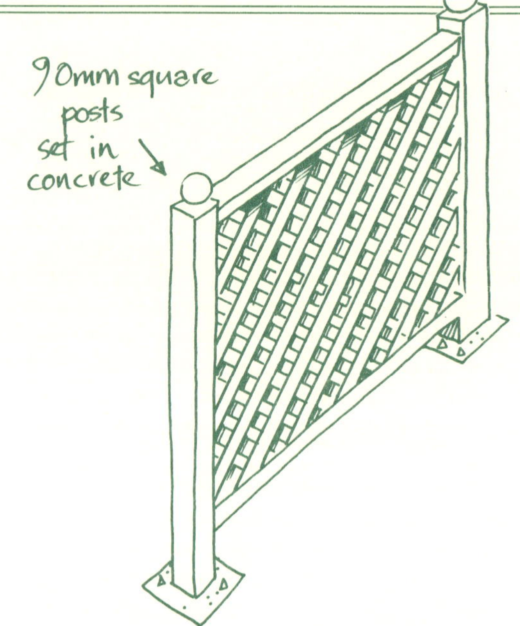

The posts should be vertical and the cappings and rails horizontal. Space the rails to cappings to suit the lattice panels to be used: 750 (2′6″), 900 (3′), 1 250 (4′2″), 1 500 (4′8″), and 1 800 mm (5′8″) are panel heights to consider. The lattice should be manufactured from durable timber battens such as treated pine, western red cedar, some European or Australian hardwoods. The battens should have a minimum width of about 30 mm (1¼″) and a thickness of at least 10 mm (⅜″) with 12 mm (¼″) thickness for the higher fences.

The lattice is trimmed to fit into the space between the posts and between the capping and rail with about 10 mm (⅜″) tolerance. The lattice is fixed using timber beads or metal channels. All fixings should be stainless steel or galvanised steel. Some timbers will give longer life if oiled, stained or painted. Lattice panels made to be easily removed can be carried to a convenient place where they can be spray painted.

Post-and-rail fences vary from the rustic split timber posts with sliprails fixed into holes in the posts to elegant white-painted dressed timber fences which have become part of the images of thoroughbred horse studs.

There is a theory which hypothesises that natural timber fences built from timber felled in the immediate area of the fence will last longer than a fence built from timber brought in from another area. When this theory is combined with the theory that split timber is more durable than sawn timber and the fact that a sliprail fence has no metal fixing to rust, this type of fence should last for a very long time. They do, and in rural Australia many fences of this type have outlasted the people who erected them.

Unfortunately the sliprail fence is restricted to internal fences and has limited use in an urban garden for few neighbours will accept them as boundary fences. The smarter white-painted post-and-rail fence with a diagonal top rail is suitable to define the front boundaries in outer suburban and near-rural environments.

Paling fences are the traditional fence which separates residential allotments in suburban areas. They are universally a blight on residential areas as they are too high and too blank to give any quality. They are a poor reflection on society, where neighbours need to separate themselves so exclusively, reducing the opportunity for the residential gardens to overlap to form an urban woodland. However council regulations in some localities insist on fences 1 800 mm (6′) where there is a swimming pool on the property.

If it is essential to erect a boundary paling fence then at least keep its height to the minimum possible, build it neatly, and grow plants along it so that the structure is obscured quickly.

The picket fence in contrast to the paling fence, is considered romantic. These can be low or high, new or old, painted or stained, plain or fancy, long or short, separated from the garden or entangled in it. They are the most versatile of fences. They are simple enough to be built by almost every gardener yet there are enough variations in design available so that each gardener can have a unique fence.

The rules applying to the construction of a picket fence are simple:

- Make sure the posts are solidly fixed in the ground
- Keep the posts close together to minimise the sag in the rails carrying the pickets
- Rails should be horizontal, unless the fence is consciously following the land's contours
- Rails should be solidly housed into posts
- Rails should have a weathering slope on their top edge sloping away from the pickets
- Keep the pickets closer together than their individual width, remember it is a picket fence not a 'gaps' fence
- Pickets should be vertical
- Pickets should be clear of the ground
- All fasteners should be corrosion-resistant

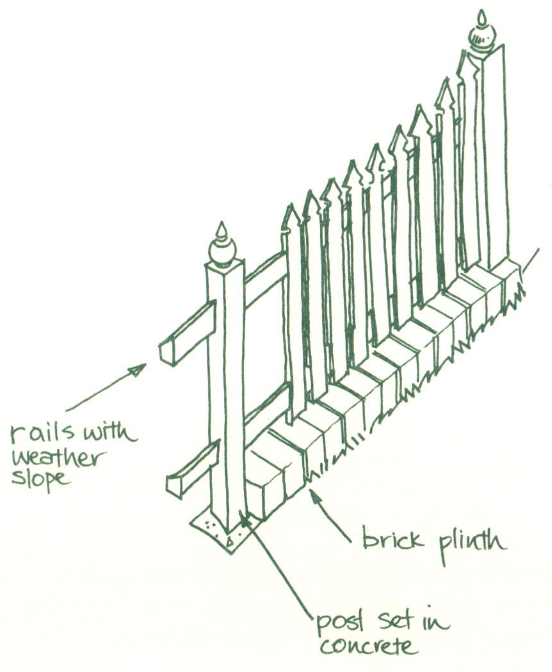

From this point individuality may have its way.

Some picket fences are enhanced by having a stone or brick plinth under the pickets. This is particularly useful as a deterrent to burrowing dogs. A plinth can also ensure that the pickets are kept out of the soil and thus reduce the danger of insect and fungi attack.

Traditionally pickets have had pointed tops and some have had extra cutouts and holes. If there is a very long fence with a complicated pattern picket-shape then a great deal of time or money can be spent on having the shapes cut. It is wise to check the shapes available from the commercial picket manufacturers as they generally are tooled up to guillotine the shapes out of the pickets. This is a much cheaper method of production than individual hand-shaping.

The posts and rails of a picket fence are usually constructed from hardwood timbers to achieve the strength and durability required, having a much higher nail grip than softwood. This is important, particularly where the fence is on a boundary where there is a risk that people may accidentally or deliberately pull on the pickets. Nails should be flatheaded to further reduce the risk of palings coming off.

The posts can be located to be a feature of the fence with finial tops or they can be concealed behind the pickets with their height limited to the height of the top rail. Picket fences up to 1 200 mm (4′) high require only a top and bottom rail for support but it is recommended that the pickets be at least 20 mm (¾″) thick. Fences over 1 200 mm (4′) high require a mid-rail or their thickness needs to be increased to 25 mm (1″) or more.

Picket fences can be built to one horizontal line if the ground is nearly level but where the ground has a slope the fence line can be stepped, sloped, or fully contour-following. When the fence is to be stepped, then consideration has to be given to the bottom of the picket. Are these to follow the slope of the ground or are these to have a plinth of brick, stone, or timber under them to adjust the slope?

It is a good idea to set out the fence with temporary long pegs where the posts will be, then to put stringlines where the top and bottom of the fence will be. Stand back and look. Slopes up to 300 mm (1′) between posts are visually acceptable and plinths will be

Metal

Many of the great wrought iron and cast iron fences were smelted to produce raw materials for armaments during world wars I and II.

Iron and steel have been the materials used to manufacture metal fences. It is possible to use other metals but their cost of production is very high. Attempts to use aluminium as a fencing material have been relatively unsuccessful and this material has been relegated to the pool safety fence sector. It lacks aesthetic beauty but has a greater ability to resist chlorine and water attack than steel.

Wrought iron spear fences on stone plinths with imposing gates were fashionable during the Victorian period and are still the preferred fence-type for wealthy property owners. These provide high quality security while the imposing mansions and gardens can still be seen from the street. Wrought iron used in Victorian fences was a different material than the modern mild steel used today. Traditional wrought iron resists rust whereas modern mild steel has an extremely low resistance to rust.

Around the beginning of the 20th century a wide range of woven galvanised steel wire fences were manufactured. These were machine-made and remained popular in suburban areas and country towns until the 1930s. Today they are no longer manufactured and cannot be hand-made.

Following on from the woven wire fences came the water tube and scrolled mild steel fences and gates, which were mostly used with low brick plinths and squat brick piers. Initially these fences (incorrectly referred to as wrot iron) were riveted together but later examples were welded.

The better wrot iron fences were hot-dip galvanised before painting but many were just painted. Rust has always been a problem with this type of fence and there are fewer and fewer examples to be seen. This style can be reproduced at moderate cost and modern galvanising and colour coatings gives the fence a satisfactory lifespan.

Modern steel fences are limited to mass-manufactured heavy gauge galvanised wire weldmesh types and those manufactured from thin-walled galvanised steel tube. The latter type is made with reproduction Victorian spear-heads and other imitated features.

These modern welded steel fences are suitable to meet the statutory requirements to fence residential swimming pools and it is easy to grow creepers through the mesh so that the fence is out of sight.

The chain wire mesh that provides the security fences around most factories is available for residential use as well. Combined with timber posts and rails, an economical fence of passable appearance is achieved. The use of wire mesh should be restricted to tennis court fences. It is available in some colours but basic galvanised grey is probably most appropriate.

Other

There are many other types of fences to choose from simple post-and-strained wire through to precast concrete. All fence types have their place so choose the fence that is in keeping with the residence and the surrounding garden environment.

OPENINGS AND GATES

Wherever there is a fence there are openings which are most commonly used to allow the passage of people and vehicles through the fence.

Defining the opening

To gain their place in the environment it is important that gateways are well defined as the point of transition between two separate places.

The design of the gateway gives the first clues on what is to be expected beyond the gate, conversely the gate also marks the end of a journey. Gates have two sides, of arrival and of departure and it is important that these two functions are expressed.

Visually fences stop on either side of an opening or gateway in a fence but the pathway or driveway continues through. Most openings in a fence are simply the stopping of the fence so that an opening is created. Most openings have some form of post or pier on either side. These define the end of the wall and provide a strong point from which to hang any gates.

Some openings in walls are more like doorways than gateways, this is when there is a head left in place over the opening. These heads may be flat and square, rounded, and arched or even full circles as used in Chinese gardens. This opening type increases the sense of enclosure within the garden and increases the sense of security from without.

Some openings are designed to be concealed. Consider a design where two parallel fences overlap allowing the opening to have little visual impact by placing it at right angles to the fences. Other openings are overemphasised. A design of heavy piers, curved return fences, and elaborate iron gates, placed in the centre of a long imposing fence and leading to a double avenue of mature trees can be overstated.

In the latter example even if the residence concealed at the end of the avenue of trees is a modest cottage, most people passing such imposing gates would be influenced by the symbols of wealth and power this opening in a fence promotes.

Openings in fences and the gates that commonly protect them are personal statements of the property owners. If the imposing gates in our example were never shut, if they were replaced by a cattle grid, or if the gates were demolished then people's responses to them and property would be different.

Size and shape

Openings come in many sizes from narrow pedestrian openings to wide vehicular access ways. Most people are quite happy to walk through pedestrian gateways of 900 mm (3′) to 1 200 mm (4′) wide and a car access between 2.5 metres (8′) to about 5 metres (16′6″) if two cars must pass.

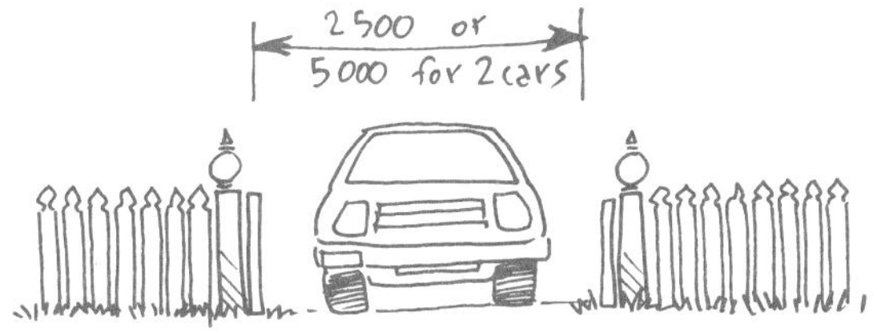

If the opening has a head, beam, arch or roof over the opening, the minimum height required for both people and cars is about 2.1 metres (6′9″). When the vehicles are people movers, four wheel drives, or commercial vehicles then heights in excess of 2.5 metres (8′) may be required.

Style

What style should an opening in a fence be? This is surely a very strange question, for it is about the non-existent, that is to say it is about the opening not the fence.

In fact the hole will be considered at least as important as the fence, for there would be little point in having a fence if there was not also an opening. When a fence is being planned the first item to be considered is where to place the openings.

The style of an opening can be achieved by consciously designing the threshold, sides, and top of the opening. The threshold can be raised one or more steps and can be paved in an interesting material. The sides can be made from stone or brick piers or have timber posts. The opening can project forward or be set back, the posts can be higher than the fence they terminate or they can be lower and they can be constructed from a wide range of materials and finishes and even be surmounted with light fittings.

Some openings even have their own roof which adds the final touch to converting a hole into a whole.

Gate posts

The gate posts are most important components of an opening in a fence for without them the fence cannot end and the gates have nothing to swing off.

The styles of gate posts are very often linked to historic periods or geographic locations. Other gate posts are simply functional.

When designing gate posts it is important to consider the garden and any buildings that there are within the garden when deciding how a gate should be designed. A Georgian country house surrounded by a formal garden is going to need a different gateway than a modest cottage in a rambling garden.

At first the choice here seems obvious; use formal classic stone, stucco or brick piers as gate posts supporting wrought iron gates for the Georgian house and timber posts with a picket fence and a picket gate for the cottage. This seems a safe choice, but the Georgian country house may have a rambling garden and the cottage a formal garden.

Some residential styles demand a particular type of gate posts. The Spanish Mission style of houses, so loved by Hollywood during the 1920s and 1930s, should always have a fence portal reminiscent of the gate of the Alamo fort, also of film fame. There are many alternatives available. A feature splash-on stucco, cordovan roof tiles, semi-circular arches with optional candy-stick columns.

This is the ideal gate for a Spanish Mission house. The garden should also have cacti and ponderosa pine. This is a special case where the house, the garden and the gates are all just a Hollywood image.

Gate posts do not need to reflect the architecture of the residence or the style of the garden as they could all be products of different periods, different people, and different socio economic circumstances. A house built during a period of economic depression may be austere and plain. This does not mean that the garden and fences that surround it need to be austere, in sympathy. Examples of a lone rose in the centre of a lawn surrounded with a two plank fence and cheap wrot iron gate hung on a textured brick pier still exist in front of houses of this type.

The gate post identifies the point where entry is made to a personal domain and it is important that there is a balance between the garden and residence composition.

Stone

Stone gate posts or abutments can be constructed from rustic dry stone through to extremely elegant polished granite and marble. There are many possible materials in between.

Stone gate posts are especially grand and the house the gateway leads to appears to be well constructed and permanent.

Dry-stone gate posts which provide a natural definition of the gateway to a cottage must be built with great care if they are to carry the load of a swinging gate. By extending steel straps from the hinges well into the stone work and cogging them over solid support can be achieved.

The easiest way to achieve good support for the gate, if it is desirable visually to have dry-stone abutments, is to concrete galvanised steel gate posts into the ground and attach the hinges to them. Usually it is not difficult to build the dry stone so that the steel post is concealed.

Gate posts built of stone rubble in mortar bedding will provide a sound gate post if constructed with care. The posts should be built on a concrete footing with two to four steel reinforcing bars extending vertically from it. The stone work should then be built around these bars. Other bars should be added horizontally as stones are added and soundly mortared in place. The hinges should be welded to steel reinforcing bars that have cogged ends and are built into the mortar. The bars attached to the hinges can even be welded to the vertical steel bars if the gate is heavy.

Rubble gate posts can be finished with a neat cut rubble capping, or topped with flagstone, or topped off with a dressed and moulded capping stone. The latter option gives a good definition to a pair of matching posts and good protection from the entry of rainwater into the top of the post.

Solid stone gate posts fashioned from large dressed and moulded blocks of stone have, for many years, been the gate posts of the rich and powerful. They are often fabricated from sandstone, limestone, granite or basalt in three component parts; a plinth or base, a shaft or pier, and a capping.

The base and shaft may be smooth polished stone or may be worked to provide an interesting appearance. Favoured over time are the tooled, rusticated, and vermiculite stone work finishes for stone gate posts. The capping is usually smoothly dressed, with a curved, gable or pyramidal top to shed water and projecting *eaves*. The shaft often has period details and features Classical fluting or panels.

Mostly the base is of a more durable stone than the shaft and capping and projects beyond the line of the shaft so as to take percussion from vehicle wheels.

Many gate posts are constructed with a brick core veneered with thin sometimes less than 20 mm (¾") thick sheets of expensive stone. Polished marble and granite are the most common stones used for this type of construction. Although many old stone gate posts look like solid stone, many were clad with thin veneers of stone and some are stuccoed with fake stone.

The quality of fake stone applied in the Victorian era is so good that few people can distinguish the difference. The technical skills of the tradesmen of 100 years ago were quite high and at least on par with the best of today's tradesperson. Tradesmen spent many hours mixing aggregates with crushed stones from appropriate sources to produce, as if by alchemy, high quality renders that provide a finish and texture so close to the original that few people know the difference.

Today there are still a few tradesmen who can produce high quality stone-like render. There is also the fully faked stone that can be purchased from garden suppliers. This material is so good and durable that it is an economic substitute for real stone.

Although available in abundance real stone is expensive to work and quarry and this adds to the cost of delivery to the site.

Brick

Brick gate posts range from the very simple to the very complex, often rivalling stone in style and sometimes including components or panels of stone or stucco.

Some cottage fences used exposed bricks for gate posts centuries ago but face bricks which would resist external climatic conditions and give a long maintenance-free life were not commonly available until late in the 19th century.

Once face bricks could be produced in large numbers at comparatively low cost, these were used in gate posts. The special moulded bricks which became available when most bricks available had moved from being underburnt hand-made callows to control-fired machine-pressed hard bricks.

Many shapes in bricks were manufactured, often of more than one colour. This availability led to the heavily modelled polychrome brick gate post of the late Victorian and Edwardian periods.

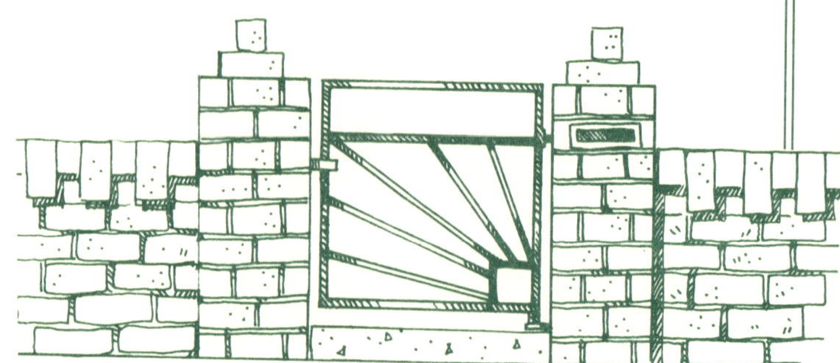

Today most brick gate posts are short and relatively simple, a shadow of what brick gate posts were at the height of their popularity.

When building a brick gate post ensure the brick pier that is representing the gate post is tied back to the wall against which it stands. Brick course reinforcements will do the job satisfactorily, but make sure that it is built in every third course.

Timber

Timber posts to support gates have been in use since the days the first metal hinged gate was hung. The posts need to be both durable, insect and fungi resistant, and tough. Posts are a target for all the children of the world who want to swing on them. Many cars sideswipe posts when coming and leaving the driveway.

If a tough durable timber is selected and the gate posts are kept to a sensible height it should be problem-free. To keep the timber posts plumb they must be set deeply into the ground. A timber plate with braces from the sides of the post to the plate is a normal method. With the post (with the base) placed in the hole and the ground backfilled in layers and well tamped a sound gate post is achieved.

The modern method is easier to use. Suspend the gate post with sound temporary braces, into a hole dug in the ground, then fill the hole full of concrete. Better still dig a trench across the opening created by the gate posts and then concrete the posts into place, by doing this the posts are unlikely to move independent of each other.

Timber gate posts can be logs stripped of bark; in some species the bark can be left on. Log gate posts can look good supporting an old chain wire gate into the compost yard in the back corner of the garden. This rustic approach will suit some country garden images.

Some timber species are extremely durable when stripped of their bark and suitably coated. Certain Cypress pines will make interesting gate posts. Treated pinus logs which are now often used in gardens are also appropriate for gate posts. Pinus logs should be of sections at least 200 mm (8″) in diameter as smaller sections are often brittle and snap if bumped by a car.

Log gate posts should be shaped or capped to reduce the entry of water into the natural splits and shakes in the timber. Log gate posts are ideal for wire fences where the wire is threaded through a hole in the log. When rails are used, these should be fixed deeply into the heartwood of the log as the outer layer of any log is sapwood, which will not season to the same strength.

Square sawn section timber gate posts are the simple alternative to the log gate post. These should be constructed from a durable hardwood. Most log posts are pine.

To reduce the danger of splintering along the sharp edges of a square timber post it is traditional to finish the corners with a chamfer or other moulded edge. Particularly handsome timber gate posts can be made with thoughtful use of stop chamfers, tapered chamfers, scottia moulds, ovolo moulds, and even scalloped bevelling.

Square timber posts can have the faces fluted and panelled, or have grooves cut around them and be surmounted with a limitless number of caps. Posts may be capped by a skillion cut or they may have a pyramidal cap, a ball cap, or even a cap shaped like a pineapple — there is no limit.

Timber posts can also be turned and moulded on a lathe. Square sections turned in some parts can produce gate posts that have square sections in convenient places to fasten hinges and rails and fancy-turned sections elsewhere. Turned timber is seldom of a quality which can be left untreated or even oiled for external use. It should be well primed, preferably by the dip and drip method, before painting.

Gate posts can be built up from a number of sections of timber to be as complicated as a Classical pier or column. For a gate post to work it has to be a cantilever up out of the ground or be solidly supported by a fence abutment. Built-up timber posts can look quite large and solid but may be hollow and weak. In many cases it is wise to treat the styled built-up posts as decoration. Conceal a stout steel or timber post within them.

For a built-up timber gate post to last always prime all faces of timber before assembly, use only non-corrosive fasteners. Use only water and weather-proof glue, only durable timbers, and if possible, have a cap cover made from soldered zinc or copper sheeting.

Metal

Gate posts made from a length of water pipe capped at the top and concreted into the ground have been a type for a long time. They work very well and generally have as much style as red textured bricks.

If the gate posts are for a gate into a yard hidden away in the bottom of the garden then the circular or square section galvanised steel tube post is an answer as there is no maintenance, it is robust enough to deflect a fully laden wheelbarrow of compost, and relatively inexpensive.

At the entry gate to the garden there is a different requirement. This is where guests arrive at the garden and first impressions are important. Traditional cast and wrought iron posts used with antique metal gates are beautifully grand but are almost impossible to reproduce today even on a wealthy gardener's budget.

Use steel for its strength to reinforce other materials in gate posts and as posts for secondary gates and gates in safety fences around swimming pools.

Gates

This is the door into the garden. The gate swings open to reveal all the work that has been expended to design, plan, and construct the garden. This should be a special experience. The gate must complement the garden and the personality of the garden owner.

Gates define a limit. There would be little use for gates if they were not required to clearly define crossing points in boundaries. Gates provide security against uninvited people or neighbourhood dogs. They are the first line of defence for the residents of the house in the garden.

Gates can be friendly and inviting as well as providing any necessary security or they can be impersonal and foreboding. In medieval times when a stranger arrived at the stout timber gate of the castle studded with iron spikes, and knocked — a small person-sized door was opened within the gate and a guard came through this to welcome or turn the stranger away. There was at least personal contact.

Today the gates of the rich, powerful, and insecure have massive faceless gates concealing gardens. These may be patrolled by savage dogs — the same dogs which most people are trying to keep out of their gardens. Or so says the image projected on our television screens. To get through the gates guests are expected to press a button, look into a security camera, and give a reason why they should be allowed in.

These forbidding gates and impenetrable gardens are not what is being proposed here. Here the gate is the way to the garden and on to the residence.

Often gates are simply a hinged section of a fence in a boundary and there are places where this approach is most suitable. A white picket fence to a shady country-style lane with a cottage and flower garden beyond does not need an overstated gate and a simple white picket gate in the fence is ideal.

For a cottage further away from the lane and concealed in the shade of large trees there may be a better site for the gate. The gate could be closer to the house by forming a fenced path into the garden. This way visitors can feel as though they are already in the garden before they reach the gate. This provides a very friendly arrival. The same concept applies if the garden is allowed to spill beyond the fence line. This may require the front fence to be built back from the titled front boundary of the garden.

Gates reflect the personality of the residents of the garden and they are the first and sometimes the only icon of this personality that is seen by other people. Everything about a gate is capable of communicating something to others; the height, the shape, the colour, the style, the openness, the latch, the hinges, and its state of repair.

The height of a gate can be from almost token height, which can be stepped over, to gates of excessive height of 3 metres (10′) or more. Gates from about 800 (2′6″) to 900 mm (3′) height will keep out most dogs but children can still see over the top. Gates from 900 (3′) to 1 200 mm (4′) high are in a middle range which is neither welcoming nor particularly secure. When the

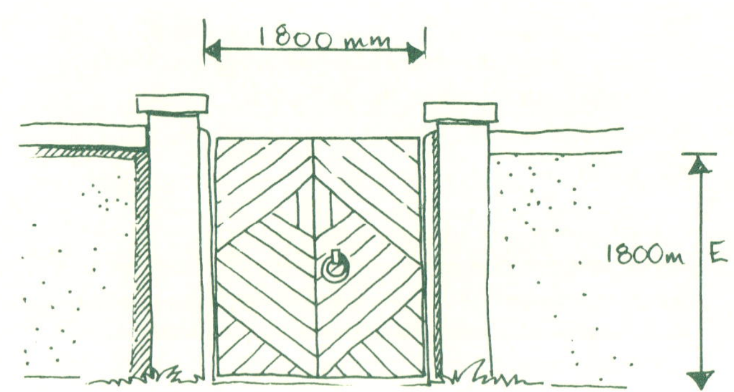

gate exceeds 1 500 mm (5′) to about 1 800 mm (6′) there is a real sense of security; gates over 1 800 mm (6′) are obviously to keep unwanted people out — or keep inmates in.

When considering the shape of a gate it is the top of the gate one thinks of but the proportions can have a bearing on the gate's shape. It is in the choice of style that the gate should be in harmony with the garden and the residence that it surrounds.

Colour is a very important element. The same gate is less welcoming when painted black than it would be if it were painted white. Red can communicate joy or anger. There are those people who would consider red to be an alien colour in a garden environment — particularly local government planning officers who seem, at times, to view the world through olive glasses. Yellow gates can shine in a shady avenue, blue gates complement a garden of annuals and hold the memories of summer skies through the depths of winter, brown gates tell of accountants and bank managers, and grey gates indicate places of pacifists. Green gates seldom work as they conflict with the colours of nature without adding any dimension.

Gates can have extreme degrees of openness which, when combined with height, completes the security image. A high gate of solid timber boards is exclusive, unwelcoming and obscures any image of what is beyond the gate. A high gate of open steel railing construction may be as secure as the former but because the view into the garden is not restricted a judgment can be made of the residents. They will not seem so remote if their children romp behind the gates on lawns covered with daffodils. Sometimes a high gate with a small viewing hole can add a special type of mystery to a garden particularly if there are many large trees in the garden beyond.

If the latch is on the outside of the gate and easily accessible the gate is much friendlier than one which can only be opened by putting a hand through a hole and searching around for the catch. Few people will risk opening a gate of this type if there are canine sounds on the other side. A big swinging ring latch handle invites entry.

Sometimes gates should be left to mellow with age. A picket gate with peeling paint can complement an old, slightly out of control cottage garden. Gates falling off their hinges are a nuisance and cannot be excused

as artistic mellowing. Old wrought iron gates carrying the patina of age sometimes complement a garden environment much more than a blasted, scraped, and enamelled gate.

Timber

Timber gates can all sag on their hinges whether simple braced ledge rails with pickets or large-framed, panelled, boarded and studded chateau gates. Timber used in gates will be subjected to many climatic variations throughout the seasons and over many years, is likely to cause a change in moisture content. If this is the case the timber could shrink or expand.

To make a gate choose timbers which have suitable durability. Try and use timbers which will remain stable and not be subject to large shrinkage or expansion rates and are unlikely to twist and warp.

If a timber gate can be constructed using morticed joints, peg or dowel fixings and bolt, washers and nut fasteners then the gate will generally give long service. A gate which relies too much on screw and nail fixing and fastening is not likely to last so long. Small diameter fasteners may, over time, cease to have an effective grip on the timber. Most small diameter fasteners, even of low corrosive materials, do eventually corrode and disintegrate.

How to stop gates sagging is not easy. Most gates will have at least a small amount of sag. There are three basic ways to stop gates sagging, and they can be combined with each other;

• Fit anti-sag braces which are usually fitted to extend from the bottom of a gate near the hinge to the top of the gate near the outer edge. This way the brace acts in compression to work against the natural force of gravity.

• Build the gate with a rigid frame. Very rigid joints need to be built at the corners of the frame. Even when steel angles are used this method is seldom absolutely successful.

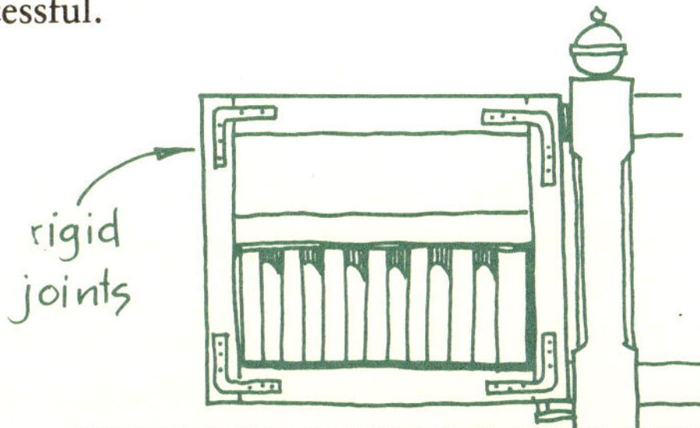

• Use a rigid panel as the basis of the gate. Here a sheet of marine grade plywood is the most popular material.

It can be used over the whole gate but as this requires cutting holes into the plywood if any gaps are needed in the gate it is more common to use the plywood panel in the bottom half of the gate and to use a rigid frame to form the upper half, which then can be fitted with bars as required.

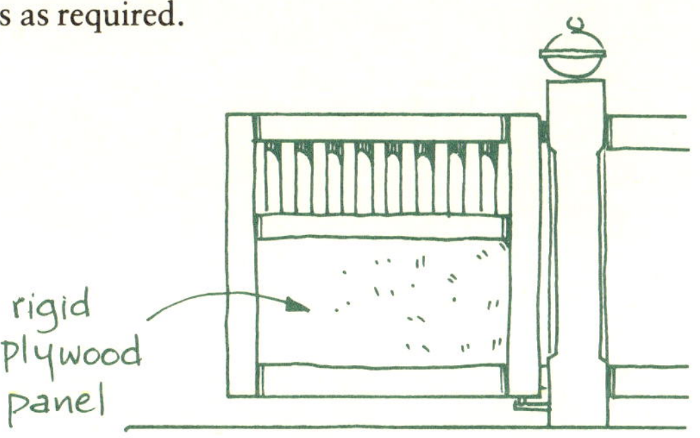

Although western red cedar dents quite easily and is not a particularly strong or tough timber, it is very durable, stable, and light. Gates made from western red cedar will give a long life if they are not subjected to excessive loads. People climbing over them can be sufficient to cause major damage. Western red cedar can be left for long periods unpainted without major structural deterioration.

Treated pinus provides a good general gate timber but is heavier than western red cedar and is not very attractive. Selected deciduous hardwood species and some durable conifers can be used for gates. Some of these timbers need to be worked and the joints cut before they are seasoned as they are often very unyielding once seasoned. In all cases the material should be carefully selected and allowed to season before being hung.

Combining a galvanised steel frame with timber cladding, spindles, mouldings and other dressings is a very satisfactory way to get the visual qualities of timber with the strength of a steel frame.

Metal

Many different types of metal and metallic alloys have been used to construct gates over the centuries. Durable gates built of the bronze and brass alloys of copper have been used since before recorded history and iron has been used to build gates or to reinforce timber gates from about the same time.

Though it is still possible to have gates made from bronze and brass the cost of these alloys has become very high and the availability of red alloy artisans very scarce.

Most metal gates are fabricated from steel or aluminium now. The steel is cut, shaped, and welded to the design required and then cleaned and primed or hot-dipped galvanised. With zinc coated over the steel during the galvanising process, the steel is able to resist rusting for a long period. Galvanised steel is not an aesthetic finish on its own and is generally painted to look better.

Aluminium gates are often fabricated with aluminium extrusions that are screwed or riveted together. Aluminium is not as flexible as steel when it is being worked and is much more difficult to weld. Aluminium gates tend to be less curvilinear and more straight extrusions. Expanded metal grid is often used in aluminium gates. Sometimes period reproduction aluminium castings, mimicking Victorian cast iron lace, are used.

Whereas steel gates can be painted with a brush on site, most aluminium gates will be prefinished at the fabricators. Powder coat, baked acrylic enamel, and anodised finishes are used on aluminium. All these have long lives but need re-finishing at a later date.

Furniture

The furniture on a gate needs to be of a type specifically manufactured for exterior use. Many handles and latches available are unsuitable and the durability of fittings must be checked out at the supply store.

Hinges

Hinges for gates should be of a non-corroding metal and be of large components. There are many ways to hang gates on hinges but the most important thing to remember is that the hinges have to be fixed to the gates during construction and in some cases the other part of the hinge must be built in to the gate post. As this takes some coordination take care with the order and needs of each procedure. Where hinges have to be permanently connected to both the gate and the post make sure that the hinges or pivots used are designed to be split apart and be re-connected.

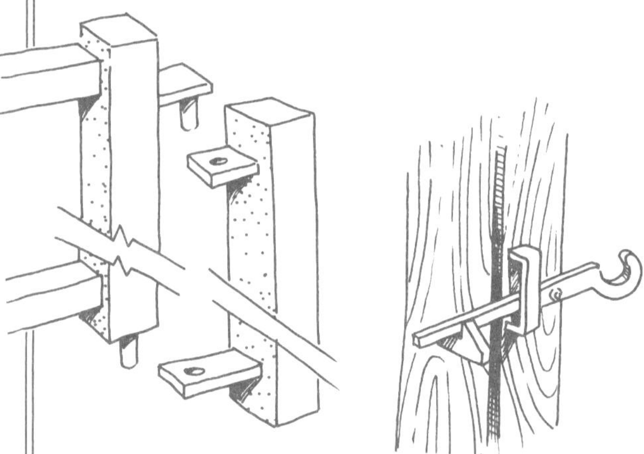

Latches and bolts

It is generally better to use a latch type lock with an exposed mechanism which can be cleaned and lubricated easily. There are good external locks for gates but these are often quite expensive and most people are happy to use padlocks for areas which are not for public access.

LIGHTING

Most modern gardens use exterior lighting to extend the times in which the garden can be enjoyed and to allow safe passage through the garden after dark. Lighting in gardens can be broken into three main components;

- Pathway and driveway lighting
- Lighting for outside leisure activities
- Lighting to display the garden

In the past lighting used mains power through cables carrying up to 240 volts. These were buried in the garden. Now most garden lighting uses much safer 12-volt system. This has become an international standard and a wide selection of light fittings can be purchased from around the world.

Installing the cables

A scale diagram of the location of every length of cable and every fitting should be drawn when the cables are installed. When the work is completed the diagram should be copied, the copy covered with laminated plastic and fixed to the wall in the garage or other convenient location near the electrical distribution system. Put the original copy with the deeds and other documents relating to the house here.

All cables should be installed in locations where they will remain accessible, easy to find, and not damaged by plant growth or normal gardening. To assist in locating cables later they should as far as practical run in straight lines between fittings, or follow the edge of a path, driveway, retaining wall or fence. It is also better to install the cables under a lawn than it is to place them in garden beds. Mark the mower strips at the edges of the lawn where cables pass under with their location and direction of travel.

Keeping the system safe

If the lighting system uses mains power then under most wiring rules the cables must be run underground in special quality and coloured conduit (usually orange). It is common for the wiring to be installed by a licensed electrician.

Modern earth leak detectors can be fitted to external lighting circuits. If these systems work correctly then it is impossible for anyone to be accidentally electrocuted, even if they slice through a power cable with a metal tool.

If a 12-volt electrical system is used then a transformer must be in a convenient location. The garage is a good place. In most places the authorities will allow non-electricians to install the cables to the 12-volts side of the transformer and to connect all of the light fittings.

The cables can usually be set into the ground without the requirement for conduit. This means that gardeners are able to have light fittings wherever they want them without having to have them installed by an electrician. Twelve volt cables may be very safe but if they are cut or dug up by the gardener they still cause inconvenience.

Area lighting

Areas like patios, terraces, decks and other outdoor entertainment areas need good overall lighting, so do

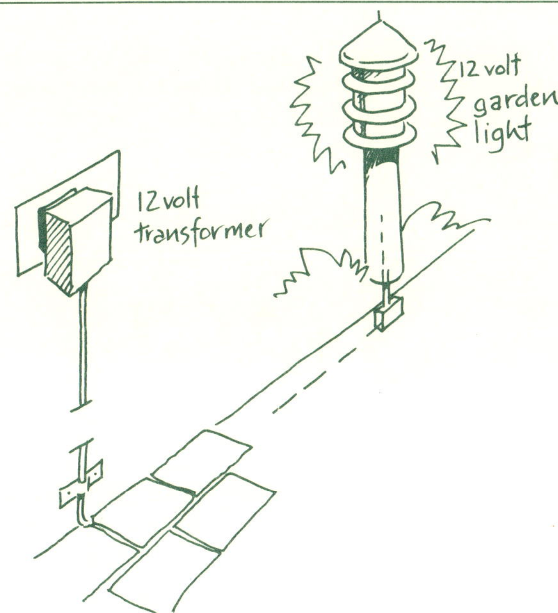

tennis courts, but they are not talked of here because in most locations it is necessary to obey strict municipal conditions if they are installed.

There are two general ways to light outdoor spaces; they can be lit from overhead or from low down sources near the ground. In most places a combination of the two sources will give a well-balanced approach. Always locate light fittings to get the most value from the light source and to avoid light dazzling anyone — including the neighbours.

All fittings should be approved external fittings. No fitting which is not designed to operate in all weather conditions should be used. Overhead fittings should be about 3 to 4 metres (10' or 14') above the ground. Where overhead fittings are at the perimeter of the area to be lit they should be spaced at between 2 to 4 metres (6'8" to 14') apart, keeping them close together where the most light is required and spaced out where light is only needed for convenience.

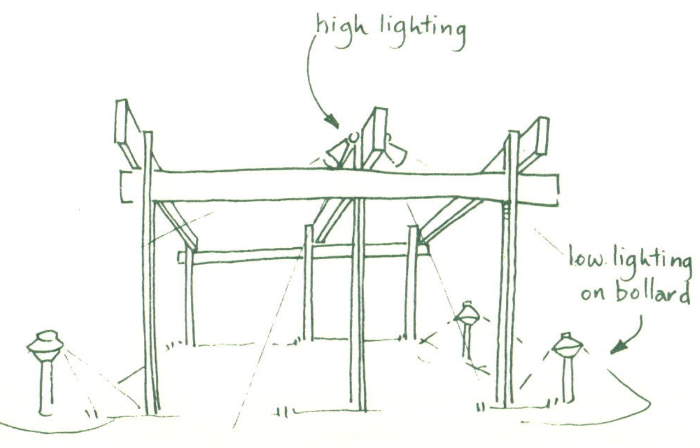

The use of low height lights also around the perimeter of the area can give a high quality of light to a terrace with minimum chance of glare; they also can be integrated into the garden and during the daytime be unobtrusive. The low height fittings can be bollard types or they can be simple box types concealed under over hanging shrubbery.

Lights can be fastened to buildings, particularly under eaves but care must be taken to avoid glare if the eave is relatively low; they can be fixed to trees which is often a good solution because the scattered horizontal light is diffused by the leaves or they can be mounted on a light pole. Light poles are convenient particularly if they are of a design that complements the garden.

Local lighting

The garden plans should be carefully considered so that lights are provided to the odd spots in the garden which need special local lighting. The entry gate and the area where guests park their cars are obvious places as is the pathway from the front gate to the house.

What about the other special places like any summerhouses, sculptures, exotic plants, the follies, the dark corner where there is always a hose to fall over when the dog has to be found at night? Many of these places will not require high levels of lighting, in fact one of the important considerations when planning a lighting system for a private garden is to make sure it does not become a Tivoli Gardens extravaganza.

The things that can be done with lighting systems is limitless, particularly when working with low voltage direct current systems which allow many gardeners to purchase components from their local electronics shops.

Spotlighting

The use of spotlighting in gardens should be limited to very special locations as the lights are more likely to be a nuisance to the neighbours than a benefit in the garden. It can be effective to spot light a special sculpture or a focal tree but the results are seldom subtle.

Back lighting

It is much more subtle to hide the general garden lighting in the trees and behind the shrubs where possible even strings of mini-lights can have a place in a well-designed garden.

Soft lighting can also be concealed behind the shrubs near a residence so that soft light can be washed over the outside walls.

Underwater lighting

Underwater lighting is a very effective way of bringing light into a garden. Pools which are lit from within give opportunities to provide soft light into corners of the garden.

Lights that shine through waterfalls and cascades can be used to create interesting grotto areas.

All underwater lighting should be of the safety low voltage type and must only be installed by, or with the assistance of, an electrician or electrical engineer.

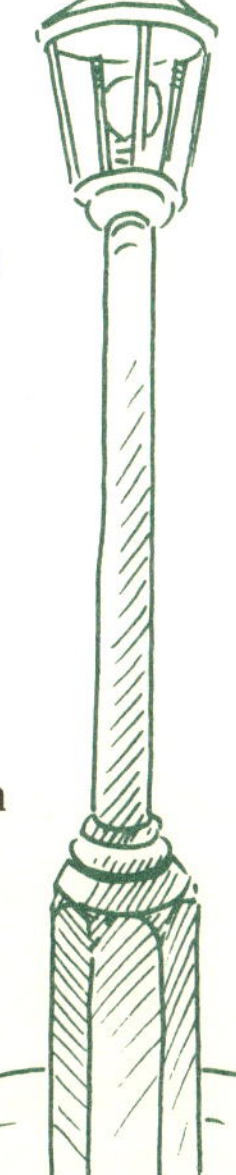

THE PLANTING STAGE

ROCKERIES

When rocks are used, often in raised mounds or on
sloping sections of a garden, as part of a planting bed,
these are called rockeries. The rocks are placed carefully
to provide an interesting display of plants. Often
succulents, small flowering perennials and prostrate
shrubs contrast well with the rugged rocks.

Rockeries can be used as a method of containing
enriched soil in gardens that have poor soil, as well as
separating different kinds of planting, one from the
other.

Selecting the rocks

The selection of rocks for a rockery must be careful as
sometimes the minerals and salts held in rocks, can
leach out into the surrounding soil. This means the
plants receive unsuitable additives.

The rocks should be of a type that does not
breakdown when exposed to the weather or change to
unacceptable colours. Many forms of sandstone are
used in rockeries from naturally occurring boulders to
quarried stone which is rumbled in a large steel drum
to give a well-worn look.

The natural sandstone boulder is favoured,
particularly if it contains iron and is covered with
interesting lichen. Natural boulders taken from the
ground surface are more likely to keep that appearance
than excavated stone which is more likely to split or
exfoliate than natural boulders. Also it may turn a dirty
mouldy colour before building up a suitable surface for
the growth of lichens and mosses.

Limestone and marble will counteract acidity in soil
because of the calcium content but some plants may
react to this and die, or fail to flourish. Some limestone
does not withstand weathering well and there are
varieties which become quite badly discoloured.

Granite boulders are successful for a rockery and
some types look very attractive, particularly when they
are wet.

Basalt and other volcanic stone boulders often have
very interesting pitted surfaces and sometimes have
glass-like inclusions.

Slate and shale can be used. Some types will
deteriorate very quickly when exposed to the weather.

Others have organic hydrocarbons within them which
may affect some plants. Hard slate is a very colourful
rockery material and if it is used carefully it can often
be laid to give the impression of exposed natural stratas.

Unless rocks are available from within the garden
being prepared they should only be obtained from
approved sources. Farmers can sell or give away rocks

which they have dug up while preparing their fields, but in many area it is illegal to remove rocks from the countryside, where they often fulfil an important ecological role.

Preparing the base

Rockeries must be well drained but some moisture must be retained in the rockery. If the rockery is built on a natural clay base lay down a layer of sand or sandy loam before any rocks are placed.

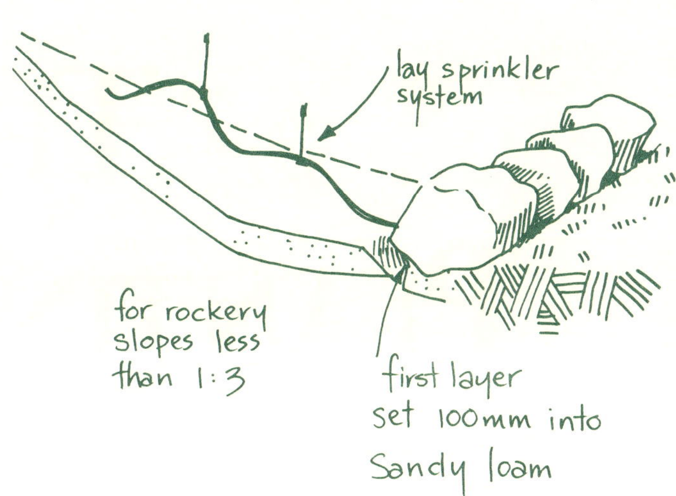

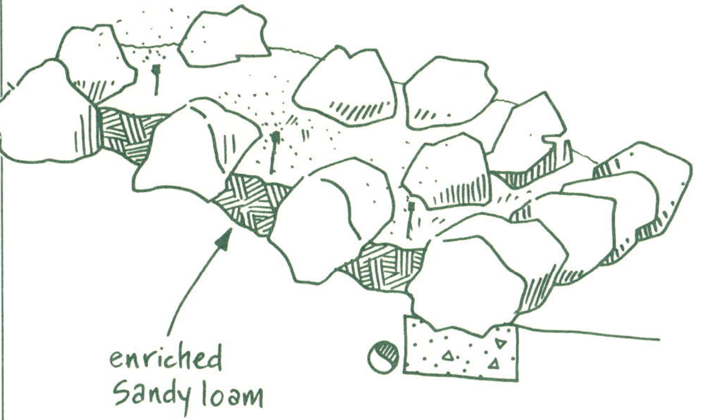

Rockeries need to be watered, but can be disturbed and made to look untidy if a normal garden hose is used. Where an underground watering system is laid out as the rockery is constructed, fine spray water can be delivered to the parts of the rockery where it is needed, without damage or overwatering in the future.

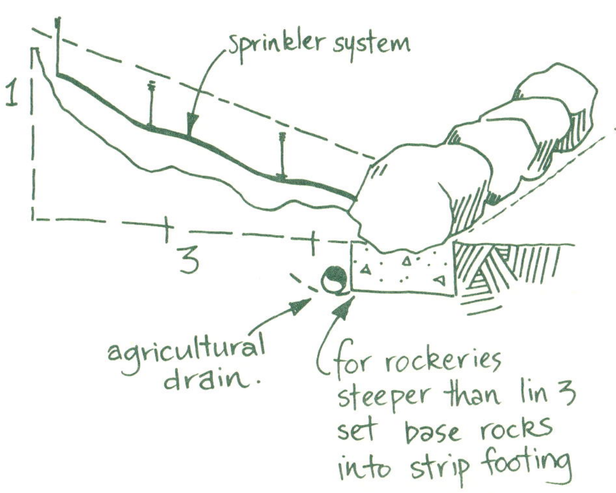

Building the pile

Starting from the lowest point of the rockery or the front of the rockery if it is on nearly flat ground the rocks should be laid. The first row of rocks should be set into the sand base by a depth of at least 100 mm (4″), more, if the available rock sizes allow. These rocks should be set close together as they will retain part of the weight of the rocks and stones above.

If the rockery planned is to be steeper than 1 in 3, that is that it is 1 metre (3′) high for every 3 metres (10′) horizontally measured, then the base row of rocks should be set in a concrete strip footing extending 300 mm (1′) into the ground and as wide as the rocks being used. An agricultural drain should be placed on the rockery side of this footing and be taken down to the same level as the bottom of the footing. This will drain away excess water and reduce the danger of footing settlement and movement.

The rockery is then constructed by progressively placing good quality-enriched sandy loam soil and rocks as required, to give the desired mix of area between rocks and soil. At least half of the volume of every rock used to build the rockery should be below the finished level of the soil in the rockery. There should be no space below the soil level in the rockery — all rocks must be fully bedded into the rocks.

The sprinkler system should be tested for leaks and spray cover before any planting is carried out. The rockery can then be planted out.

LAWNS

As lawns can be a large part of a garden the appearance and easy maintenance of them is most important. The groundwork for sowing a new lawn needs to be carried out very carefully.

The ground where the lawn is to be laid should be cleared of all vegetation, other than trees or shrubs that are wanted. Clearing vegetation to a reasonable depth is essential so that all old roots (particularly from weeds which can ruin a new lawn) are removed. After the removal of weeds a controlled spraying with an approved selective weed killer can be applied to the garden. This should be used only in compliance with the strict recommendations of the manufacturers and to the rules and regulations controlling the use of agri-chemicals in the area.

After the ground has been de-weeded than the base can be prepared. Scrape the top of the base soil to the level for the finished lawn, and always allow some fall across even a level lawn. Water will be trapped and allow the lawn to become soggy after heavy rain otherwise.

In heavy rainfall areas where lawn is being prepared and the base ground is heavy clay with very low water absorption properties, then a layer of crushed rock with agricultural drains should be considered. At most places this is unnecessary and the topsoil for the lawn can be laid directly over the prepared base.

Where the lawn will have mower strips it is better to install them at this point. They will help contain the topsoil and assist in maintaining the design level and contours.

The sandy loam

A clean guaranteed weed-free sandy loam topsoil should be laid over the whole of the area and the final contours of the lawn established. Make sure that there are no places where water can pond and that all areas of the lawn surface will be able to drain easily.

The loam can be watered and left to dry. This will reveal any spots where the loam was poorly filled as these will fall as the water dries out. Refill the lawn with extra loam where required. At this stage it is better to add more loam than to attempt to re-rake from the high spots to the low spots. If loam is raked from one point to another the process of reaching even contours will be more difficult and the surface on areas which are being consolidated are better left alone.

After loam is added, re-water the area and allow it to dry. Repeat the process until the lawn is at about the required levels and contours.

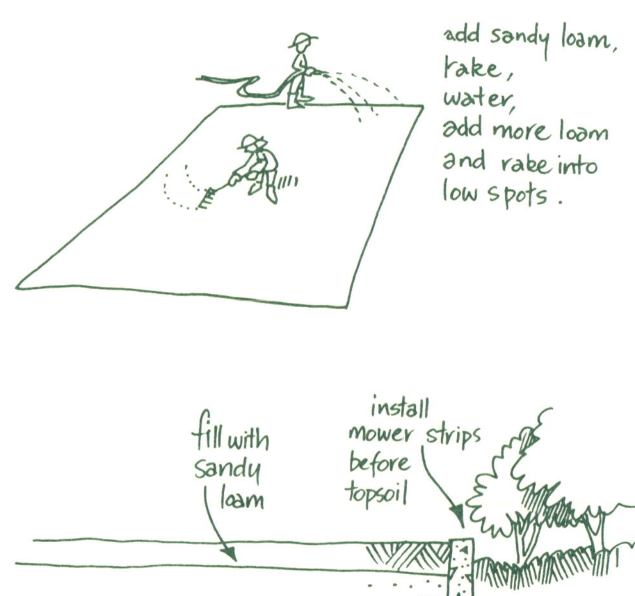

Raking and rolling

When the loam is well dried but still holds some moisture the surface can be rolled. Start from a point and roll back and forth in 50 per cent overlapping parallel passes, then roll at right angles using a similar action. Check the levels and contours when all the lawn area has been rolled in both directions.

Fill the hollows and gently rake the whole surface, then water again and allow to dry. Repeat the rolling in the reverse direction. By now the loam should be well compacted, level and contoured.

Seed or turf

If the lawn is to be planted with grass seed then rake the surface or otherwise prepare it to the recommendations of the seed supplier.

Roll the seed in, when and if recommended by the supplier, and water as instructed. Sit back and watch the lawn grow, applying extra seed to any bare areas as it grows. Water as directed.

If turf is chosen instead of seeded grass then make sure an allowance has been made to accommodate the thickness of the turf rolls. Unroll the turf on to the prepared base loam, then fill any gaps with small sections of turf, trying not to leave any gaps.

Carefully spread loam on to the top of the turf to fill small gaps and to take out localised unevenness in level, roll, and water.

Alternatives to grass

It is possible, and in some areas highly practical, to use plants other than grass to make a lawn. Some herb lawns are fragrant and will grow under trees where many lawn grasses fail from lack of sunlight.

Mowing

The choice of mower a gardener uses is personal. Some people expound the quality of reel mowers while others say a well-maintained modern rotary mower will cut lawn equally well and do the job faster.

When designing the contours and slopes of a lawn assess if a lawn-mower can cope with steep slopes. There can be problems with tight changes of level in a lawn and too sudden a concave-shaped change in level may mean that the mower has difficulty cutting the grass short enough; too convex a change in level could lead to the mower cutting through to the soil.

HEDGES

Hedges are living fences and preparation for planting must be careful. Almost any shrub and some trees will grow to form a hedge. Consult the local horticulturalist to determine the best hedge plants for the area and the site you intend for the hedge. Some will grow fast and give good early visual and security barriers. Unfortunately they may continue to grow fast and a scraggy hard-to-maintain hedge may result which could grow wildly at the top, but look dead and dirty at the bottom.

Some hedges, often the most desirable ones in appearance, like an English box, take a lifetime to reach a mature height.

An alternative to fences

Hedges are an alternative to hedges, or is it that fences are an alternative to hedges? Hedges can be grown, if the correct plants are chosen, to provide low and narrow hedges, only 600 mm (2′) or so high by 300 mm (1′) wide, or they can be planted in some species of pine to provide a living barrier over 10 (30′) metres high.

No fence could be over 6 metres (20′) high and look like it was part of a residential environment. Where as a fine-trained and clipped Cypress pine hedge of this scale can provide a wind and security barrier that no fence can match and still be a thing of beauty.

Hedges allow sections of gardens to be divided up internally more subtly than a fence. Screening the back corners of the garden with a hedge is more successful than doing it with a fence.

Setting out

The setting out of a hedge is critical. It will determine the density and quality of the hedge at maturity. If the individual plants are located too close together then they may be come entwined and force the hedge to grow too thickly. When planted too far apart, the hedge may never grow close enough, for the shape of the individual plants to merge and become a single face to the hedge.

Growth speed

Some hedge species are notoriously slow-growing and others are quite fast. Check in the local area where the hedge is to be planted for indications of local growing conditions. Never be the first to plant a new type of hedge in a neighbourhood, unless there is overwhelming evidence that it will flourish in the chosen location.

Clipping

It is important that a hedge can be trimmed to maintain the desired height and thickness. Few plants will stop growing at a certain height.

PLANTING CONTAINERS

It is not always possible or desirable to put all the plants in a garden in the ground, some are displayed better when separated into individual plant containers. Plants which need special soil mixtures or plants that have root systems troublesome in a garden bed, are more successful and controllable in a container.

Planting containers vary from small single plant urns, bowls or pots, to very large specialist containers for many plants or for a large shrub or tree. The soil in a container must be controlled. Only the water, soil, and nutrients that are in the container should be available to the plants. Plants in a normal garden bed can send explorative roots searching for better sources of nutrients or for the most reliable water source.

Where plants require moist soil, and there is any chance that manual watering being unreliable, then fitting a time clock or moisture probe controlled water supply is sensible. Many plants flourish in a container but lack of water can mean that a cherished plant will die much quicker than the same species in a bed. Obversely care must be taken not to overwater plants in containers as the water can be trapped in the bottom leading to rootrot and similar problems.

The soil mix used in containers will vary to suit the plants grown in them. Some plants will require better

A hedge may die at ground level, then progressively die-off-up the trunk. It is necessary to check the core of the hedge. If this dies it is a major task to clean out the dead heart and there is then the risk of having a hollow hedge.

draining soils than others but in most cases a soil that has a high content of rotted vegetable matter and some cohesive clay material, will hold water longer and allow the roots to take up what the plant requires before it drains out of the container.

Nutrients must be added to most containers to maintain the plant as there is little chance of these being added naturally. Take care only to add the nutrients required by the specific plant and only add processed nutrients strictly to the manufacturer's instructions. Too much nutrient will kill the plant eventually.

Containers should be large enough to contain all the roots the plant will produce. If there are too many roots for the size of the container then there is danger of the plant becoming root-bound. If a plant appears to becoming root-bound then replant the plant in a larger container or prune the plant above the soil and prune the roots below.

Most plants will survive being transferred to a larger container, if it is carried out at the correct time of the plant's growth cycle. Plants that can have their roots pruned are not as common but check with a horticulturalist on whether a specific plant can be root-pruned or not.

Remember some plants can grow to be rather large and may be too big to be transferred to a larger container without mechanical assistance.

Styles

Containers can be made or built from a wide range of materials. It is essential they are able to contain soil, support the weight of a growing plant, and be durable.

In a garden, terracotta and concrete are the most favoured materials for large pots and urn-like containers. The kiln-fired terracotta may be in its unglazed pink-orange colour, salt-glazed in browns and greens, mixed with manganese to be a dark brown, or glazed in any colour and design fashion demands.

Terracotta is a strong kiln-fired clay that has been used for centuries to manufacture plant containers from the simple plant pot to gracious Grecian and Roman-style urns. Few gardeners have the facilities to manufacture terracotta products, so it remains an off-the-shelf selection of traditional designs.

Mass production plant containers are manufactured in reinforced concrete. They range from the kitsch through the bizarre to elaborate Classical and Romantic reproductions. Some are covered in river pebbles, others are stippled and stencilled, and there are those that are of artificial stone.

Unlike terracotta which needs skilled artisans to produce it, concrete is an easy-to-work-with material that many people can use. The instant garden container businesses, making thousands of poorly designed and manufactured concrete containers has despoiled this useful product.

Gardeners should not despair as they can use concrete to make containers to suit their own garden for very little expense. Most concrete containers are made by rendering layers of weak concrete over or into a pre-made mould. Often these moulds are simply put over containers which will provide a suitable base shape.

To make fancy patterned concrete containers:

first find a container that can be copied
use fibreglass reinforced resin to make a female mould
the mould may have to be cut in sections so it can be removed and then reassembled to make a concrete container

To make a replica concrete container:

spray the inside of the mould with a material which will not adhere to concrete, this is so the new container will be able to be released from the mould when it is made

render the inside of the mould with a coating of fine render, this will be the material that is visible on the outside of the new container

while the render is still wet apply overlapping sections of chicken wire to the inside of the render and pull it into render enough for it to remain in place but not be pushed through to the mould

apply a coat of concrete render, to the inside of the container, containing crushed bluestone of about the size that would pass through a 10 mm (⅜″) sieve

allow the concrete render to set, then render the inside with a slurry of cement rich render

cover over with wet bags sheeted over this plastic and allow to cure

remove the mould after 3 to 4 days and keep damp for about another week

finish the outside in a material and colour to suit the garden environment, fill with soil and add plants

Always leave a weephole in the bottom of the container. The overall thickness of the new concrete will vary and experimentation will be needed before high quality durable pots can be made. Initially allow about 25 mm (1″) to 35 mm (1½″) of thickness and remember concrete is heavy so try not to make containers that cannot be moved, practice with a small one.

Containers can also be built in place using stone, concrete, bricks, concrete blocks, and timber sleepers or other large section durable timber sections including treated pinus.

Portable

Portable planting containers should be moved easily from place to place but many portable containers are very hard to move. When they are full of soil and have plants in them this is so but often they were not designed to be moved.

A container that is 750 mm (2′6″) in diameter and 600 mm (2′) deep contains about a quarter of a cubic metre (10 cu. ft) of soil and weighs at least 100 kg (240 lbs), even more if moist. It is not something that can be hugged and lifted by the average gardener. If the container has handles, that can allow two shafts to be used in the manner of a stretcher, then two or more people can apply their combined lifting strength.

A garden which contains many portable planters so that plants can be shifted around to suit special seasons or even at whim are well advised to design a planting container which is designed to be moved with ease. If there are smooth pathways in the garden a pallet jack, which is a hydraulic devise designed to lift and move shipping pallets, is a valuable piece of equipment.

A timber planting container can be made on a base about 900 mm (3′) x 900 mm (3′) with three parallel battens made from 75 mm (3′) square timber supporting it above the ground. On top of this base any sort of container built of timber with a plywood, metal or plastic lining can be designed to suit the garden environment. A pallet jack or a fork-lift can be then used to move the container.

The pallet jack can lift and move a maximum of about 1 000 kg (2 400 lb) (1 tonne) or a container of about 900 mm (3′) square by 600 mm (2′) deep, that is half a cubic metre (18 cu ft). A container of this size is generally the maximum that would be required in a residential garden.

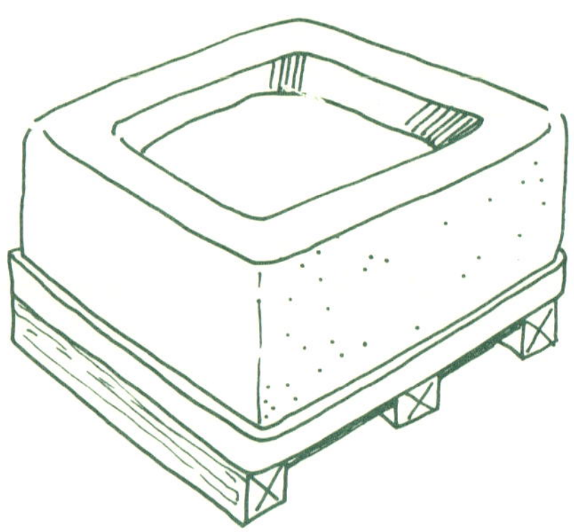

Permanent containers

Fully enclosed containers can be built from any durable material which is strong enough to contain the soil and resist the thrust of growing roots.

Stone, brick, and concrete block containers normally have to be rendered on their inside faces with a waterproof render or face with another impervious membrane. This is to reduce the loss of water from the soil into the stone, bricks or blocks and to avoid this water carrying impurities through the supporting walls of the container.

If water does seep through the walls of the container it may stain the outside of the container or leave unsightly salt or chemical crystals on it. Care should also be taken not to overfill a planting container as this will also tend to soil the exterior.

Timber railway sleepers, round logs and other suitable section durable timbers can also be used to build planting containers. If timber battens are nailed vertically to the inside face of the timber log-cabin style container and then lined internally with waterproof

plywood, a well-ventilated rot-resistant container will result.

Permanent planting containers do not need a bottom so they are able to be drained easily, this drainage should never be overlooked. The sides of a permanent container may be extended deep into the ground, to reduce the chance of roots from the plants in the container and roots of adjoining plants interfering with each other.

Planting containers can be built into fences, onto walls, suspended above the ground or wherever an imaginative gardener will design and use the many different types of containers to fill out a garden. Combine planting containers into the design of buildings in the garden, including the residence.

An interesting way to use planting containers is as a roof for smaller garden buildings, a shed with a blooming roof can be really quite stunning and the whole shed can be designed to complement the planter.

WATER FEATURES

Water is vital for any garden. Without it plants would die. Water is responsive to the environment in which if finds itself, it reflects the life of the garden.

Water is

Still	Rushing
Calm	Rippled
Quiet	Gurgling
Running	Swirling
Spraying	Bubbling
Dripping	Splashing
Falling	Cascading
Flowing	Ponding
Meandering	Dammed
Frozen	Misty

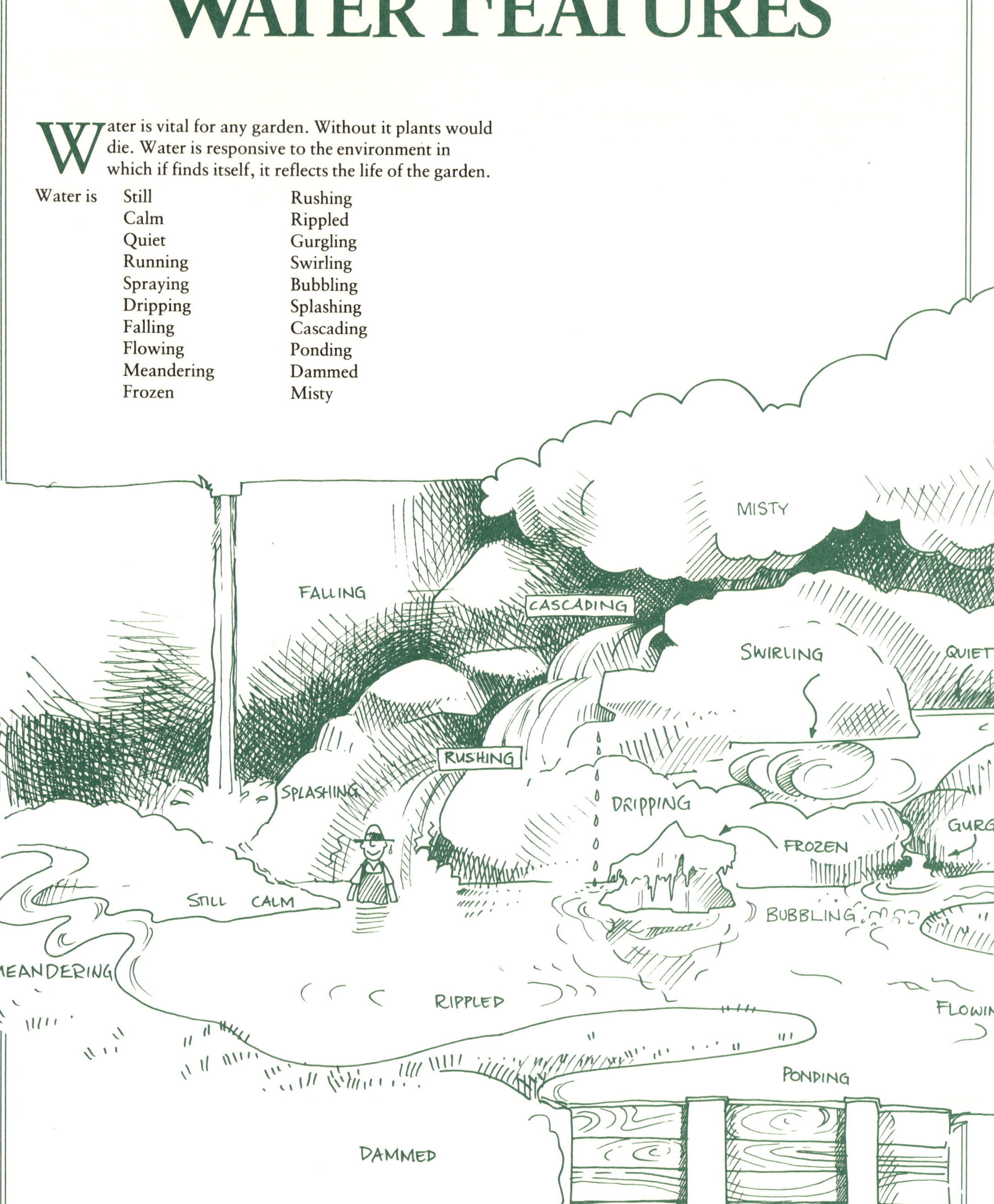

NATURAL WATERWAYS AND PONDS

Few gardens have the benefit of permanent creeks or rivers running through them. Where gardeners do have these natural watercourses to use it must be recognised that the environments will be affected upstream and downstream and that such watercourses belong to everyone.

The natural waterways are an important component of the ecological balance of the world and everyone who has a garden on the banks of a watercourse has a special responsibility.

Gardeners should check with all authorities which have jurisdiction over the watercourse that passes through their gardens before they do anything that will change any part of its course or its quality. Nothing

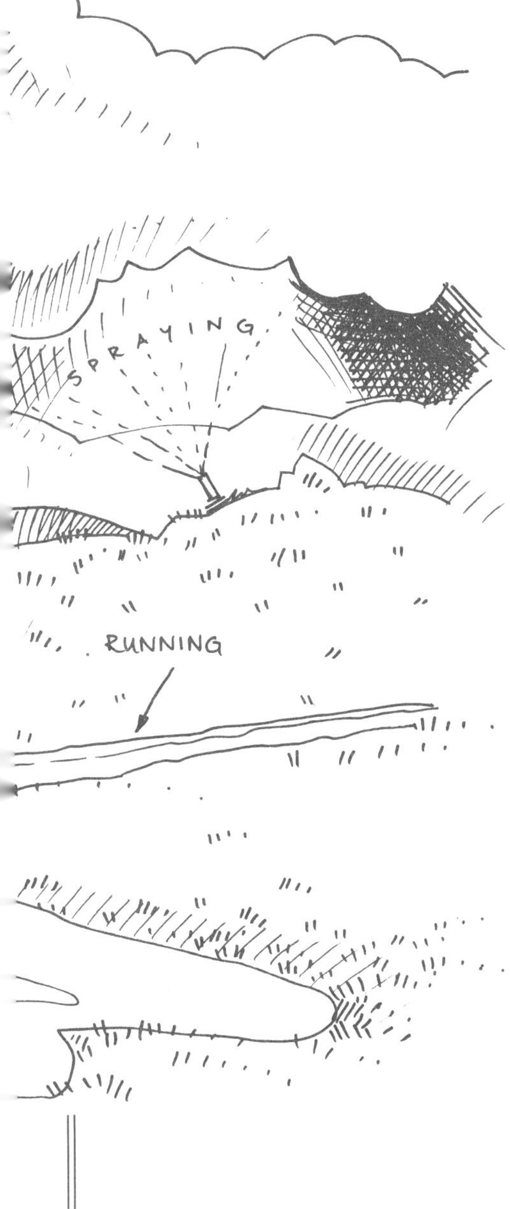

must be added to the watercourse that would degrade it or the environment in any way. It is the gardener's responsibility to make sure that no pollutants enter the watercourse. This not only means the chemical and biological pollutants that are dealt with elsewhere but also silt deposits. The simple change of the land use to that of residential garden can have major effects on a creek. A garden adjacent to a watercourse where once there was bushland or pasture will change the micro-environment in the area of the garden.

If the regulations affecting the watercourse are not strict every gardener has the responsibility to the overall environment.

Progressively as the land adjacent to a watercourse is developed for residential development and gardens there will be an increase in the speed of stormwater run-off. This means more water will find its way down the watercourse immediately after rain and the watercourse will run with higher volumes than it did previously but for shorter periods of time. Large volumes of water followed by periods of lower volume means that banks will be wetted then allowed to dry. This leads to soil erosion.

In the watercourse if the water flow is increased significantly the gardener may need to make changes to the watercourse to accommodate the increased volume. Any such changes should only be carried out with the approval of the authorities. It is recommended that any changes to a continuously flowing watercourse be designed by a civil engineer as there are many hidden complications in damming, ponding or creating a spillway.

There are a few simple rules for gardeners who tackle alterations to smaller stormwater-fed watercourses:

- Never lower the bed level of the watercourse where it leaves the property — if the level is lowered the water will be dammed up causing water to remain ponded with no drainage. This can lead to stagnant water which will breed mosquitoes and there is a danger that water flow will undermine the neighbouring property.
- Always maintain the bed levels of the watercourse to be a downward progression from where the water enters the property until it leaves the property — if an upstream level is lower than any downstream level, water will pond. If the difference is large enough the water will be dammed.
- Where ponds, pools or billabongs are formed in the re-design of the watercourse, these should be located in positions and at levels that allow the water to be drained from them, back to the watercourse by a simple gravity flow trench or pipe.
- Always form a temporary water flow around any earthworks that are being carried out, sand bags will often be suitable for this purpose. Take care to avoid any loose soil releasing into the watercourses that will be swept downstream in the next heavy rain. This adds to silting the watercourse system.

Stabilising the watercourses and banks

Where watercourses flow over a natural stone bed quite major work can be carried out to the flow pattern of the watercourses without great risk. If the levels allow, it is possible to shape rapids, cascades and even waterfalls into watercourses flowing over rock.

Watercourses bedded on rock may have banks of soft earth. These are prone to erosion, particularly if there is an increase in volume flow in the watercourse or if there is insufficient root growth in the banks.

These banks can be stabilised by growing species of trees and shrubs which will bind the soil but while these grow other types of bank stabilisation will be required as a temporary measure.

Often banks can be stabilised by covering them with large section crushed rock aggregate from the bed of the watercourse to a level on the bank above the highest calculated flow level. Take measurements over a wet season to ascertain these. The crushed rock should be, as far as practical, silt-free and of a size and mass that will not be swept away by the water flow.

Another way of stabilising banks is by using stone boulders, rubble or cut stone pitchers. These should be laid from the bed to above the maximum flow level and can be laid from the near vertical to shallow walk-down banks. In most cases stone banks will not require mortar courses but where the banks are very steep, a bed-course will often ensure a greater degree of stability.

If a cement mortar bed-course is used to bed stones for a bank stabilisation scheme to a rock watercourse bed take care that the cement mortar is only used where it is required. Cement mortar will set underwater and does not wash off so any mortar smeared on the rock bed will remain visible for a long time.

Where watercourses are flowing over clay or gravel beds stabilisation is often simpler than rock as there is often no problem in trying to accommodate the junction between two different materials.

When modifying these watercourses it is often easy to rebuild the bed and banks from natural material except where these are not stable enough, like loose sand or soluble clay, or unattractive. Imported river gravels can be used as an overlay. Crushed quartz and limestone is favoured by gardeners who want a white bed to the watercourse; river pebbles can be used for a similar effect.

In extreme conditions the bed and the banks may need to be lined with bedded stone, brick or concrete. In the construction of a fully lined watercourse it is important that the base under the new bed is well prepared. Normally this means excavating out all the silt material and replacing it with good quality crushed rock. The stone, bricks or concrete are placed on a layer of stabilised packing sand over the crushed rock base. Grade lined watercourses towards a centre-line gutter.

The banks are built to even slopes where possible and all voids between the new stonework, brickwork or concrete should be filled with a well-consolidated packing sand.

Generally lined watercourses are required when the water flow is intermittent which means when the watercourse's main function is to dispose of high volumes of stormwater. Any watercourse is potentially dangerous particularly for young children but channels carrying stormwater can become raging torrents without warning. Fencing to keep children out of the channel is desirable.

Re-routing existing watercourses

When a natural watercourse is not conveniently located in a garden consider re-routing it to achieve a better garden plan. First ensure if you have any rights over the watercourse. In some places the rights will be limited to controlled stormwater disposal, restricted irrigation rights, and a requirement to maintain the watercourse in good order within the property.

Where permission will be given to re-route a natural watercourse engage a civil engineer. This is not necessary if it is a minor modification, of a very small creek, in very simple topography, with stable geological conditions.

Occasionally a natural watercourse will not fit into the proposed garden design. Then application can be made to have the watercourse piped through the garden. This may be quite expensive but in some cases the final result is worthwhile.

When a natural watercourse is piped, it is normal for authorities to require a shallow floodway in the ground, over the line of the pipe to allow the passage of water if there is a greater-than-design-capacity flood. This floodway can be planted with lawn and some other limited species of plants but no buildings or fences can be erected in the zone.

ARTIFICIAL POOLS AND CREEKS

It is often easier to construct artificial pools and creeks than to make use of natural watercourses as upstream and downstream ecology is somewhat reduced.

Environmental considerations cannot be ignored but such constructions are easier understood and controlled.

Many of the factors discussed under natural watercourses apply when dealing with artificial watercourses and pools, but as the latter are closed systems, that is the water is mechanically re-circulated, you need to take greater care to avoid loss by absorption.

Unless the soil is bedrock or some of the very dense types of clay, most artificial creeks and pools will have to be lined with waterproof materials. A fissure in a rock in the wrong place can be a major point of leaking and so careful choice must be made of stone.

Water only flows downhill, it only rises if mechanically assisted so in a closed system waterworks there must be a pump or a series of pumps to reticulate water from the bottom of the system, back to the top.

In choosing the size of pumps check the volume of water to be moved in any given period (litres per minute), and the height that the pump has to lift the water (in metres).

Source of water

There must be a suitable water supply when pools, ponds and creeks are to be constructed in a garden. In some areas the street water supply will be sufficient but this can often be restricted (or expensive) in dry periods if large volumes of water are required to make up for evaporation and other losses. Underground water may be an alternative but it is important to have permanent water before embarking on major waterworks projects.

Choosing the route and location

The route of the waterworks is critical to the efficient working of the system. Creeks which are too steep will circulate the water too fast and there will be no gentle water flow. Creeks on the flat will have no sparkle to the water and so there will be no babbling brook.

A water system in a garden must be cool, sparkling and reflective and it should be heard. Water in creeks that are close to the natural ground level, with gently sloping banks and of a reasonable width can be seen while water in deep narrow crevasses are little better than common drains.

Creeks do not need much fall to flow, and will circulate in a system which as a fall of 1 in 100 between the inlet point and the outlet point. Remember that the top of the water flowing in a creek has a slope between the inlet and the outlet only when there is water flowing, when it stops flowing, the water has a horizontal surface. A pool at the bottom of the system must be capable of holding all the water that is needed to operate the system, except if there are intermediate dams in the creek.

Intermediate dams allow the garden designer to have slow-flowing creeks, dams, waterfalls or cascades to change the level to another creek and dam. When the dams are expanded to appear as pools and ponds and there are cascades between levels, then waterworks are visually beautiful, reflective, and sparkling noisy displays.

A header dam is required at the top of waterworks and a catchment pool is needed at the bottom of the system. There can be any number of dams, pools, ponds and changes of level in between. In a well-designed system it is unnecessary to pump water around the system constantly as the water at rest in the pools and ponds will give a satisfactory appearance.

You can have shortened systems where the water is pumped between some of the staging ponds, allowing some waterfalls or cascades to flow, without moving all the water in the system.

In locating all the parts of a closed waterworks system it is important to make allowance for disposal of extra water entering the system during periods of rain. It is sensible to design the artificial system completely independent of the normal stormwater drainage system as stormwater can introduce silt and other pollutants into the water. To do this, surface drains are necessary along any natural run-off area which could introduce water into the artificial system. These should be designed to connect into the garden drainage system.

In periods of very heavy rain, particularly where ponds with a large surface area are in the system, extra water will be introduced. It is important that the system will flow naturally to dispose of excess water into the garden drainage system. Local flooding can cause damage to garden beds and plants as well as other structures if provision is not made for excess water.

Excavating the creek and pool

Excavations for creeks and pools must be taken down to stable foundations as damage to the lining of the watercourses and dams can result from uneven foundation support. This precaution is critical when any dam wall or other structure is to be constructed.

Design the waterworks system so that the excavated soil can be used as fill in other parts of the system.

Tanking

Tanking or methods of making watercourses and pools waterproof and to achieve a leak-proof system needs a lot of thought. There are a number of ways to achieve satisfactory waterproof linings from natural earth to reinforced concrete.

The natural ground method will only work in un-fissured rock areas and in soil of workable clay that can be used to line the excavations. The use of clay lining has its limitations as there is a problem in keeping the water clean and clear; also it will dry out and crack causing leaks to occur if it is not covered with water.

In some cases clay lining can be covered with clean sand and gravels to provide a clean water environment. Remember these materials, no matter how clean they are guaranteed to be, still seem to produce clouds of very fine particles which take a period to settle to the bottom of the water system.

Reinforced plastic liners over a layer of packing sand can give very good results if installed with care. If there are any holes, these must be repaired before the watercourse or pool is filled with water. Once a plastic liner has been under water for sometime it will become covered with normal algae growth and it is very hard to find any holes. Even quite small holes can allow large volumes of water to escape and this escaping water can scour out the sand under the liner, further adding to the problem.

Many modern specially manufactured plastic liners will give many years, even decades, of trouble-free service. When installing a plastic liner, it is normal that the liner be taken up the bank to a level well above the maximum expected water level. If a trench is excavated along the line of the edge of the plastic liner, its free ends can be turned down into the trench, which is then backfilled with crushed rock.

This method of terminating the edges of the plastic liners reduces the danger of stormwater getting under the edge of the liner and damaging the sand bed. Also surface water will flow into the trench, if it is properly constructed, and not into the artificial waterworks system, thus reducing silting.

Starting just below the calculated minimum water level, the plastic liner should be covered with flat-bottomed rocks and these should extend up to a level higher than the highest calculated water level. Above the rocks single width sheets of galvanised chicken wire should be laid down, the sheets are to be turned up along their edge with the rocks. This chicken wire can be filled over with garden soil and the wire will assist in retaining and binding the soil along the banks of the watercourse or pool until planting sends down roots and takes over the binding role.

Bitumen can be used as a tanking for watercourses and ponds if applied over a well-established base. If used in conjunction with special felt sheets it can be built up in layers to provide a strong long-lasting membrane. The main problem with bitumen tanking is that if it is perforated and water gets behind it, large sections can be damaged beyond repair in a very short period of time.

Bitumen is normally a charcoal colour in its natural state, this suits some ponds, but if a lighter colour is required crushed quartz or river pebble aggregates can be applied to the top layer.

Always consult a well-established company which specialises in the use of bitumen or other proprietary membranes; read carefully the warranty that they are prepared to provide over the material, and only use the product strictly in accordance to the manufacturer's and installer's recommendations.

The longest lasting of the materials available for lining watercourses and pond is concrete. There are a number of ways in which concrete can be used and many ways that it can be finished.

Gardeners over time have used hand-mixed concrete trowelled into light (often chicken wire mesh) reinforcement to line watercourses and ponds, with variable success. If the concrete is poorly mixed, of incorrect material proportions, incompletely cured, traversed with fissures or is on an unstable base, cracking and leaking can occur.

The simple rules that apply to making a hand-mixed and trowelled concrete pond are:

• Do not tackle too large a pond, 3-metres (10′) diameter and 1-metre deep, is as large a pool as should be tackled by one person.
• Always make sure that the excavation is into a stable and dry foundation.
• Always line the excavation with at least 50 mm (2″) of packing sand.
• Always cover the packing sand with a plastic membrane. This will assist in waterproofing the pond and allow the concrete to cure more thoroughly as water from the concrete is not lost to the ground.
• Always space the reinforcing mesh away from the membrane by at least 50 mm (2″); 75 mm (3″) is preferred for larger ponds. The preferred reinforcing is weldmesh sheets carefully cut and shaped to fit the excavation. It is a good idea to have a couple of steel bars of at least 10 mm (⅜″) diameter going right around the pool within its lip. Chicken wire can be used for reinforcement but it is recommended only for small pools.
• Always mix the concrete thoroughly to a consistency that is neither too stiff nor too sloppy. It should be able to be applied to the reinforcing with no trouble to pass through it, then as it is built up, flow around the reinforcement. At the same time it should be stiff enough not to slump to the bottom of the pool when the sides are being constructed.
• Always construct a scaffolding over, and into the pool so that the person applying the concrete can work without contact with the reinforcement or the concrete.
• Always mix and apply the concrete as continuously as possible. If a part of the concrete is allowed to set before the next part is placed against it, the danger of fissures is greatly increased.
• Always make sure that the concrete has a full contact bed to the plastic membrane. Use a blunt steel rod to work it through the reinforcement and against the membrane.
• Always cover the reinforcement with at least 50 mm (2″) of concrete, this will give a 100 mm (4″) minimum thickness to the concrete. The minimum recommended cover over the mild steel reinforcing weldmesh fabric of 75 mm (3″), this is needed if rush burst-out is to be minimised.
• Always trowel-finish the surface as the work progresses as concrete can set very quickly, leaving a rough unworkable surface.
• The golden rule is never attempt to apply concrete to a pond if all of the work cannot be completed in about one 8-hour period.

The interior can be left as placed if a reasonable job has been done of trowelling the surface as the work proceeded. It can be rendered or covered with an aggregate finish. Exposed aggregate finishes can either be applied as a render allowed to set partially and then have the surface render matrix hosed off to reveal the aggregate, or the aggregate can be bonded onto the surface of the concrete with a chemical bonding agent.

Other methods of constructing concrete tanks for ponds include concrete poured into formwork or concrete sprayed into the reinforcing. Concrete using formwork may be used to pour watercourse channels but most are better constructed using precast concrete sections, moulded fibrous cement, or formed plastic channelling.

The sprayed concrete method is used extensively for constructing swimming pools and generally is the most suitable method of lining a very large pond. It is probably not economical to hire the specialised plant and equipment if the pond has less than 30 square metres (323 sq ft) of water surface.

Stabilising

The construction of watercourses, ponds and dams normally means that quite an amount of earth banking is created which is not consolidated or stabilised fully.

To avoid potentially damaging settlement and erosion these banks must be stabilised. Planting trees and shrubs in the new banks will provide roots to bind the subsoil and the surface should be covered with grass or a densely planted rockery as soon as practical.

Other methods of stabilising are dealt with elsewhere (see 'Preparation').

Reticulation

To work out the size of pumps and pipes required it is important to work out the volume of water in the system and the flow rate you intend. If the volume of all ponds and watercourses is worked out in cubic metres, to convert this to litres, divide by 1 000. (A cubic yard contains 27 cubic ft or 170 gallons.)

A pond 3 metres (10′) in diameter at the water surface, has sloping banks so that the bottom of the pond has a diameter of 2 metres (6′8″) and 0.5 metre (1′8″) deep measured vertically, has a volume of a little over 3 cubic metres or (4 cu yds) or a water capacity of 3 000 litres (600 gallons).

With two pools of the size calculated above, joined by a brook which as a cross-section of approximately 0.1 of a square metre (0.6 sq ft) and a designed flow of 10 metres per minute (33′ per min) over a distance of 10 metres (33′) the brook then contains 1 cubic metre (a little less than 3 cu ft) of water; that is 1 000 litres (200 gallons) of water flows down the brook every minute.

When the water is flowing in the brook the lower pond, which has a capacity of a little over 3 000 litres (600 gallons), can only have 2 000 litres (400 gallons) in it. If the pump is switched off, the 1 000 litres (200 gallons) in the brook will drain into it.

The pump required for this system will have to pump 1 000 litres (200 gallons) per minute to the height between the inlet in the lower pond and the outlet into the upper pond. By an adjusted weir where the higher pond supplies the brook the flow rate between the ponds is controlled by the slope of the brook and the rocks and other devices in the brook restricting the flow.

If the more complex waterworks system is required then these calculations have to be carried out for all ponds, watercourses, and pumps required. There will also be a certain amount of on-site testing and tuning of the system required before it will work flawlessly.

Fish

There are a few things that must be considered before fish are let into a water system: make sure that the water is chemically and thermally suitable for the fish and that the water is mechanically safe for the fish, that is, the fish will not be sucked into pumps or tumble down waterfalls or cascades.

Aquariums can supply water-testing kits and the chemicals needed to adjust the quality of the water. Ensure that, if there are adverse chemicals in the water, it is known where these came from, and that they will not re-occur. In concrete-lined water systems certain chemicals will continue to be leached into the water for a period of time, although these can be corrected to a certain extent. Monitor the water quality for an extended period of time for the fish's safety.

The thermal condition of the water cannot be altered easily but if fish are to be left in an outside pond over a winter period, particularly in an area where freezing can occur, a heating system may be required. The simplest way to heat pond water is with thermo-statically controlled electric immersion heaters but these are very expensive to run — the fish could be sent on a tropical holiday for the cost. A modern alternative is to use the black absorption-plate thermal collectors which, if connected through thermostats and pumps, will keep the water temperature at a level suitable for many fish.

It is important that ice on ponds does not spread right across the pond, become thick, and exert pressure onto the carefully constructed banks. To avoid this problem and to make it easier to break up the ice, if that is required, float sealed sections of flexible plastic pipe,

about 30 to 70 mm (1″ to 3″) in diameter, in the water. The sections should be part-filled with water so that they will float deep enough at the surface to be caught in the ice and not forced up onto the surface where they would be useless. An alternative to the tube is to throw a few logs of wood into the water as these will give a similar result.

The mechanical safety of the fish can be maintained if good quality mesh or perforated metal grilles are used to keep fish away from any suction inlets and any currents. In many areas cats and birds are a danger to fish that are kept in external ponds, so place a bird-proof grille over the pond in which the fish live. If a grille is impractical then at least build-in ledges under which the fish can shelter out of the searching eyes of birds. Water plants also afford some protection — the family cat that has tried to walk on waterlilies soon becomes less attracted to a fish dinner.

All fish require oxygen in the water for them to survive; it is important that the water be circulated and that it be allowed to be sprayed through the air, as in a fountain, or fall or cascade as white water.

WATERFALLS, CASCADES AND FOUNTAINS

Water in ponds, pools, creeks and brooks adds a special serenity to a garden but waterfalls, cascades and fountains add drama. Waterfalls and cascades need a significant change in levels to allow for the drop of the water and this is more easily achieved in a sloping garden than in a flat garden. Sometimes an artificial waterfall or cascade is a way of livening up a flat garden and they are easy to construct.

Few gardens are endowed with natural waterfalls and some are so endowed that the gardeners wish they were not. Natural permanent waterfalls seldom come in the scale suitable for a residential garden and in most cases it is simpler to construct a waterfall in the location and of the size which suits the garden.

The same can be said for cascades and rapids as these are generally in rocky inaccessible country far from where most people live. Cascades and rapids do not

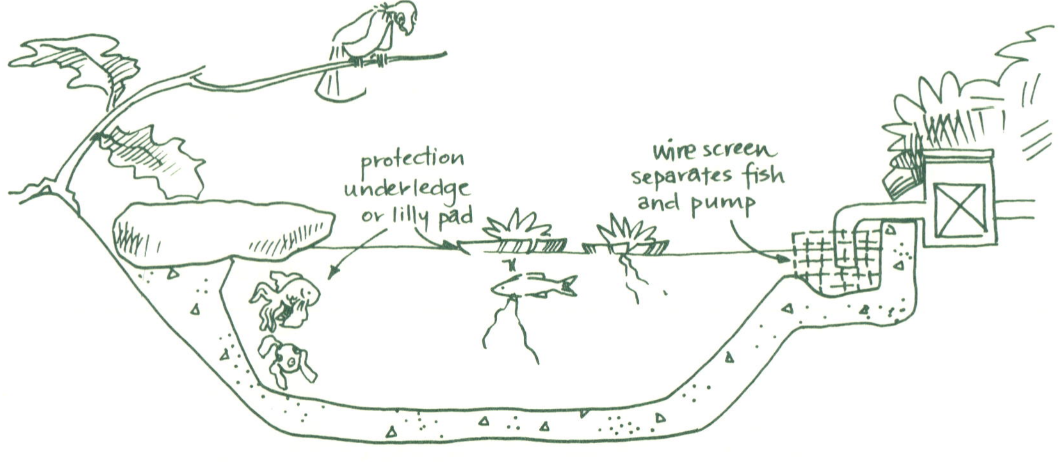

need the same fall as a waterfall but they need fall over a distance if they are to present an effective display.

Fountains can be placed anywhere where there is a supply of water and a re-circulating pump.

Calculating water volume

Waterfalls can range in size from small falls of 1 metre (3'4") or so into small ponds to falls of many metres. The water volumes vary from a few litres (less than a gallon) a minute to very large volumes indeed.

A drop of water takes about a second to fall 10 metres (32'). If the water being released from the header pond into a waterfall is 0.5-metres (1'8") wide and 50 mm (2") deep and has to fall about 3.5 metres (12'), then the fall will contain about 90 litres (20 gallons) at any instance in time. If the water takes about half a second to fall 3.5 metres (12'), then 180 litres (40 gallons) fall every second or over 10 000 litres (2 000 gallons) per minute. The pump to operate this hypothetical waterfall would have to have the power and capacity to lift 10 000 litres (2 000 gallons) of water through 3.5 metres (12') vertically every minute.

A pump of this size requires significant power and should not be installed in a garden where the cost to operate it would mean that it would be used occasionally. Install a waterfall using a pump which can run regularly without the power bill becoming prohibitive.

Cascades and rapids use much less energy and less water, and if these are well located can provide as interesting a feature as a full drop waterfall.

Fountains also vary significantly in size and water capacity. The requirements of every individual fountain has to be calculated. An important aspect of fountain water calculations is to ensure that there is an adequate water basin and that the basin is filled up automatically from a mains water supply. On a windy day a significant volume of the water in the fountain can be blown away from the catching basin. If this water is not replaced as quickly as it is lost there is a danger that there will not be sufficient water in the fountain for its requirements. If the pump runs dry damage to the bearings can occur and the pump will be destroyed.

Selecting the location

The location of waterfalls, cascades and fountains in a garden is extremely important from aesthetic and functional considerations. They can be located to be major visual foci in the garden or they can be located more subtly so that they are heard first and then discovered in a walk through the garden. Both these location types are equally valid and they can even be mixed in a garden where there is sufficient space.

If a water feature can be constructed so that it can be seen from a number of different locations in the garden then its value is increased manifold. A glimpse of a waterfall in the distance through a break in the foliage can be just as special as standing on a terrace watching a waterfall without visual restriction.

To hear water babbling over a cascade of rock in a brook that is concealed from view, adds mystery to the

garden and increases the delight when the brook is finally discovered.

To feel the mist being blown from a fountain that is out of sight over a fence is a special experience that can lift the sensations available in the garden to include all the senses. A garden that looks good is only partially complete, consider how much greater is the experience if the garden also smells fragrant, has interesting sounds, varying tactility and even has the occasional fruit that can be plucked from the branch and eaten, thereby completing a full sensory experience.

Subtlety is the most important factor when combining sensory experiences in a garden, if the view is too busy, the fragrances too strong, the noises too intrusive, the textures and water sprays too varied or disruptive and the fruit well formed but inedible, then the plot is lost.

Building the base work

In nature waterfalls, cascades, and rapids are located in rocky country where the elements have reduced the watercourses to their most fundamentally suitable location over time. This is hard to duplicate in a garden and as has been stressed here — the most important factor in constructing a waterfall, cascade or rapids system is the foundation and the base.

Water will leak from the smallest fissure and if it soaks down into the base and foundation work of the waterfall or cascade system there is a risk of uneven ground movement. This can cause more fissures to occur in the water carrying system, allowing more water to escape, further adding to the risk of the whole structure becoming unstable or even ceasing to function.

Unless a waterworks system is being constructed on and into solid base rock the whole of the foundations should be excavated to the same sound stable strata. If the stable foundation is deep in the ground then a series of reinforced concrete piers may have to be excavated and a series of beams poured to support the works.

If the ground has good bearing capacity at a level near the surface but is of a reactive clay type, then the whole area under the waterworks systems should be excavated and filled with a suitable roadbase material.

To build up the height that is required for a waterfall it is almost certain that the internal core of the high level structure should be built to form solid masonry of poured concrete. It is possible to build an earth-filled structure but usually this requires a stone-batter or crib-type retaining-wall system.

With the solid core method it is easier to construct a natural-looking garden from rocks and earth around it because the garden component only has to provide the appearance required and a bed for plants. It does not have to carry the mass of an upper pond which is required to supply the waterfall with water.

The masonry work does not have to be of high visual quality as it is not seen but it should be engineered to provide adequate support. The masonry core can incorporate a chamber for the location of pumps and other plant required to operate the system.

Consider the total system that has been designed and look for weak points in the system or parts which are under high levels of stress. If possible install an overflow drainage point near the points that have been identified. With this precaution taken any failure of the system which is accompanied by a large volume of water, can be drained away before major damage to the base system occurs.

Forming the watercourse

For waterfalls, cascades and rapids the watercourses must be carefully designed to make sure the water is contained within the system. While water can be lost by leakage through the bottom and sides of the water-courses, it can be lost through spray or water spilling from undersized watercourses.

Leakage through the bottom and sides of the watercourses can be controlled by careful construction but loss from spray and spillage requires careful design. It would be simple to make the watercourses so large that there is no danger of any water escaping from the system. However, the garden would be dominated by the earthworks and construction associated with the waterworks system.

The aim is to design a waterworks system which will contain all water without loss and with the minimum visual impact on the garden. If too much of a safety factor is allowed in a watercourse the water level is so far below the top of the banks that it can be lost in a dark shadowed crevasse. If the water level in the watercourses is raised to a level which is close to the top of the bank then the danger of overflow increases but so does the visual exposure of the water.

Constructing agricultural drainage systems along each side of all watercourses and around all ponds will allow water which overflows to be picked up and either re-introduced to the system downstream, after being filtered, or allowed to run safely to waste. If a bank of crushed rock or river pebbles is constructed over the agricultural drain there should be no puddling at the edges of the watercourses and no muddy spots in the adjacent planted areas.

Where it is impractical shallow surface spoon drains can be built into the garden as close to the watercourses as possible. An open drain system will work better where the ground is undulating and unsuitable for the construction of agricultural drains.

Control of spray, particularly at the bottom of waterfalls, along cascades and rapids, and around fountains, is a serious consideration. A significant volume of water can be lost from a system because of spray. If too much water is introduced to a garden then it will eventually become waterlogged and plants will cease to flourish.

At the base of waterfalls very careful design of the basin is necessary to catch all the water, with enough spray to add interest. Putting it where the sun's rays provide mini-rainbows increases its charm. The banks of the basin can be surrounded with rocks, sandy beaches or a combination of both, it is possible with careful design to have hardy lawns overhanging the basin.

The most important component of the design is to predict what will happen when the water passing over the falls hits any projections on the way down and what effect any wind will have.

Fountains spread their spray a significant distance from the fountain on a windy day and some spread quite a volume of spray around even on relatively calm days. The problem is easily overcome if the area around the fountain is imperviously paved and provided with grated drains to collect the water. Wet paving can be very slippery and potentially dangerous. Paving, however, will not always be acceptable aesthetically.

Paving with radiating mini-gutters and a roughened low-slip surface can be manufactured from stone, kiln-fired clay or concrete. These can provide reasonable compromises. Another method is to use special turf over a base of crushed gravel and agricultural drainage pipes. This allows the water to drain away with the minimum of slush.

A wind monitor can be connected to the pump of the fountain and if the velocity reaches a speed which will cause excessive spray the fountain can be shut down automatically. Placing a fountain in a pond or pool is another solution.

Reticulation

The reticulation system for the water in waterfalls, cascades, rapids, and fountains is not as easy to design as a simple waterworks system using header ponds with connecting watercourses to lower collecting ponds. The variable factor of water loss as a result of overflow and spray is difficult to calculate.

A small-scale waterfall into a fishpond can be designed by having water gush from a pump-fed pipe over the fall. This type of waterfall works only when the pump is operating. A smaller secondary cistern attached to the fishpond can have a top-up water supply controlled by a simple float-activated valve.

If the system is larger with combinations of water-falls, cascades, rapids, and sprays then the reticulation system is much more difficult to design. An hydraulic engineer can be employed to design the size of pipes, the piping system, the location, and size of pumps, the method of topping-up lost water, the filtration, and water-conditioning system, to satisfy any local water supply regulations.

This is not to say that gardeners cannot design and install their own water reticulation system for very large waterworks but an engineer may assist in bypassing many of the problems that gardeners may not be able to predict.

Waterworks of a major scale should be constructed early in any garden development and should be com-missioned as early as possible to allow modifications to be made to the system to tune its operation. Making a waterworks system function at high efficiency while providing an interesting sensory component of the garden is a very satisfying achievement.

Finally gardeners should always remember that the local water authorities are concerned about all matters of water use if it is connected to the supply mains. Most authorities will accept a complete break in the supply line, that is the water from the main feeds the system in a manner whereby no water can be siphoned into the main supply under any circumstances, as the end of their responsibility. Other authorities will require detailed information on any proposed waterworks system and require that approval is given for the whole design.

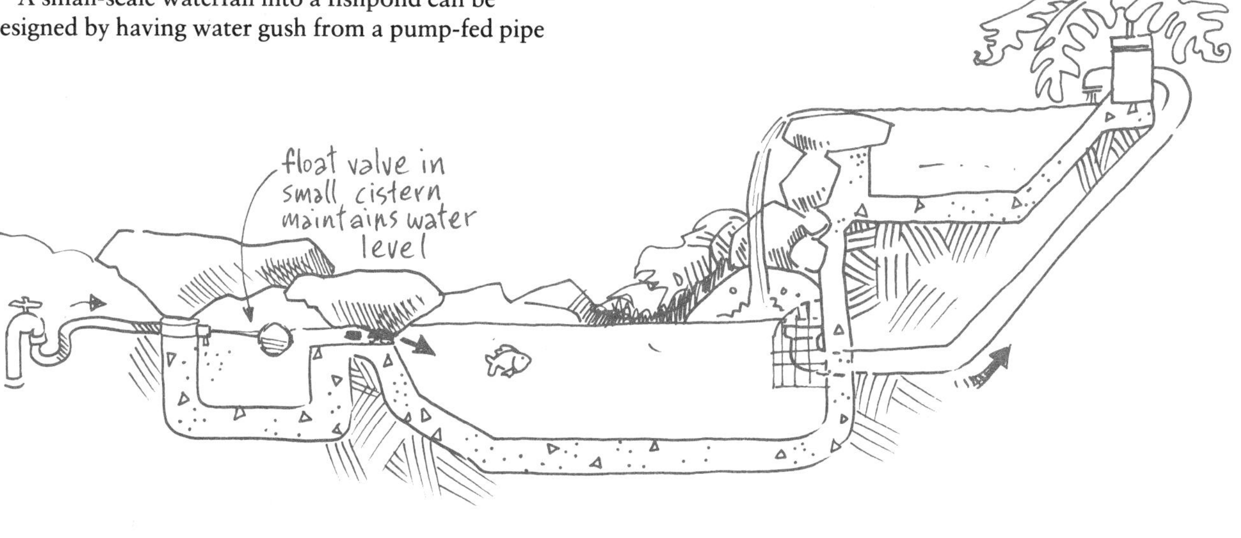

DAM WALLS

Dam walls have to resist higher pressures the deeper the water, and any dam wall, whether of earth or masonry construction, requires excavations be taken down to sound foundations. Most dam walls used in gardens are constructed with a stone core covered with gravel and formed to include a cascading spillway in the exposed face.

Selecting the site

Dam walls require stable foundations and abutments, and if they are to hold back water being supplied from a natural catchment or permanent watercourse these should be located so that they contain the volume of water required in the most acceptable location.

A dam wall across a normally dry gully that only collects local run-off during periods of rain is under less complex forces than a dam built across a permanent creek which can turn into a raging flood torrent with little or no warning.

The most important factor in locating a dam wall, after making sure the foundations and abutments are suitable, is to consider what would happen if the dam wall were to fail. Where a dam is not consistently full of water but has a varying capacity, there is always a risk that the dam or its supporting base and abutments could fail because of unseen sub-wall deterioration. Dam walls should be checked regularly and maintained to design requirements. They should not be considered as build-and-forget structures.

A dam holding back a pond of water with a surface area 6 metres (20') in diameter and averaging 1 metre (3'4") deep, contains 28 cubic metres (989 cu ft) of water with a mass of 28 tonnes (30 tons). It is wise that the route this water would take if it were released suddenly, is clear of all buildings and other critical improvements. Not only should the improvements on the immediate property which contains the dam be considered but a downstream survey should be undertaken to make sure that there is minimum risk to life and property.

Calculating the capacity

Never guess the capacity of a dam. It should always be carefully calculated. This information is required to safely design the wall but it is also required to make sure that the water area does not cover more ground than anticipated. It is not easy to stand in a gully and visually determine the extent of the pond that will be retained by a dam.

Using an accurate optical or laser level the contour representing the maximum water level of the dam should be marked out on the site. Generally it is much safer to do this on location than to try and plot a dam

on a drawing, using surveyors' contours. On many occasions the contours on a survey drawing are interpolations taken from point levels and these could be on too coarse a grid to give an accurate diagram.

Once the full volume level is plotted, work out where the water level will be if the dam is quarter, half, and three-quarters full. It is important to do this as it will show how much of the banks will be visible.

Engineering the wall

Dam walls can be constructed in many ways. The most common is to form an earth wall across the gully or watercourse to be dammed. An earth wall must be constructed from material that will not leak and will hold back the dammed water. The most common material has a high clay content but earth dams can be constructed from gravels which have been stabilised by the addition of slaked lime or cement.

However, earth walls have very shallow sides and take up a significant area on the ground so they have to be carefully designed into the garden. Where there is sufficient room and the garden is totally new this is less of a problem.

In the basin of the dam, the shallow slope of an earth wall is difficult to be made attractive when the water level is below maximum capacity. No plants can be grown underwater which still present well when exposed. It is possible to batter the inner bank with stones and river gravel which will improve the low water appearance but water in the dam needs to be treated to restrict the growth of algae, otherwise the rocks may be a slimy smelly mess when exposed.

If an earth wall is used as a buttress for a masonry wall then the shallow bank is restricted to the outside

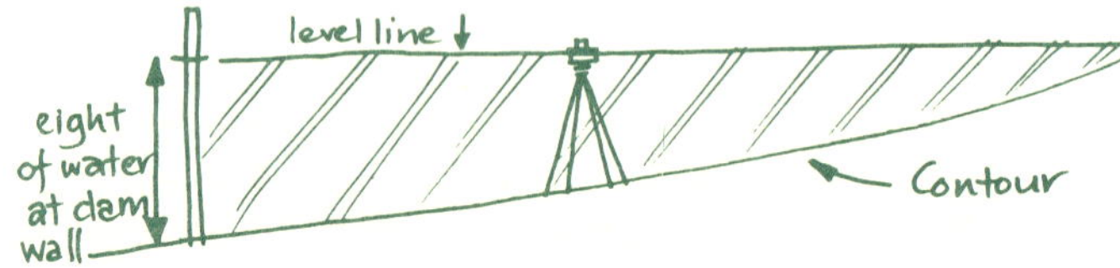

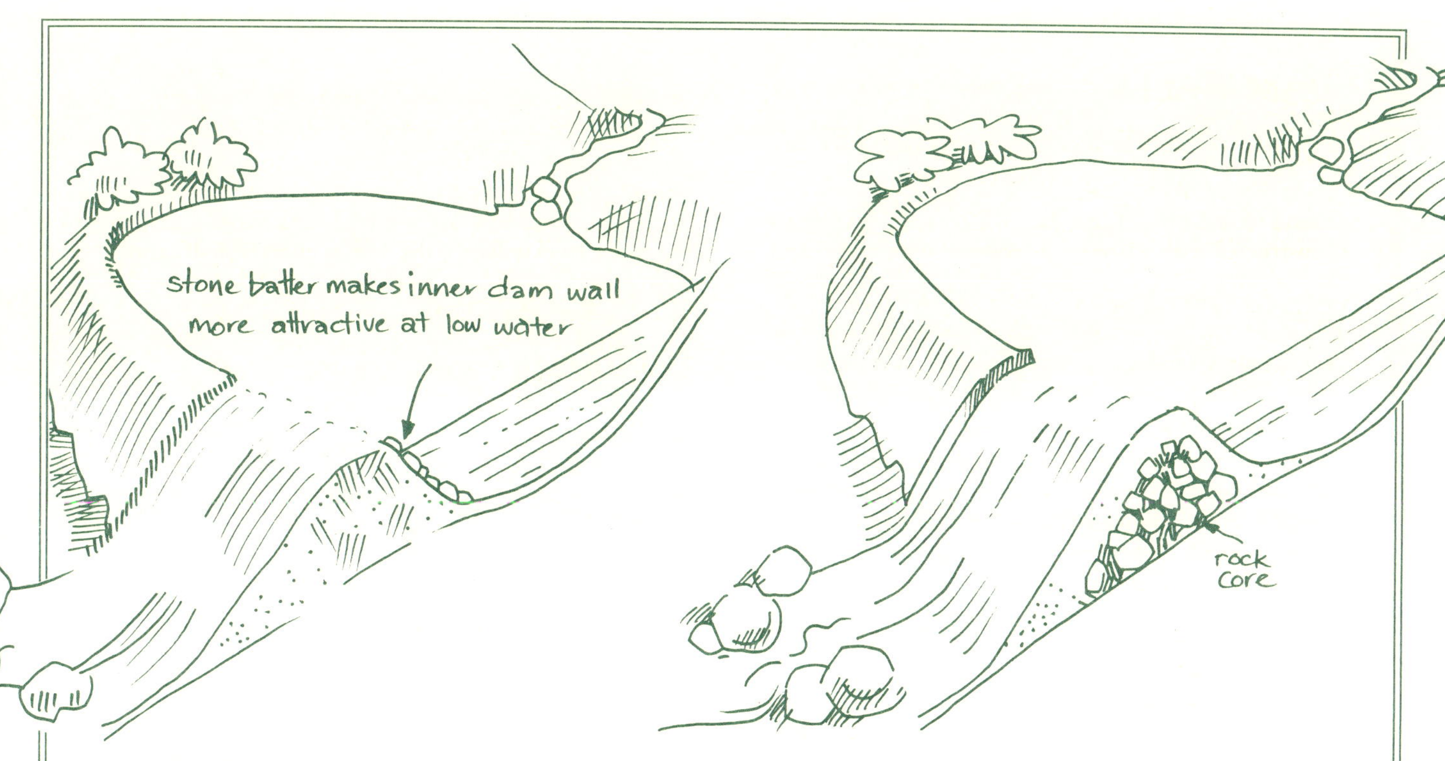

of the dam which can be developed with an interesting creek, cascade, and rapids as part of the overflow spillway. The inside of the dam wall can then be vertical or near vertical and have less visual impact.

engineer and a full geo-technical survey should be carried out.

Masonry dam walls constructed of bricks, concrete blocks or of reinforced concrete can be of three main types: gravity, vertical cantilever, or arched. In general terms a dam wall works in the same way as an earth retaining wall but with the added dimensions of containing a body of water.

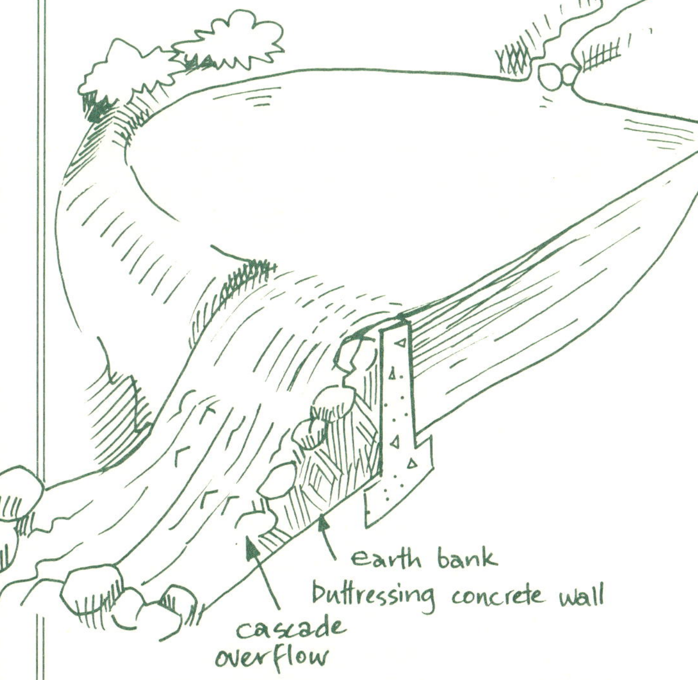

An earth wall for a small dam can be designed and built by a gardener if a conservative approach is taken to the engineering. Gardeners should not undertake to build an earth dam wall higher than 1 metre or so, or one that is supporting a pond with a surface area of over 30 square metres (330 sq ft). Even then realise the potential dangers involved if a wall fails. Larger earth wall dams should be constructed by an experienced civil

Gravity dam walls should be limited to places where there is a very sound foundation material, preferably bedrock and should be restricted to very small volumes of water. The wall should be constructed on a reinforced concrete footing and the wall should be fully bonded stone, brick, or reinforced concrete block or poured concrete.

The ratio of thickness to height of a gravity wall should be 1 to 1. At any point in the wall the thickness of the wall should be the same as the height. The wall can be stepped or sloped but the 1 to 1 ratio should be

maintained. The top of any wall should be at least
300 mm (1′) thick.

Spillways should be allowed for at least 20 per cent
of the length of the dam wall and be set down about
300 mm in a small dam. This allows a 300 mm (1′)
freeboard to the top of the dam wall.

A cantilever dam wall is constructed so that the mass
of the water being retained is utilised to hold back the
contained water. To achieve this a reinforced concrete
slab is poured on the bottom of the dam extending back
under the water for a distance about the same as the
proposed height of the dam wall.

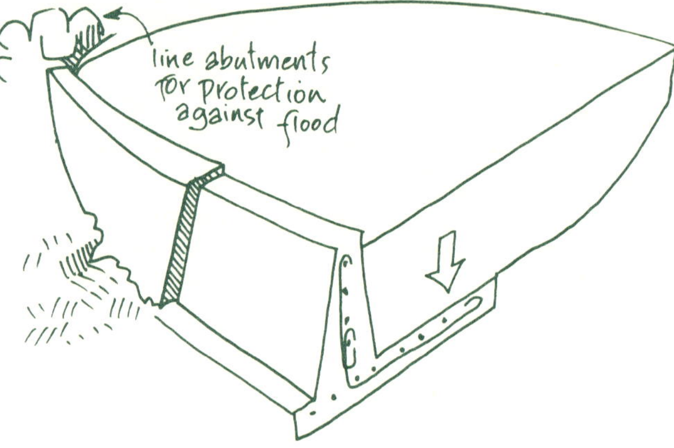

Reinforcing rods are left extending out of this slab
on the line of the proposed dam wall. The dam wall is
then constructed in reinforced concrete or reinforced
concrete blockwork. When the work is complete the
dam wall, which is fully integrated with the base, acts
as a cantilever to hold back the water. The wall can be
much thinner than an equivalent gravity wall but such
walls should be designed by a civil engineer in all
circumstances or at least constructed by a company
specialising in this type of work.

Arched dam walls can be constructed only between
two bedrock faces which are on opposite sides of the
watercourses that is to be dammed. The construction is
in effect a masonry wall which is arch-shaped in plan,
with the arch curving in towards the water.

These dams, if constructed with care, have very good
strength to mass ratios as the water pressure acting on
them is a component of their strength. Small arched
walls up to 2 metres (6′8″) long and 1 metre (3′4″) or
so high damming a small water pond can be designed
easily and built by gardeners. The wall should be well
bonded together and all joints must be completely full
of mortar. The curve should be approximately the arc
of one-quarter of a circle and the wall thickness should
be at least equivalent to three thicknesses of brick — not
less than 350 mm (1′2″). The design should be checked
by an engineer.

Because an arched dam wall makes use of water
pressure to assist its retaining strength, this should be
checked carefully if the water level is well below its
maximum design capacity to ensure it remains sound.

It is important that the base of all dam walls are
designed so that water cannot force its way under them,
undermining the structure, and causing the wall to fail.

It is possible to build small dam walls from timber,
rubble and clay but these tend to be unpredictable
structures with a short life and are not recommended.
It is better to build a fake beaver dam in front of a
masonry wall if this feature is part of the design of a
conifer garden.

Spillway design

Dam walls must incorporate a place where water above
maximum capacity can be released. This water is often
used to dramatic effect as a waterfall, cascade, or
rapids. If the dam is fed from a pumped source then the
maximum flow that can occur over the slipway can be
calculated to within a few litres. However, if the dam
is fed from a natural source it will be more difficult to
predict the maximum flood condition.

Pump-fed dams need only to have spillways of the
size and position that is required to operate the downstream water display. These spillways are normally a set

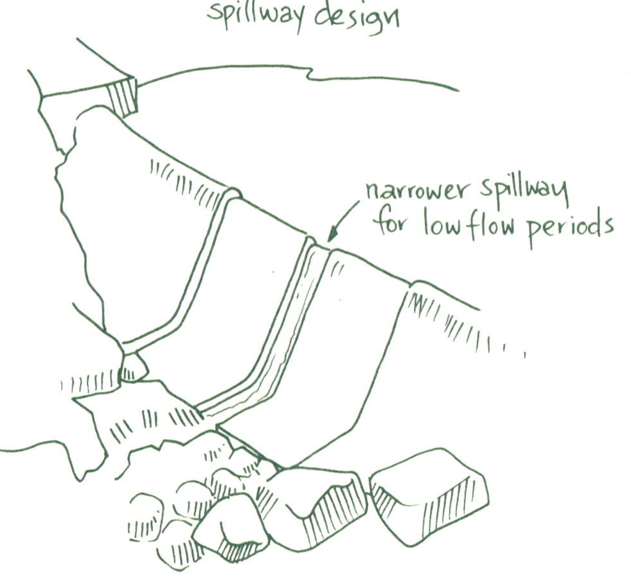

down in the dam wall often with a simple gate to tune the water flow.

Dams across natural watercourses must be designed to accommodate the normal water flow and extreme flood flows. If the normal spillway is constructed with a set down from the top of the wall of, for example 500 mm (1′8″) and a series of other spillways are set at 400 mm (1′4″), 300 mm (1′) and 200 mm (8″) down from the top of the dam wall, they would begin to flow in turn, giving a gauge of the flow of water entering the dam.

Flood protection and safety

Check that the water flowing over the spillways can be collected and routed safely downstream without causing damage. Remember in a full flood condition that it is possible for water to be cascading over the full length of the dam wall. Anti-erosion measures should be taken at either end of the dam wall at the abutments to avoid scouring of the ground and the possible reduction in structural sufficiency.

Mechanical floodgates can be incorporated into a dam wall but these need to be opened manually and should be avoided if a suitable passive flood-control system can be used. Careful consideration should be given before a watercourse is dammed. A creek with a history of flooding may be unsuitable for damming in a residential garden.

A flood alarm can be fitted to the dam wall to alert the residents if the water flow exceeds what is considered normal.

BRIDGES

One of the side benefits from having a watercourse in a garden is that bridges can be used. Images of the bridge on Willow Pattern china conjure up a feeling of serenity.

Bridges are structures that can provide both function and beauty, and can introduce an agelessness into the garden. A rustic timber bridge or a humped-back arched stone bridge are free from the rigours of time casting and assisting in the garden-scape to provide spatial links to another part of the garden which are much like crossing a time threshold.

Although bridges are commonly thought of as a way of crossing a watercourse they are also useful for crossing a gully or for levelling out a pedestrian walk-way through an undulating part of a garden.

Selecting the site

The first thing to consider when selecting a location for a bridge is that there must be a need to cross a watercourse or a gully. Usually bridges are placed where they are needed. If a pathway link is needed between two places that are separated by a depression in the ground that cannot sensibly be walked through or around, then a bridge is needed.

Once it is agreed that a bridge is needed work out the best location to bridge the obstacle. A number of basic

aspects can be considered: where is the narrowest point between the banks; where is the bank at the same level on either side; where is it possible to bring the paths to on either side; where are there suitable abutments for a bridge; and where will the bridge look best in the garden environment?

The shorter a bridge, the cheaper the cost but where the budget allows, available bridges in a garden should not be governed by being as short as possible; this makes for an insignificant bridge.

Bridges normally span places of a smilar level, but it is not essential. It is possible to design very interesting, even whimsical bridges which spring from different levels. The bridged pathways that climb up the mountainsides in the European Alps are forced to link different levels and are very romantic.

The slope of the pathways that service the bridge should not exceed a fall of 1 in 8, if practical. It is where the land begins to fall at a slope greater than this that it is obvious that a bridge is needed. Sometimes, in a formal garden, the pathways can arrive straight at the bridge, but in most gardens serpentine paths will be more interesting.

Bridges are only as good as their abutments and these may be the two most important things to be found when considering the location for a bridge. When selecting the abutments for a bridge, isolate the spots that cannot be used, then compare the sites where there are suitable abutments on both banks. Then and only then combine this with the other available information on potential locations for a bridge.

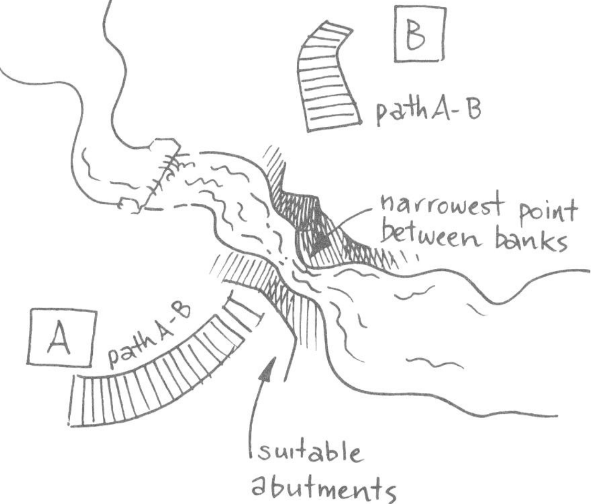

By finding the narrowest point, with the banks at the same level, with easy access pathways and sound abutments, logic says this is where to build the bridge. This may not be the case, another site may be the best location because the bridge will look better if it is built there. Compromise between the head and the heart.

Vistas from, views towards

Bridges in a garden are to be crossed although they do not have to be crossed. It is legitimate to build a bridge simply to complete a picture. There is no rule that says bridges must be functional.

Most bridges are functional and visually pleasing and do much to add dimension to a garden. What is often overlooked is that a bridge is also a viewing platform, a place to stop, to ponder and to take in the garden's beauty.

There is something very naive about leaning on the rail of a bridge and looking for fish in the water, or sitting with dangling feet in water on a bridge's edge. Bridges seem to attract the longest dragonflies and the most colourful butterflies.

Abutments

The great bridge that spans Sydney Harbour would just be another grey steel truss bridge if it did not have such impressive towers at either end. These towers do not provide structural support but give balance above the huge hinged joints at their bases. The towers rise to clearly show that the bridge is contained between the two banks at the mouth of the Parramatta River.

In a residential garden the dramatic abutments of the Sydney Harbour Bridge may not be so forcefully required but many small bridges are a let down visually for lack of suitable abutments.

The abutments support the ends of the bridge and absorb the horizontal thrust. It would be easy if all bridge abutments were solid rock but many are clay and gravel. For lightweight bridges a slab of durable timber or a concrete pad will carry the loads transferred from the bridge with minimum movement and no problems.

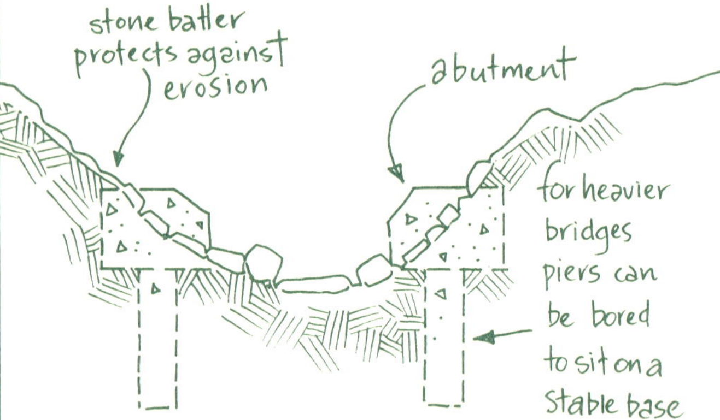

If a bridge is of heavier construction, particularly masonry, then the abutments should be taken down with piers to a more stable level outside of the influence of the watercourse. Piers bored into the ground with a truck-mounted machine can be taken down as far as necessary. Many boring rigs will take holes down over 10 metres (33′).

If there is any danger of erosion of the abutments at the banks under a bridge then consideration should be given to covering the banks with a stone batter. A batter will reduce the erosion and give a visually stronger looking abutment.

Timber bridges

Timber bridges can be a plank across a brook or a fully engineered trussed structure. The most common, however, are those constructed of beams, props, and decking.

A purist may still consider that the correct way to build the abutments for a timber beam is to drive great timber, telegraph pole size piles into the ground and to build to bridge from these footings. Piles of this type are still available and they are very efficient but are no better than concrete piers or even a simple brickwall abutment.

Bridge-building timbers must be of sound hardwood timbers to give the best results. Take into account that large sections of timbers exposed to the weather are likely to have high shrinkage factors.

An alternative to solid sections of timber is to use glue-laminated (glulam) timber beams. These have a number of advantages. Glulam beams are significantly stronger per unit of cross-sectional area than solid timber beams and they can be fabricated with permanent curves making them ideal for bridge construction.

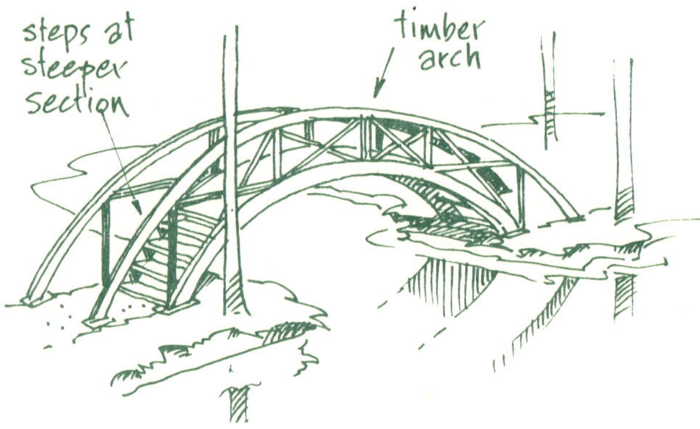

Jarrah timber from Western Australia is used extensively in the manufacture of glulam beams for local and export use. Jarrah is a very good timber for external use and when used as curved beams in bridges has few peers.

Timber bridges can span up to about 6 metres (20′) without too much trouble, but over this span consideration of bounce in the members has to be considered. Bounce can be reduced by placing props from the face of the abutment to the underside of the bridge timbers. This effectively reduces the span of the main timbers and allows for spans to extend to over 8 metres (26′). These spans assume the use of commercially available timber sections. Spans beyond 6 metres should be designed by an engineer to gain the greatest efficiency from the material.

Bridges for people seldom need to have a greater width than 1.5 metres (5′) and widths of less than 1 metre (3′4″) can be used successfully. The main spanning timbers are normally spaced from 300 (1′) to 500 mm (1′8″) apart and are then planked over with timber decking. The decking planks should never be less

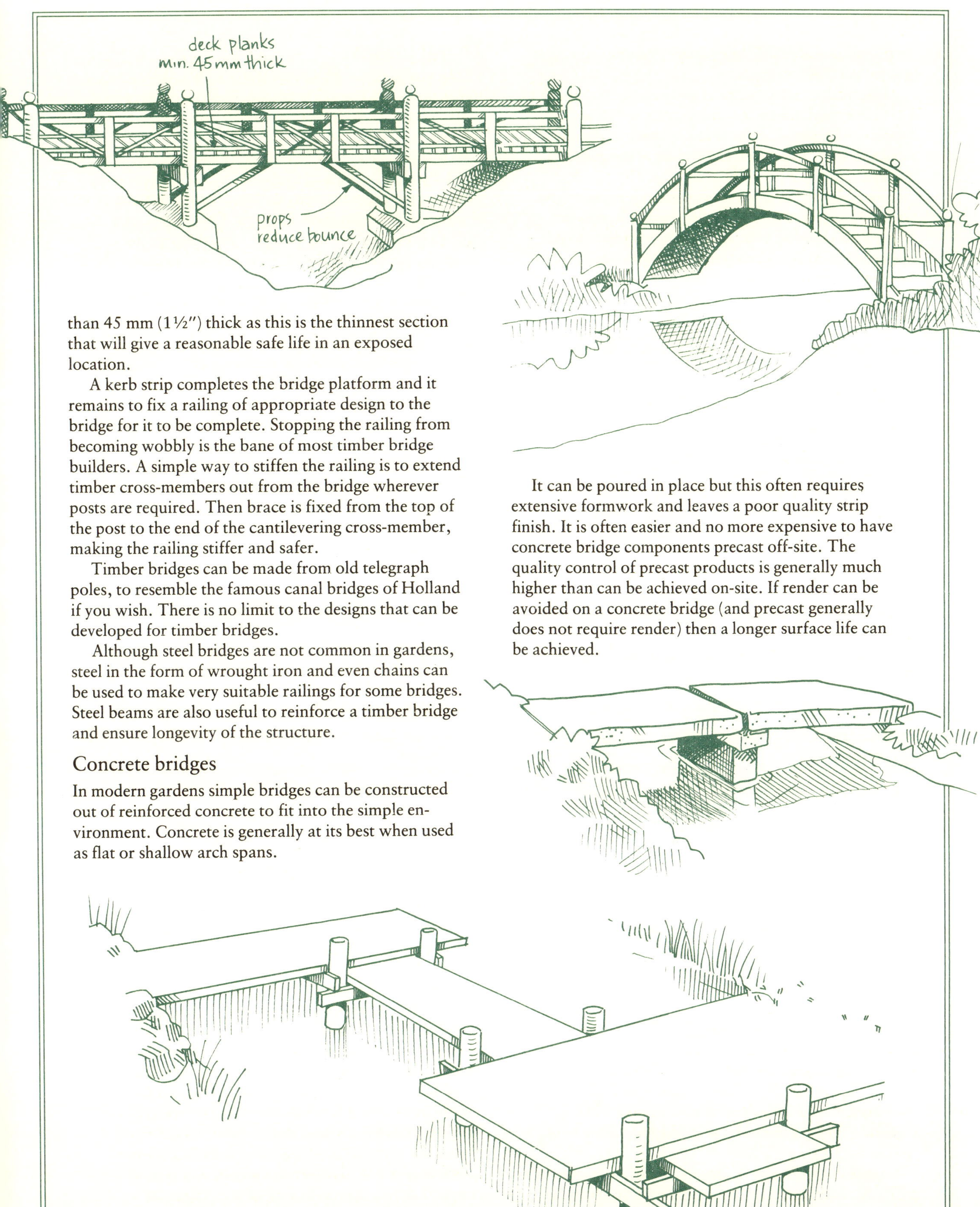

than 45 mm (1½") thick as this is the thinnest section that will give a reasonable safe life in an exposed location.

A kerb strip completes the bridge platform and it remains to fix a railing of appropriate design to the bridge for it to be complete. Stopping the railing from becoming wobbly is the bane of most timber bridge builders. A simple way to stiffen the railing is to extend timber cross-members out from the bridge wherever posts are required. Then brace is fixed from the top of the post to the end of the cantilevering cross-member, making the railing stiffer and safer.

Timber bridges can be made from old telegraph poles, to resemble the famous canal bridges of Holland if you wish. There is no limit to the designs that can be developed for timber bridges.

Although steel bridges are not common in gardens, steel in the form of wrought iron and even chains can be used to make very suitable railings for some bridges. Steel beams are also useful to reinforce a timber bridge and ensure longevity of the structure.

Concrete bridges

In modern gardens simple bridges can be constructed out of reinforced concrete to fit into the simple environment. Concrete is generally at its best when used as flat or shallow arch spans.

It can be poured in place but this often requires extensive formwork and leaves a poor quality strip finish. It is often easier and no more expensive to have concrete bridge components precast off-site. The quality control of precast products is generally much higher than can be achieved on-site. If render can be avoided on a concrete bridge (and precast generally does not require render) then a longer surface life can be achieved.

Reinforced concrete also makes a good structural core to masonry bridges.

Brick bridges

Bricks can be used in a number of ways to construct bridges but the two most useful ways in residential gardens is as abutments for bridges of all types, and as arched bridges in their own right.

A traditional brick arched bridge should make good use of abutments to make the arch span as wide as practical. As brick bridge arches are normally semicircles or quarter circles they will rise to be as much as half the width of the span out of the water.

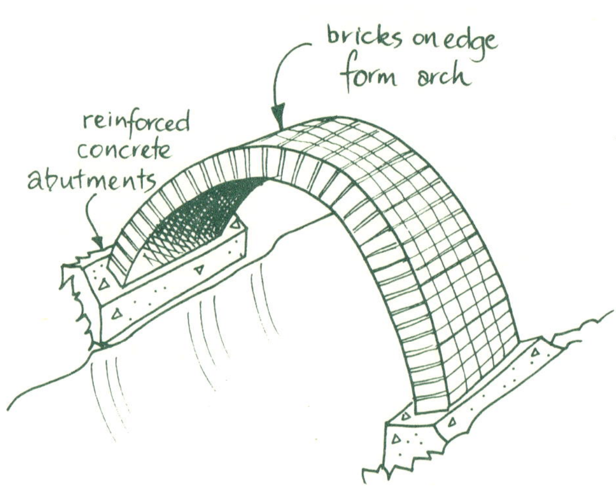

The arches should be built as vaults and with the bricks on edges, two rings are sufficient for arches up to 1 200 mm (4') span but larger spans should have three rings. The arch then has the sides of the bridge above the arch filled with brickwork to at least the height of the kerb of the pathway over the bridge.

The pathway, and therefore the line of the kerb, can be humped. It is important if the bridge is to be humped the line of the kerb must be a very smooth curve.

When the sides of the bridge have been built up to the kerb with at least double brickwork then the pathway across the arch can be constructed. This can be filled with brickwork or with sand and then paved over.

The side brickwork can be extended higher than the kerb but care should be taken on small arched bridges that there is not too much exposed brickwork as a proportion of the bridge. A nice touch is to use stone flags as coping on the kerb.

An alternative to constructing a whole vault to support the bridge is to build the arches and the sides of the bridge including the kerbs as a facing to a reinforced concrete bridge. Although not as pure a method as the traditional one, this leads to significant cost-saving in most cases. Make sure the brick sides are well tied onto the reinforced concrete structure.

Stone bridges

Stone bridges have much the same requirements as brick bridges. Stone can be used as abutments to bridges of another material, or as the primary material in an arched bridge.

Stone abutments complement timber and arched brick bridges very well and provide suitable bases onto which lamps can be mounted. Abutments can be built with vertical or sloping sides. Often they can look stronger if they have a slope of 5° to 10° off the vertical.

Rubble, strata stone, squared rubble, rusticated stone, and ashlar can be used in the construction of stone abutments, or they can be used in combination. The stone used to build abutments is sandstone, granite or basalt because these are long-lasting and have high strength.

To build a true stone arched bridge is a very expensive project as every stone has to be cut and trimmed individually. The result is exemplary but not worth the expense in most gardens.

If a concrete bridge is built, it can be faced with a veneer stone to give the appearance of a solid stone bridge for a fraction of the cost of the stone. Facings can be of sandstone, granite, limestone, and even marble, sawn or split.

When designing the stone facings to go onto a reinforced concrete bridge there must be solid concrete behind the areas that the stone veneer is to be fixed. The facing veneers should be planned so that the finished effect is of stone construction not just a jumble of stone pieces.

The stones forming the arch should be cut to the same shape as real arch stones and there should be neat full-width stones to form the coping.

A stone bridge can look more interesting if the ends of the bridge are opened out to sweep the users on with style and elegance.

Covered bridges

Covered bridges are most popular in locations where timber bridges are used in snow areas, to stop the snow blocking the bridge. Also the risk of the bridge collapsing under the weight of the snow is reduced.

Bridges with roofs can be used as picturesque rustic elements in a garden and provide an interesting place to shelter on a rainy day particularly if the creek below the bridge is in full swirl.

Alternatively Classical or Romantic structures can be built on bridges which can provide a special vantage point from which to take in special waterworks or to rest on a stroll around an adjacent artificial lake. The combination bridge and folly was a feature of many Victorian gardens and adds an interesting dimension.

LAKES

Lakes need space. There is no absolute size which separates a lake from a pond. Small boats should be able to use it, even if the boat is a simple small flat-bottomed punt then the pond can be called a lake.

A surface area of 200 square metres (2 200 sq ft) would be about the minimum size that could expect to be considered a lake. The banks would have to be landscaped thoroughly to support the environment associated with lakes.

On a property under 2 000 square metres (22 000 sq ft) in area it would be difficult to have a lake with

any sort of supporting environment, and a residence. In some places using cluster title or community title legislation, developers are able to provide a lake to be shared among a number of householders. In those cases the individual has little or no input into the planning of the lake and the garden environment that surrounds it.

The modern community title systems which are becoming enacted in many places allow landowners to come together and subdivide their properties into private and common areas. People who live in especially beautiful areas, and even not so beautiful areas, can band together to create lakes and other grand garden schemes. There should be a future in sharing the scarce land resources between families to the benefit of more people.

Again it must be mentioned that in most locations lakes will be subject to rules, regulations, and approval procedures. The most important consideration for people who own gardens with lakes is how to exclude uninvited people. Owners are responsible for the safety of all people who are on private property, trespassers or not. In the event of a mishap legal action can be taken for compensation or damages.

Views

Lakes are always horizontal, water will not stay on a slope, so they have a significant levelling effect on a garden. Water seems to attract the human eye more than the most beautiful plants. People walking by lakes inevitably look at the water, rather than the immediate garden-scape.

Views across lakes are critical. The planting and improvements on the rim of a lake give value to a lake. Few lakes have unique value in their own right. Some do, but water is water, interest is added by what can be seen across a lake or in a lake.

Islands and jetties add interest to a lake, particularly an island with an interesting summerhouse and a small jetty to tie up a rowing boat. Isolation within the garden within the city, no one can be disturbed when they are surrounded by water.

More adventurous gardeners may put a shipwreck in their lake. This will work only if there is a small chance that the observer can be made to believe that a ship could get there in the first place.

The path that surrounds a lake should be planned carefully for maximum effect and for continually changing views. It does not matter if the changes of view are subtle; many people would consider this the best approach. It is important that the walk should be satisfying.

Reflection

Still water is a good reflector and wherever possible a lake should take advantage of these reflections. To achieve this, interesting stands of trees or other special features have to be located close to the water's edge. These should be where they can be observed from a high point overlooking the water in front of the place of special interest.

Skilled designers will be able to use special planting or carefully designed features or buildings to provide a staged optical illusion. Semicircular arches rising out of the water, when viewed from particular locations, will give the images of full circles.

Glare

A small problem but sometimes a very important one to consider is the amount of glare that can come off the surface of a lake. This is at its worst when buildings are very close to the water's edge, facing into the setting sun.

Glare is a problem but there are few more beautiful sights to see than the sun setting behind a grove of trees on the banks of a lake, with the reflection of the trees, and the sun shimmering on the surface of the lake.

Boats

Rowing boats, and even the Oxbridge punt will add movement, nostalgia, and romance to a lake. Boats will need a small jetty jutting out into the lake. This will double as a place to sit and contemplate. A small boat-shed will provide an interesting feature at the lake's edge.

Remember safety. People can drown in small, shallow lakes, ponds, and cascades.

Boats should be fitted with flotation systems so that they will not sink and should be self-righting, if possible. It is easy to say that people should wear life jackets when boating, even in a small lake but most people will take the risk and go boating without a life jacket. Fit an alarm to the boat in a position where it can be operated easily even if the boat has capsized.

Children should always wear life jackets.

Swimming

Unless the lake is specifically designed as a swimming pool, swimming should be discouraged as the bottom of a lake is likely to be uneven and unpredictable. Also, the water in most lakes will not be treated in the same way as water in a swimming pool and the risk of infections is much higher.

Maintenance

The maintenance program for any lake is major and there are many things to be considered.

All aspects of lake maintenance cannot be covered here as they are often specific to one lake but the main considerations are:

- The lake water should be clear and free of algae and weed build-up at all times
- The banks of the lake should be kept in good condition and all erosion treated promptly, even if minimal
- The surface of the water should be cleared of all leaves and other debris. If it sinks to the bottom it provides fodder for unwanted vegetation
- The water should be checked for pH levels and other chemical measurements regularly and imbalances should be corrected, if necessary
- The water should be checked for its oxygen content regularly

Fish and fowl

If the water is kept in good condition many freshwater fish can be kept in the water with some for fishing and eating, others for weed and algae control, and those which simply add colour and movement to the water.

The koi is a fish which is colourful and a suitable lake fish in many parts of the world. It has the advantage of being large enough to be seen and to resist many birds.

Always check with the government departments of fisheries and wildlife to determine which species of fish may be released into open lakes. Certain fish are banned in some locations but not in others. Take care not be a link in the chain of environmental risks.

Ducks love lakes and if there are any ducks in the vicinity of the new lake a colony will probably take up residence. Other waterbirds like geese, swans, pelicans and the smaller breeds will fly in if there is a stretch of water to land on, and a suitable supply of food.

Domesticated ducks may also be added to the lake but nature will probably provide all the fowl needed to create an interesting and varied stock.

Aquatic flora

Water plants are a natural component of lakes and reed beds and other water-tolerant plants, if controlled, will provide natural environments for fish and fowl. Choose introduced plants carefully. There are many species that will spread uncontrollably if they are uninhibited by their natural control agents. The water hyacinth is one such plant.

As it takes time to learn what are the best plants to introduce to a wetlands environment, gardeners should move slowly when introducing plants to the lake. Constant monitoring of the growth patterns is essential, as is undertaking whatever control methods are required, if a particular species begins to overgrow. Many water plants can be grown in underwater containers. This controls their proliferation and allows for specific maintenance and fertilising.

Birds will bring seeds from other places and water-weeds may turn up unexpectedly in a lake. Gardeners must be aware of such introduced weeds and be ready to deal with them as soon as these are noticed.

Minimum water flow

Lakes contain many thousands of litres of water. A mini-lake with a surface area of 200 square metres (2 200 sq ft) and an average depth of 1.5 metres (5′), contains 300 cubic metres (330 cu yds) or 300 000 litres (65 000 gallons).

If a milko delivered two litres (3⅓ pints) of milk every day it would take over 400 years to fill this lake with milk. The petrol pump that puts petrol in a car, pumps about 20 litres (4.5 gallons) a minute, therefore a pump of this capacity would take 11 days to completely circulate the water in a lake of this size.

A lake, like any body of water, needs to move and be aerated to keep the water from becoming stagnant. If the lake is fed from a stream then there may be sufficient flow to keep the water sweet. Meet with a consultant who understands the water flows and chemical content where the lake is planned, to assess the maximum volume of water it can contain.

Mechanically circulating, aerating and conditioning a lake is a major undertaking using vast amounts of energy and significant doses of chemicals from time to time, to keep the water sweet.

Bank design

Lakes in gardens may have been artifically created but they can only be considered to be lakes if they appear natural. The most important consideration in attempting to achieve a natural appearance for a lake is the design of the banks.

In nature the banks of lakes may be of rock cliffs, grassy slopes, rocky edges or sandy beaches, they can also be reeded swamps or mangrove-like. Garden lakes can draw from any or a mixture of the clues from nature. It makes sense that the banks should represent what would be found around natural lakes.

Banks of stones, sand and lawn are generally suitable for lakes in gardens as rock cliffs, swamps and mangroves normally require more severe topography and space than is available even in a very large garden.

Lakeside trees

When choosing trees to line the banks of a lake these should be of a species suited to this environment. Trees by a lake perform a number of tasks: from providing the roots that bind the banks together, to the aesthetic consideration of providing the backdrop, and often the reflections in the lake.

Always consider the position of the sun when planning the trees so that they can be displayed at their best, whether this is when they are highlighted by the morning sun or silhouetted against the sunset.

Traditionally weeping willows have graced the banks of English lakes, and the lakes of Canada always seem to be located in pine forests. These traditional images can be used in a garden lake but the use of smaller tree varieties may be more in proportion to a residential garden lake.

Consider also the use of local indigenous species. In Australia there are many eucalypts which thrive on the banks of rivers and lakes. Always discuss choices with local horticulturalists before making a selection.

SWIMMING POOLS AND BEACHES

There was a time when a private garden swimming pool was the domain of the rich and famous, only the homes on films had one. Then there was the period that every family had to have one if they lived anywhere where the summer midday temperature climbed over 20°C.

Now that initial demand for family pools has settled down, a wider range of options are being explored by those families who must have a swimming pool. Pools are being designed to fit in with the garden environment. In the past many were just stuck in the middle of the backyard where they were most obvious.

Modern pool designs enhance the garden environment and add a number of different leisure activities associated with water, to a family's lifestyle. The humble backyard pool may now include beaches, spas, waves, sprays, underwater music, and a light show as well as serve the simple function of swimming.

With the increase in the numbers of private swimming pools came an increase in the number of children who accidentally drowned in pools. In many locations this has led to rigid rules about pool safety and a general requirement that private swimming pools should be surrounded by a high, unclimbable fence, and a childproof gate.

Regulations about installing swimming pools and the safety requirements can be obtained from local government offices.

Above ground

Above ground pools sold as a kit generally consist of a steel frame, galvanised steel walls, tailored plastic liner, a portable ladder, and a pump with filter. These were sold originally in simple circular shapes to families who could not afford a full in-ground model.

These were put in backyards on beds of packing sand over one weekend by dads and their friends. The pool satisfied the children's needs to splash about in cool water on a summer's day. Ugly, often these lasted only a couple of seasons before succumbing to rust, leaks, pump failure and disinterest, not to mention a lack of weekly maintenance, which is an essential part of pool-owning.

For a while the above ground pool improved and was popular, and competed with the in-ground variety by added luxuries such as elevated timber decks, extended oval shapes, and deeper excavated diving ends. There are still a few above ground pools manufactured and if they are placed in a garden carefully they can fulfil a useful purpose without being as unsightly as when they occupied the centre of the backyard.

The danger of an above ground pool collapsing (particularly during wet stormy nights) and releasing 20 000 (4 000 gallons) or 30 000 litres (6 000 gallons) into the neighbours' gardens, has discouraged many potential buyers.

In-ground

It is logical to place a swimming pool in the ground, where it appears more natural. There is no limit to the size of an in-ground pool. A small pool has a surface area of about 20 square metres (217 sq ft) while a full-length Olympic-size pool is 50 metres (165') long and can be up to 25 metres (82') wide. The latter is larger than many residential building allotments and is extravagant for a residential swimming pool.

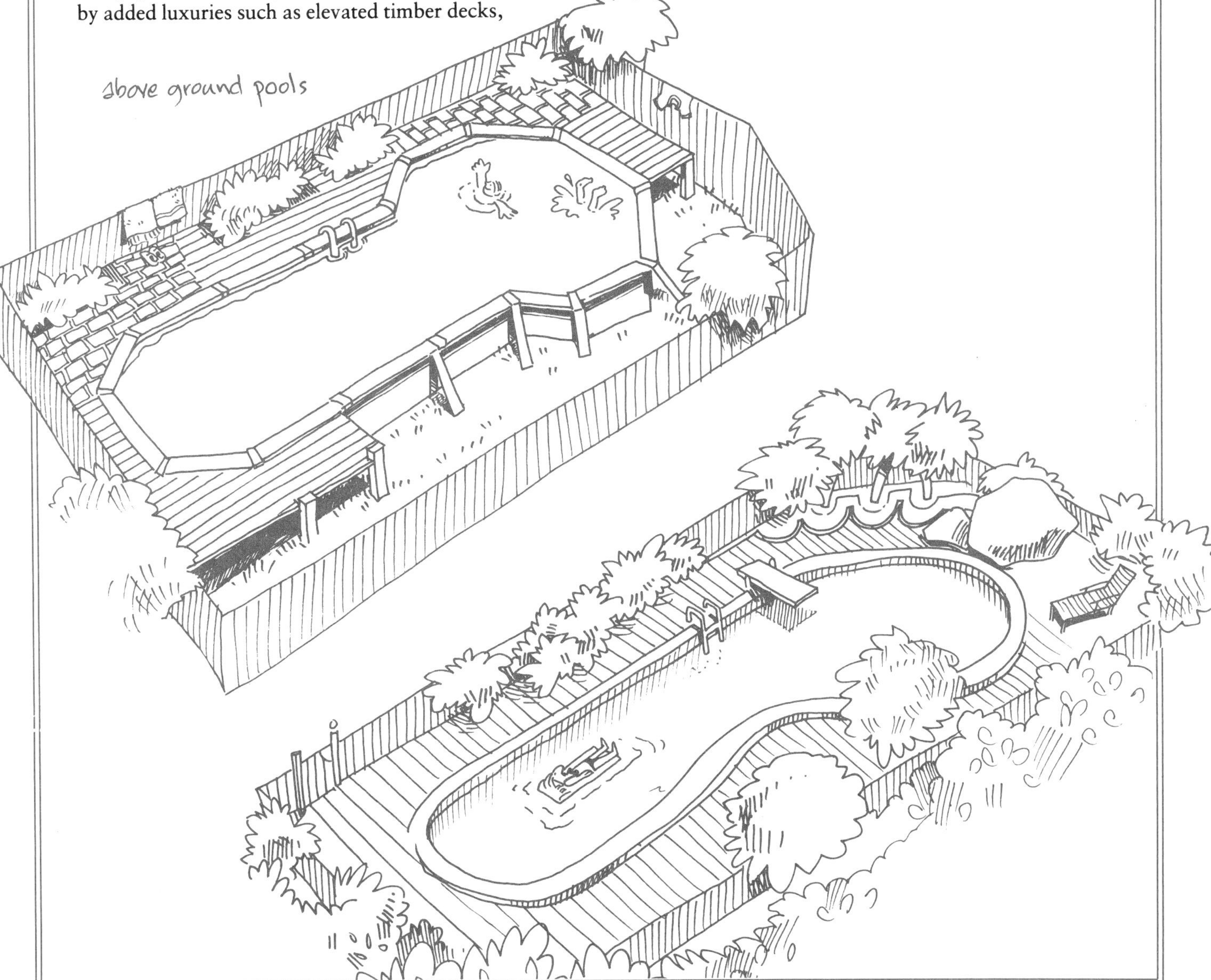

The traditional in-ground garden pool is rectangular, 10 metres (33′) long x 5 metres (16′) wide, with an average depth of about 1.5 metres (5′). If fact most garden swimming pools are around 40 to 70 square-metres (450 sq ft to 800 sq ft) in surface area with a capacity of between 50 000 to 100 000 litres (10 000 to 20 000 gallons) of water.

The shapes of in-ground pools vary from rectangular to kidney-shaped, to the free-form shapes which are becoming increasingly popular.

Most early in-ground pools were constructed of reinforced concrete, fibreglass pools followed these. The market varies from place to place but the concrete and plastic (fibreglass-reinforced plastic) pools dominate the market over the modular and membrane-line pool systems.

Reinforced concrete

Those early pools were made from reinforced concrete that was cast into timber formwork shuttering, and then backfilled on the outside, and rendered or tiled on the inside. It is still possible to build a pool by this method but it is a more expensive and is more prone to leaks than the modern sprayed-concrete technique.

That technique is where a hole the size and shape of the desired pool is excavated into the ground deeper, wider, and longer by the thickness of the concrete that is to be used. When the excavation is complete a steel reinforcing mesh and rods are placed in the bottom and around the sides of the excavation to an engineer's design and then concrete is sprayed through, around, and over the reinforcing.

The concrete is finished to a standard ready to accept a proprietary sprayed or rendered finish. The finishes range from what is little more than thick paint, to crushed quartz renders and small river stone pebbles, bonded to the surface of the concrete.

When sprayed concrete was used first for pool construction bottom to sides junction of the pool were constructed with a large radius corner to suit the technique but the plan, shapes of the pools at the surface remained standard rectangles, or in the traditional shapes seen in pools in Hollywood films.

Modern concrete pools are less formal in shape and are tailored to fit the function and fit into a particular garden environment.

It is possible to design free-form reinforced concrete swimming pools with deep diving zones, lap swimming straights, safe toddler zones, and even small islands. These can be constructed for little more cost than for a more traditional shape.

Flexible membrane

Some in-ground swimming pools can be constructed using heavy-duty reinforced plastic membrance tailored

from specially manufactured sheets or using sprayed-in-place plastic or bitumen membranes.

There are limitations to the use of these flexible membranes and rely on the pool being filled with water for the membrane to keep its form. If the pool is emptied the membrane can be pushed up by subsurface pressure. Flexible membranes are a good option in well-drained sand or gravel soils but are unpredictable in clay soils. Some of these products have not been tested over a sufficiently long period to prove their durability.

Filters and pumps

All swimming pools should be fitted with an efficient filter and re-circulating pump system. These are essential if the water is to be kept clean and well aerated. Usually water is taken into the filter system from a number of skimmer pick-up points at the surface of the pool around its perimeter. This way much of the light floating debris that lands on the surface of the pool such as leaves will be skimmed off and filtered out of the pool water. Once this debris sinks to the bottom it is difficult to remove.

A pool pump and filter should be operated daily. The duration of the filtering period will be dependent on the amount of rubbish landing on the surface of the pool, and also on the capacity of the pump.

The pump should be located so that it can be easily accessed for maintenance and service but should be in a position where any motor noise will not disturb neighbours or the residents of the garden. Remember when planning the services to allow electricity supply for the pool equipment. In many locations the approval to build a pool requires the applicants to show where they are locating the motors and how they are keeping the noise within acceptable limits. Any electrical cords used near pools should have automatic circuit breakers which cut the power within seconds of a short circuit or contact with water.

Over the years there have been many accidents caused by the suction at skimmer boxes which are parts of the filter/pump system. It is important to be careful when installing high volume pumps of many kilowatts of power, that small children cannot under any circumstance have any part of their bodies sucked into these.

Automatic crawling vacuum cleaners can be installed in the pool to collect the debris from the bottom of the pool or this task can be carried out manually.

Bacteria and algae control

Pools can be filled with fresh water or salt water. Fresh water pools are a misnomer, as the pool has to be treated with very high doses of chlorine to keep bacteria and algae growth to acceptable levels. Salt water pools use the chlorine that is contained in common salt, sodium chloride, to carry out the same task.

There is much debate over which is the best system. This will not be entered into here. However, gardeners should take care that any plants in the splash or spillover zone adjacent to a pool should be chosen for the tolerance to chlorine or salt.

Modern pool systems automatically monitor the level of chlorine or salt in the pool and add more chemical as necessary. There is always a risk that too much chemical will be added. While this is not a major problem in a salt water pool it can be of some consequence in a chlorine system. If there is a high chlorine smell at the pool then take a reading before entering the water.

Water conditioning

The water in the swimming pool should not be mixed with water from any other source until that water has been cleaned, sanitised, and conditioned. There should never be any plants growing in, or even dragging in the water, used for swimming.

The cardinal rules for swimming pool water is that it must be kept at as close to a neutral pH as possible and it should be free of all living matter, particularly bacteria and algae. To maintain a soft water condition, that is to reduce the tendency of the water to be made acid by the addition of chlorine or to be made alkaline by metal oxides, chemicals will need to be added to the water from time to time.

Never add chemicals to a swimming pool until a test is taken and then add these strictly to the instructions on the containers. It is advisable to wait until the chemicals have been thoroughly distributed through the water and the condition re-checked before allowing anyone to enter the water.

Heaters

Heating outdoor swimming pools was a very expensive option when the only available method of heating was to use a fuel or electrical heating system. This has changed since the development of more and better solar-collector and thermal-transfer systems.

An average family swimming pool can be maintained at a comfortable swimming temperature all year-round in most temperate zones of the world by the use of black pipe or black panel atmosphere to water thermal-transfer systems. Even where temperatures fall below freezing point the use of these systems, which are normally mounted on the roof of the residence, and an efficient insulated pool cover, can provide pool water at a suitable temperature for swimming.

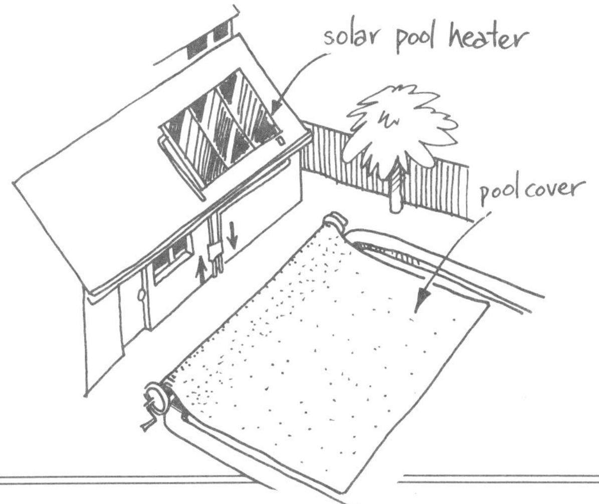

The installation is modestly expensive but a well-designed and manufactured system should give many years of free heating energy with only minor regular maintenance.

Steps and ladders

Most pools today use swim-out platforms formed into the pool or have shallow slopings edges to the pool in convenient locations to emerge from the water without having to resort to in-pool steps. Steps in a pool are a nuisance to engineer and of little value if there are efficient swim-out points provided.

Ladders remain a necessary part of the pool's components. These are needed to provide safe egress from a pool where there are steep sides, and a bottom deeper than the height of the people who will use the pool. Many materials have been used to make pool ladders but only stainless steel combines great strength with a long corrosion-free life. Some of the modern composite plastics are also very efficient but these should be checked carefully before purchase for price and proven durability.

Finishes

Tiled pool interiors have given way to more natural-looking finishes and now a modern pool in a garden can be designed with finishes and surrounds that make it appear like a naturally occurring lagoon.

Modern internal finishing coatings can be purchased in a wide range of colours which can be used singly or combined to provide a pattern to the inside of the pool.

Coping and paving

The coping of the top of the walls of a swimming pool was a very important component of the pool's appearance but as pools have become more natural in appearance the use of a coping has become less. It is now common to take the edge of a swimming pool and slope it so that a continuous skimmer gutter is installed back from the edge of the pool sides. This makes it appear as though the water merges into the surrounding paving, lawns or gardens.

The use of low-slip materials is essential for any paving adjacent to swimming pools where there is any chance that water can lie on it. In most cases water splashed out of a swimming pool should be drained away from the pool and be collected in a separate gutter and run to waste.

Beaches

With the demise of the upstanding coped edge to swimming pools have come some other changes. One of these is the use of sandy beaches as part of a private swimming pool. It is important that the sand used is as free of salts and organic matter as possible and is installed by people who understand what they are doing.

A sandy beach at the end of a lawn beside shady trees and a fragrant rockery can be an interesting environment, particularly if this is a suburban garden far from the seaside or any large waterway.

Spas, bubbles, and waves

If a wave machine is installed in a swimming pool it is possible to surface ashore onto the artificial beach on an artificially generated wave.

To add further enjoyment while swimming, air bubbles can be released into the pool at strategic locations. These provide refreshing tingles.

When the swimming is over, a spa built into a swimming pool, or constructed in another location in the garden is where people can relax in a bubbly, foamy pond.

These options and many other products can be used in conjunction with a modern garden swimming pool, but try not to get so carried away with the special effects of the pool that the surrounding garden environment is ignored.

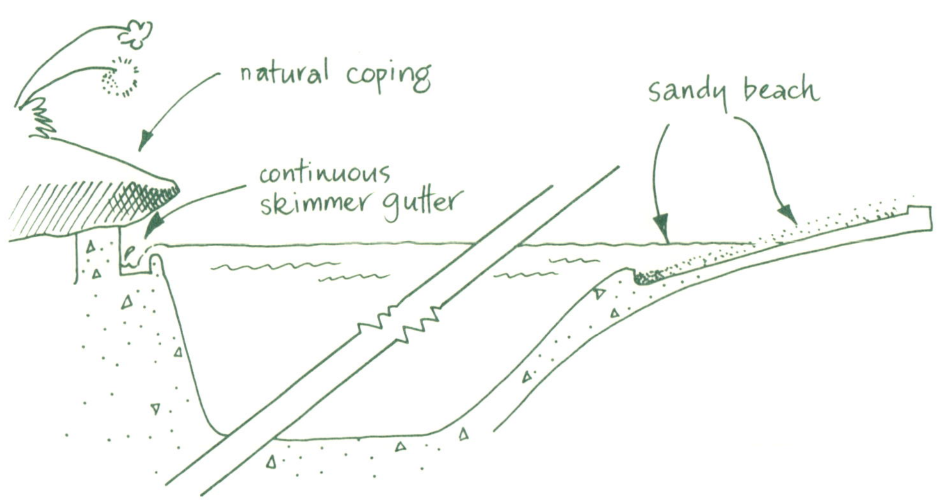

BUILT FEATURES

Gardens are incomplete until they have been used. To use a garden there need to be built features which can extend the usefulness and enjoyment of the overall plan and the plantings.

Interesting entries to a garden can be reinforced by roofed gateways; pathways can be arched by roses growing on specially designed arbours.

Pergolas provide shade for people while supporting vines which would grow only on the fences. There their natural growth is limited.

Trellises can add shape and form to courtyards within the garden. These can carry climbing plants so they can give their maximum display to the garden.

Follies are rare in modern gardens. They were lost to gardens full of native plants. Exotic and Romantic gardens are returning and the folly can again become a part of the garden.

Statues are also a part of the new garden such as abstracts, Classical marbles, and the highly contrasting Postmodern pieces.

Sundials are a great contrast to the flickering digital watches of the 1970s and the overpriced 'designer' watches of the 1980s. Such a gracious Victorian ornament as a sundial must have a place in every thinking person's garden. Time is for reflection, not for keeping.

Lych-gates and arbours

Lych-gates are a legacy of the past when the entries to the graveyards of parish churches in Europe were provided with a roofed gateway where mourners rested on the way to the graveside or had the pre-interment service during inclement weather.

Modern lych-gates are considered to be roofed gateways, associated with elegant residences in leafy garden suburbs, not as places to rest a coffin.

Some local government authorities will attempt to block the building of a lych-gate on the grounds that it is a building. This is because of an old building law which bridged health and safety and town planning. If you wish to build a lych-gate and meet with local authority opposition then appeal to the local environmental planning authority for support.

The lych-gate should have a comfortable bench, at which passers-by may rest. It can be an external display of goodwill at the entrance to a well-planned and beautiful garden.

Arbours are precisely arched trellises for the purpose of training climbing roses to form a freestanding arch over a pathway. Arbours can be a two-dimensional threshold or can be extended three-dimensional vaults of considerable visual delight and perfume.

Nowadays any shaped arch for the training of climbing plants is called an arbour, at least in the privacy of a garden.

Choosing a style

The traditional lych-gate is linked to medieval England in many people's minds. This seems a fair judgment as such gates were common at this time. Fallen from favour during the industrial revolution lych-gates were revived as part of the Arts and Crafts Movement's reaction against the grimy mill towns of the early industrial revolution — the Garden Suburb.

Traditional lych-gates are of a Tudor style and their late 20th-century revival is also loosely based on the English vernacular architecture often considered to be Tudor-inspired.

This style is manifest in a stone base, oak posts, beams and rafters with a slate roof. It is in keeping with the 'stockbroker suburbs' at the better end of town. There is no reason why Georgian, Regency, Italianate, Victorian, Edwardian, Intra-wars bungalow, Art Deco, Modern, Postmodern, and vernacular styling cannot be applied to suit the garden and residence.

In a heavily planted garden a lych-gate may be the only building that people passing by the property will see. This means that it can be used to provide an image of the style of the residence within the garden.

Arbours are effectively style-free. They are fabricated usually from steel rods and often borrow motifs from the Victorian foundry styles of the late 19th century.

Arbours and lych-gates can be brought together in the modern timber lattice gate frame. An interesting way to use the ubiquitous timber latticing that is invading suburbia, is to design a lattice gate frame that uses a style of the past, and build it as open lattice.

By doing this a very interesting gateway which projects itself as a ruin through which climbing roses, grape-vines, ivy, wisteria, or bougainvillea can grow and flower.

Integration with planting

The use of lattice is one way to integrate lych-gates into the planting. However the lych-gate can be built in a well-kept hedge, rather than a fence. Lych-gates can use the thickness of a hedge to advantage by being sited forward or backwards of the hedge.

On arbours plants must grow through them but often only the plants climbing on the arbour are considered. The arbours can be used as reference points from which to extend overplanting.

If a series of arbours are set up to form an arcade then points of interest can be linked together. It is possible to have a line of view which would frame special trees or plants in the centre of the arbour.

Samples

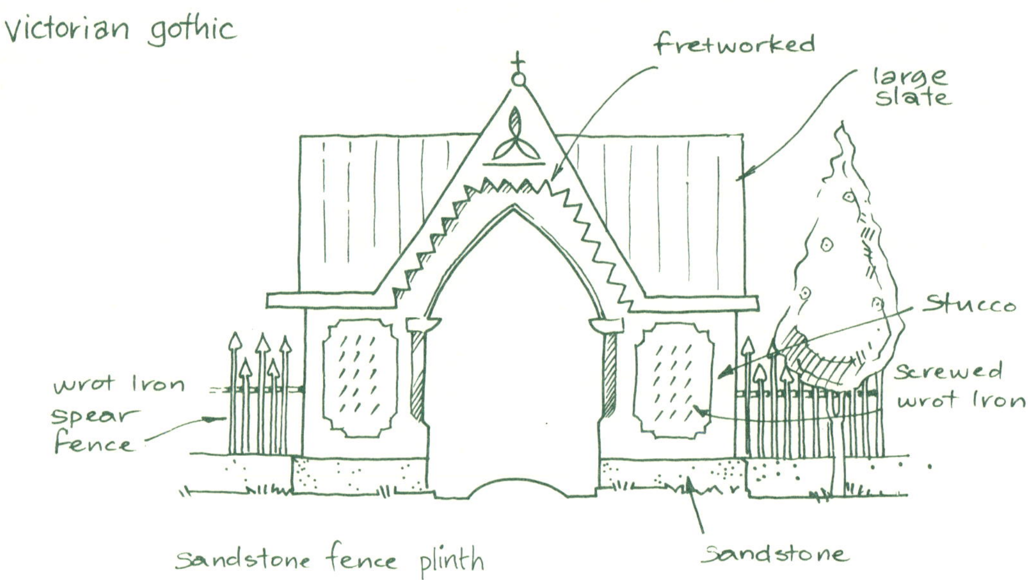

georgian
slate
tuscan Column
timber

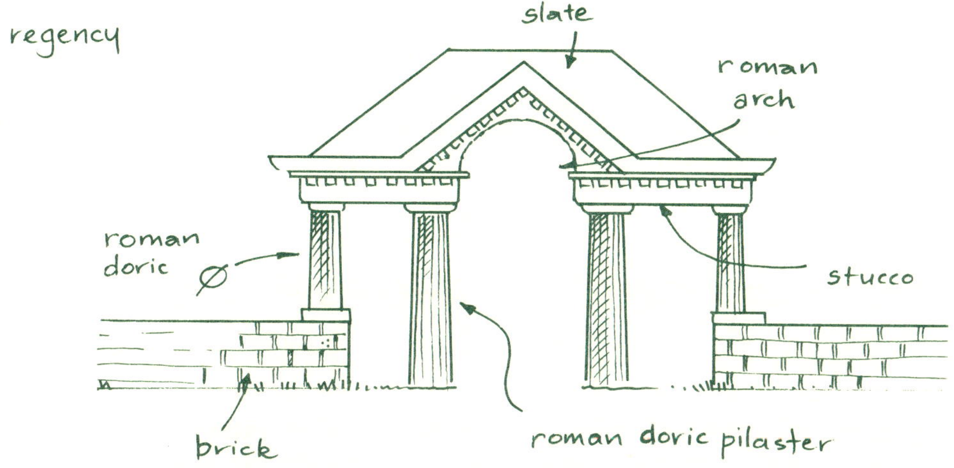

regency
slate
roman arch
roman doric
stucco
brick
roman doric pilaster

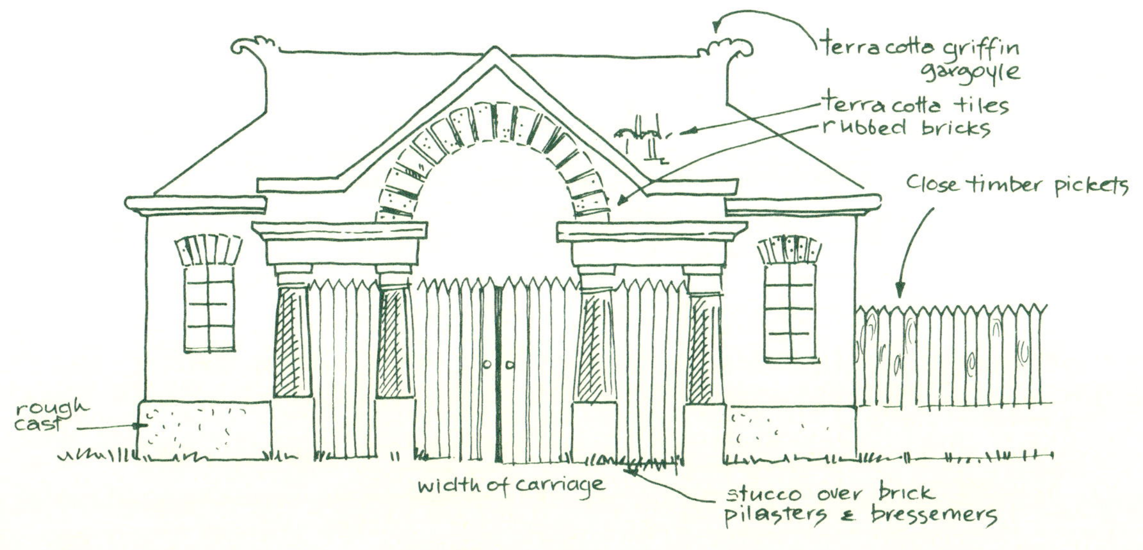

federation
terra cotta griffin gargoyle
terra cotta tiles
rubbed bricks
Close timber pickets
rough cast
width of carriage
stucco over brick pilasters & bressemers

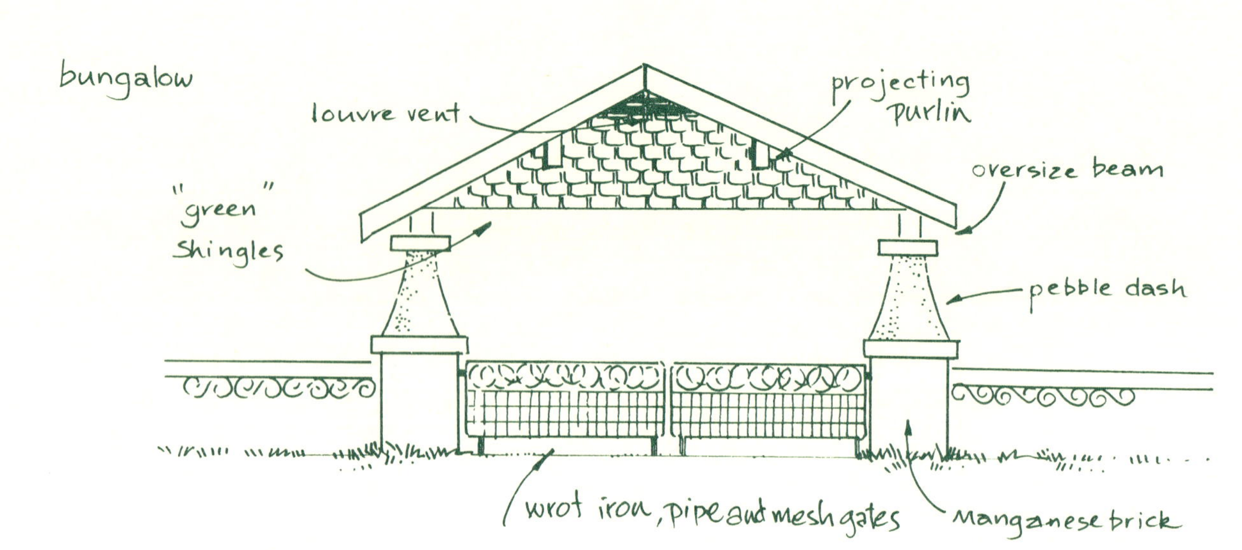

bungalow
louvre vent
projecting
purlin
oversize beam
"green" shingles
pebble dash
wrot iron, pipe and mesh gates
Manganese brick

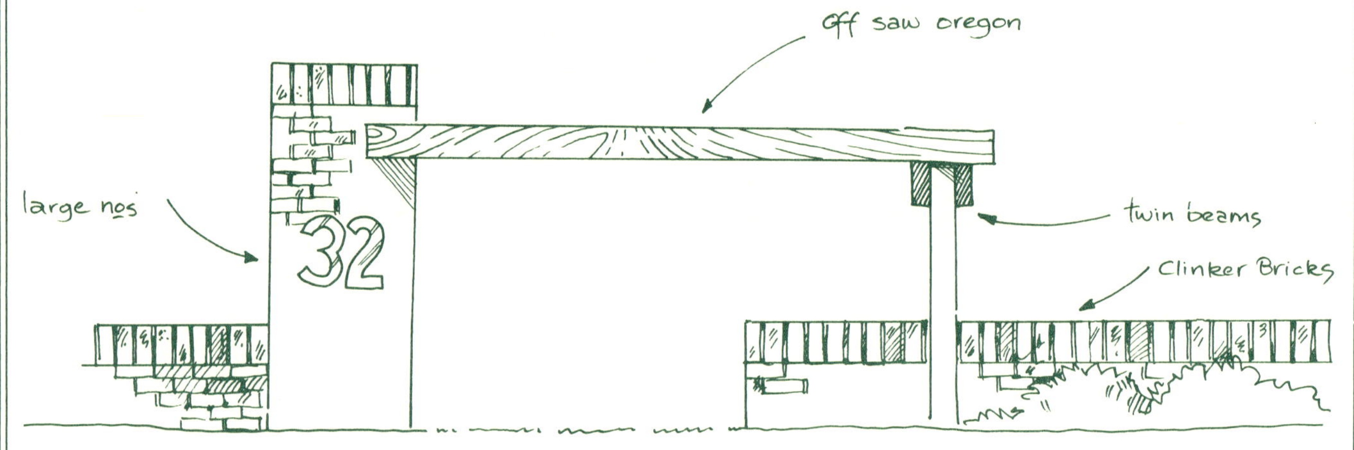

modern 1960's
off saw oregon
large nos
32
twin beams
Clinker Bricks

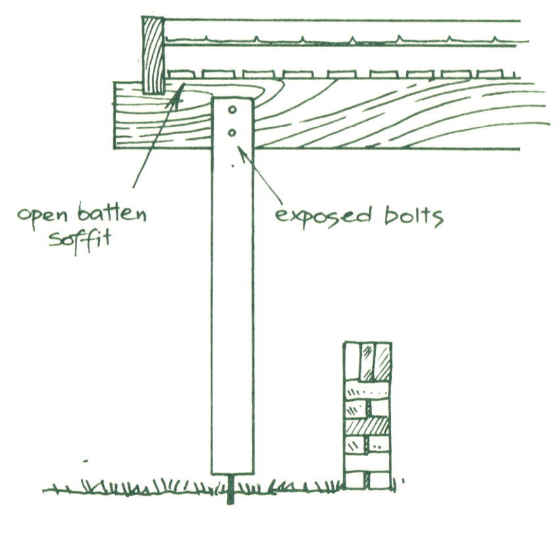

open batten soffit
exposed bolts

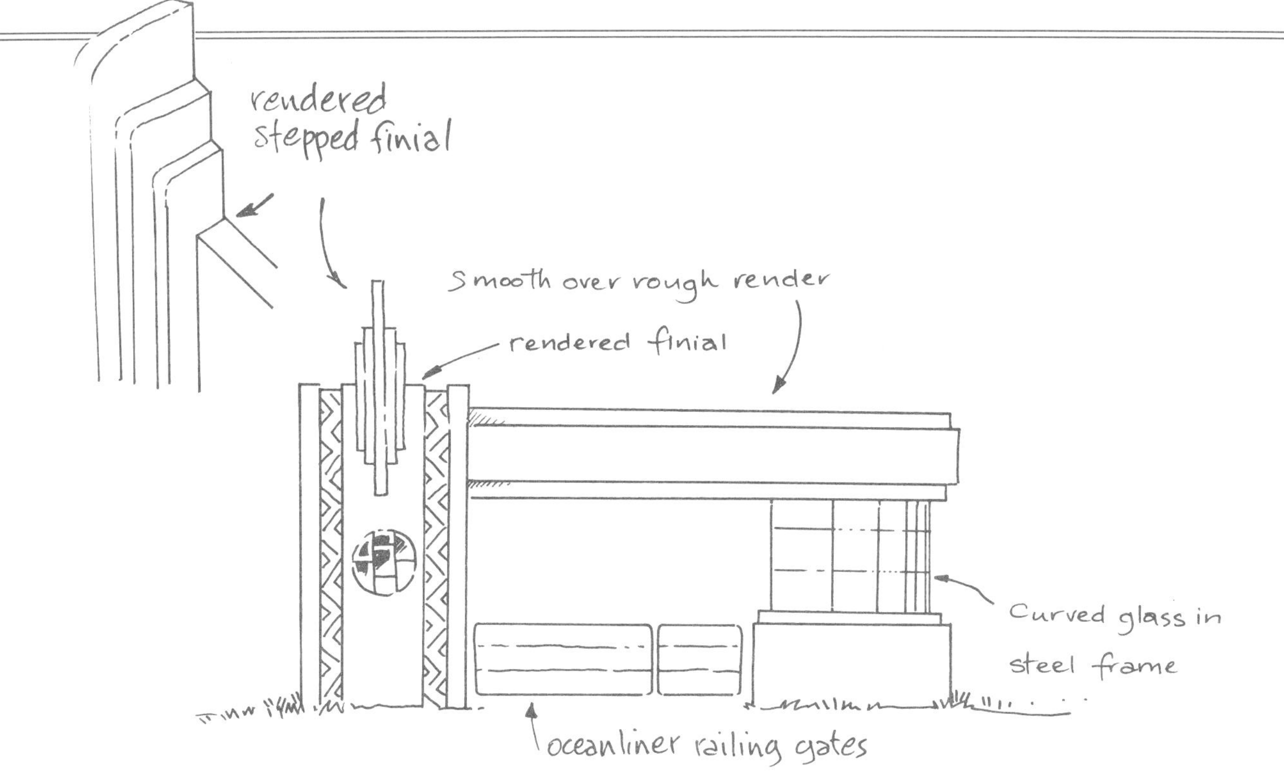

PERGOLAS

Pergolas can be freestanding or attached to an existing building and are about shade and climbing plants. Pergolas can be used to provide shade to windows and parts of the garden while waiting for new garden planting to become established.

A pergola is a simple structure of posts and beams, sometimes with battens over. They can be as small as a couple of square metres (10 sq ft) or extensive, covering a large area.

Choosing a style

The style chosen for a pergola should be in keeping with the style of the residence: there should not be a major conflict structurally. Pergolas are simple structures, therefore the style chosen for the posts and the beams is very obvious.

Pergolas have appeared in most parts of the world from very early times, probably as rustic structures used to support grape-vines. By Roman times some pergolas were decorative and for shade, and made of marble and other stone.

Few examples of pergolas have been handed down through history as they are structures of quite a short life. The shady pergolas of Tuscany still carry the same vine-stock that their predecessors did many centuries ago.

Plotting the shadows

If a pergola is to be used for shade it is important to contact the local bureau of meteorology and find out the angle of the sun at midday, mid-winter and mid-summer, as well as the bearings and times of sunrise and sunset at the solstice.

This will give enough information to plot the shadows cast by any pergola. Gardeners who cannot make these calculations should see an architect who will be able to plot the shadows on a drawing for anytime of the day on any day of the year.

If the sun shading and shadows are not understood there is little point to erecting pergolas. Pergolas are most efficient when used to shade the northern sun (the southern sun in the Northern Hemisphere) as this is where the sun is high enough in the sky to be precisely plotted, and the shadows predicted. In the Western and Eastern Hemispheres the sun varies its position in the sky significantly from summer to winter, and it is so low to the horizon at dawn and dusk, rendering pergolas a less effective sun-control mechanism.

Freestanding or attached to another building

It matters little if a pergola is attached to a building or is freestanding. Some of the most attractive pergolas are freestanding but some of the most effective are attached to the walls of buildings. In the latter the wall provides bracing for the pergola structure. If a pergola is free-standing it will need to have posts which cantilever out of the ground to provide the rigidity necessary, or have post-to-beam joints which are rigid. This is difficult to achieve in timber structures but is possible in steel frames. External cross-braces between some of the posts, which can be unsightly and dangerous, is an alternative. Another is to use diagonal latticing as bracing adjacent to some posts.

Integration with planting

Make sure there is a suitable site for vines or climbing plants to be planted at the point where they can be trained to attach themselves to the pergola. Usually this is adjacent to a post so the plant can climb to the pergola beams.

You can position the plant so that it is trained up a guide wire or cord until it is well established on the pergola. This method keeps the posts free from vine entanglements and shows the link of the vine to the soil clearly.

To assist some vines to extend more or less uniformly across the pergola, battens or wires can be attached between the pergola beams. Lattice work and shade cloth can be added to the top of pergola beams if these are considered appropriate.

Often translucent sheeting is attached over the beams of pergolas. This should be used only if there is a special need as it is a major task to keep wet leaves from sticking to the sheets and to avoid capillary action sucking dirt collecting in the laps in the sheets. If a translucent roof is required design it carefully to avoid visible overlapping of sheets.

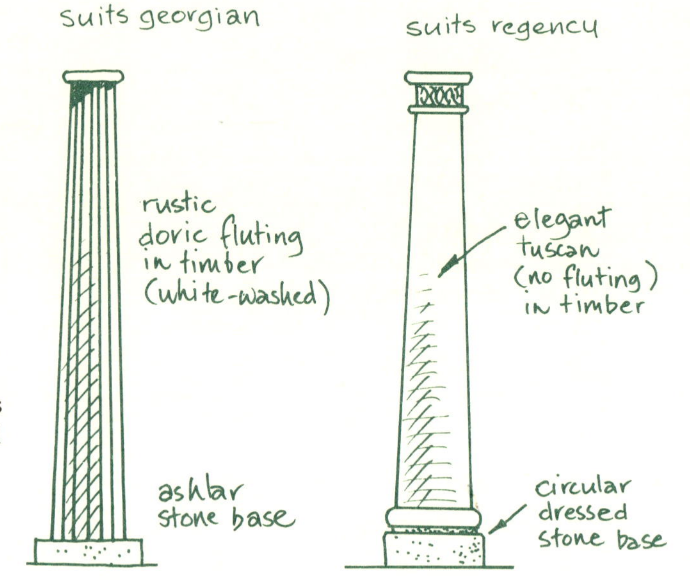

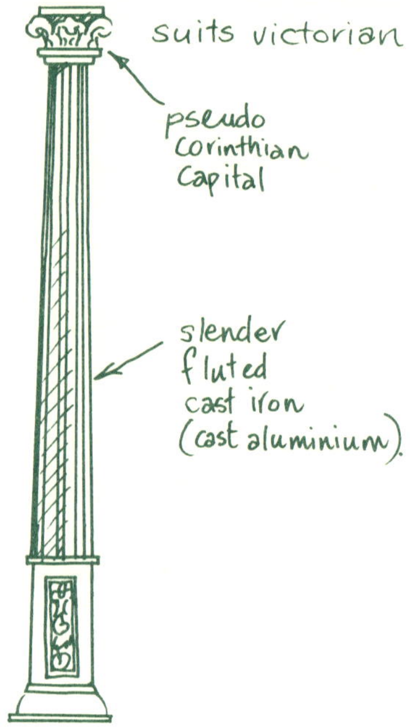

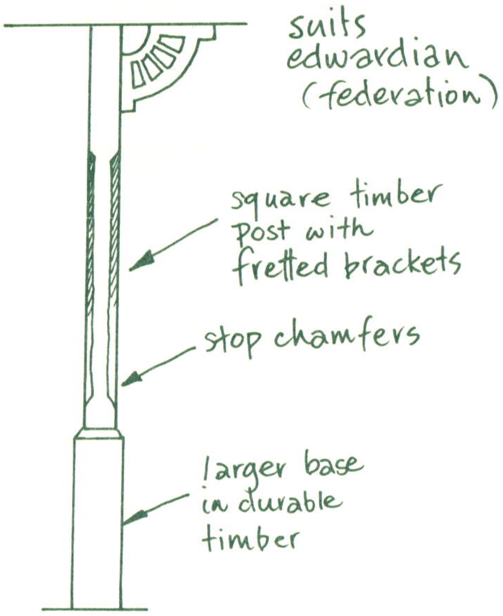

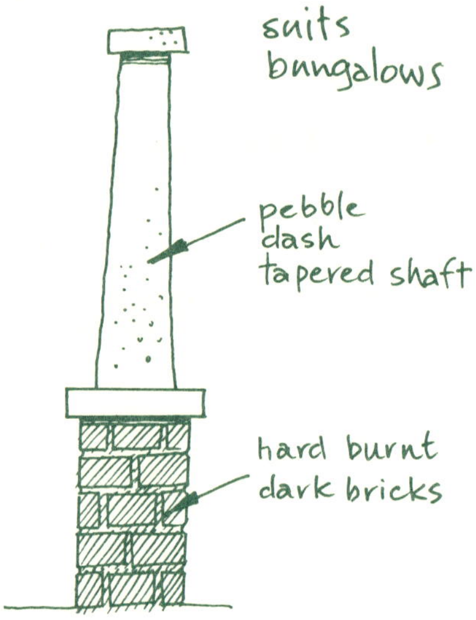

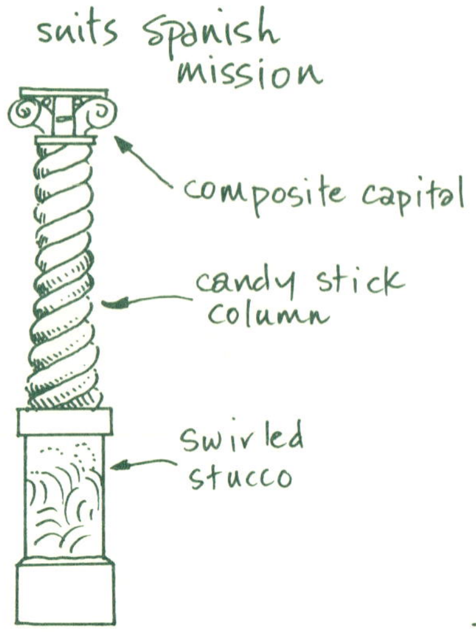

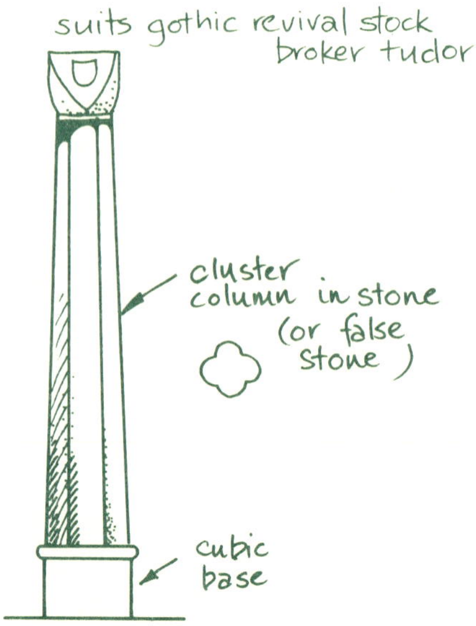

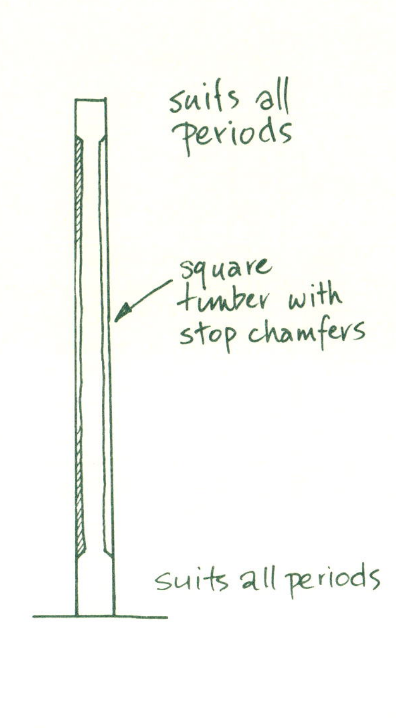

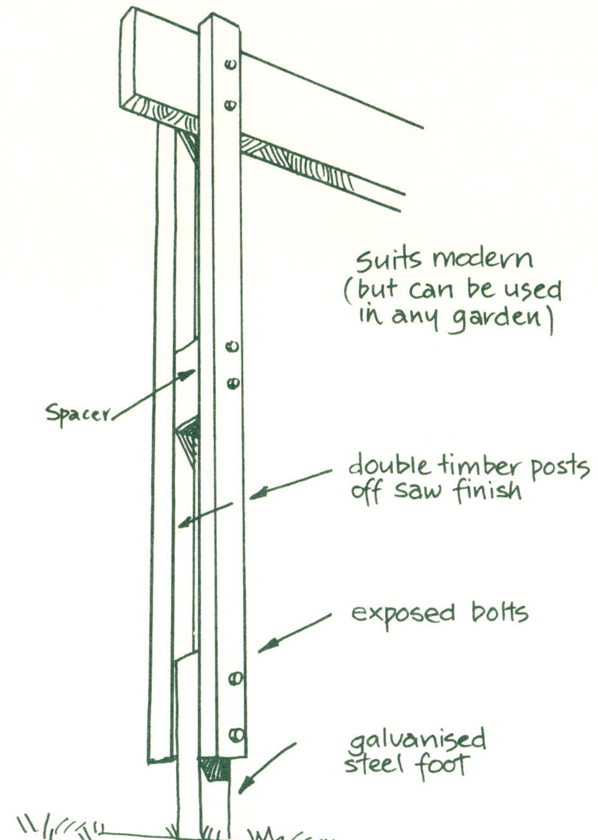

beams are
mainly in timber
but wrot iron or
cast iron
(fixed to timber or
steel tube)

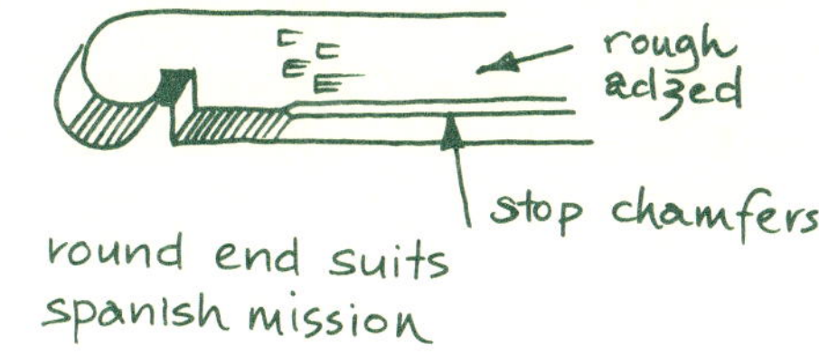

round end suits
spanish mission

stripped logs
suit rustic cottage

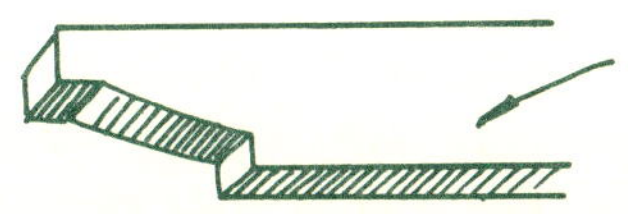

splaycut end suits
bungalow and
art deco (moderne)

'roof' end suits
georgian/regency

adzed oak (eucalypt)
suits federation arts
and crafts

TRELLISES

Trellising is a specially made lattice or other frame which can be used to support plants which are predisposed to climbing. They can be used as a decorative feature and can often assist a garden achieve an atmosphere.

Choosing a style

The style of trellis selected is a personal choice. As with all design components in a garden the shape and style of the trellises should not conflict with the residence and the rest of the built environment.

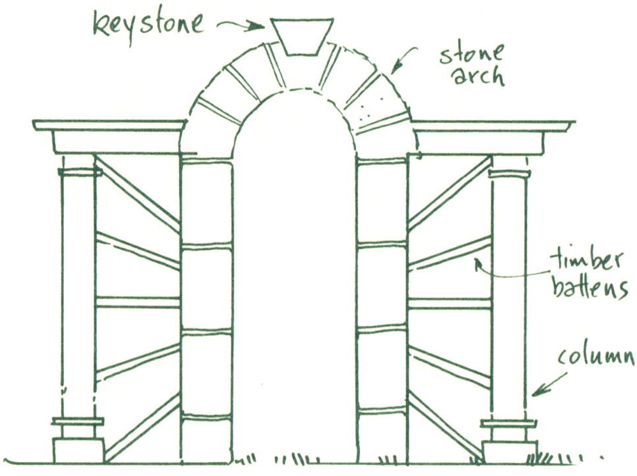

As a screen

Trellises make useful screens on which to grow plants. They separate different sections of a garden visually and provide privacy for sun terraces or other areas which otherwise may be overlooked by passers-by or neighbours. A trellis used as a screen must be soundly fixed to posts of sufficient strength and securely attached to a base. The trellis needs to be able to resist all wind and other climatic conditions experienced in the garden.

On a wall

When fixing a trellis to a wall use only corrosion-resistant fasteners to avoid marking the wall with rust stains. Affix the trellis to the wall so it does not touch the ground as this will lessen the chance of rot and insect attack.

Always check the growing patterns of the plants using the trellis for support. The trellis has to be large enough to accommodate the plants and be of sufficient strength to support their weight.

Always fix the trellis a reasonable distance off the face of the wall so that the gap is large enough for the diameter of the largest branch of the plants to fit.

Bought or custom-made

Off-the-shelf trellises are available but, in general, they are not as well built or as attractive as trellises which are made especially for a plant or location.

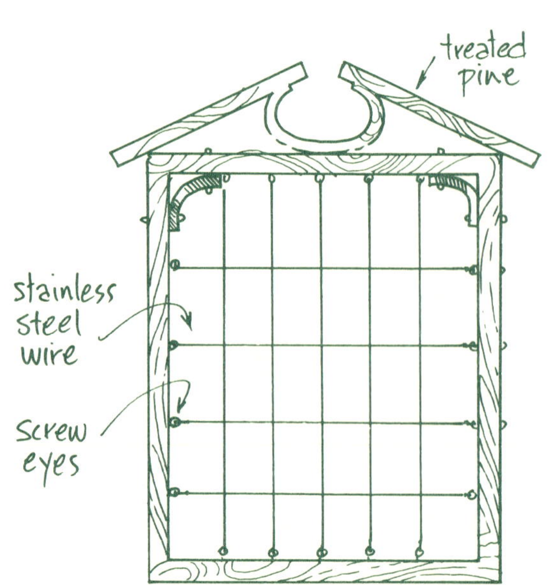

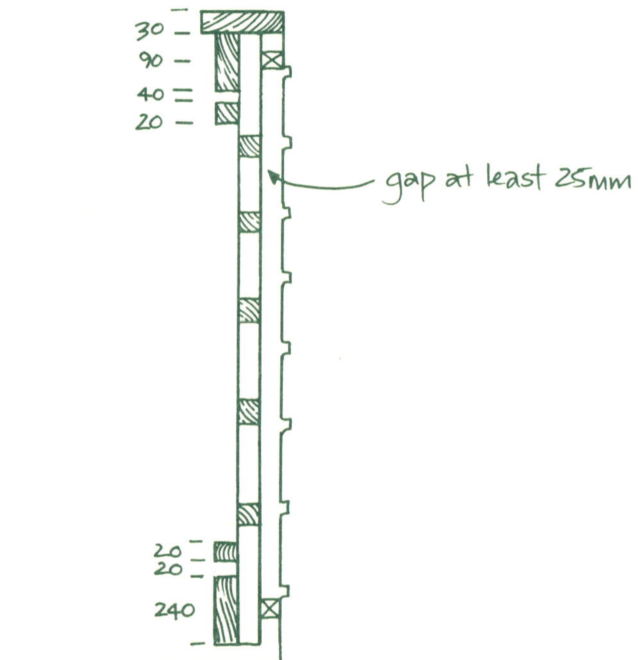

Given that good quality durable timber approved for external use with non-corrosive fixings are used, a trellis will give long service and can be made by most gardeners. While some illustrations of ideas for designs of trellises are included here there are many books which give ideas for other designs.

Integration with planting

Trellises should be designed to suit the proposed planting. However if you want a special design of trellis then choose plants to complement that trellis. If the main rising trunk of the plant enters the trellis from behind, then allow it to grow forward into the trellis.

Normally climbing plants bend easily when they are young and supple, and this is when they should be shaped to complement the trellis. Some branches will have to be pruned off the plant to maintain the plant's proximity to the trellis. Give some time to caring for, training, and pruning the plants on the trellis so that the combination enhances the garden.

FOLLIES

For this section a folly will be considered to be any building in a garden that is specially designed and located for effect. A folly may or may not have another function but its primary reason for existence is to provide a specific visual impact.

Traditionally follies are of historic buildings and monuments, often faithful copies at a reduced scale. Greek and Roman ruins are great favourites as follies and in some USA parkland gardens full-size reproductions of the Parthenon and other Grecian ruins have been constructed. Gothic church spires, castle keeps, Egyptian temples, and Chinese pagodas also have their adherents and make suitable models for follies.

Follies are used most often as a centrepiece of a long view across an open section of garden or avenue. They are used also as features to add romance and intrigue to a grotto or pond side. A pile of Roman marble column and capital sections or the remnants of a medieval tracery arch can turn a boring corner of the garden into a place of dreams.

Follies can be of any material but durable maintenance-free materials are preferred. Stone is a much-favoured material for the construction of follies and if the natural varieties are too expensive then there are a number of firms which offer off-the-shelf follies to be assembled from artificial stone. Some of the artificial stone follies come complete with artificial lichen and other antique tokenism.

Surveying for a location

Follies can lose their value as a visual element in a garden if they are not located carefully. Follies need to be seen from a number of different aspects. There is increased interest if the folly disappears and then reappears during a stroll in the garden.

Sun on a folly can be of special importance. Decide when the sun should be seen shining onto the folly.

Some prefer morning sun, others take great care to provide planting in locations that masks the sun so only a few rays will cast light onto a folly, and only at pre-determined times.

Other follies can be designed so the sun is behind the folly. Then the shadows can be cast onto the foreground. The sun moving across the sky behind a spire can be used as a giant sundial if there are shadows of plants or other markers on the ground. These can be translated into time by an aware observer.

A folly should not be treated lightly; if it is only a pile of stones which have a very crude representation

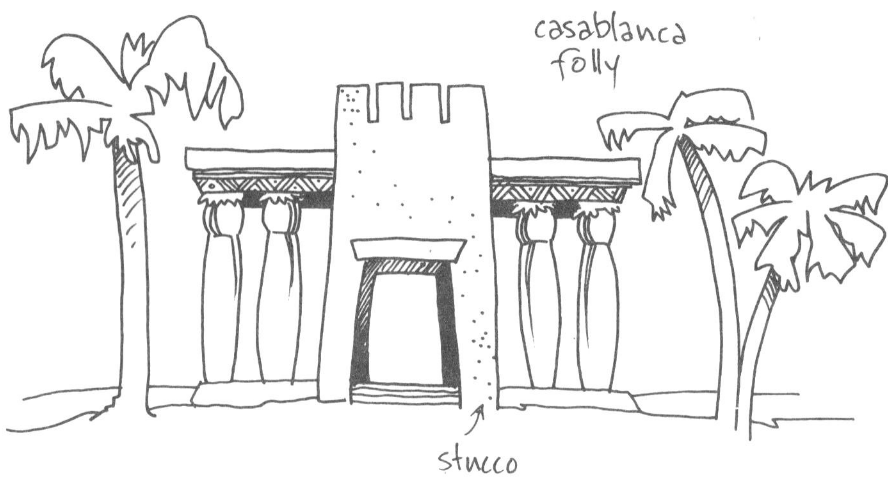

of a historic ruin it will quickly become boring. Take care in locating a folly so that the best factors of available sunlight, shadows, vistas, and topography are incorporated into its design and thought is given to any other local factor such as fogs, mists, and rain. Gathering storm-clouds and forked lightning have greater moment when a spire is in the foreground.

Careful choice of location can widen the impact of a folly. If a Greek temple front is visible from a grove of trees across a hollow in the garden how interesting it would be to set off to explore the ruin, only to arrive at it from behind by following a path that progessively provides more and more clues to the location of the temple ruin.

Follies can add special excitement to a garden. In a very small garden it is hard to get maximum value out of a folly but just the corner of an interesting ruin peeking out from behind a clump of trees only a few metres away, can add a romantic touch.

Playing the perspective game

When placing a folly in a garden location may be the most important factor but by distorting distance by playing with perspective is the way that a scaled-down folly can be used in a vista to appear as a full-sized representation.

Using a reduced-scale folly will make it look as if it is further away from the observer than it is. Only if the observers have a clear measurement in their heads of what size the original is will this be effective. Unless a person has been to the Acropolis and stood in front of the real Parthenon the chances are that they will not appreciate the perspective distortion.

Now if a few trees are planted beside a folly of the Parthenon which are small-scale reproductions of trees that are normally seen as a larger size then these will help to reinforce that a folly is larger than it really is and therefore make it appear further away from the observer.

If the reduction of a folly and the planting in its immediate vicinity are used with other perspective-altering devices like diverging lines, normally expected to be parallel, away from an observer. Prune the trees that make up an avenue running towards a folly so that the closest tree to the observer is higher than the furthest tree. This will exaggerate the perspective.

When deliberate effort is made to distort perspective the scheme must be followed through all the possible viewing points to see if the distortions may backfire in some places. If effort is only made to distort the perspective looking from a terrace of a residence looking towards a folly, there is a problem if the observer walks to the folly and looks back to the terrace, it will appear even closer that it is.

If a folly can be placed on the skyline then the need for the perspective manipulation is reduced.

Designing a ruin

It has been said that the strength of the design of a building cannot be seen until the building has been reduced to a ruin. A significant component of the strength of the Parthenon is that it is a ruin. In its prime it was probably a gaudy pagan temple; now it displays the purity of a ruin.

To design a ruin the design has to be complete first and then sections cut away to reveal the true strength of the building with the fragile but durable sections scattered around and the decayed materials lost forever.

Most ruins will not have roofs as usually these are constructed of wood which decays and falls in, or are destroyed by fire. Here stone domes and vaults together with pagoda roofs are the exceptions.

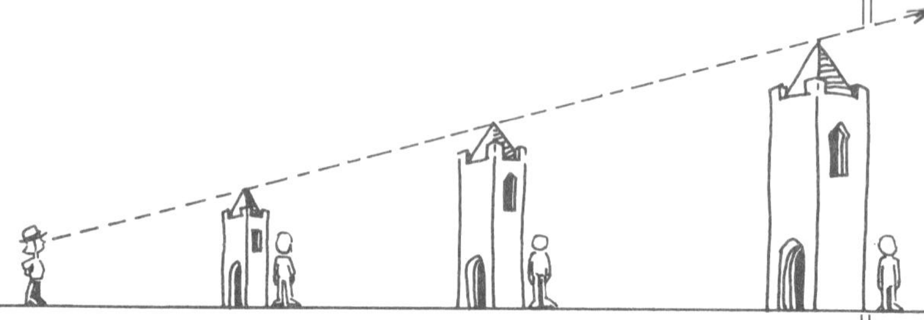

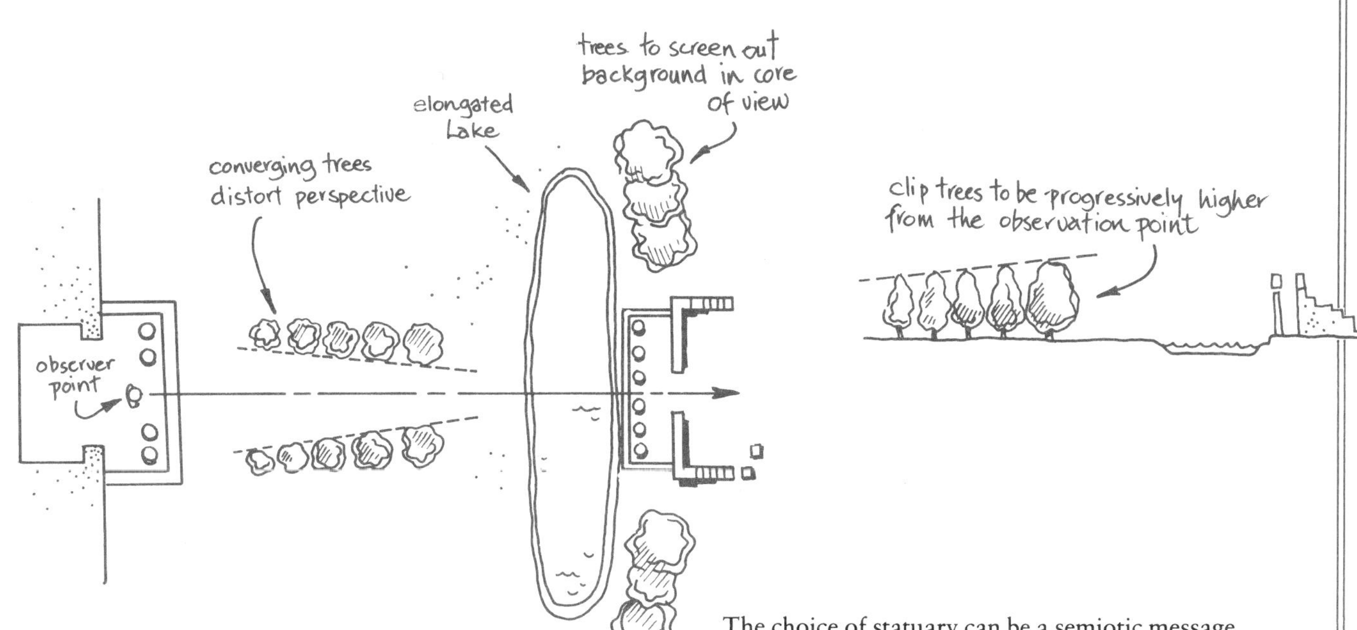

Windows are without glass, though a small fragment of stained glass in a Gothic ruin can be left and the only window frames that survive are those of stone tracery.

Greek and Roman ruins should appear to have failed by erosion or the Samson effect, Gothic churches to have succumbed to fire, Norman castles were reduced by gunpowder and weeds, Oriental pagodas have been bleached and leached so only their tiles have any colour, and Egyptian temples have peeling hieroglyphics but are otherwise intact.

The folly is a fake so the materials can also be fake but this is not a film set and the folly should be constructed of durable materials to provide a lasting pleasure in the garden and be safe for visitors to the garden.

Can it have a function?

Follies can lose impact if they become functional elements in their own right. It would seem bizarre to sit in a one-tenth scale reproduction of a Greek temple, drinking coffee from a thermos flask while waiting for a summer shower to pass — but gardeners who read Agatha Christie may respond to this.

A picnic lawn as the focus of a ruined amphitheatre would work but attempts to find uses for ruins of temples, churches, pagodas, and castles seems a waste of time except maybe as a storage shed for garden tools and equipment.

STATUES AND SCULPTURES

Statues belong in gardens. They are the human way to say to nature that no matter how beautiful it is, we will always be trying to compete.

Do statues immediately bring images of David and Venus or of gnomes and trolls? Does it matter? Gardens are an expression of human individuality.

The choice of statuary can be a semiotic message to others of the personality, culture, and status of the garden owner. How many people have a small grey gnome which quietly sits in a corner of the garden, just for luck, and a reminder of their humility?

Statues can be small, though any object less than 300 mm (1′) high can easily be lost in a garden environment. They can be large and there are people who have huge Henry Moore bronzes on their lawns.

The only criterion for a statue in a garden is that it must be weatherproof. Stone, bronze, iron, brass, copper, ceramics, artificial stone and even concrete are suitable materials under most circumstances. Fibreglass statues have been constructed and there are some stunning artistic triumphs in this material.

Sculptures can be figurative, when the subject of the sculpture is clear, or non-figurative when the subject is open to some conjecture or is completely subject-free. Always statues are figurative though often mannered and abstract.

Identifying nodes

Statues and sculptures must belong their place in a garden. They should be able to be viewed in comfort. On a terrace or near a sheltered sitting place are good locations.

They are by their nature 'nodal' that is, they are a point of convergence where visual lines are concentrated. Statues and sculptures are reference points or loci for pathways, enclosures, and other garden linear or planar features.

Nodes in a garden pinpoint features and should be identified and defined with great care. A plan of a garden on paper may suggest a particular point as being the node but when the place is investigated on-site, final tuning of the location often will be required.

It is important to know approximately where a sculpture or statue is to be located in a garden but it is equally important to adjust the location to display the item at its best. The final location should not be determined until the sculpture or statute has been observed in the morning, at midday, in the evening and at as many times in between as possible. It should be seen at night when artificially lit. These observations should take a whole year to complete so that all of the seasons have added their impact.

Classic, Romantic or Modern

European sculpture has its roots in the states of Ancient Greece and the Classical style of sculpture from this period was developed by the Romans and revived during the Renaissance to remain a force even now though its fashion status varies. This is the sculpture of gods, goddesses, and heroes — it is a sculpture of marble.

In contrast there is a large body of European sculpture that deals with the Romatic — the sculpture of dogs, deer, and adventure.

Modern sculpture is abstract and where figurative it is often distorted by elongation or plumped up in a Rubenesque manner. It is often designed to be at its visual best in a garden environment.

Exotic or erotic

Exotic sculptures from the Orient, South America, Africa or any emerging society are much prized in gardens where totem poles and death masks mix it with Buddhas and Krishnas.

Some of the very best garden three-dimensional art and craft pieces come from the equatorial regions of the world where marvellous weathered timber objects were

always modelled to fit into an external environment. An erotic sculpture from India or New Guinea can be secreted in a small clearing to bring fertility to the garden and make all plants flourish.

With fountain, in a pond, in a niche

Sculptures can be used as fountains if they are made with water pipes built in or if they are set on a pedestal which contains the water sprays. Make sure that that sculpture is resistant to water and will not deteriorate.

Ponds environments are suitable for some sculptures, those that can be mounted on the edge coping or on special pedestals at the edge of or even within a pond. Sculptures which provide interesting images when reflected on water are most suitable beside water.

An interesting location to place a sculpture is in a niche specially constructed in a brick or stone wall. A niche gives some measure of protection to the sculpture and adds interest to a wall or fence.

SUNDIALS, URNS, AND VASES

Sundials have been part of a garden environment for many centuries only being replaced by mechanical clocks in many places during the late 19th century. Many gardens were designed around the sundial rather than the other way around.

Most sundials are mounted on pedestals about 700-mm (2'6") to 1-metre (3'6") high and are made of brass or a similar metal. Other sundials can be very large and use figures engraved onto terraces.

Locating for best sun

A sundial has to be located in full sun. In the Southern Hemisphere this means it is located on the north side of a building usually and on the south side in the Northern Hemisphere.

Trees to the east and west of a sundial can cast very long shadows late in the afternoon and these need careful plotting.

Sundials — should they tell the time?

Many sundials in gardens are not mounted correctly nor do they give a clear reading of the time. A sundial is a pleasant decorative item but if it is set up correctly and does tell the time it is much more interesting.

Choosing and locating

Choose a sundial that suits the residence and the garden. Its location, if possible, should be so that it can be seen and read from a study, main bedroom or living room. It is very elegant to walk out through French doors onto a terrace to read the time on a sundial in the morning and it is less jarring than a digital alarm to the nervous system. And what is the point of rising before the sun has risen?

Urns and vases are a further method of creating period identification pieces in a garden, and are useful in establishing the corners and axes of specific areas. Put in these plantings of special significance or colour, and keep them looking neat and weed-less.

Urns and vases can be made from many materials including stone but most are made of concrete or terracotta clay. They must be planted carefully as the soil can dry out very quickly. Always consider the nutrient requirement of the plants very carefully and use drain holes, porous content, and internal linings to suit.

PEOPLE FEATURES

Gardens are planned to provide quiet enjoyment for people so include a range of people features be built into a garden. From simple seats to elaborate gazebos, barbecues, play areas, passive post-boxes, and flapping clothes lines, are some of the essential features of a modern garden.

GARDEN SEATS

Garden seats must have a history as long as when the first human sat on a fallen log, breathed in the sweet smells of nature, listened to the song of the birds, and considered the complexity of falling leaves, and wondered if they would grow back again.

The history of sitting in a naturally beautiful place is prehistoric and could even be pre-human but the delight of sitting in a secure place taking in the sights, sounds, and smells of nature is a pleasant experience at any time.

Choosing the location

Garden seats should be located to take in the best places for sun, for shade, for gentle breezes, for aspect and for vista. It is often better to have two or three simple seats in strategic locations in a garden than to spend a fortune on a hand-made Chippendale or Voysey reproduction garden seats.

Always choose the locations with care:

- A seat that is upwind of the autumn leaves, downwind of the autumn roses, and bathed in the warm sun of early autumn or
- A seat that is under the dappled shade of a spreading broadleafed tree, overlooking at a pond surrounded with the colourful bulbs, and inhabited by a clutch of ducklings during spring

are some things that should be considered when locating a garden seat.

Timber

Timber is the traditional material for a garden seat, even a well located fallen log can be a very comfortable resting place. Timber seats can range from the naive styles of half-log benches, rustic styles using carefully selected gnarled twisted branches, to the classic oak or teak seats of the English country gardens.

The timber used for garden seats should be strong and durable when left out in the weather. Most of the dense deciduous hardwoods like oak, some of the eucalypts (particularly jarrah), the western red cedars

and redwoods of North America, and some of the denser pines are suitable, as are many other timber species, if they have been treated against the ravages of the weather and insects. Teak and other high quality rainforest timbers have been used in the past but their supply is now severely limited as the world attempts to protect the last of the great tropical rainforests.

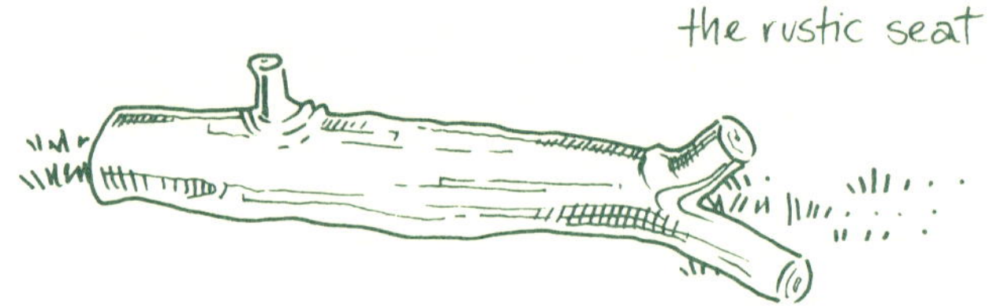

A timber which will last outside without painting is a distinct advantage and some of the best species will allow this, but most will need at least an annual coat of linseed or similar oil preservative while others must be painted.

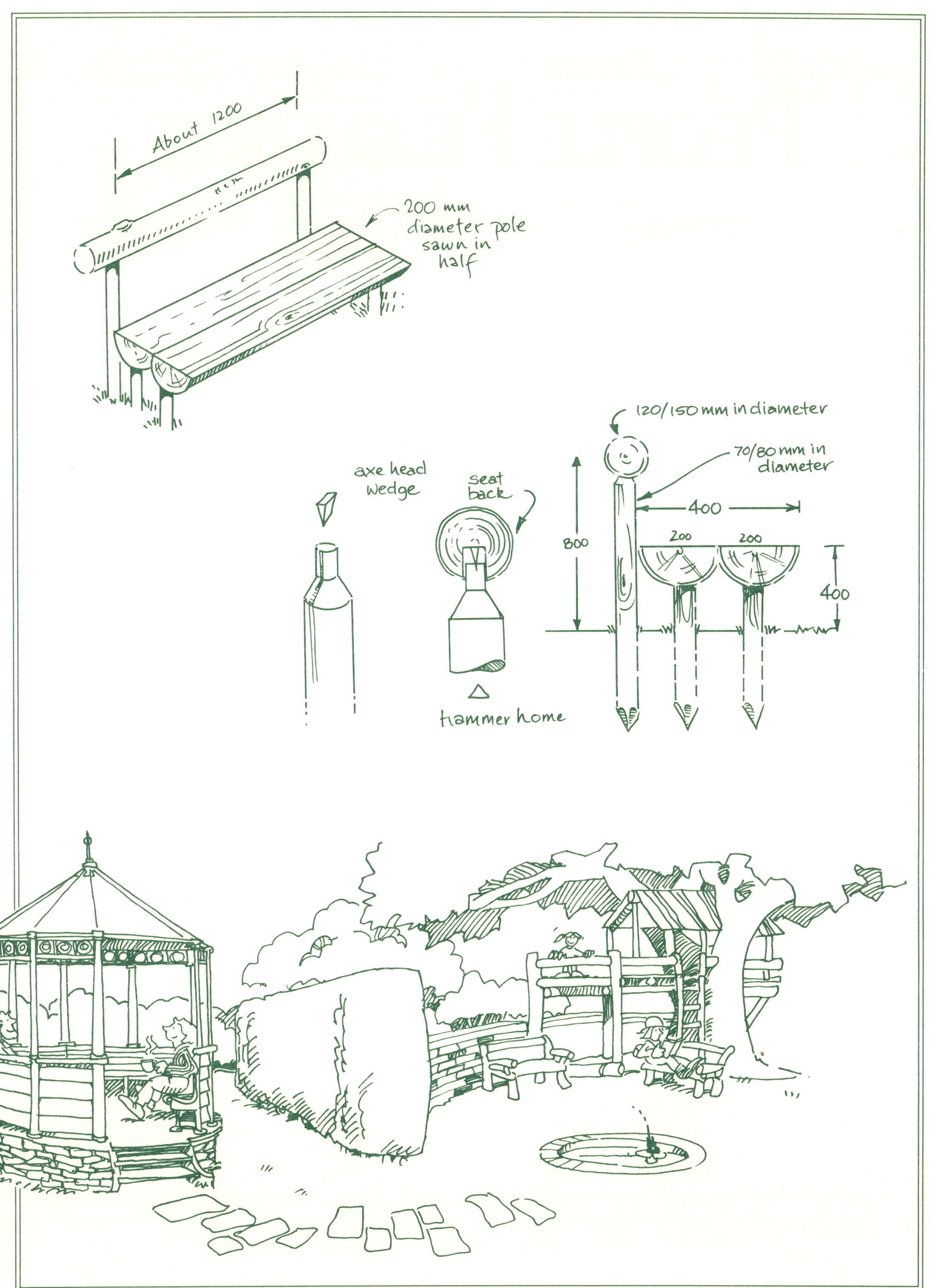
About 1200
200 mm diameter pole sawn in half
axe head wedge
seat back
hammer home
120/150 mm in diameter
70/80 mm in diameter
800
400
200
200
400

Timber is a poor conductor so it seldom becomes too hot to sit on in summer and in winter does not feel too cold. It can be worked easily to provide a passable ergonomically suitable seat and back profile and in most cases can be repaired if it is damaged.

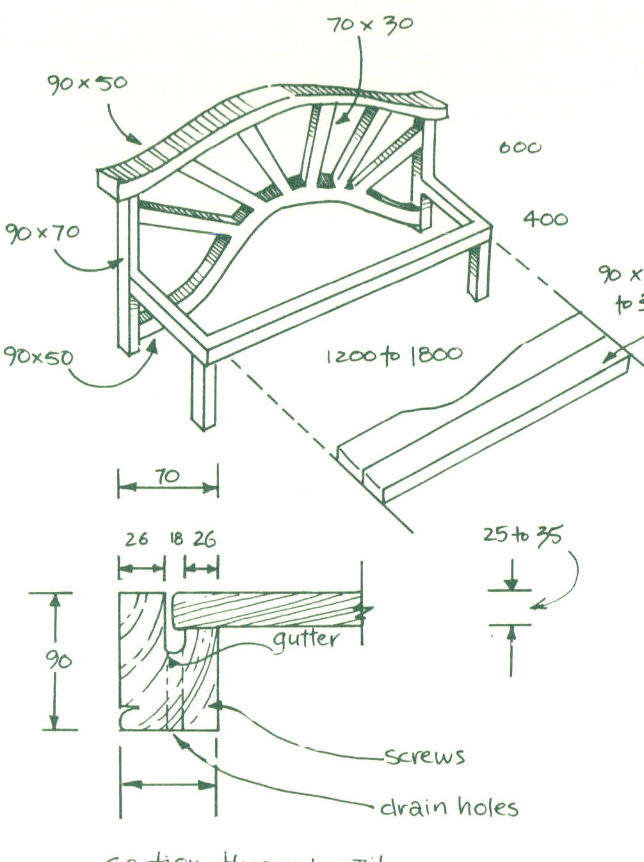

There are some traditional forms for timber garden seats and these should be considered before making a final selection but take care of the designer-label garden seat looms.

Metal

Designer-label timber garden chairs are one thing but would anyone purchase anything but a genuine Coalbrookdale cast iron metal-framed garden seat if they could, preferably a Victorian one?

Metal garden seats range from those made in the birthplace of modern foundry to simple welded steel frames for a wooden slat seat. The ergonomics of the fabulously elaborate expensive cast iron seats are often worse than a basic garden seat.

The metals used for garden seat frames and, in some cases, for the seats and backs as well, are normally iron, steel or aluminium. New cast iron outdoor furniture is expensive as it is only made in a few factories and has been severely affected by the introduction of relatively cheap cast aluminium products. Both cast iron and cast aluminium give long-term service and have good resistance to corrosion, though neither will perform as well as timber in salty atmospheres.

Formed and welded mild steel frames for garden furniture can be made to mimic older more durable wrought iron designs but few manufacturers supply premium wrought iron reproductions. Make sure that any mild steel product to be used outdoors is galvanised and guaranteed against rusting for a extended period of time. There are still blacksmiths who can make genuine wrought iron frames and a price from one of these tradespeople may be worth considering.

Aluminium can be used for garden seats but it is normally restricted to the fold-up and put-away variety. Light gauge steel tubing is offered in a number of modern ranges of garden seats and if too thin a gauge and of carefully designed and engineered construction can last for a reasonable time. It is not recommended to purchase bargains in metal outdoor furniture. There is a simple test, if a three-seat garden bench seat can be lifted easily by one person then check how well it is designed and constructed before purchasing.

Having custom-made steel is not always as expensive as many people seem to believe. Visit the local steel fabrication shop for prices. Often they are relieved to make a garden seat rather than to fill another builder's order.

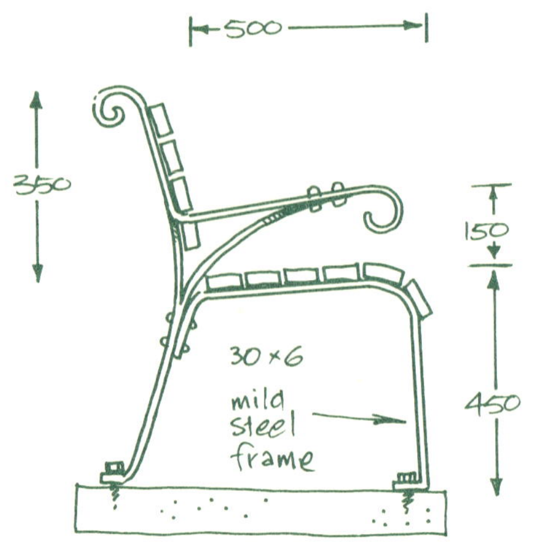

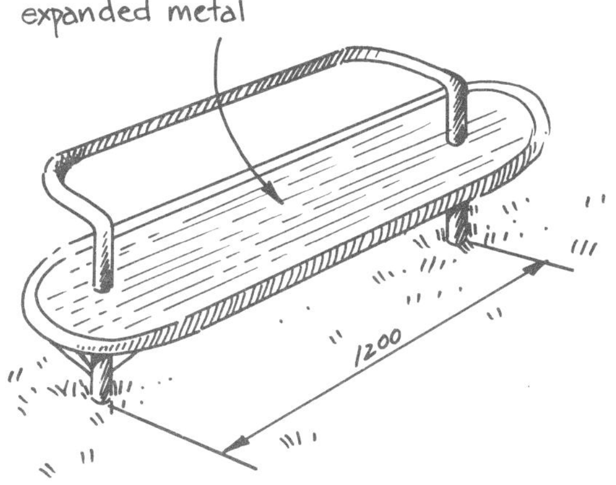

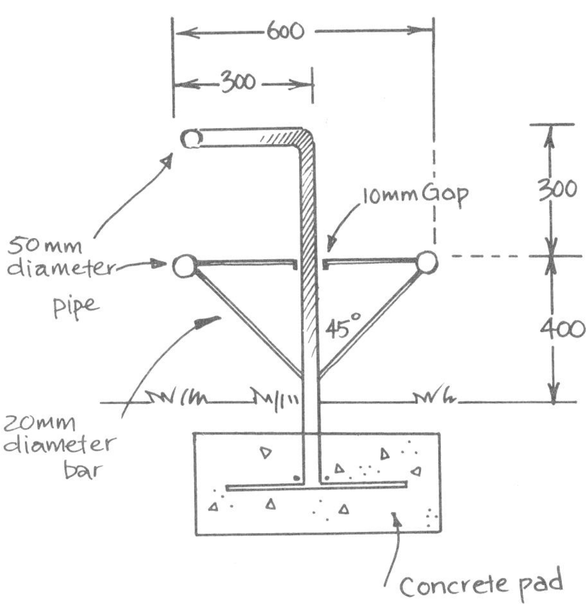

Masonry

Seats made from stone or brick are permanent. Where you place such a bench should be well researched before construction goes ahead.

The advantages are that they do not rot and can be made to fit into a garden environment. If the seat and back is tiled (particularly on those constructed of brick) a certain style can be added to a corner of a garden.

Such seats should always be shaded from the height of summer sun. Stone is a good conductor of the extremes of temperature.

Antique or modern style

Except for the grand Victorian extravaganzas which included garden seats complete with cast iron trellis shading, most garden seats have been reasonably style-free, not venturing too far into the fashion stakes.

Garden seats should look as if they grew in the garden at the same time as the plants, so choose styles and materials that show the patina of age with grace, then it does not matter when a seat was made.

Only gardens which are attempting to reproduce or create a purity of style should be concerned about style-matched garden furniture.

Buy or make

If a seat of the size and style required can be found in a store, at a garden supplier, or by attending an antique auction at the right price, that is good. However if you do not buy one at one of these venues consider having a seat made.

Many people who are handy could make their own garden furniture. It is pleasant to sit in a seat or in a chair designed for, and built in, a garden.

BARBECUES

Barbecues are often touted as a great garden activity.

Choosing the location

A barbecue in a garden should be placed subtly. Few modern families cook their meals on an oversized range in the dining room so modern families should give equal consideration to the siting of the barbecue.

Barbecues should be sized to suit the likely demands. A good size for a barbecue top is between 600 mm (2′) and 900 mm (3′) long by 300 mm (1′) to 400 mm (1′4″) wide. Such a top will grill enough meat for from six to 20 people. The level of the grill needs to be about 600 mm (2′) to 800 mm (2′8″) above the ground.

A unit of this size can be built into a terrace wall and double as a pedestal for a planted urn on the 364 days of the year when it is unsuitable for barbecues.

Open fire or gas?

The use of open-fire barbecues has become less a requirement for all but the most dedicated barbecue purists. It is they who believe that smoke, cinders, and charcoal are still essential ingredients of barbecues. Most barbecue chefs have succumbed to the ease and predictability of the built-in or portable gas-fired barbecue.

If town gas is not available then bottled LPG gas will do the trick, particularly when it is connected to a modern-purpose designed barbecue grill which can be purchased with such options as hot coals grilling and grill-level smoke extraction. Some units even have a built-in cappuccino machine.

Portable

Portable barbecues are often very rustic, looking more like a log cabin on wheels than a cooking appliance. Not a permanent component of the garden, these can be wheeled out when required and just as quickly wheeled away.

Permanent

Permanent barbecues should be built of stone or brick and designed so fat and dirt does not run down the faces of the unit.

Concrete blocks are a suitable material but the combination of heat and fat can leave this material looking very soiled.

If the unit can be integrated into the garden in a manner that it is as unobtrusive as possible this is a distinct advantage visually. The grill of the barbecue should be located below the level of the masonry walls and the well should be lined with smooth render or ceramic tiles for easy hygienic cleaning. Allow a drain hole to let cleaning water out.

A weather-tight lid should be lowered over the grill area when the barbecue is not in use to keep out the weather and vermin.

Sample designs

A few design ideas have been included but care should be taken to locate, adapt, and scale these to suit the location and the garden for which it is intended.

PLAY AREAS

A garden used by children is a different place from that solely used for the quiet enjoyment of adults. Children have special needs and these should be catered for as a component of the overall design. Play areas with such equipment as swings, slippery slides, see-saws, and climbing devices should be considered for their durability, appearance and safety. It is important that these are actually wanted by the children.

In a residential garden a tough lawn is a suitable base on which to put play equipment but most children also appreciate a free play area which has bare sand in which they can allow their imaginations to take over. A sand-pit should contain sand which is a compromise between a clean, sharp and well-drained type and an easy-to-handle type which has a high content of clay. Children generally prefer a sand which will allow for them to build miniature houses, castles, roads, and walls without the structures falling down too easily. Parents prefer sand that does not stain, washes off easily, and does not become a bog in wet weather. Find a suitable compromise.

A sand play area should be at least 2 metres (6'8") square to be effective. It can be sited under a pergola or even have its own roof. Using a roof is more effective than covering the sand with a lid as it allows the sand to breathe and stay fresh. At the same time the roof gives the children protection from the sun which is a growing concern.

If there are dogs and cats in the garden then a fence and gate may be needed to keep them from turning the sandpit into a litter-tray.

Manufactured

There are basically two types of play equipment that can be used, that which is designed for a specific purpose such as swings and slides, and equipment that is for free play. The specific purpose equipment can be purchased from many supply sources or it can be custom-designed and fabricated. In general it is advisable to purchase well designed and manufactured pieces of equipment usually made to suit the ergonomic requirement of children. These are durable in all weather and satisfy the safety regulations.

Often equipment for free play is overlooked in a children's garden play area. An assortment of robust specially made boxes, wheel shapes, planks and ladders can provide children with relatively safe materials while allowing them to explore their own creativity. All these help with their spatial and coordination development.

Natural

Including some garden trees for shade and (in carefully considered circumstances) the use of strong established trees for climbing and the construction of a tree house would be a bonus for the play area. It is important that a garden is for all the family to find enjoyment and one of the most pleasant sounds in a garden is the sound of children happily at play.

CLOTHES LINES

Locate them out of sight but in a well-ventilated corner
of the garden, please.

Rotary

Rotary clothes lines once dominated many back gardens and their legacy lives on. There are modern rotary
clothes lines that can be stored in a shed or garage when
not in use. This not only removes a foreign object from
the garden, it also saves many people from being
garrotted.

Designed

Once upon a time clothes lines were made of a few posts
with galvanised wire or clean white rope strung between
them. These were simple and worked well. The white
corded rope line was only obvious when it was in use.

Now it seems that every industrial designer has
produced a folding clothes line of greater or lesser
efficiency. Why must they be manufactured in bright
green paint with yellow plastic coating over wire lines?

Gardeners should start a revolt against designer
clothes lines and return to the post-and-cord variety
where flapping bleached linen adds a romantic flavour
to a family garden.

POST-BOXES

Post offices have some regulations to do with post-
boxes. The box must be located where it can be easily
used by the delivery person. It must have a slot that
takes standard envelopes and displays the property
number or name.

Beyond these requirements post-boxes should be
weather-tight, have appropriate security, a newspaper
receptacle and be robust and durable. Too many post-
boxes are made from poor quality materials and need
to be replaced regularly. Such boxes also detract from
the whole presentation of the residence and garden. The
post-box is often the first item seen by passers-by and
indicates the personalities of the residents.

There are many manufactured post-boxes available,
from simple metal boxes to elaborate excesses of con-
torted rocks, pebbles and wrought iron that defy all

bounds of visual acceptability. Even if the choice is to
purchase a simple metal post-box it is important to
check that it is corrosion-proofed as the light gauge of
steel used in some post-boxes can rust very easily.

Where timber is used in a post-box it should be of
a durable species, preferably treated with preservative,
and assembled using non-corrosive fixings — brass or
stainless steel are preferred — and glued with
weatherproof adhesives.

The most durable post-boxes are built into masonry
pillars, with a cast aluminium or a brass slot. Choose
the post-box to complement the garden and the style of
the residence but consider durability as well.

Freestanding

A freestanding post-box can be designed as a feature.
If the box is in a masonry pillar its size should be in
keeping with its immediate environment.

If the post-box is mounted on a timber, steel, stone,
cast iron or cast aluminium post or pedestal, the most
important factors to consider are: stability, strength,
and style. Determine the appropriate material for the box.

Timber posts can be de-barked logs which can give
a simple but attractive rustic look if well chosen, or they
can be worked timber. Sawn timber posts are acceptable on a house which also has exposed sawn timber
but dressed and worked timber is a better choice
usually. A simple post with stop chamfered edges is
universally acceptable. However with grooves, flutes,
and turning more care needs to be taken in achieving
suitable style and proportions.

If a timber post is to be set in the ground it has to
be of a durable species or it may quickly become a
larder for wood-eating insects or decaying rots. It is
often better to cast a galvanised steel angle vertically
into a concrete footing and then to bolt the timber post
to this, keeping a gap between the bottom of the post
and the ground. This has two advantages, the post is

kept clear of the ground and the post can be unbolted and replaced easily.

Steel posts can be circular or rectangular hollow sections or they can be built up of welded bars. In all cases it is advisable to use galvanised steel.

Often stone pedestals are fabricated with a base, shaft, and capital which are bonded together. This allows for less stone to be used in the manufacture, and some mixing and matching of the three components. Stone pillars can be used and are constructed either with solid stones laid one on top of the other, or they can use a brick structure which is then clad with stone veneer panels such as sandstone, limestone, and basalt used in the stacked type with marble and granite.

It is possible to build strata stone pillars but these are not natural in appearance and are bizarre if they are lacquered.

Cast iron and modern reproduction cast aluminium posts are often in the shape of elongated Classical or Gothic column styles and make suitable posts where a particular stylistic period is desired.

In-fence

If a post-box is built into a fence then it loses much of its individuality but is more durable. Post-boxes can be built into almost any type of fence.

GAZEBOS

A gazebo or summerhouse is a small building in a garden which is specifically constructed to gain maximum enjoyment from the garden environment. They can consist of four posts and a roof, or they can be studio-type buildings where an author or artist chooses to work.

Freestanding pavilion-like structures have long been components of garden environments where shelter from the elements, whether blazing sun or rain, has been required. The designers of gazebos and other pavilion-like buildings always have had the opportunity to make architectural and contextual statements, often raising these seemingly modest structures to works of art.

Gazebos are important components of the garden design and should never be treated flippantly. They must be well designed functionally and aesthetically. As part of the garden they should appear to belong.

Choosing the location

Before a gazebo can be sited think of the reasons for its erection. Is it to be functional or is it an aesthetic object — a folly?

A gazebo is a visual element in a garden and a place from which vistas are observed. In the middle of a large lawn a gazebo can be sited in the manner of a Victorian bandstand, against a stand of trees or in a quiet dell, away from the main activities areas of the garden.

The general rules for locating gazebos are:

- They should be in a position to obtain maximum advantage from the sun
- They should be sheltered from the wind but benefit from a gentle breezes
- They should be located on a high, rather than a low point in the garden
- They should have short, middle, and longer distant points of interest in their vista
- They should have a feeling of intimacy, to be on display when sitting in a gazebo is not acceptable
- They should be approached along a path of interest, to join a residence to a gazebo by a direct straight path can work in some gardens but to arrive through a hole in a hedge may be more interesting

Choosing a design

Designing a gazebo in detail is particularly important. Often a gazebo is a freestanding structure which can be seen from all sides, and from high and low elevations. A gazebo can be sited near a hedge or wall, or be attached to a suitable garden wall.

The traditional gazebo usually has a reasonably steeply pitched roof. This gives a visually strong profile to the structure but it is not an absolute rule. A well-proportioned flat-roofed gazebo can suit many gardens.

The gazebo was popular in the Victorian and Edwardian periods. When to dress in one's Sunday best and lounge in the summerhouse was considered an act of extreme pleasure. This was before cars and mass communications changed the concept of leisure.

The Victorian and Edwardian gazebos are valid today. A typical Victorian gazebo was polygonal in plan having six, seven, eight, or nine sides. It was framed of timber or cast iron and had a slate or zinc roof. The timber-framed construction had decorated timber posts and bresummers in a style often referred to as 'carpenter's Gothic'. If there was a balustrade, it was often in an open cross pattern or was of jointed timber boards. Inside there was a seating bench facing inwards against some of the walls.

The cast iron gazebo used cast iron posts in a pseudo-Classical style and had cast iron lace work to the bresummers and the balustrades. The seating benches were timber on cast iron brackets. There are some examples of circular cast iron designs given in this book. Both styles had steeply pitched roofs.

Edwardian gazebos were either in a Queen Anne revival style or a style that has been loosely described as Arts and Crafts. The Queen Anne style had much in common with carpenter Gothic but included more lathe-turned and fretworked timber bracketing to carry an overhanging roof. Arts and Crafts style often had a stone balustrade and simpler timber work in what was considered to be a reflection of vernacular craft.

There is also a style of gazebo which is a cross between a summerhouse and a folly. These were often constructed on a circular plan with six or eight stone columns (of the Tuscan order) supporting a stuccoed domed roof. Inside these domes were often finished in *trompe l'oeil* (a clouded sky painting) and the bench seating was of real or fake marble.

The style chosen matters little for the gazebo but there is a tradition that suggests multi-sided designs with peaked roofs have the greatest acceptance.

Selecting materials

Modern gazebos are mostly timber framed, few are of stone or cast iron. Timber is the most flexible and easiest to work with. One of the most appropriate is Douglas fir which is a strong light long-life timber in exposed structures if it is well primed and painted or stained with an appropriate oil-based stain.

The floor of the gazebo can be at ground level or raised. At ground level it can be either flagged with stone, use pavers on a sand bed or quarry tiles on a concrete slab. All are equally acceptable. Raised floors also can be in quarry tiles on a raised concrete slab but a floor of timber decking is often more suitable.

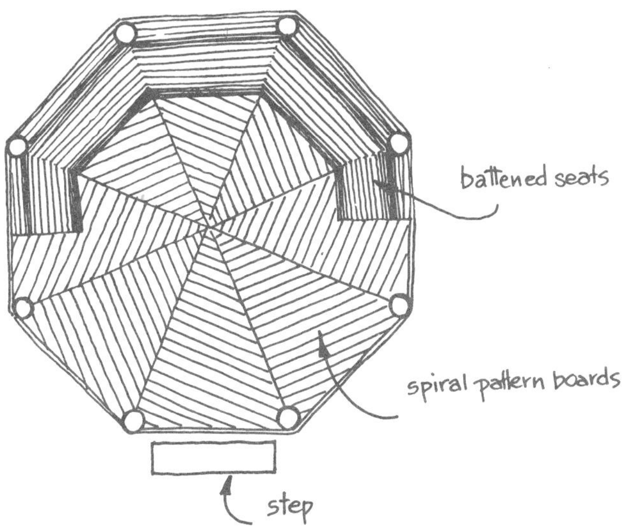

The roof structure can be exposed to view or a ceiling can be installed. The former is spatially more interesting. The lining to the internal roof space can be flush-jointed fibrous cement but timber lining boards are traditional. The roof cover is nearly always corrugated galvanised steel but slate and terracotta tiles are also acceptable.

A simple summerhouse

The traditional summerhouse or gazebo has a polygonal plan which has sides of 1 (3′4″) to 2 metres (7′) in length, making a hexagonal structure from 2 (7′) to 4 metres (13′6″) wide. The floor can be at ground level but the summerhouse often looks better raised 300 mm (1′) to 400 mm (1′6″) with a rise of two steps.

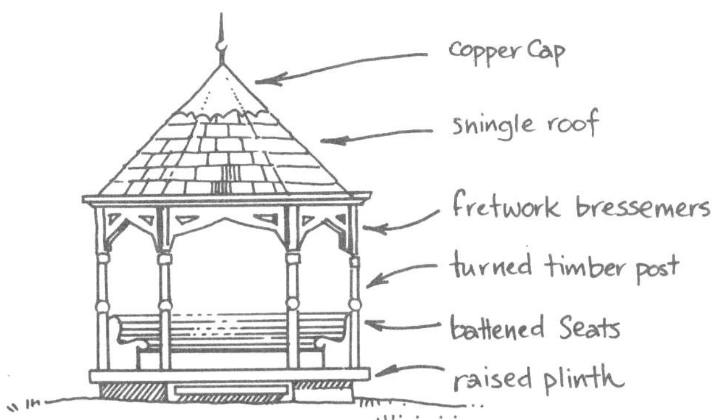

The height from the floor to the eaves should not be less than 2 100 mm (7′) and seldom need to exceed 2 700 mm (9′). Roof pitches of between 35° and 50° give good proportions and balance to the massing.

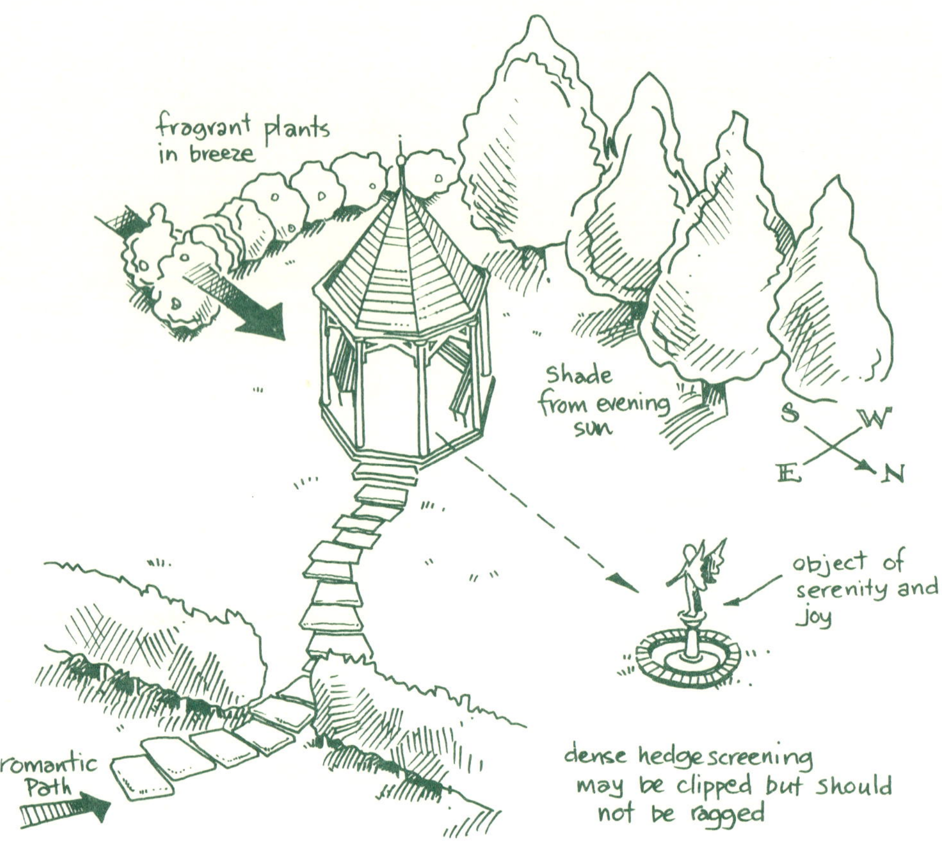

Most modern summerhouses have open sides but where the summer climate can be sometimes chilly a few of the sides can be enclosed to shield occupants from wind. A popular method of enclosing a summerhouse is to use a hexagonal or octagonal plant and place walls with windows in alternate bays, then affix shutters that can cover the windows or swing to enclose the normally open bays.

Latticework also can be used to screen some sides and when combined with timber framing, can produce interesting visual effects. Aromatic plants can be trained to grow up lattice providing extra shade and wind shelter, as well as introducing natural perfumes. Some species of roses have fragrant flowers and leaves.

Seating can be built-in against the balustrade or walls but this is very restricting and formal. Many summerhouses now are used with more comfortable portable seating.

Structurally the timber is visually more interesting if it is expressed inside and outside the building. This requires quite complicated timber structure and jointing. If the timber frame is fully cut, jointed and tested before final erection there is less chance of materials wasted by incorrect cutting.

A summerhouse can be constructed of latticework so that it can be completely overgrown with vines and creepers. This is very romantic but not in zones with high summer rainfall.

In the more tropical climates a roof of brush, laid over a waterproof plywood sub-roof, can bring the look of a Pacific island hut to the garden. Roofs of this type will become waterlogged and smelly in cooler zones with high winter rainfall.

A year-round pavilion

A pavilion-studio in the garden is a place where the relaxed atmosphere of the garden will improve the creative spirit of the user and assist in a great painting or the definitive novel coming to fruition.

A small pavilion-studio with room for an easel or a typewriter (read Word Processor — but who would want to read a novel written on word proccessor), an easy chair or two, an old couch, and a pot-belly stove. This is the stuff that dreams are made of.

There also has to be a veranda-ed porch to complete the fantasy.

The room should be in the order of about 150 (1 615 sq ft) to 200 square metres (2 150 sq ft) in floor area have wide opening glass doors as well as strategically placed windows to catch glimpses of the garden. If it is to be a painting studio the main windows light should be to the south in the Southern Hemisphere, or the north in the Northern Hemisphere).

The interior of such a studio should be representative of the artist's personality but on the outside it should be in harmony with the garden environment. Keep the style simple and direct in the manner of a bungalow cottage. The studio should be cheerful and inviting and have the smoke from a wood fire drifting out of chimney flue on cooler winter days.

Use natural materials such as timber, stone and shingles with some bricks and unpainted but weathered corrugated steel. Aluminium products are usually unsuitable.

The appearance does not have to be rustic to be contextual and it certainly does not have to be of gingerbread to be a cottage.

The legal requirements

In many areas approval is required from the local building authorities to build a gazebo, summerhouse, studio or similar building. Preparation of full architectural drawings and specifications may be required.

Gazebos are a piece of garden furniture and the authorities will want to know only where it is, how large it is, and that it is structurally sound.

Studios can be classified as habitable spaces and therefore require approval of their structural integrity and quality for human habitation.

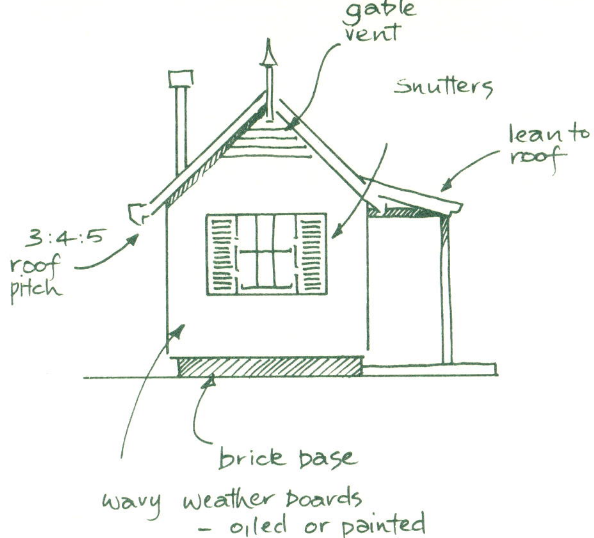

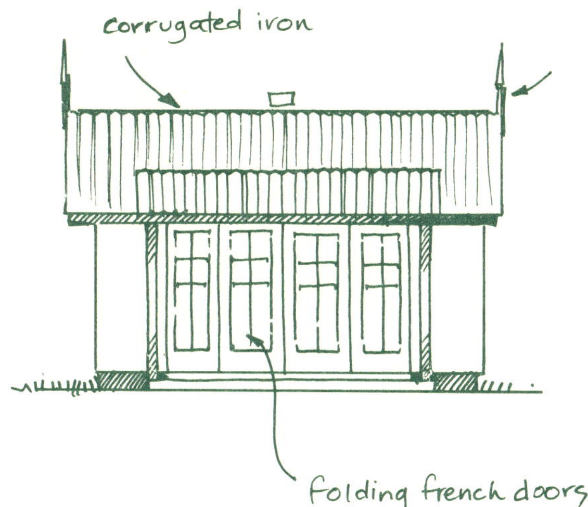

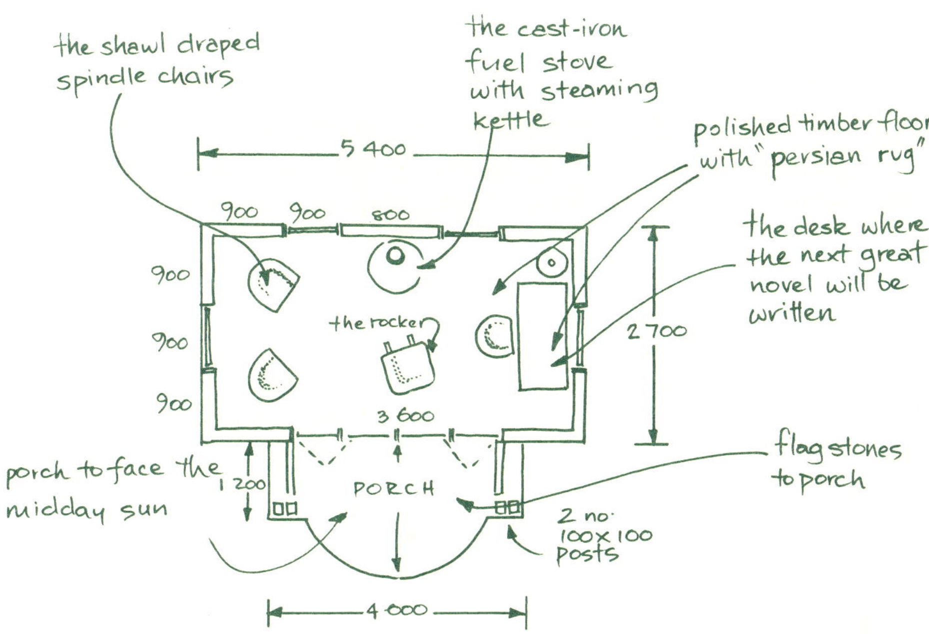

GARDEN BUILDINGS

GARDEN SHED

No garden is complete without a storage area for all the tools and accessories needed to work a garden. The size of shed depends on the individual household but too small a shed will become overcrowded and untidy; individual items will be hard to find, and some items will be left in the weather. Sheds which are too large take up more space in the garden than is needed.

A shed is generally not a building that would be featured in a garden. Sheds have been utilitarian structures of minimum quality and even less style. A box of fence palings with rickety door and a corrugated iron roof is the norm.

A garden shed can provide a base for the wisteria and rambling rose and become an attractive building tastefully set in an unobtrusive section of the garden.

A well-designed shed can still be rustic but it should be weather-tight and structurally sound. Start off by building the shed on a reinforced concrete slab, which is raised at least 100 mm (4″) above the surrounding ground and falls at least 1 in 50 to the doorway.

The slab should be 100 mm (4″) thick, it should have integral edge beams, about 200 mm (8″) wide and 300 mm (1′) deep. These need to be reinforced with steel mesh.

A shed should contain a stout workbench, at least 1 500 mm (5′) long by 600 mm (2′) wide on which to carry out potting and other indoor tasks. There should be a wall of shelves to stack all those bottles and boxes

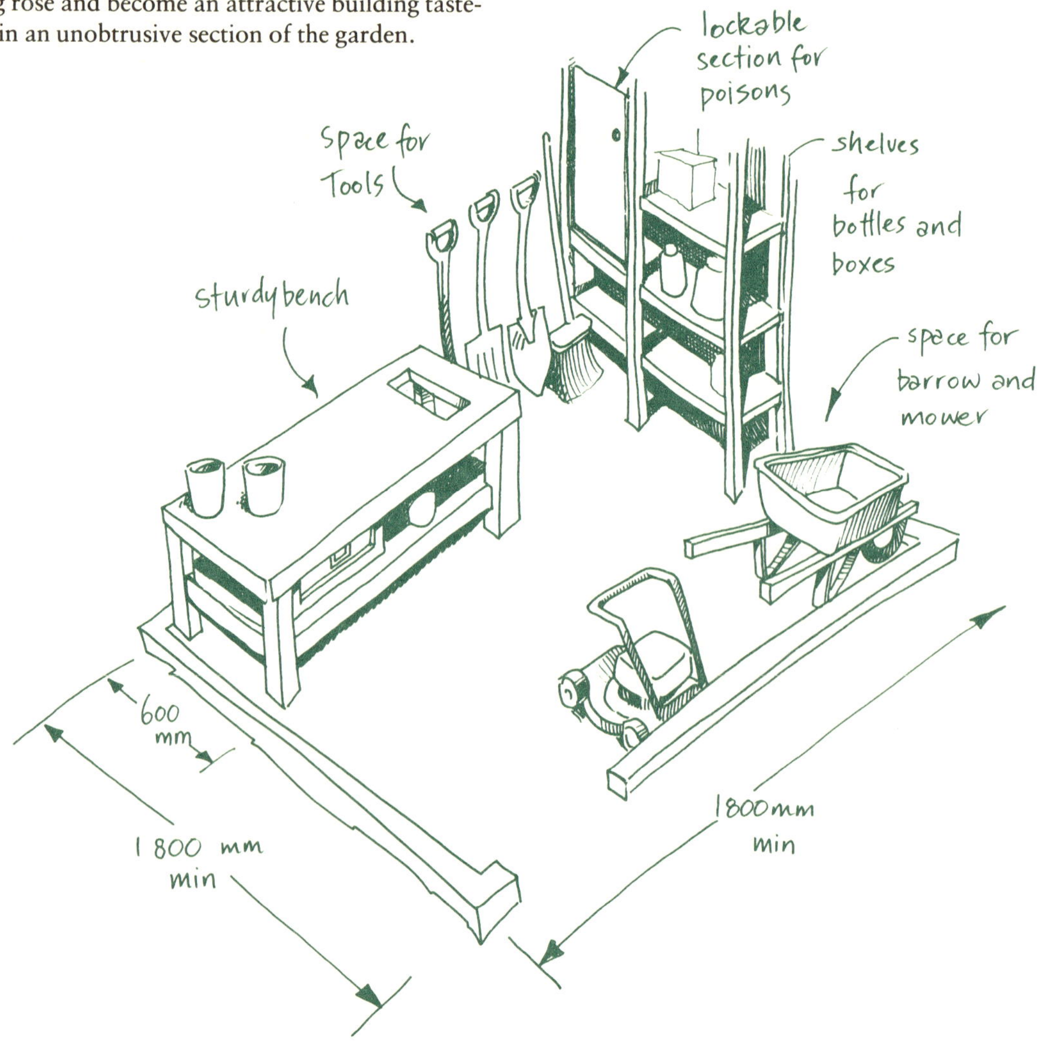

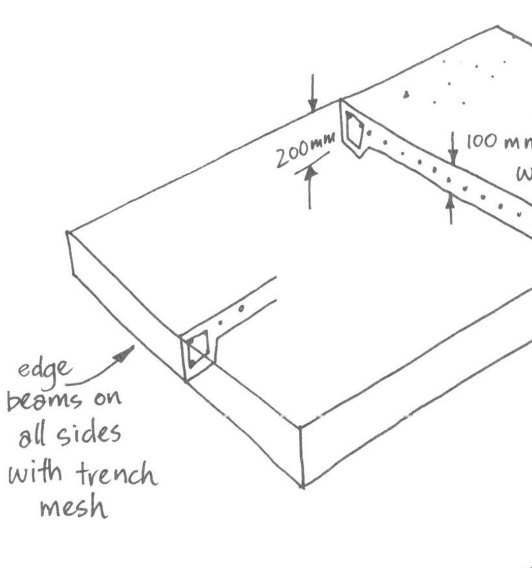

of garden preparations; a section of wall to hang spade, rakes, and mattocks; and there must be room on the floor for the lawn-mower and wheelbarrow.

This means that a minimum shed size is about 1 800 mm (6′) square, it should be at least the same height or more for taller gardeners. Isolate a section of the wall shelves and fit it with a secure lockable door. Use this to store poisons safely out of the reach of children. The shed door should be locked as most items stored there are dangerous in some way.

Ensure that the shed is weather-tight to protect the contents of the shed. It will still get damp if it is not well ventilated and ventilation reduces the risk of vapours from chemicals being trapped in the shed's air and becoming concentrated.

Choosing a location

A shed must be conveniently located but not dominate the garden; on or near a boundary, out of sight from any vista points where the site is well drained and well served with paths and other access ways, seems ideal.

Where the shed is used for potting or similar bench-top tasks then some natural light is an advantage. If possible locate the shed door on the leeside, that is away from the prevailing wind and rain.

It is convenient to have an electric light and a power outlet in the shed although this can affect its position in the garden. Consider also the convenience of a hand basin in the shed with a small hot water heater. The gardener can wash up easily and have a convenient supply of water when working in the shed.

Gardeners are more likely to wash their hands after handling garden chemicals thereby reducing the danger of poisoning.

That a simple basin is required to connect to the main sewer, means that cost often prevents the installation of this useful device. In most cases the dirt and chemicals in the waste water were from or for the garden, so there should be no reason why they should

not be absorbed into the garden soil by way of an absorption trench. There would actually be a reduction in the amount of chemicals entering the sewer system.

Prefabricated

There are many prefabricated garden sheds sold, which are often economic and made from pre-finished sheet steel. Some of these sheds are decorated with painted panels and scrolls. If your budget can only stretch to buying an olive green tin shed, hide it at the bottom of the garden.

Some timber prefabricated sheds are available ranging from poorly designed and poorly finished sheds using low quality materials to quite well-designed solid timber sheds, often of treated pinus.

Ask to see the instructions when purchasing a prefabricated shed, to identify what extra materials, fittings, fastenings, and time will be needed to erect the shed. Any guarantee under five years is meaningless. Waxed cardboard will last for six months, even a year in a drought.

Most prefabricated sheds will require a concrete slab to be built by the gardener. This is the most complicated and expensive single item in the construction of a shed so make sure its cost is added on. Cheap floors for sheds like concrete flagstones or second-hand bricks will seldom give the satisfactory service a concrete slab does.

Custom-designed sheds

In many cases it is just as cheap to build a purpose-designed garden shed than it is to purchase a poorly designed prefabricated one. By the time a gardener adds erection time, a concrete slab, a bench, shelves and racks to a bare prefabricated shed, you may as well construct one which fits into the environment and function of a specific garden.

Garden sheds traditionally have been built with weatherboard or paling sides; these must be fixed correctly to exclude weather. More durable materials are available in many sizes and patterns of planks and shingles made in fibrous cement. When painted or acrylic-stained the material looks like solid timber. Fibrous cement shingles are suitable for a shed roof.

Sheds roofs are often skillions, that is, they have a single slope. A gabled roof, however, may suit the roof of the residence better. Vents, of louvres or lattice, can be built into the gable ends to improve ventilation in the shed. These can be protected from the weather by a roof verge.

The shed door can be made in many ways but the traditional boarded, ledged, and braced type is suitable, durable, and repairable. This is a door that has a face made from tongue and grooved timber boards, which are often flooring boards as these are of durable timber species. The boards are nailed to three boards called ledges and the ledges are braced diagonally with timber boards cut into the ledges to reduce door sag. In hardwoods the nails should penetrate as far as possible into the ledges without coming out the other side. With softwoods, and it can be done with hardwoods, the nails should project through the ledges and be clenched over to maximise their grip.

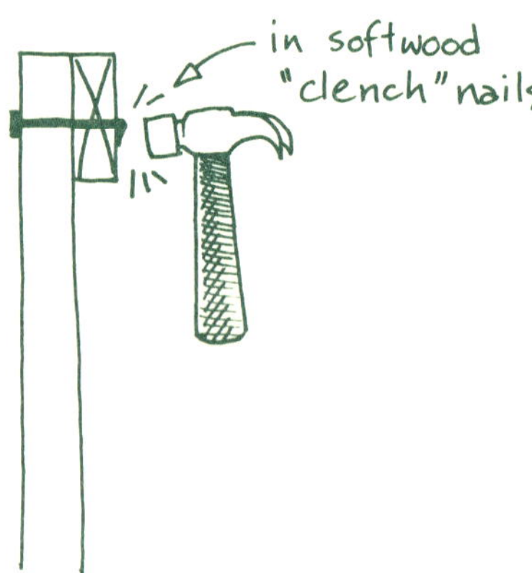

Strap hinges on the line of the ledges and screw or bolt to these gives a good strongly hung door. A galvanised steel padbolt and a brass padlock are suitable for locking sheds as these are easy to adjust if the door drops a little on its hinges and such metals resist the ravages of the weather.

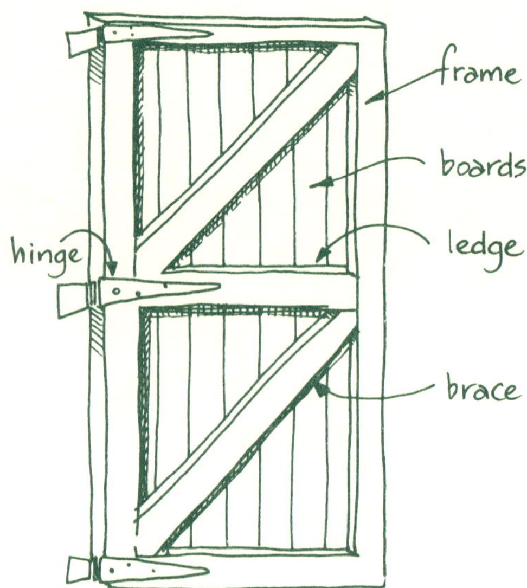

Some gardeners put windows into sheds and many second-hand lead lit casements have graced humble garden sheds. Other gardeners prefer to use hinge-up hatches to allow light and ventilation into their sheds when they are working. Build these hatches as for doors hinged at the top and locked at the bottom, a simple timber prop will hold them open.

The advantage of the fully opened hatch is that there is sufficient ventilation to mix garden chemicals on the bench in the shed. If a chemical says that it should only be mixed in open air, then this means outside the shed but many a gardener tackles this kneeling on the ground, crouched over the dangerous chemical. If poisonous chemicals are to be mixed in the garden, fix a small bench to the outside of shed for this purpose, it can be on hinges so as to swing down when not in use.

Timber frames should be separated from the concrete slab by a waterproof strip or by an air gap of at least 10 mm (say half an inch). Many garden sheds lean because their builders forget to brace them. Bracing is simple: run strips of hoop iron diagonally from corner to corner of the walls and roof frames and nail there with clouts at every stud or rafter.

The authorities

This is just a reminder that many local authorities will require a permit to construct a garden shed. Check the local requirements. **Note:** even prefabricated sheds that can be bought at the local supermarket are considered buildings in some locations.

CONSERVATORIES

Conservatories are buildings that are specially built to provide a stable environment for the propagation and growing of plants that would not flourish in the natural environment. They are an invention of Europeans who wanted to grow tropical and subtropical species in

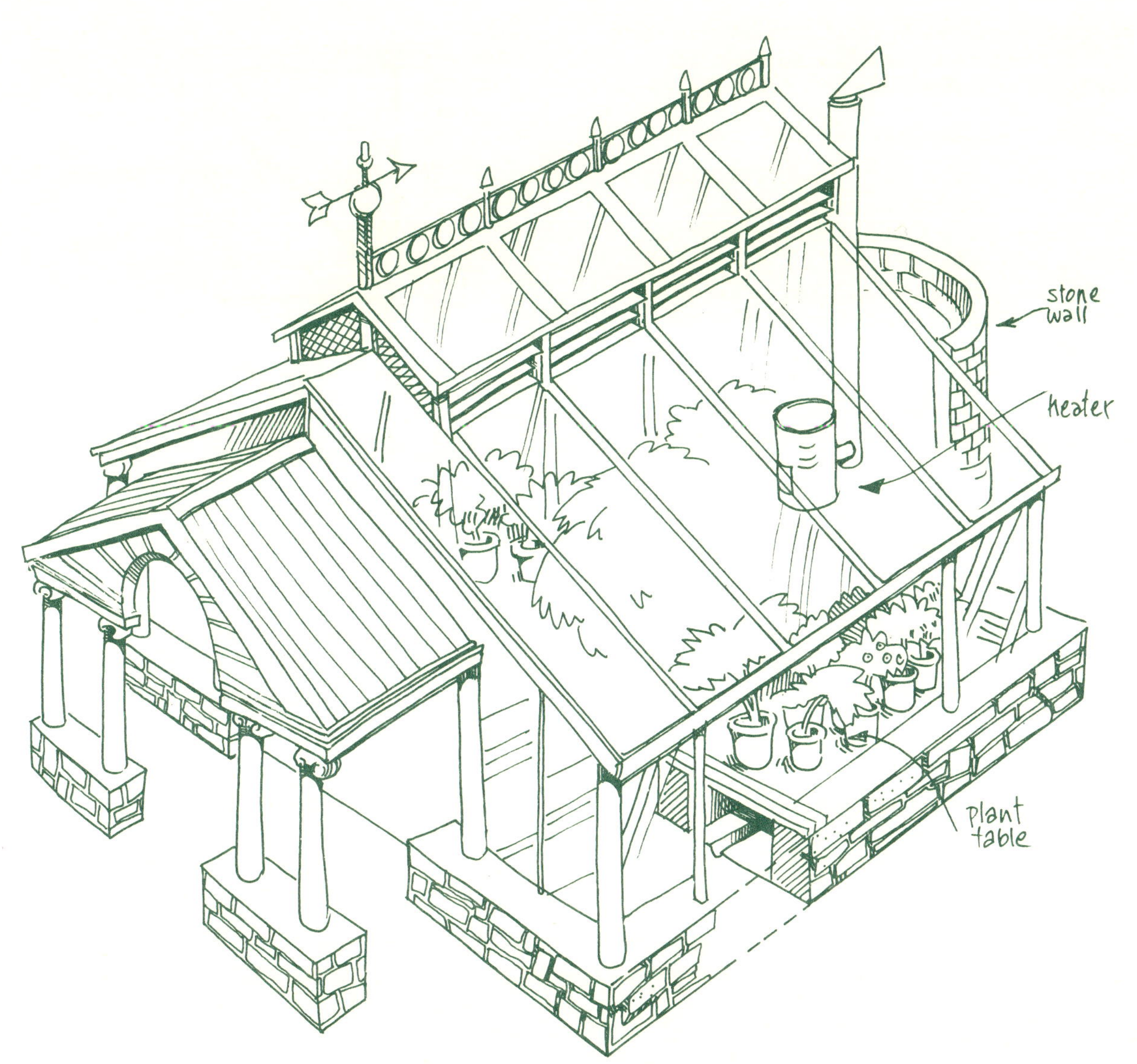

Europe. They are to be seen, even in small gardens, in many northern countries where vegetables and fruit can thrive in this artificial environment.

Most conservatories are built with roofs and the upper part of the walls sheeted with glass. The radiant heat of the sun passes into the conservatory and is trapped within the glasshouse, so extracting the greatest possible advantage from the solar energy.

To control the temperature in the conservatory the gardener can adjust canvas roller shades over the glass if the temperature rises too high. Doors can be opened and heat flushed out through high level vents. When the weather is cold a stove can be lit or hot water piped heating can be turned on.

The plants in a conservatory are irrigated by both drip systems into the soil and by spray systems into the air usually as tropical and subtropical plants require a higher humidity to survive than is normal in the Mediterranean or temperate latitudes.

Where the amount of daylight is insufficient because of overcast conditions, then banks of colour-corrected lamps can be used to increase the available daylight conditions. Information on conservatory equipment is available through large nurseries, building information centres, and special outlets for garden buildings.

In modern conservatories it is possible to program the temperature and humidity gradients, irrigation requirements, and lighting levels into a computer which controls the shades, the vents, the watering system, the heater and even banks of growth lights. These refinements are found in conservatories of very keen gardeners or horticulturalists, and are costly to set up and maintain.

Many plants are grown in portable containers so that these can be moved into the garden on special occasions or taken into the house for decoration particularly when they are in flower. In warmer climates conservatories are used to grow specimen plants primarily but they provide an environment for the cultivation of some food crops, the most common of these is tomatoes.

The conservatory has always been a place to go to observe plants that would not normally be seen in the surrounding natural environment but also a place where people can relax. In recent times there has been an interest in conservatories as places for leisure and relaxation. This type of conservatory may have many less plants than those for propagation. Too many plants make the atmosphere unfit for human occupation. Such a building or addition to a residence is sometimes called a solarium.

Conservatories are being built where natural conditions are suitable for many of the plants to grow without assistance. Conservatories have become a status symbol for some but this should not be seen as a debit against their construction as they provide a very pleasant environment. In the cooler months the hothouse heat trap can increase human comfort and provide a pleasant almost-in-the-garden feeling.

Freestanding or attached to house

If a conservatory is to be used for its traditional purpose, as a place to keep and raise special plants which would not otherwise survive, then it is preferable that it is a separate building in an area where it can make the best of nature's benevolence.

Conservatories that are specifically glass-roofed extensions of residential living space are more convenient if they are attached to the residence. They can be used as a link from the residence to the garden or serve as a second entry to the residence.

If a conservatory attached to a residence is constructed with a concrete floor it can be tiled. It can be used to store solar energy which will be released into the residence in the evening by opening the door between the conservatory and house which encourages a flow of warm air to come in.

Glass in a garden, if it is kept clean, is like water and reflects the planting around it. However be careful as it also reflects sunlight and, if poorly located, may reflect the sun towards places where it is not wanted. Consider neighbours who do not want a dazzling light directed at their dining room window at dinner.

Choosing a style

Many conservatories are designed with a pseudo-Classical or Romantic main elevation behind which is a simple light-framed structure to support a gable-roofed glass box. This, in effect, is a folly. The front is intact but the ruined rear is outlined by the glass.

As glass to build conservatories was not available until glass began to be mass-produced, the rise of conservatories was during the Regency and Victorian periods. The greatest conservatory being the Crystal Palace Exhibition Building erected in London in 1851.

During the Victorian period the conflict between the Revival styles of the architecture of the period and the rise of functionalism in engineering is evident in the design of many of the conservatories of that time. These featured decorated stuccoed fronts and the remaining structure of the building is in finely detailed cast and wrought iron.

The plan shape of most conservatories is normally a rectangle, although there are examples on many other plan shapes including squares, circles, cruciforms, and polygons. Many rectangular conservatories have internal aisles, and apse ends in the manner of a basilica.

Roofs are mostly gables of slopes between 25° and 50° but there are numerous examples of barrel-vault shaped roofs. Where a conservatory has an apse end and a gable roof then there is a half cone-shaped roof over the apse. This is a very common conservatory feature. The apse can be a true semicircle but is more often a semi-polygon, where the sides are seldom more than 600 mm (2′), the roof over then is more correctly described as a half-polygonal pyramid.

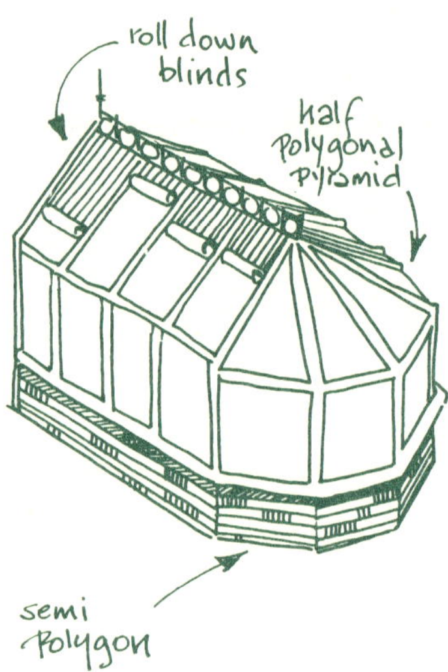

It is possible to produce a free-form conservatory but these present problems of engineering, cutting glass panels, and the unpredictability of the reflected sunlight. A common modern shape is a square pyramid. This is associated particularly with followers of New Age theories. For them anything within a pyramid is affected by pyramid power and flourishes.

The style of a conservatory is inhibited by its function and the use of glass. Clear plastics can be used but these are limiting. A conservatory attached directly to a building should be in harmony with that structure.

Prefabricated

Most house and garden journals advertise a range of prefabricated conservatories. This is so particularly of English and North American publications. Some of the firms seem to be able to trace their history back to the invention of glass, it's odd that being *Established . . .* seems to mean so much.

It is a trusting person who orders a prefabricated conservatory on the strength of an advertisement. A small conservatory is quite an expense so prudent people would only purchase by mail order if they were very sure of the supplier.

If possible go to the display centre of the manufacturer and have a careful look at the finished product, and do this with other manufacturers. Only order a conservatory when it is absolutely clear that the kit will be delivered and it can be erected without complications — if the manufacturer has an erection service consider this carefully.

A kit to adjoin a residence needs flashing and fixings to be included although in most cases the kit will not include floors (normally a concrete slab is required), electrical, plumbing or erection. Some just provide the frame and no glass.

Pre-cut, kit, modular or prefabricated conservatories are the easiest way to purchase a conservatory and if they are well designed and easy to erect they can be good value for money.

Custom-designed

Custom-designed conservatories are very complicated to design so that they remain weather-tight and structurally sound, while displaying a minimum of structure. It is not easy to design an individual conservatory as a good visual design is only a fraction of the exercise.

Producing a structurally and mechanically efficient design is limited by the availability of specialist components which are often restricted in use to the prefabrication companies.

A planned conservatory of less floor area than 10 square metres (110 sq ft) is suited to being offered as a kit, up to 20 square metres (220 sq ft) it can be custom-designed or a kit. Where the floor area exceeds 20 square metres (220 sq ft) engage an architect to prepare an individual design.

Conservatories have an open exposed structure, if not well designed and detailed a conservatory will appear ugly and could be dangerously unstable. Unless you have suitable experience you should not attempt to design a conservatory. Prepare a brief for an architect by writing down what functions are required for the structure and provide an idea of the style you consider is appropriate.

Conservatories should be built to last as long as the residence so the quality of the initial construction is extremely important.

Watering and heating systems

All conservatories will require water fittings and most will benefit from a heating system. A tap and a

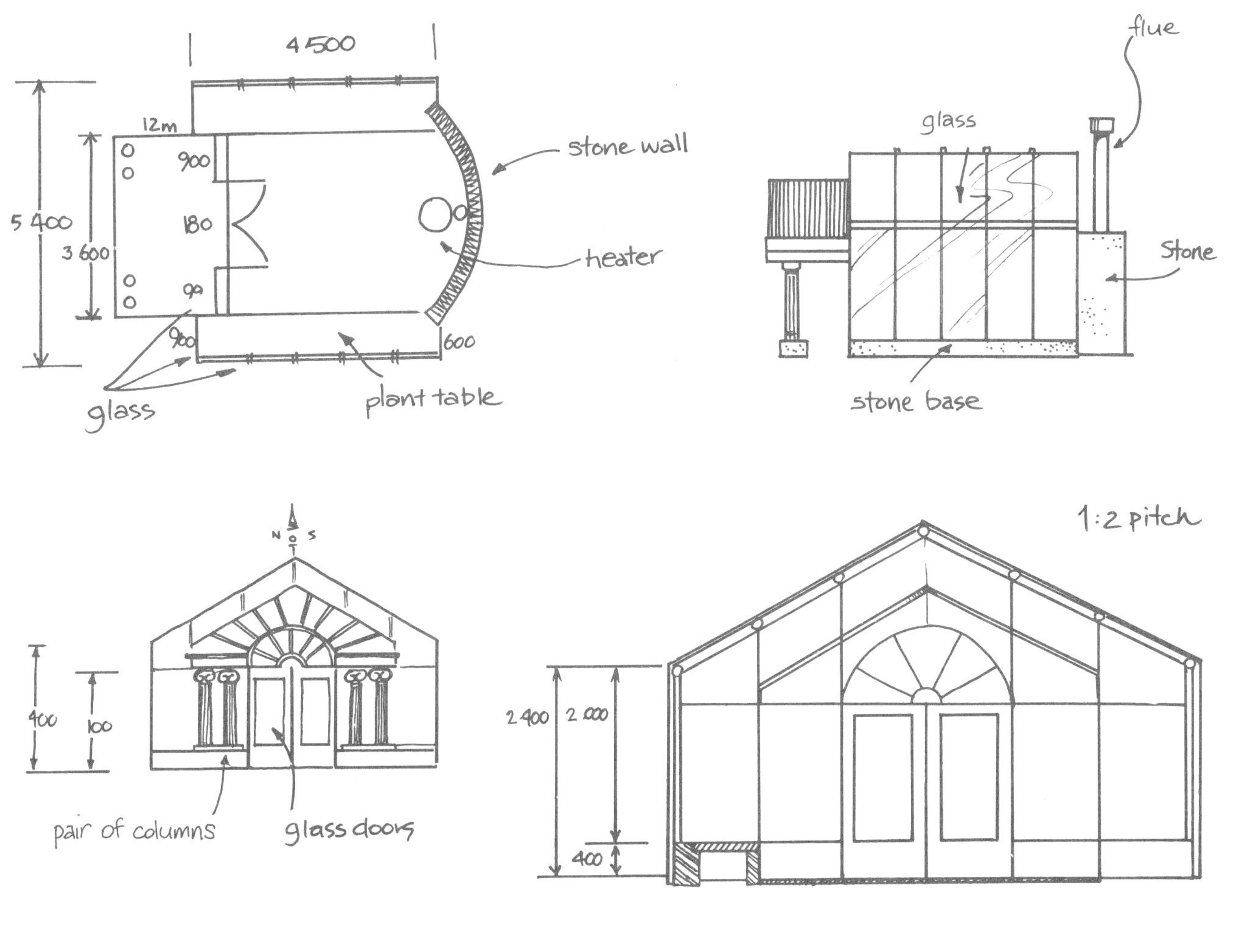

watering-can or hose will only work if you have the time to water the plants in the conservatory regularly. Pot-belly stoves may look the part in a conservatory but few gardeners want to be stoking a stove all night when there is frost in the air.

A good drip, flow or spray watering system can be installed easily by most competent people. The system can be connected to a timer valve on the tap and set to operate automatically requiring inspection only from time to time. Even more sophisticated systems that measure the moisture content of the soil and the humidity of the air can be installed. These systems need quite a lot of specialist equipment including a small computer to control the water flow.

The water that is dripped, flooded or sprayed in the conservatory needs to be collected by an adequate system of drains. In a conservatory used for the propagation of plants then floor drains are the normal way the waste water is collected.

This is not satisfactory in a conservatory attached to a residence and used as a special room. Here construct masonry benches on which the plants may be placed and install drains into the top of these. This would prevent water from draining onto the floor.

The best form of heating in a conservatory is one which operates automatically and provides good even heat. A system using piped hot water is very satisfactory as there is no danger from open flames and the heat source is maintained at a relatively low temperature. The hot water can be heated during the day by solar radiation, stored in an insulated tank, and used to heat the conservatory at night. Supplementary heating should be available if there is insufficient solar radiation to heat the system.

A simple thermostatically controlled system will work efficiently but remember that most plants need some variation in temperature from day to night and from season to season. Only grown plants in a conservatory will thrive in the same conditions.

The authorities

Few local authorities will allow the erection of a conservatory without their approval, particularly ones that are attached to residences and accessible from them. Check the local requirements and if someone else is erecting the conservatory make sure that they have obtained the necessary permits as the property owner is normally the responsible party.

In some places gardeners who erect their own conservatory are required to obtain an owner-builder's permit and if the conservatory is attached to a residence its erection may be allowed only by a licensed builder.

SHADE HOUSES

Shade houses are structures which are specifically designed to provide a shaded environment for plants that do not thrive in direct sun. These are particularly important in areas which have strong summer sun.

A shade house is a simple structure of posts and beams rather like a pergola covered with brush, saplings, battens, latticework or shade cloth. The purpose of the shade house will determine what design is applicable although it is possible to build more elaborate shade houses.

If the shade house is to be a small shady area at the bottom of the garden where a few plants are propagated, then a simple shed which gives shade and wind shelter is sufficient.

Where a garden pathway is routed through a shade house then it can be integrated into the garden and provide an environment in which to grow those special plants which only require partial sunlight. A shaded garden walk can be used and designed together with a shaded sitting area where not only your plants but you can enjoy a respite from the heat of the midday sun.

Choosing a location

Choosing a location for a shade house needs care as they are not only to shade the plants — and you, but they should also provide temperature control and, in some cases, wind and weather screening.

A simple shade house may be located on the edge of the garden where it is easy to access but not in full view. A walk-through shade house can be an important feature of a garden if it is well designed in keeping with its environment.

A walk-through shade house can be very satisfying if it follows a contour around the garden. Shade houses should be located with their long axes in an east to west direction, maximising the available shade.

For some plants shade houses should be located so that the summer sun is cut out but the winter sun is allowed to enter, and this requires careful calculation of local sun angles if a passive design is required.

Preparing a design

Shade houses do not have to be simple flat-beamed timber frames draped with green shade cloth; they can be designed with three-dimensional frames. Shade can be provided by the use of brush or sapling shading to give a rustic appearance, timber battens or lattice in geometric designs, or shade cloth in one of the new colours — fawns, beiges, and even stripes, complement the ubiquitous greens and black.

Brush should be fire-resistant. It is very easy for accidents to happen and you want to avoid regular replacement. A brush roof is very dense and little sun will filter through.

Saplings provide excellent shade when used as battens because their round sections allows more subtle sun control than square or rectangular stock. Some saplings can be used with their bark intact which over time gives interesting colours and textures. Use saplings of between 25 mm (1″) to 75 mm (3″) in diameter. The most popular are saplings that are nearly parallel but tapered saplings are an alternative.

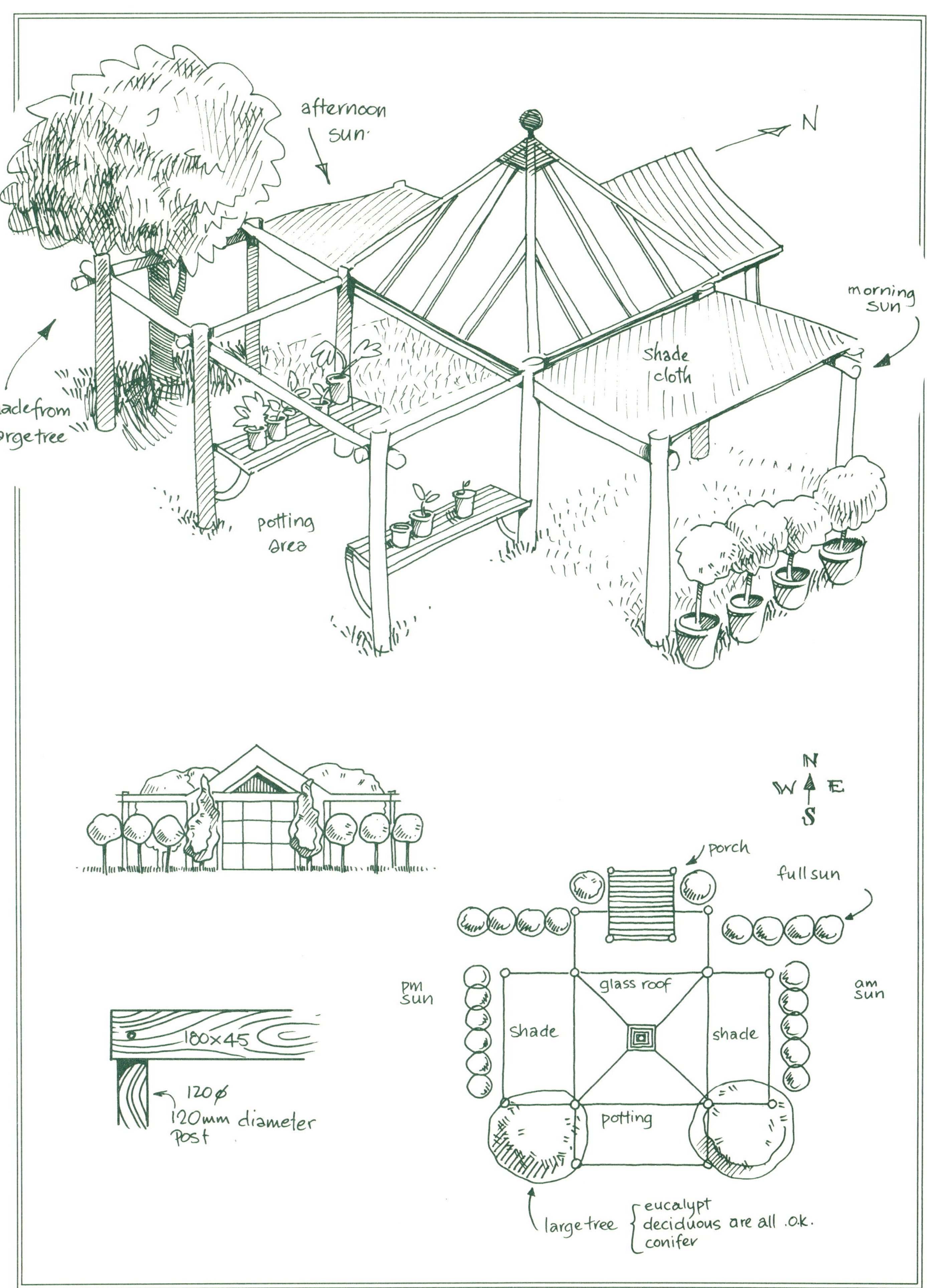

afternoon sun.
N
morning sun
shade from large tree
Shade cloth
potting area
glass roof
porch
full sun
pm sun
am sun
shade
shade
potting
large tree { eucalypt / deciduous are all .o.k. / conifer
180×45
120 ø
120mm diameter post
N W E S

If square or rectangular section battens are used then their spacing and direction requires careful detailing to achieve dappling of the sunlight. In some locations battens are running east to west and north to south. Contact the local meteorological service to find out the angles of the sun at various times of the year and day.

Lattice can be used on the *roof* of a shade house but it is generally more suited to providing shade and a frame for climbing plants as *walls*. Lattice, when used as walls, can look very interesting and enhance a shade house, turning it into a feature of the garden.

Active shade houses are ones where roof panels can be opened on hinges to let in light and to allow the passage of a cleaning breeze. Sides can be made with colourful canvas awnings, roll-up shade cloth panels or durable exterior quality venetian blinds or louvres.

With a little imagination most gardeners can turn a simple shade house into a garden feature, they can be cheap to construct and forgiving of simple errors with climbing roses, wisteria or ivy soon able to hide all but the most gross mistakes.

Remember again, the shade house should be in sympathy with other garden and residential buildings.

Natural shade or manufactured shade cloth

Remember that thoughtfully planted trees and shrubs will provide high quality shade in most gardens without the gardener building a shade house.

To build an ugly shade house is unforgivable, it is better to plant a spreading oak tree. Where trees are used to shade other plants care must be taken that the plants can be grown in the same soil consistency as the trees. As trees have roots just below the surface of the ground soaking up the nutrients, plants under trees need to be planted in soil that is separated from the soil of the tree by containers.

Watering systems

Mister sprays can be attached to the beams so that on extra hot days a fine mist of water can be sprayed in to the shaded environment to reduce the heat in the atmosphere.

The authorities

In most areas shade houses are regarded as a simple garden item and do not require approval. If the shade house is larger than, say 10 square metres (110 sq ft) it may be considered a building and require approval by some authorities.

AVIARIES AND DOVECOTES

It is no longer fashionable to keep caged birds in a garden and many people consider it cruel to contain any wild creature. There are, however, many breeds of birds which have been bred in captivity and there are no free-flying varieties. These birds would cease to exist if they were not bred and cared for in aviaries.

An alternative to having caged birds in a garden is to provide wild birds with facilities that will attract them to a garden. Dovecotes are an example of this approach as are feeding tables. Once a wild bird has found a regular and easy-to-access source of food it will return often while it does not feel threatened. The danger of the wild birds becoming dependent on the supplies of food from people means they will stop fossicking for their own natural foods. However if the person who feeds them stops doing so then the birds could perish. If you are absent from your residence often it is unwise to set up feeding facilities for wildlife.

Aviaries must be of the size, shape, and design recommended for the species and number of birds to be kept. They should be built of the highest possible quality materials and of an attractive design. The value of a beautiful bird song is severely reduced if the birds are housed in tatty cramped cages.

Dovecotes should be spectacular in design; multi-level apartments atop tall catproof poles. All feeding tables and other apparatus used to attract birds will be as nought if local cats can use the garden as a killing field. Birds and cats do not mix, cats are born with thousands of years of genetic programming which identifies birds as food.

Choosing a location

The most important consideration in deciding the area for birds and bird features in a garden is to make sure it is a feline-free zone.

Think why you want the birds in the garden: for their songs; personal beauty; and to be observed at play, and when eating. Birds are soothing in a garden, so have them where they can be easily heard and observed.

Make sure with aviary birds that they have the correct exposure to sunlight, are protected from the weather, and provided with a habitat which closely resembles the one they would use if they were wild.

Preparing a design

In the Regency and Victorian periods garden aviaries grew to be very large structures often over a 100 square metres (1 100 sq ft) in area and tall enough to enclose fully grown trees. Others from this period were small and lavish in appearance; gilded cages within conservatories were common.

A modern aviary is a cage-like building that is divided into a number of units where different species of birds can be displayed. Adjoining the display cage is a weatherproof enclosure where birds are held for breeding, nesting, and roosting.

These types of aviaries may be useful for bird breeders but do not add to the environment of a garden.

In a garden, there seems to be little point in having a few birds in cages, where they are kept only because they have striking plumage and can be observed through the wire. It is better to attract wild birds or to have ducks and fowl walking about in the garden — a side benefit is that ducks eat snails and spiders and also lay eggs.

Peacocks will make their home in a garden happily if it is a suitable environment. They will welcome a few peahens. Such breeds of birds look beautiful and add a special dimension to a garden but they can be very noisy and they do fly — being hit by a low-flying peacock is too frightening to consider.

If a walk-in full-flight aviary can be built in a large area then a special bird environment can be created. However an undertaking like this should be very carefully planned.

Vermin-proofing and hygiene

Birds produce copious quantities of droppings and these should be collected and disposed of appropriately. Never allow bird droppings to build up, as they will smell and will kill some plants if the uric concentrations are high.

Some birds eat mice and rats. A rodent-infested aviary, where vermin romp around in bird litter, eating fallen seed and attacking hatchlings must not happen. Always design aviaries to be completely vermin-free by using very fine-gauzed chicken wire. Another precaution is to clear the aviary daily of food debris.

All caged birds should be checked by a veterinarian once a year at least. The birds and cages should be clean at all times and all parasitic infestation must be treated immediately. Birds suffer from many afflictions and viruses and an aviary can become disease-ridden very fast if health of the birds is not monitored regularly.

The authorities and neighbours

In many areas there is a limit on how many birds can be kept without a permit. In some closely settled areas poultry are not permitted but how an inspector can identify a wild duck which arrived on its own wings from one that arrived in a carton is open to debate.

Some birds are protected and in some places exotic (not indigenous) birds are banned completely.

Neighbours are seldom as enthusiastic about birds as their owners and there are many suburban confrontations, over what level of noise and smell is tolerable and how close aviaries are placed to dividing fences.

KENNELS AND CATTERIES

Dogs and cats have been part of gardens since earliest times but this has not changed their disposition to dig holes and kill birds respectively.

It should be obvious that there is a relationship between the size of a garden, the size of dogs which dictates the sensible maximum number of canines that can comfortably inhabit a garden. It is also sensible to choose a dog that will complement the garden — to have a huge golden retriever bouncing in and out of the waterworks of a garden may be fun for the dog.

When providing a kennel or cattery for pets to shelter consider an enclosure so that the animals can be sensibly restrained when needed. The dog enclosure can be part of the service area of the garden, but not where any manure is stored as some dogs just cannot resist rolling in this stuff.

Catteries can have the appearance of a small summerhouse in a sheltered part of the garden. Provide cats with a warm snug box out of the weather and snoozing platforms above the ground in dappled sunlight: this is a feline palace. If the outside perimeter of the cattery is planted out with catnip mint, it is a feline heaven.

Choosing a location

Dog and cat houses should be in a sheltered part of the garden with good exposure to warming sunshine. With animals that are noisy at night put them where the neighbours will not hear the dogs barking, or the cats calling.

Few dogs will use a path if there is a more direct route. Watch for dog paths appearing in the garden. The dogs may damage plants or the paths may be unsightly. Erect fences or plant thorny hedges to act as diverters. The entry to a dog kennel should be from a paved part of the garden so that the constant entry and exit of a dog will not chop up a lawn.

Preparing a design

Both dogs and cats need dry draught-proof shelters in which to sleep. The traditional dog kennel with a gable roof and an arched door works very well. Make sure the floor is above the ground and is made of a suitable material. Plywood manufactured as formwork for concrete is very good for this purpose.

Most cats appear to wish to sleep on their owners' beds, but many owners believe a basket filled with old quilts in the corner of the garage is a suitable alternative. A small shed with a dog-proof catdoor, a window to let in the sun, and a series of sleeping platforms is a suitable cattery for a few cats. If this has access to an enclosed run then the cats can have their own safe haven from the family dogs.

The floors of cattery sleeping areas should be impervious concrete and the enclosure should be river stones or other material that will allow water to drain away easily. Plant a pot with lawn grass and put it in the enclosure to give the cats greens to chew as this is essential if the cats are contained for extended periods.

Hygiene

Dogs and cats do *it*, but not always where they should. Make sure that their sleeping quarters are easy to wash and disinfect. Kennel roofs can be removable and the inside of catteries should be able to be hosed out.

Avoid all cracks and crannies inside an animal enclosure where dirt can build up and vermin and parasites breed. Cover all floor and wall junctions if possible and build in solid material with no exposed framework if possible.

The authorities and neighbours

In many places there are restrictions on the number of dogs and cats allowed on one property and in most areas local authorities require dogs to be licensed. There can be restrictions on the breeding of domestic pets for sale at a residential property as well.

A combination of laws, regulations, and common law actions has effectively made owners totally responsible for the actions of their pets. If a dog jumps a fence and destroys the neighbours' prize roses the dog's owner is likely to be held responsible. In some places the emergency services will send owners a large bill to bring a cat down from a tree.

HUTCHES AND COOPS

Once upon a time every garden had hens in the backyard, laying the family's breakfast. Those days have passed and few hens are kept. Restrictions on the number of hens allowed may be to minimise noise and odour. Most areas do not ban the keeping of hens in a suburban garden absolutely but they do not encourage it.

Other backyard livestock has also disappeared from most suburban lots. In sub-rural and rural areas it is possible to keep one cow for fresh milk, to keep horses for transport, and to breed rabbits for the table.

Rabbits are proclaimed vermin in some places and it may be illegal to have them. Check before purchasing animals for the table or as pets.

PRACTICAL GARDEN PLANNING —

BEHIND THE SCENES

WASTE DISPOSAL

Gardens produce piles of lawn trimmings, mountains of leaf litter, and stacks of prunings. Once this was all piled in to an incinerator and the fragrant smoke often filled autumn skies. The trouble was that the fragrant smoke also contained smog-creating contaminants.

Many environmental authorities now forbid the burning of garden refuse in backyard incinerators.

Gardeners should recycle as much of the refuse from their gardens as possible, not only to avoid polluting the atmosphere but because if vegetable matter from a garden is composted and recycled, there will be less need to add externally sourced material to a garden.

The prunings can be shredded and chipped, then spread back on the garden beds as mulch.

Lawn clippings are the nuisance factor as they are hard to break down into a clean, non-slimy, mulch or compost. Where a garden has large areas of lawn compared to garden beds, the lawn clippings will need to be removed from the garden and responsibly disposed of in an environmentally sound way.

Designing a sanitary garbage area

With the trend towards the separation of garbage into different components, glass, paper, aluminium, steel, plastic, vegetable waste and general refuse the area of the garden is no longer the only place to leave the garbage cans.

Build a well-constructed roofed enclosure of masonry with a smoothly rendered and painted interior. This should be insect and vermin-proof. Inside is room for the temporary storage of the above items.

The refuse shed should be located in a cool part of the garden but needs to be conveniently located to the residence and not too far from the pick-up point.

Vermin-control systems

No one wants rats to infest their garden but they will be attracted if any food scraps are left around; this is the basic requirement for vermin control.

The enclosure where the garbage is stored should be constructed to effectively exclude the entry of rodents and insects. Flies that get in can be dealt with by spraying the enclosure with an insect spray.

This area must also be out of reach of pets and birds. Cockroaches will seldom be killed by the general application of insecticide, they can only be eradicated from the garbage storage area if it is spotlessly clean.

COMPOST HEAPS

Compost heaps were once an essential part of every garden. With the development of proprietary suppliers of compost and fertilisers and their convenience compost heaps were discarded.

With an increased awareness of the benefits of recycling and other environmentally responsible considerations many gardeners are composting their own vegetable matter once again.

A traditional compost heap

A traditional compost heap generally consists of two or three bins built of stout timber planks. The bins have earthen bases, though they can be on concrete if required. The bins are constructed with only three sides. These are about 900 mm (3') to 1 200 mm (4') square in plan by about 600 mm (2') to 900 mm (3') high.

There are many regional variations using many materials and forms. It is possible to make a successful compost heap on the ground or in a slight hollow.

The process is that vegetable matter is loaded into one bin until it is full, then the next bin is used. The first bin is turned over occasionally and so on until all bins are in use.

The vegetable matter is covered over with soil when it is added, reducing infestation by insects and vermin. This provides the dark environment for the slow breakdown of the vegetable matter and reducing the strength of the final compost to a useable level. Some gardeners have added lime to compost to neutralise acids and control the speed of decomposition. Seek local advice on how much lime is suitable for the material being used and the plants which the compost will be applied to.

Take care if lawn clippings are added to compost heaps as these often cook to a slimy useless mess.

The older the compost, and the more decomposed the vegetable matter is, the better the resulting material.

Modern proprietary systems

There are many modern easy-to-use clean composting bins available. Check what is available locally with suppliers and users. Never buy a composting bin unless someone who has used one recommends it.

The other consideration is how to fit a number of large plastic bins into a garden, without them being a visual disaster.

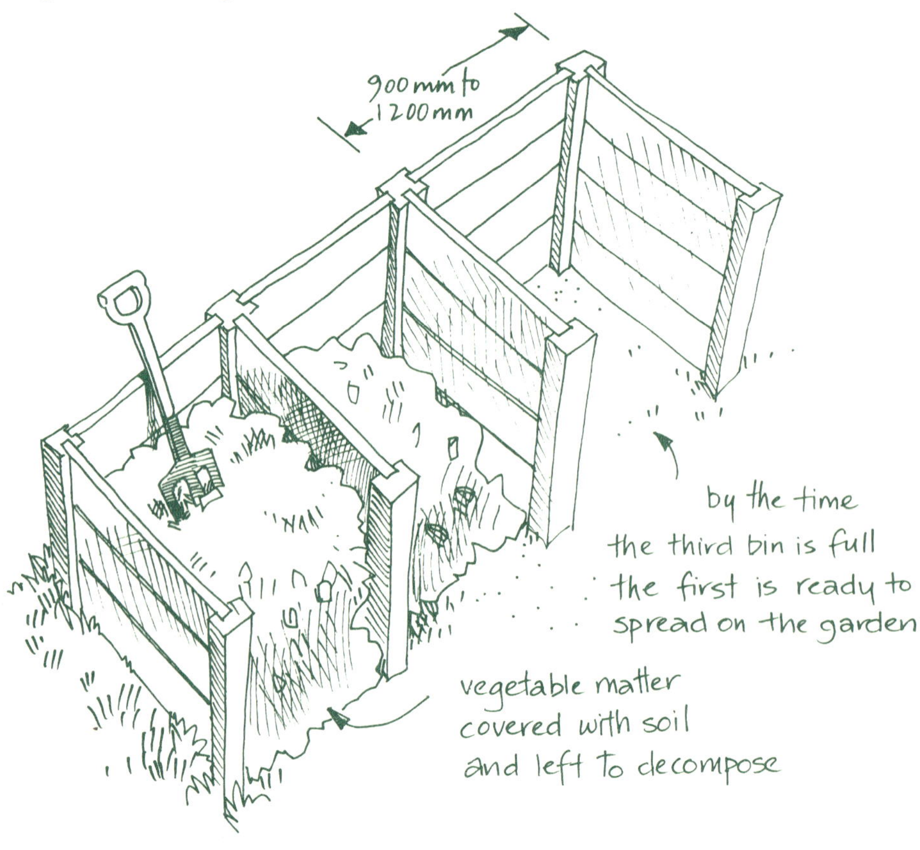

SEEDLING AND BULB RACKS

It is important if a garden is to raise its own annuals and bulbs that well-designed, well-placed seeding and bulb racks are provided.

Location

Seedling racks should be in a warm sheltered part of the garden, or in the conservatory. They need to be protected from driving rain, hail, and frost.

Bulb racks should be located in a dry, cool part of the garden under trees or in a shed. Some bulbs need to be dug up every year after they have flowered and die back. Separating the new bulbs stops overcrowding in the beds and increases the number of available blooms.

Construction

Traditionally seedling and bulb racks have been timber batten shelves attached to timber frames. Onto these racks the seedling boxes and the bulb baskets were placed. The baskets were often made of woven cane.

Modern racks are now more likely to be plastic baskets hung from a steel frame. It is doubtful that these are more efficient or even longer than the traditional timber type but they certainly are less suited to a garden variety.

Keep the plastic baskets out of sight in sheds and use timber frames outside where applicable — this is an aesthetic judgment based on the traditional values of a gardener, that is, that nothing in a garden should compete with the plants.

GLOSSARY

aggregate   the hard material added to cement and water to make concrete, particularly sand and crushed rock

aquifer   a porous subterranean rock strata which contains water

ashlar   is structural stone that has been dressed so that it has square corners

backfill   the refilling of an excavation after a section of structure is completed or a utility service has been installed

batch mixed   a term usually used to denote concrete made from cement, sand and course aggregate that has been carefully measured by volume or weight

battered bank   an earth bank which has been stabilised by the use of a weather- and erosion-resistant facing

bed-course   the lowest course of any masonry construction

bed level   the lowest level in a construction

bond   the overlapping of masonry units to increase the integrity of a wall

bresummers   exposed beams particularly in verandas, gazebos and pergolas

capping   a continuous finishing component fixed to the top of any wall or fence

cleaning eyes and pits   capped openings or formed pits in an underground pipeline specifically for the purpose of rodding out any obstructions in the pipes

coping   a continuous finishing component particularly where fixed to the top of a masonry wall or at the edge of a swimming pool

coursed rubble   is stone laid with regularly spaced horizontal bed joints in an otherwise random-pattern stone wall

crossfall   means a shallow gradient slope perpendicular to the direction of travel of a pathway or driveway

cured   the term used to describe fully set full strength concrete

cures   the term used to describe the process by which wet concrete changes to solid full strength concrete

cutting   this is the term used to indicate that an area is to be re-contoured by excavation. Generally used to denote where hillsides are to be terraced or mounds are to be levelled

datum point   a reference point of known location from which measurements can be taken

dimensionally stable   a material which does not vary in size or shape

diverter valves   are valves that allow water flow to be directed into two or more pipes or outlets

even bearing   is the requirement that the supporting foundations are capable of supporting evenly distributed superimposed building loads

fall   the direction of slope of a roof or terrace from the high point to the low point

female mould   a mould into which the material to be cast is poured. A male mould is one around which material to be cast is placed

free board   is the distance between the water level and the top of the banking or tanking

frog   the depression in the top of the pressed clay brick

going   is the horizontal distance measured across a stair tread from the nose of one tread to the nose of the next tread

grade line watercourses   are watercourses that follow the natural slope of the land

gravity flow trench   is a trench which has a downward sloping bottom, allowing any liquid to flow without pumping

grow   this refers to the phenomenon of brick growth where some clay bricks become longer after they have been built into walls

header pond   is the pond at the highest level of a watercourse system, from which water is allowed to flow into the system

hurdles   are two pegs driven well into the ground with a horizontal member spanning between them and extending a short distance beyond. They are used to hold stringlines accurately in place when setting out any earthworks or construction

laser theodolite/laser level   these are modern surveyors' instruments that make use of the ability of a laser to emit a straight line of light which can be directly read on a levelling staff or can be reflected back to the source allowing automatic level and distance calculations to be made

massing   is the term used to describe the visual effect of building up a close-grouped collection of individual units

mixed media roadbase   where more than one material is used to construct a roadbase

no-fines   a term used to describe a concrete mixture which does not contain any fine aggregate (sand)

nosings   are the projecting overhangs of the edge of stair treads and of copings

off-form surface   particularly refers to the finishes which can be obtained when the formwork is removed from concrete

offset   a measurement taken perpendicular to a known point on a known line

optical level   a horizontal telescope fitted with levelling hairs mounted on a tripod stand which can be swung through a full circle

passive design   is design where the concept is to allow a gentle evolution of the environment to take place

pebble dash stucco   is a mixture of river pebbles in a cement mortar which is thrown against a prepared surface. When the mixture sets the result is a surface which shows the pebbles visibly standing out on the surface

perpents   the vertical mortar joint in masonry construction

pilasters   are piers, columns or pillars that project from the face of masonry walls. They are generally located for style as well as function

plan dimensions   the measurements on the horizontal plane used by tradespeople in construction

plinth   a proportionally low, base unit to any construction which is often wider than the structure it supports

plumb-bob   if a string is held at one end and the other end is weighted then the string will be vertical, this is a plumb-bob

point levels   are levels taken at predetermined points on the surface of the ground and plotted on a survey plan. Sometimes the surveyor will interpolate between the point levels to draw contour lines

power-take-off-implements   are implements designed to use the motor power generated by another machine to provide their motive power. Many implements have been designed to be used in conjunction with tractors

private treaty   is an agreement between two people. It is a contract

reactivity   is the property of clay foundations to expand when wet and to shrink when dry

reduced level   a level expressed as a height above or below a known level (a datum level)

reflux valves   are special valves used in water drainage systems to allow fluid to flow in one direction only. They stop waste water being sucked into clean water supplies and sewage being forced back up a line

set down   describes the level of an area which is a small distance lower than a control level

setback   a statutory distance from a property boundary within which no buildings can be built

silt trap   is a pit in a stormwater system that is specifically designed to separate silt in the incoming stormwater and allow only silt-free water to flow through

spacers   are components with the sole purpose of locating other components at a set distance apart

stiffeners   are functional components of structures that make other members stiffer and more able to withstand superimposed loads

stone-batter   an earth bank that has been stabilised by covering the sloping faces with stone blocks or rubble

strata-stone   is a method of masonry construction which consists of layers of thin courses of split stone, thought by some to resemble natural rock strata. This is seldom structurally sound except with low superimposed loads

string level   this is a light aluminium tube that can be fastened to a stretched piece of string by two hooks located at its ends, a spirit level is built into the tube and if the string is moved until the spirit level indicates a level tube, then the string is also level

stringers   are the sloping pieces of timber or steel used to support stair treads

stucco/stuccoed   a render applied to masonry made from lime, cement and crushed rock fine aggregate (sand), exact composition and application varies from place to place

surface spoon drains   are shallow drains located to collect water running across the surface of the ground, they are generally constructed of concrete and are often semicircular in section

the run of the fence   is the full length of a fence

tight dry jointed   mortar-free joints in masonry that are worked to give close contact between the blocks

uPVC   unplasticised polyvinyl chloride, a durable plastic used to manufacture sewer pipes and many other water pipes and fittings

verge   the edge of any slope

voussoirs   wedge-shaped masonry units used to build archways in walls and to construct spiral and fan-shaped paving

weepholes   a term usually used to annotate holes left in masonry to allow moisture to pass through or to flow out, often they are unfilled perpent joints

well draining base   a supporting bed generally of crushed stone gravel which is both structurally sound and porous so that any water that collects can be drained away

ACKNOWLEDGMENTS

About the artist

GREG GAUL

Greg Gaul has a thriving commercial art and design studio, G-Raffics, in
Katoomba in the Blue Mountains, west of Sydney. This family business produces
artwork and cartoons for a number of newspapers and a variety of brochures.
The studio employs a number of talented local people such as illustrator
Beth Norling.
Greg worked in Canada and Britain for a couple of years and on his return to
Sydney he worked in a commercial art studio before becoming self-employed in 1976.
He started G-Raffics in 1988.

About the author

GEORGE WILKIE

George lives in the picturesque village of Leura in the Blue Mountains, 100
kilometres (60 miles) west of and 1000 metres (3300 feet) above Sydney.
He and his wife, Lyn, share their 1000-square metre (half-acre) cottage garden
with four exotic cats, magpies, currawongs, satin bower birds, many native
parrots, the occasional rabbit, and a wandering peacock.
Educated at Royal Melbourne Institute of Technology, Sydney Teachers College,
and the University of Sydney, the author consults in Town Planning,
Architecture, and Interior Design. He was head of the department of Interior
Design at the University of Technology, Sydney, and is now developing a Centre
of Research and Information in the field of Tourism Destination Design for the
University. George was heard on a commercial radio station, where he discussed
listeners' queries on architecture and design. He also contributed a section on
selecting and evaluating houses in the *Sydney Morning Herald.*
Building Your Own Home — a comprehensive Guide for Australian Owner
Builders which George wrote and illustrated in association with Stuart Arden
was published by Lansdowne Press, 1984 (now Weldon Publishing).